THE WORLD OF SEX
VOLUME 4: SEX IN ETHICS AND LAW

Also by Iwao Hoshii (in English)
THE ECONOMIC CHALLENGE TO JAPAN (1964)
THE DYNAMICS OF JAPAN'S BUSINESS EVOLUTION (1966)
JAPAN'S BUSINESS CONCENTRATION (1969)
A FINANCIAL HISTORY OF THE NEW JAPAN (Co-author with T.F.M. Adams, 1972)

Other volumes in this work
VOLUME 1   SEXUAL EQUALITY
VOLUME 2   SEX AND MARRIAGE
VOLUME 3   RESPONSIBLE PARENTHOOD

PERSPECTIVES ON JAPAN AND THE WEST

THE WORLD OF SEX

Volume 4

Sex in Ethics and Law

IWAO HOSHII

PAUL NORBURY PUBLICATIONS LIMITED
Woodchurch, Ashford, Kent

First published 1987 by
PAUL NORBURY PUBLICATIONS LTD
Woodchurch, Ashford, Kent, England.

ISBN 0-904404-57-9

British Library C.I.P. Data
Hoshii, Iwao
The world of sex.
Vol. 4: Sex in Ethics and Law
1. Sex——Philosophy
I. Title
306.7'01   HQ21

ISBN 0-904404-57-9

Set in Bembo 10 on 12 by Visual Typesetting, Harrow.
Printed and bound by A. Wheaton & Co. Ltd, Exeter, England.

Contents

9 RAPE

Foreword

THE EVALUATION OF SEX has fluctuated between two extremes
— unrestrained pursuit of sexual pleasure and blind suppression of sex.
Although the puritanical condemnation of sex has not disappeared,
pleasure for pleasure's sake in the uninhibited enjoyment of sex is by far
the prevailing attitude in many societies. This book attempts to show
that human dignity can only be preserved if the affirmation of sexual
lust is paired with the responsibility for sexual conduct. The categories
of good and bad apply also to sexual behaviour. A man who catches
herpes from a prostitute and infects his wife is just as much a louse as a
boy who makes a girl pregnant and leaves her in the lurch. The
condemnation of irresponsible conduct implies that good and bad are
not just words or labels affixed arbitrarily to what a certain society thinks
desirable or undesirable. It supposes that there is a foundation for such
a distinction and that it is man's duty to do the good and to avoid the evil.

The intellectual emancipation of our age has destabilised the
traditional value systems, and sexual morality has been one of the
persuasions most aggressively challenged and often peremptorily
contradicted. The tendency has been to date a 'scientific' understanding
of sex from the time of Freud and the attempt to free sex from the
restrictions of Christian morality by removing the traditional taboos has
been the main thrust of this scientific understanding.

The sexual revolution which shocked the United States in the sixties
and seventies and which had repercussions almost everywhere did not
and could not change the inherent meaning of sex, that is, the meaning
which sex has in and by itself. Nowadays, the claim to understand what
something is in and by itself is considered entirely unscientific. There is
a host of epistemological objections denying the possibility and validity
of an 'objective' understanding. 'Objective' does not mean absolute or
unconditional, and the limitations on human understanding implied in
the distinction between what we think and the way we think do not
negate the realiability of our intellectual faculties.

The moral convictions of a given society reflect its image of man.
Social conditions or religious beliefs may indicate the image of man
prevailing at a certain time in a certain country. In western thought, the
image of man was greatly influenced by the attempts to arrive at a
metaphysical understanding of man and the world. These intellectual
pursuits started with Greek philosophy and the Scholastics carried on the
inquiry into the meaning of man and man's destiny with the confidence
that human reason can find the truth. A metaphysical understanding of

man's existence leads to the recognition of a value system based on the nature of man. The nature of man provides a universal and unchangeable standard of good and bad, right and wrong. This standard was systematised in the doctrine of natural law which asserted that there are things, situations and relations in which the question of right or wrong does not depend on any positive rule, order, command or prohibition but is settled by 'the nature of things.'

The traditional morality held that its injunctions and prohibitions were based on the inner meaning of sex and the inherent rationality of the institutions regulating sexual relations, marriage and family. The evaluation of sex rested on a deep understanding of man and fathomed sex in the context of the entire personal and social values of man. Modern 'sexology' suffers from its 'clinical' approach. For sexology, homosexuality and sexual deviations constitute important fields of study. Sexual phenomena formerly considered aberrations of an abnormal minority are relied on for gaining insights into the basic problem 'what does sex mean for man?'

Scientists have an inclination to disregard the boundary lines of science and to stray into alien territory. Metaphysics is one of the fields into which such excursions are particularly frequent. Scientists undoubtedly have the right to make metaphysical assertions, but they should not make them in the name of science and present them in the garb of scientific conclusions. Nor should they be astonished if philosophers point out bad logic or bad metaphysics in their ostensibly scientific deductions.

I think that the meaning of sex is to be understood first and foremost from the 'normal' rôle of sex in 'normal' human life. I readily agree that there are great differences in what people believe to be normal but I deny that what traditionally has been treated as 'deviations' (particularly homosexuality) can establish a claim to be considered as normal. Pathology can provide valuable information on the functioning of man's body and soul, but pathology supposes the possibility of ascertaining a standard by which the pathological can be defined. To my mind, the knowledge gained from the study of aberrations in sexual behaviour can 'supplement' the findings based on 'normal' sexuality but cannot 'correct' these persuasions.

Sexuality belongs to man's constitution, his nature, but also to his conduct, his actions. I am convinced of the intelligibility of man's nature but man's actions take sexuality into the sphere of irrationality and man's freedom creates the possibility of immorality. Irrationality and immorality are human possibilities which show what man can do but the recognition of the range of what man can do does not negate the limits on what man ought to do. Facts have no normative value, and the physical possibility of human conduct does not provide its moral justification. This position, which seems so obvious in everyday life, is strangely controverted in the realm of sexuality where certain behaviour is vindicated by the assertion that it is within the reach of man's capacity.

The validity of religious doctrines on man and mankind as such depends on postulates which are hardly self-evident. Father Pierre Teilhard de Chardin's synthesis of natural science, theology and mystical experience professes a christological evolutionism combining a theistic interpretation of reality with the evolutionary tenet of an ascending complexity of the organic world. The assertion of a christological destiny of mankind is based on revelation which remains outside the considerations of this book. On the other hand, the moral traditions of the West cannot be understood without reference to Christianity in general and the position of the Catholic Church in particular. Christianity represents the most important spiritual movement of the West which has shaped or influenced thought and institutions in many parts of the world. The moral teaching of the Church contains what for many centuries were considered the norms of man's duties and especially his obligations with regard to marriage and the family. Much in Christian morality reflects universal human values which can be affirmed and adhered to without any theological implications but the position of the Church on issues such as birth control, artificial insemination, abortion and divorce has given rise to fierce controversies. I have stated the problems as objectively as I could but, as in many other instances, I have set forth my own convictions. I have used the Bible as a source of information and evidence of Jewish and Christian thinking.

A widely held position asserts that the West's political, economic and social systems are based on pluralism. Pluralism appears as the premise as well as the expression of the liberty and liberties deemed essential to the individual and society. On principle, pluralism means a variety of opinions, attitudes and convictions that are tolerated and are supposed to tolerate one another. Pluralism, however, cannot be equated with absolute indifference. Human societies cannot exist on a merely physical, biological and instinctive commonness. They require the recognition of some values, principles and rules by their members. Such values and principles may be incorporated expressly in constitutions and similar documents or they may be acknowledged implicitly in the institutions and laws of a given society. Whatever their form, such basic principles must be recognised by every individual and group in a given society if that society is to exist and function.

The values and principles on which society is founded do not belong to the realm of science. They have not been deduced from theoretical propositions nor formulated on the basis of compacts or conventions. Theory may influence the formulation of constitutions or laws but the social and political reality has more to do with what men believe. Just as political revolutions are not the outcome of new political theories, so the sex revolution was not shaped by new theories on sex but by changes in the attitudes towards sex.

Self-fulfilment was one of the buzz-words of the sexual revolution. The belief that hard work, self-denial and moral rectitude were their own reward gave way to the notion that 'self' and the full realisation of its potential were all-important pursuits. Americans, in particular, came to believe that they could have it all — wealth without work, sexual freedom without marital problems, self-absorption without loss of community. The human potential faddists indulged in the self-destructive tendency of confusing 'needs' and 'desires.'

The advocate of an open society sometimes overlook man's essential limitations. As Karl Popper understands it, an open society rejects all taboos and is, in conformity with the ethos of modern science, willing to question all convictions, all attitudes, and all social and political institutions. It will only maintain those that are likely to prove enduring and to survive even the most radical criticism. The open society, therefore, is an alternative not only to totalitarianism but also to societies that rely on their traditions.

A view of the universe repudiating the purely mechanistic interpretation of reality by the natural sciences and the social and economic structures based on such an interpretation has been proposed by Fritjof Capra. A disciple of Heisenberg, Capra became interested in oriental mysticism, particularly in the cosmic intuitions in Hinduism, Buddhism and Taoism, and its conception of the universe as an organic whole. Capra thinks that the old western culture and its technologies and social organisations have become petrified and unable to cope with the emotional and existential crises underlying the protest movements of the 1960s and 1970s, such as feminism, ecological consciousness and the peace movement. The mechanistic, materialistic and deterministic ideologies of the natural sciences and the existing social systems do not correspond to the harmonious connections in the universe accessible to contemplation and mystical experience. The solar era advocated by Capra proposes to replace the 'hard' technologies with their irresponsible exploitation of natural resources and economic science reducing man's needs to the accumulation of material goods by a new paradigm of life and action which relates to man's place in the planetary ecological system.

A true understanding of man and his destiny cannot be gained from a single science or a single point within a science, from the instincts in psychoanalysis, evolution in biology, or the class struggle in sociology. Reality has many facets, and the reality of man is no less complex than the reality of society or that of the universe. Problems are not solved by violence; revolutions, struggles and war only create additional chaos. Human problems must be approached in a frame of mind willing to accept the total reality of man and to affirm sensuality as well as morality, instinct as well as reason, and inclination as well as duty.

IWAO HOSHII
May 1987

1

Sexual Morality

Should There Be Sexual Morality?

THE BASIC QUESTION of sexual morality is whether there can be or should be something like sexual morality. There are undoubtedly a number of ethical systems that include commandments or prohibitions related to sexual behaviour but the existence of such systems does not decide the question of their validity. The authority and binding force of norms regulating sexual conduct has been denied by authors such as Engels and Reich, and Sweden's guidelines on sex education are almost an invitation to unrestrained sexual licence. In practical terms, many of the rules and conventions regulating sexual behaviour of individuals as well as society in the beginning of the twentieth century have faded into oblivion.

The Russian Revolution led to a sex revolution which, however, soon gave way to a counter-revolution. Marxism had proclaimed that with political revolution should come sexual liberation. When true human forces were finally released by socialism, sexuality, too, would be set free.

In the first wave of revolutionary elan, marriage and divorce became simply a matter of registration. People had themselves inscribed as man and wife and their names stricken from the register; everything was allowed to everyone with everyone. The communes which were to replace marriage and the family were founded on the view that sexual relations were not to be restrained. Free love was to liberate women from male despotism; actually, it led to the most outrageous contempt of women by men. The school was to take over the educational functions of parents but teachers were powerless to get the children under control. Hordes of abandoned children roamed the cities, stealing, drinking and killing.

Something had to be done to prevent complete social disintegration. In a conversation with Clara Zetkin (German communist and feminist, 1857-1933), Lenin formulated the problem as follows: 'The changed attitude of youth to the questions of sexual life is, of course, a matter of principle and appeals to a theory. Some call their attitude "revolutionary" and "communistic." They sincerely believe that this is so. I, an old man, am not impressed by that. ...They (the young and many older people as well) certainly know the handy theory that in a communist society, the satisfaction of instinctive life and the need for love is just as simple and irrelevant as drinking a cup of water. This cup-of-water theory has made part of our youth crazy, completely crazy. It has become a tragedy for many young men and women. Thirst will be slaked. But will a normal human being under normal circumstances lay himself in the mud of the road and drink from a puddle? Or even out of a glass whose brim is greasy from many lips? More important than all this is the social aspect. Drinking water is an individual action. Love requires two, and a third life may arise. In this fact lies a social interest, a duty to the community.'

Unrestrained Sex

The cup-of-water theory reappeared in the warnings of the official Chinese press against sexual licence. The sex revolution has no place in socialist China, declared the *Beijing Daily* in July 1981. The 'sluice gates of passion' should be kept securely shut until matrimony. Sexual permissiveness is giving love the cup-of-water treatment. 'It is regrettable that some young people take a nonchalant attitude and treat love as an object to be disposed of at will.' 'Play friends,' as the paper calls them, change lovers all the time. Others lose control of their 'sluice gates of passion' soon after engagement, prematurely overstepping the bounds of pre-marital relations. 'Such attitudes and behaviour are extremely harmful to oneself, to others, and to society.'

In Sweden, schools carry out sex instruction with zealous thoroughness. Every pupil knows how you get children and how you need not get them. An adolescent can obtain contraceptives without any difficulty. Sweden's Board of Education provided the following guidelines for teachers on sex instruction to children below teen age: 1. Do not try to deter the start of intimate sex relations. 2. Give pupils detailed information on sexual stimuli and responses as well as on various intercourse positions. 3. Discourage racial sex discrimination. 4. Discard any reasoning that women are in some way inferior to men. 5. Do not discourage sex deviates.

'Free marriages' qualify officially for exactly the same social benefits as formal marriages. The Swedish bishops have branded extra-marital and pre-marital intercourse as sinful but, according to a survey, 95 per cent of all Swedish women have had pre-marital sex. Sweden is one of the countries with the relatively highest number of illegitimate children, unwanted pregnancies of girls under 14 years of age and abortions involving girls under 15, a growing number of minors convicted of rape and of children under 14 suffering from venereal disease. The situation is almost the same in some American states. According to a study of Johns Hopkins University of 1980, 50 per cent of all girls between the ages of 15 and 19 and 75 per cent of all boys between 17 and 21 in the region of Washington, D.C. had had sexual intercourse. Generally speaking, pregnancies and abortions of girls in this age group are on the increase despite the greater use of contraceptives, while the spread of venereal disease is alarming. A study published in March 1981 reported that in the United States, four out of ten girls between the ages of 14 and 19 had at least one pregnancy, although two-thirds of the girls used prophylactics. Of 29 million young men and women between the ages of 14 and 19 in the United States, 7 million young men and 5 million young women had sexual intercourse; the average age at the first sexual experience was 16.

In Africa, the weakening of traditional rural values due to rapid urbanisation and the breakdown of the extended family has had a destructive impact on sexual behaviour. In Zimbabwe, for example, a baby boom has been accompanied by 'baby dumping.' Most of the women charged with infanticide are young unwed mothers whose boyfriends refuse to share responsibility for the pregnancy. Despite the country's strict anti-abortion law, hospitals report numerous cases of complications from illegal abortions. As many as 20 per cent of the urban population suffer from some form of venereal disease and in 1983, more than 1,200 school girls between the ages of 13 and 15 became pregnant.

Failure of Sex Education

The liberal attitudes towards sex reflect the rootlessness of late twentieth-century society. People no longer live all their lives in the same community where aberrant sexual behaviour is not tolerated. Religion no longer plays a major rôle in keeping married couples together and single couples apart. The effects of early sexualisation suggest that the unrestrained satisfaction of the sex instinct creates problems for society which raise serious doubts on the soundness of the claim to unlimited sexual freedom.

The failure of education to infuse norms of decency can be attributed to two developments. First, the framework of socially desirable and acceptable conduct has become so rickety that it can no longer support educational injunctions. In other words, the image of man forming the guiding principle of education has become so blurred that it can no longer serve as a directive norm. Secondly, education has withered into mere instruction, and sex education, in particular, has become information without value judgements, description without differentiation, and rules of conduct without motivation,. The old Japanese custom allowing pre-school children of both sexes to bathe together in public baths acquainted them in a natural and casual way with the bodily differences between men and women and accustomed them to the naked body. Women felt no inhibition against nursing their babies in public. Sex education in today's schools runs the risk of inciting a lustful curiosity which, without an effective indoctrination to self-control and respect for one's own and one's neighbour's body can have devastating results. Only a rehabilitation of customs appropriate for today's society and a strengthening of social coercion on the basis of a new spirit of community can arrest the failure of education.

Systems of Morality

Generally speaking, it may be said that each group expects of its members that their conduct will conform to certain norms which correspond to the values on which the group is based. The norms that claim to regulate human conduct have no uniform character. Today's western societies generally recognise three kinds of norms: moral, juridical and customary.

Norms based on religious doctrines or convictions form a religious moral system usually propounded in moral theology. The observation of these norms is considered as good and virtuous and their violation as sin. There are also philosophical systems of ethics, actually, there are almost as many systems as there are ethicians. Scholastic philosophy asserted that there are norms founded on human nature which indicate the difference between good and evil, moral and immoral in human behaviour. Moreover, there are social norms expressing what kind of behaviour society considers desirable for the relations among its members. They show what prevails as custom, manners and courtesy which may differ for different classes or strata of society. Behaviour conforming to these rules is considered as polite or decent, their violation is censured as impolite, vulgar or insolent. All these norms are upheld as 'traditional' and in many cases, their observance is expected as a matter of common sense. People not conforming to accepted usage run the danger of being judged queer or, depending on the seriousness of the matter, of being ostracised.

The counterpart to the commandments and prohibitions in the moral order form the laws in the political order. This is not the same as the social order. There are moral norms regulating man's conduct in all social relations but laws do not extend to all aspects of the social order. Actually, today's laws have little relevance to the ordinary life of the citizen, except those imposing taxes and regulating traffic. What society considers desirable in a certain culture is, as mentioned above, usually referred to as manners which form part of social customs and usages observed by society for ensuing smoothness in social relations. Different from the organised coercion of the state, the coercion of custom which Rudolf von Jhering called social coercion is unorganised. Von Jhering thought that the objective of social coercion was the realisation of morality but this is a misunderstanding. Morality cannot be enforced because freedom is essential to morality. But social coercion can contribute to the observance of moral norms in man's external conduct. On account of the dissolution of modern society, social coercion has lost much of its effectiveness. Today's bitterly deplored depravity is primarily a problem of custom and not of morality. The atomisation of society has made social pressure ineffectual so that the norms which were to uphold decency have evaporated. The revolution resulting from the secularisation of society has completely altered the views on sex and this change has been more radical than the transformations in politics and economics.

Man's Rational Nature

Man is ordained towards the development of body and soul, and this development can be partially controlled by man's free determination. For man, whatever contributes to this development is physically and objectively good, whatever is in conflict with it, is bad. For the morally good, the 'harmonious' development must be considered as norm. Man must be seen as a whole and the inherent structure of the values proper to man must be recognised. Good is what is in accord with the essence of man and human society. To the question what the essence of man is, Aristotle answered with the definition of man as 'animal rationale,' a living being endowed with reason and free will. Reason and free will distinguish man from all other living beings and provide the foundation of the priority of the spiritual over the corporeal. Reason and free will are also the hallmark of man's personality. As a person, man can understand himself as an intelligent and independent being and in this self-understanding can dispose of himself and determine his own development to the extent that it is subject to his control. Although man's development as an organism (the 'animal' in the definition) is beyond his control, his development as a person is entrusted to his free decision. Human society, too, is based on the rational nature of man; man's reason can apprehend what goals society should pursue and the ways these goals should be achieved by free cooperation.

Freedom

Freedom means man's faculty of self-determination as well as the conditions under which he can use his freedom. In the first sense, freedom implies the absence of internal physical necessity, the freedom from inner determination or compulsion; positively, the freedom of choice. In the latter sense, it refers to the absence of force, violence, threats and other external physical coercion. In its positive aspect, the freedom from external restrictions denotes the freedom to act in accordance with one's own discretion. Freedom of conscience, freedom of religion, freedom of speech, academic freedom and similar freedoms fall into this category. In addition to internal and external physical constraints, there are moral restrictions imposing limitations on the freedom to act through obligatory norms.

Freedom is a dynamic faculty but it does not include its own regulation. Freedom is part of man's rational nature, the power of self-determination proper to man as a person. Freedom gives man the possibility to form himself, but this possibility also involves the responsibility for the proper use of freedom. Freedom forms the basis of morality. Although a great part of man's development constitutes a necessary natural process, it also involves man's free action. By reason, man can understand his ordainment to develop in accordance with his nature, that is to say, he is a human being and has to live as a human being. By reason, man also understands that his free actions in accordance with his nature are good and his free actions in conflict with his nature are bad. He understands that 'the good is to be done and the evil to be avoided.' He knows what is good and bad first and foremost by his conscience in which he becomes aware of the conformity or discrepancy of his actions with what he 'ought' to do.

Although man cannot ignore the basic difference between good and bad and his obligation to do what is good and avoid what is evil, he can be ignorant of some moral norms or err on the morality of certain actions, their relation to the objective order, the order of nature as well as the positive order of the society or societies to which he belongs.

Responsibility

Responsibility is an irreplaceable premise of morality. Modern psychology shows that conduct and attitudes that seem extremely anti-social were created by an unfortunate chain of circumstances. Psychological and psychoanalytical studies emphasise the significant rôle played by hereditary defects, an unhappy and loveless childhood, and the lack of models and support in adolescence in the genesis of asocial or anti-social behaviour. The conscious and subconscious motives that can be discovered in the analysis of an individual may make his conduct understandable, but this understanding does not imply that the individual is not responsible for his actions. When President Reagan's would-be assassin was found not guilty by reason of insanity, a wave of indignation roared through the United States. Psychologists have to learn that man's free decisions are beyond the parameters of their inquiries.

Social Morality?

The formal object of morality is the 'good,' that is, what agrees with man as a rational being and is in harmony with human nature. The good to which morality refers constitutes the specific object of free personal decisions related to man's development as an individual, including his conduct in social relations. The problem of group morality has been discussed mainly in connection with the question of corporate liability. In criminal and international law, three problems present themselves:

Can a corporate body as such be criminally liable? Can a corporate body be liable for the criminal actions of its individual members? Can an individual member be liable for the acts of the community? But morality is a question of conscience, and a corporate body has no conscience. Objectively, therefore, there are norms embodying the essential requirements of human nature, considered not only in itself but also in its relations, comprising its social relations and its connections with other 'things.' But subjectively, there is no corporate morality, and morally good or bad actions are imputed to the individuals responsible for corporate decisions.

In connection with the 'theology of liberation,' the concept of 'social sin' has been widely discussed in recent years. Social sin means the injustice of social, political and economic structures which result in oppression, persecution and poverty. Often, the meaning of social sin has been extended to comprise eroticism and sexual permissiveness allowing the spread of prostitution and pornography and the manipulation and corruption of public opinion by the media which, in addition to giving prominence to violence and sexual licentiousness, propagate distortions, half-truths and outright lies. The abuse of power by totalitarian and authoritarian régimes as well as by economic aggregates is mainly responsible for the disregard of justice in the public sphere. In the final analysis, individuals are responsible for social sin, not only by their actions instigated by lust for power, greed and pride but also by their failure to correct injustices when corrective action was within the sphere of their duties and competence.

Obligation

Morality differs from good manners and customs by its obligatory character. Moral norms must be observed. Metaphysically, this obligation is based on the nature of man as a being endowed with reason and free will and ordained towards a development by his own action. Moral philosophy explains the duty to observe moral norms by the nature of man and his ordainment towards unfolding his personality by his own free actions in conformity with his nature and the order of values implied in his nature. Here lies the difference of philosophical ethics from moral theology which, as mentioned above, is based on the norms of human conduct contained in revelation.

Objective Order

In an article entitled 'The Rediscovery of Human Nature' which appeared more than ten years ago, *Time* magazine wrote: 'There is a sneaking reappearance of the old notion that certain fixed elements in man (once unscientifically known as "human nature") are not susceptible to environmental changes' (2 April 1973, p. 25). Considering expressions such as 'by nature' or the 'essence of man' as unintelligible, philosophers have discussed the meaning of man's existence without giving a definition of man. In the West, the human values inculcated by the traditional moral code intimated an image of man that could be understood even without reference to an explicit formal definition.

The old morality was founded on the premise that there exists an objective order and that on the basis of this order, man can know what is morally good and bad. This view presupposes the theistic explanation of the intelligibility of man and the universe so that man can know what he is, why he exists, and what he is living for. Man can know the objective order of values, and he is bound to form his conscience according to this objective order. In his conscience, man can measure the action he intends to do against these objective norms and thus discern whether it is in conformity with the right order or not and thus whether it is right or wrong. Morality regulates not only action but also inaction: to omit or refuse an action to which one is obligated can be just as immoral as to do what is contrary to one's duty.

In the realm of the physical being of organisms, good is synonymous with healthy, but it is fundamentally wrong to locate the meaning of morality in the health of the community and to define the good by its well-being. The 'good' man cannot be identified with the 'socially healthy' man, that is, the individual whose conduct contributes to the preservation of the community. Aristotle said that man is by nature a social being, but that does not mean that he is an 'organ' or 'part' of society. The relations of the individual to the community are entirely different from those of organs to the organism; the individual is morally bound to the end of the community to which he must contribute by his free actions. Man is ordained to live in society and depends on it, so that a completely independent individual is impossible.

Albert Schweitzer, who gained fame and worldwide recognition for his work at the medical mission at Lambarene but who was also a theologian and a musician, based his ethics on the respect for life. He formulated the principle 'good is what preserves and promotes life; bad, what destroys and impairs life.' Respect for life must be all-embracing and obligates not only individuals but also groups and organisations, above all the political communities, the states. The main objection against Schweitzer's ethical norm is that life is not the ultimate criterion of right and wrong because life, at least life in our experience, is no absolute value.

Limitations on Human Development

In order to understand the personal destiny of man, it is necessary to see the essential limitations of man's development. Aristotle and other philosophers have often spoken of perfection as the inner goal of man, but such a thing is beyond the bounds of our experience. As in nature and history, there is no rectilineal, least of all a straight upward development in human life. The curve of bodily growth rises sharply in the beginning but slows down later and can drop very suddenly. Mental development can go upwards during the entire span of human life but there may be differences for the various mental faculties (observation, judgement, reasoning, memory, and so on). This implies that man's development may have several apogees but there is an inevitable end — death, which is not the same as perfection.

Death is the end not in the sense of a goal but of a terminus. As an irremovable limit to life, death constitutes a permanent yet unidentifiable threat to human existence. In thinking of death, man must be considered not only as an individual but also as a social being. The death of the individual is part of the metabolism of the race which, as a whole, continues to exist. But different from other living beings, man is not merely a specimen of the species but possesses a unique value as an individual so that every individual makes a distinct contribution to human history. This contribution may not mean much but there are men whose influence outlasts their earthly existence and whose activities remain fruitful long after their demise.

Man's Natural Ordainment

Aristotle's thinking was thoroughly teleological. His practical philosophy affirmed morality as the basic human value because only a moral life could assure the development of reason, the specifically human capability. Life according to reason is what is divine in man. By his inner form, his 'humanity,' man is ordained towards the realisation of this form as his inner goal. Since Aristotle ascribed individuation to matter, he did not adequately deal with the problem that the individual never reaches his perfection and that at least in our experience, man's individual existence ends with death. Nevertheless, self-development remains the goal of human life, and in its inner spiritual structure, human nature's ordainment towards this goal determines the direction of man's spiritual activities.

This natural ordainment of man for a development as a personal being can be elucidated by an analysis of his higher faculties. Man's intellect is intrinsically structured in such a way that it seeks the truth, man's will intends the good, and man's feeling pursues the beautiful. In Scholastic terminology, the true is the formal object of the intellect, the good, the formal object of the will, and the beautiful or pleasing the formal object of man's emotions.

The good and the true are convertible with being, according to the Scholastics, which means that every being is necessarily good and true, and every being also has its own particular beauty. Aristotle explained the transcendentals (that is, notions and realities surpassing all *genera* and categories) as aspects of the Absolute Being pertaining to other beings only by analogy. As a transcendental, the true differs from truth in the epistemological sense and refers to the intelligibility of things; good is different from moral goodness and relates to the perfection, desirability or attractiveness of a thing. The doctrine of transcendentals brings out the concinnity between the order of being and the human mind. Modern psychology has rejected this analysis as well as the attribution of specific objects, but both remain indispensable for an adequate understanding of man's mind in the context of his existence as a human being.

Intellect and Truth

The ordainment of man's intellect for truth means two things: first, that the intellect apprehends all its objects in so far as they possess intelligibility; secondly, that this natural ordainment towards the formal object acts as a kind of spring or release to set the faculty in motion. The object is grasped by the intellect precisely because it is knowable; in Aristotelian terms, the intellect discovers in the object the form which is capable of conscious existence in the comprehension of the mind. Of course, man can err, but he does not think in order to think something false. He thinks the false because he thinks that it is true. Truth is the aspect in whatever man thinks that corresponds to man's intellect and the aspect under which the human intellect tries to grasp everything.

The second element included in the assertion of the intellect's ordainment for truth regards the working of the intellect as an active and self-moving faculty. There is in the intellect a tendency towards the truth, a propensity or proneness to grasp the intelligible in everything entering man's consciousness. This is neither instinct nor command; it constitutes the active nature of the intellect which sets itself in motion by this *a priori* disposition. Nothing psychology can adduce in its investigation of consciousness, subconsciousness, awakening, attention or interest, can explain why the intellect works. We can discern the conditions which may affect intellectual activities but they do not explain the basic fact that the intellect works and always works in the same sense.

Will and the Good

Man's will is ordained towards the good. Here again, we maintain, first, that the will possesses an inner tendency towards the good and, secondly, that the operation of the will is determined by this structural ordainment. Man often errs in what he considers good, and often does things he knows to be wrong and evil. And yet, it is not because they are evil that man does them. Although they are evil from one point of view — which may be the correct point of view in accordance with the objective norms of right and wrong —, man finds in the evil something attractive. It is not the evil that attracts him but the good in the evil, for, as St Augustine said, 'There can never be any evil where there is no good' (Enchir. de fide cath., 13,4). Luther believed in the radical incapacity of man's free will for the good *(Vom unfreien Willen, Münchener Ausgabe,* p. 207). But man's experience contradicts the assertion that man wills the evil as such. The thief steals not because stealing is bad, but because he wants or needs the things he steals or because he enjoys the thrill of it or is proud of his defiance of the law. The question is not whether the subjective motive or objective is morally good or bad but whether in man's conscious representation of the object pursued by his will there is one side or aspect which appears to him individually as something good and desirable.

The Scholastics have formulated this theory in the distinction between *'voluntas ut natura'* (the spontaneous activation of the will by the appearance of something desirable in man's consciousness) and *'voluntas ut ratio'* (the deliberate choice; see S. theol., 3, 18, 3; 1-2, 10, 3). 'Will as nature' means the necessary fundamental tendency of the will towards its formal object, the good in general; 'will as reason' implies the free determination of man embracing an object which he apprehends as good but which does not necessitate his choice. The inherent tendency towards the good stirs the will to action as soon as something desirable comes into man's consciousness; but this motion of the will does not constitute man's free choice. Even after this initial natural movement of the will stretching out for the good, man can deliberate on the appropriateness of pursuing this object. He still remains master of his act, capable of self-determination. Without the natural tendency of the will based on the *a priori* orientation of this faculty, there would be no mechanism for the actualisation of the faculty; without the possibility of deliberation, there would be no freedom. This combination of natural necessity and rational freedom characterises the existential position of man who finds himself created as man and therefore limited to human possibilities, but free within these possibilities and master of his own destiny.

The natural tendency of the will towards the good implies a rational explanation of human freedom. Since Heidegger, existentialists stress the self-affirmation contained in man's decision but refuse to attribute to man's existential reality any essential meaning. Man's freedom, however, is not an end in itself. Man is free because by his freedom he is capable of striving towards perfection through his own endeavour and on his own responsibility. Man's freedom makes man's existence a moral task and gives to his actions a moral value. Freedom enables man to fulfil his destiny in a human way. By recognising the norms and assuming the obligations imposed on him by his nature — being faithful to himself —, man achieves his end. Hence the inner meaning of freedom lies in the possibility of self-realisation which it confers on man. From this it follows that there is a right use and a wrong use of freedom. Although freedom in itself is one of man's most precious faculties, it also marks the uncertainty of man's existence (which, however, is overemphasised in existentialism).

Man's Emotions

Man's emotional faculties are more complex than intellect and will. The old philosophers as well as modern psychologists have tried to systematise and classify emotions but no attempts have found general acceptance. There is no doubt about the basic dichotomy of attraction and repulsion which is manifest in the polarity of love and hatred, desire and fear, joy and sorrow. Modern authors have often tried to reduce affections or emotions to other elements which would mean that they were not acts of a specific faculty. But so far, these theories have not been convincingly confirmed. Although many of the emotional phenomena involve various factors (for example, secretions of the ductless glands like the adrenals), there remains a distinct and irreducible psychic experience which postulates a particular potentiality in man's structure. Fundamentally, it can be described as man's receptivity for the beautiful and his aversion from the ugly, hideous and horrible. The inner yearning of man goes to grace and harmony, to everything which is lovable, desirable, attractive or perfect. Dogs can be taught tricks but only man is capable of art. Man's admiration of the beauty of nature, his artistic creativeness or aesthetic enjoyment belong to a different category than the true, the good and the useful. The appreciation of the beautiful is subjective and different cultures and periods have different canons of art, but there remains the basic fact that every man can feel the attraction of what appeals to him as beautiful and can reach out for what he finds lovable, that every man shrinks away from what appears to him as frightful and is turned off by what he thinks ugly.

Naturally, man's faculties are not in separate watertight compartments and do not work in complete independence. Nevertheless, the human spirit possesses specifically different potentialities and human consciousness embraces very distinct experiences. One and the same human person is endowed with this triple structural ordainment towards the true, the good, and the beautiful, and he may experience these three attributes in one and the same object. Like the concept of entelechy, the analysis proposing the true, the good and the beautiful does not give an explanation but points out a fact that demands an explanation.

Good and Obligatory

While all actions in harmony with man's nature are good, not all good actions are obligatory (that is, man is not bound to do everything that is good). Obligatory actions are those required for man's existence (to use the ordinary means for preserving health and life) or his integrity as a person (self-knowledge, self-control, self-esteem) and those that are necessary to avoid evil. The duty to do good and to avoid evil is given with man's nature as a being that must live and grow by his own free decision. It is in man's nature to develop as a person, and because he cannot renounce being a person, he must live — and die — as a person, responsible for being what he is bound to be. Ethics, therefore, is essentially teleological, leading man to the unfolding of his personality to which he is ordained by his nature.

Protestants generally uphold ethics of intention while Catholics stress ethics of responsibility. Man may feel responsible only for what he intends, but he is responsible for all that he does — morally responsible for what he does or does not do by his own free will.

Material Norms

On principle, moral norms claim universal validity. What is valid for me should be valid also for others under the same circumstances. Different from Kant's categorical imperative ('act only on that maxim through which you can at the same time will that it should become a universal law') which regards only the formal aspect of the ethical obligation, the doctrine of a natural moral law asserts the universal validity of material norms (that is, rules commanding or forbidding certain kinds of action). It is possible to create a system of good and bad human acts and many authors of books on ethics or moral theology have done just that. But these are purely abstract considerations that are of very remote use for man's actual life, just as a handbook on driving cannot tell a driver what to do if his brakes fail. The book can tell him what to do if ..., but no book can exhaust all 'life.' Moral norms, therefore, can indicate possible choices but nobody can tell an individual what he has to do in a concrete situation.

Subjective Morality

While moral norms intimate the objective moral order, moral conduct implies man's free decision for what he considers good. Moral (and legal) norms are not self-executing. Norms can only influence human conduct if they enter into the individual's consciousness and the individual recognises that the norm is relevant to what he intends to do or not to do here and now. An obligatory norm can only be effective if the individual's conscience is aware of its obligatory character and acknowledges that he is bound to act in accordance with the norm. Subjective morality presupposes that man knows what he is doing, that is, that he is doing what he considers good and intends to do it. Man need not have the intention of fulfilling his duty or, what Kant thought necessary for morality, to do the good because it is good and for no other reason or purpose.

It is possible that man finds himself in what is called an incorrigible error and thinks that something is good which is objectively evil (so that his action is subjectively good but objectively bad) or considers something evil that is objectively good (so that the action is subjectively bad although it is objectively good). This analysis is based on the theory that all decisions can be subsumed under general principles (which does not mean that man uses a syllogistical method in the actual decisions of his conscience). Moralists further distinguish object, circumstances and purpose of human actions. In order to be morally good, object (that is, what man does), circumstances and purpose (or motive) must be good or at least morally neutral; if one of these three elements is bad, the entire action is bad (*'bonum ex integra causa, malum ex quolibet defectu'*). For instance, to drink beer is neither good nor bad in itself, but to drink beer that has been stolen or in order to get drunk is morally bad. Because it is bad to do something immoral for a good purpose, the principle 'the end justifies the means' is wrong: a good end does not make the use of a bad means right.

Perfection

Man's moral growth does not mean a continuous upward curve towards a pre-planned goal. Although man's perfection has often been represented as such a goal, it cannot be defined by certain human qualities to be attained or certain actions to be accomplished. It indicates a direction rather than a goal, a direction in which man is supposed to move rather than a goal to be attained. Man's perfection is an unattainable goal — Christ's words, 'Be you therefore perfect, as also your heavenly Father is perfect' (Matth 5,48), enuntiates an attitude rather than a norm. Man must continue to act until the end and each act must be performed on the assumption that it will contribute to man's moral growth which must go on as long as man exists. Moral growth cannot be measured in metres and moral worth cannot be valued in dollars and cents. Morality is not a question of observing certain norms — although this constitutes one aspect — but of affirming the inherent ordainment of man's nature in attitude and behaviour.

Sometimes the presentation of ethics puts too much emphasis on prohibitions, the fences and barriers, and gives not enough attention to the direction and guidance, the beacons and signposts. For man's actual life, to know what is good or bad is not enough; man needs motivation to follow his conscience, the conviction that there is nothing more important than to live up to his personal dignity. Motivation is the crux of all moral education and the point where most secular systems are woefully inadequate.

Morality and Legality

In western society, individual freedom is often asserted as a right 'beyond good and evil.' In his conduct, western man respects primarily legal, not moral restrictions, and he thinks himself entitled to go all the way to the point where his conduct meets the barrier of the freedom of others and the restraints of legal inhibitions. But the meaning of law and morality cannot be confined to the purely negative duty of avoiding evil. The observance of legal prohibitions may generally suffice for protecting human co-existence but such behaviour will hardly ensure a humanly satisfactory social climate. There are legal and moral tasks whose fulfilment demands positive action. The observation of legal norms requires only external conformity but morality extends also to man's inner life. If individual morality would consist merely in avoiding breaking the law, it would completely neglect the cultivation of moral conduct and the positive development of moral goodness.

From a theoretical point of view, popular notions of what is good or bad do not decide the morality of human conduct; nevertheless, the results of a survey sponsored by the Connecticut Mutual Life Insurance Company of Hartford and carried out by Research and Forecasts, Inc., a New York survey firm, on 'American Values in the Eighties' are interesting. Large majorities believe that adultery, homosexuality, lesbianism, teenage sex, pornography and marijuana are morally wrong. More than 40 per cent of the respondents condemned pre-marital sex and cohabitation of single people. The report suggested that 'moral issues' are becoming the most controversial problems in American politics, overshadowing traditional questions such as the welfare state, the scale of government, defense and foreign policy. Leaders as well as issues will be judged increasingly in moral terms.

Some of the qualifications used to indicate compliance with or infringement of moral norms can be used with reference to particular norms as well as moral behaviour in general. Honest and dishonest, for example, refer to conduct regarding property or truthfulness but can also convey a general assessment of a person. The tendency to equate behaviour in a certain sphere with morality in general is particularly noteworthy in the expressions judging sexual behaviour. Besides more specific terms such as chaste, continent or undefiled, we use pure, decent, virtuous, decorous and moral which gives the impression that the observance of the sex code is equivalent to a morally good life — an implication which is notoriously false. The evaluation of human conduct with regard to moral norms includes an evaluation of the personality which is not necessarily connected with the observance of social customs and is irrelevant to the fulfilment of legal duties.

Theories on Morality

The positivistic rejection of objective values reduces ethics to a system of empirically and scientifically unverifiable norms which the individual may accept on ideological grounds but which he may also disregard. The programmatic negation of obligation constitutes the gist of the anti-theology and anti-ethics of writers such as Auguste Comte, Friedrich Nietzsche and Jean-Paul Sartre. Morality, if not sheer hypocrisy, is psychologically or socially conditioned conduct. Freud's 'superego' forces alien values on the individual's burgeoning consciousness, repressing the drives of the 'id' so as to ensure a somehow tolerable co-existence in society. The occasional explosions of the repressed instincts lead to crimes by individuals and wars by the masses.

Existentialism is based on the premise that each man must define for himself his own moral code. God is being dethroned in order to proclaim the autonomy of man. God is man's most repressive constraint. As long as man does not reject this bond, he has not taken the decisive step for freeing himself from restrictive inhibitions. God's non-existence is the condition of human freedom. If there were a God, he would define the sphere of human existence. Inescapably, obedience would be the basic determinant of man's life. Only if there is no God does no creative idea of man exist and nothing predetermines who or what man is or ought to be. Only then is he truly free. Everybody must invent for himself what he understands by man and no standard should limit his choice. Man is what he makes of himself. In his *'Saint Genêt, comédien et martyr,'* Sartre glorifies a new generation of saints typified by the French thief, homosexual and author Jean Genêt. Illegal and anti-social behaviour is the mark of the totally free.

The traditional morality supposes that it is better for man to be than not to be, and that man's existence implies the duty to live in accordance with the meaning of this existence. Schopenhauer, who explains the world as the will to live, echoes a basic assertion of Buddha and holds that it would be better if this will would not exist, if nothing would exist. The world contains more sorrow than joy, and all satisfaction is only ephemeral because it generates new desires and new wants. The pain of the animal that is eaten is more intense than the pleasure for the animal that eats it. Different from animals, man possesses reason but reason is made subservient to will and a slave of hunger and sexual lust. Conscious or unconscious concupiscence also dominates a man who regards himself as a sage.

Morality is not the outcome of group indoctrination. Society, it has been asserted, inobtrusively teaches by play and education what is considered right or wrong. These values or 'programmed decisions,' the customs of the group, are 'internalised' and become the conscience of the group's members who are taught that they remain members of the group only so long as they adhere to these norms.

The psychological theory of self-suppression denounces the limitations of freedom by learned cultural rules and mores. But social life is based on self-control, and no society could exist if the observance of social rules would depend entirely on coercion.

The 'Humanist Manifesto II' states: 'We reject all religious, ideological, or moral codes.' — 'We affirm that moral values derived their source from human experience. Ethics is autonomous and situational, needing no theological or ideological sanctions. Ethics stems from human need and intent.'

Sociobiology, the latest attempt to explain ethics in terms of Darwinian evolutionism, reduces the 'moral imperative' to a feeling embodying a selective advantage at least for the group or the gene pool of the species. 'Noble' properties have proved useful for self-preservation or the survival of the species so that behaviour conforming to what has contributed to the improvement of the genes tends to favour natural selection., Robert Spaemann and Reinhard Löw have shown the inner contradiction of the sociobiologists when they deduce moral postulates from the world of pure fabrication *(Die Frage Wozu?* 1981). Selective advantage is a mere fact unrelated to the phenomena of man's moral experience such as freedom, self-determination, duty, responsibility and guilt. The 'ought to' implied in moral postulates is specifically different from all forms of biological or psychological advantages for the individual or the group. The moral good cannot be reduced to any kind of physical good.

Reviving Rousseau's thesis of man's inner goodness, the humanist psychology intends to create a new man and a new society by self-realisation. Erich Fromm thinks that man's positive forces grow if negative potentialities are not encouraged. Nature itself develops towards the good and is only vitiated by social influences. The tendency towards self-realisation operates with remarkable efficiency in nature. The organism makes mistakes, but these are corrected by feedback. Man receives the impulses to the realisation of his positive potentialities by person-related communication. There is no need for advice, admonition or commandments, and only those laws which the individual considers right are to be obeyed. Feeling is superior to intellect, intuition more reliable than science and technology. Changes in consciousness, possibly aided by drugs, can lead to the exploration of deeper and hitherto unknown zones of the ego.

Authority and Freedom

Man's life in society necessarily implies a limitation of his freedom. There are natural societies and voluntary societies (the Scholastics added a third kind, a society based on positive divine institution, the Church). The concept of a natural society means that this kind of society (family, state) corresponds to a natural ordainment of man so that it is natural and necessary for man to live in this kind of society. The actually existing societies, however, are not necessary but the result of a historical development. All members of society are directly bound to the goal of the society and directly responsible for the attainment of the goal. But the goal of society, the common good, is not the result of a necessary development but a task to be accomplished by the free cooperation of the members. What is required for the common good is not immediately evident. Therefore, it is necessary to determine what the common good actually means, what it requires and how it should be achieved, and thus guide and direct the free activity of the members to the goal. This is the function of authority. (Authority has a number of other meanings, such as the authority of a scientist, or of a witness or a document, which need no explanation here). If all members of society had a complete understanding of the goal of society and its requirements and would do spontaneously whatever is necessary (as Plato supposed for the philosopher), authority and law would be unnecessary. The prophet Jeremiah envisioned this for the state of perfection (Jer 31, 33-34; quoted Hebr 8, 10-11 and 10,16).

The bearer of authority has the task and the competence to direct the free activity of the members of society to its goal, the common good. Authority demands obedience because the members of society are bound to the common end and obliged to cooperate for its attainment., How authority is exercised is a different question. The bearer of authority can be a single individual nominated by society but authority can also be exercised by the entire society (direct democracy).

Authority is based on freedom, and freedom requires authority. Authority has no place in the necessary mechanical operations of nature. Authority appeals to free consent. The directives of authority are followed because it is rational to follow them. Without authority, man remains without orientation in society and does not know how to use his freedom in society.

Civil Authority

What man is bound to do or not to do as a member of civil society is laid down in the laws but the laws are not the reason why man should obey them. Just as man is bound to the end implicit in his nature, so he is bound to the end of the social entity to which he belongs. Man belongs to social bodies in different ways. He belongs to some kind of community constituting and organising the public order, now usually the state, necessarily so that he cannot repudiate being bound to the end of that community. But he forms or joins other groups or communities by his own free will and he is bound to the ends of these groups or communities because of his choice. In many cases, he may be free to quit these groups which will end his obligation to contribute to the end or purpose of these groups, but in other cases, his freedom to withdraw may be restricted. Man is free to marry or not to marry, but if he marries, he is bound to the end of marriage, the community of life.

Meaning and Function of Law

Civil authority has the power to make laws, that is, to determine what the public good requires and in which way the public good should be realised. (Of course, today's laws are mostly technical manuals for the operations of the bureaucracy.) Law can only control external conduct, and the task of the legislator is not to make citizens virtuous but to make society livable. The formal object of the activities of the political authority is the 'just,' that is, what is postulated by the public order and in harmony with the value system of the community. It has often been asserted that the state is responsible for 'public morality.' What we understand today by public morality is a question of 'mores' rather than ethics, that is, the behaviour considered desirable or at least tolerable in a given community. Upholding public morality was one of the functions the state took over from the Church in the Christian Occident where Christian morality had been the only universal regulation of the public order. But the state is incompetent to decide questions of morality or to determine what is morally good or bad. When you put the state in charge of morality, you get Puritan New England.

The entire criminal law involves moral issues, but criminal law is intended to protect the public order, not public morality. The individual has a moral as well as a legal obligation to obey just laws, but the moral duty is not imposed by the state; it results from the individual's commitment to the common good.

Laws, St Thomas explains (S. theol., 1-2, q. 96, a. 2), must be appropriate to those for whom they are established. It would be utopian to expect perfection in the ordinary run of people. Laws should respect the limits of what can be demanded of the morality of the ordinary citizen. Legislation (and politics) requiring for its functioning a change in man himself is immoral. So the legislator has to content himself with prohibiting the worst crimes from which the greater part of the people can abstain although human law must forbid all that would endanger the existence of human society. This includes the protection of life and health, the freedom, safety and dignity of all persons living or staying in the territory of the state and to ensure that 'justice' is observed in all circumstances. The authorities, therefore, are bound to indicate what is incompatible with the public order and people can only be arrested and punished for infringements of the rules thus established.

A recent Vatican instruction on sex education ('Educational Guidance

in Human Love') stated that it is 'incumbent on civil authorities' in view
of the public good to protect 'public morality.' 'It is the task of the state
to safeguard its citizens against injustices and moral disorders,' the
document said. This includes the abuse of minors and every form of
sexual violence, degrading dress, permissiveness and pornography. The
instruction also calls for 'juridical regulation of the instruments of social
communication to protect public morality' which is to cover magazines,
films, radio and television programmes, exhibitions, shows and publicity.
The Church can hardly expect that today's pluralistic society in which
the freedom of expression constitutes a basic value will be ready for this
kind of regulation.

Man's obligation to obey just laws does not come from his
submission to authority but from his moral duty to cooperate by his free
actions to the common good (which is not a fixed thing but, like man's
personal existence, a continuous evolution). Man's basic ordainment
towards the common good implies a moral duty inasmuch as it involves
his personal freedom. His civil liability for infringements of the law
(police and the courts have no business to intervene so long as the law
is obeyed) concerns only his external conduct. No state, therefore, can
exist without a minimum of voluntary compliance by its citizens and a
modicum of moral commitment to the goals of society.

Crimes are actions in violation of a law forbidding or commanding
such actions and making such violations punishable. These laws are called
criminal laws because they define the actions to be regarded as crimes
and stipulate how they are to be punished. They are also called penal
laws because they fix the punishment by which infractions of the law
are to be expiated. The character of criminal law as positive regulations
is stressed by some generally recognised principles such as *nullum crimen
sine lege* (no crime without law) and *nulla poena sine lege* (no punishment
without law) which intend to protect people against abuses. But the
principle that nobody should be punished for an act that was lawful when
it was performed is not observed by totalitarian régimes.

Law cannot replace morality. In a society in which the moral order
has broken down, people live in fear, in fear of falling victim to crime.
When people no longer respect moral rules and the precepts of civility,
life in society becomes a nightmare. Complaints about rudeness and
vulgarity are just as widespread as the anxiety for one's safety. The
emancipation from the restrictive morality of the past has resulted in the
moral stupefaction of society. The horrendous effects of the eclipse of
morality demonstrate its creative role in public life.

Law cannot replace man's conscience. No man should be forced to
do what his conscience forbids him to do. An individual is not entitled
to affirmative illegal action because of the dictates of his conscience (the
'right to revolution' is too complex a subject to be discussed in a few
words), but no man should be coerced to act against his conscience.

Totalitarian régimes try to abolish the individual conscience as a disturbance of social uniformity. Dissenters who refuse to comply with state orders as against their conscience are defamed as criminals. But faithfulness to his conscience is one of man's inalienable rights.

The Catholic Archdiocese of New York lost a lawsuit contesting the constitutionality of a city regulation requiring the inclusion of birth control and abortion in family planning programmes. Exclusion of such measures made the agencies of the Archdiocese ineligible for city contracts, with the loss of millions of dollars in financial aid.

Since the agencies are not obliged to conclude contracts with the city, they are not forced to recognise that birth control and abortion are at least morally indifferent. The legislature must have been well aware that the official creed of a large section of the population considers artificial birth control and abortion as immoral, and the regulation was a deliberate attempt to assert a secularist morality against 'sectarian' views. Similar conflicts have arisen from the prohibition of discrimination against homosexuals.

The concept of civil rights has not yet been sufficiently clarified. While the state may make rules that disregard the moral views of its citizens and enforce these rules in the actions of public bodies, it has no right to force anybody to conform to its disregard of moral issues and to make 'civil rights' the canon of private conduct. Still less can people, including government officials and private organisations, be obliged to act against their moral convictions.

Custom, Morality and Law

The distinction between custom, morality and law is not always clear and in some societies, there is hardly any differentiation in practice. Generally, the code of each group determines what is publicly allowed and what is allowed in private, and it may regulate the behaviour of married and unmarried men and women. In December 1980, Miss Padmini Kolhapure, a film actress (at that time aged 18), was hauled into court because she had kissed the Prince of Wales when he visited a film studio. Ansah Ahmed, a citizen of Meerut (a place north of New Delhi), who described himself as a 'pious Muslim,' submitted a complaint to Judge Sardar Akhtar in which he stated that the actress had kissed the prince with the intention of attracting cheap popularity and that she had insulted Indian womanhood. When Miss Kolhapure did not appear in court, the judge issued an arrest order. The charge was 'depraving Indian culture by publicly kissing.' Asked by western reporters whether kissing was allowed on the Indian screen, Miss Kolhapure replied: 'Oh no, this was my first kiss!'

Lately, however, a marked change has been transforming Indian sexual mores, at least in the cities. The trend towards a more open society which started under Indira Gandhi has accelerated under her son and successor Rajiv. Issues such as women's rights, inter-caste marriages and homosexual relations are being aired, largely under the influence of television, and explicit sex is appearing in the print media and in the movies. On-screen kissing which was banned as 'un-Indian' in indigenous productions and could only be shown in foreign films is now routine and even nudity is creeping in. The number of divorces, although still small, is rising and women are no longer willing to suffer in silence. Pre-marital sex is becoming more common and more unmarried women are having abortions. But the change has also its seamier sides such as an increase in drug abuse and crime.

A Kuwaiti youth was arrested on a beach while kissing and hugging his 15-year-old fiancée. He was sentenced to six months in jail but the prosecutor appealed the sentence because it was insufficient punishment for offending public decency. The appeals court upped the jail term to 42 months. The consent of the girl, the court held, was immaterial because she was a minor.

In western morality as well as law, marriage constituted the institutionalised form to which permissible sexual relations were limited. The sex revolution which rejected traditional western sexual morality asserted individual freedom against social institutions and questioned the foundations of the customary restrictions on sex and the validity of the institution of marriage.

There can be no doubt that moral norms are often felt as oppressive so that many societies condone behaviour violating the accepted rules of conduct under certain circumstances. This creates a double standard which is particularly frequent in the rules for sexual conduct of men and women. In some instances, festivals provided the occasion for forgetting all rules and prohibitions. Carnival, for example, was celebrated with unrestrained licentiousness in European countries until fairly recent times.

Catholic Position on Sexual Morality

Among the West's traditional positions on sexual morality, the doctrine of the Catholic Church constitutes one of the most rigorous, but also one of the theoretically most elaborate systems. (The Church, of course, is universal, but the systematisation of the moral code was chiefly the work of western theologians.) As moral theology, the teaching of the Church is not based on rational arguments but on revelation; however, many of the commandments or prohibitions are applications of principles of 'natural law' to certain situations.

The basic norm of Catholic moral theology regarding human sexuality is the proposition that the human semen and sexual pleasure connected with the activation of the sex organs are only intended by God for the procreation of offspring in a legitimate marriage. 'All deliberate exercise of sexuality must be reserved to a married relationship which realises the full sense of mutual self-giving and human procreation in the context of true love' (Pope Paul VI, Encyclical *Humanae Vitae*). The sexual act becomes sinful also in marriage if its inner purpose (the procreation of offspring) is intentionally impeded (either by the interruption of intercourse and ejaculation outside the female organ — the original meaning of 'onanism,' Gen 38,9, or by artificial means). This, however, does not mean that sexual intercourse is only licit if it actually leads to conception. Every voluntary procurement of sexual pleasure outside marriage and sexual acts unrelated to the lawful marital act are sinful. The sins connected with the satisfaction of sexual lust are divided into actions in which the gratification of the sexual desire is obtained in a 'natural' way such as fornication, adultery, incest, rape and abduction (kidnapping for immoral purposes), and sins against nature which include masturbation, homosexuality, anal intercourse with a woman and bestiality. Sinful are thoughts, desires, talk or acts through which sexual excitement is voluntarily sought even if no orgasm occurs.

Pope John Paul II on Chastity

Pope John Paul II created a considerable stir when, in commenting on a passage in the Sermon on the Mount ('You have heard that it was said to them of old: "Thou shalt not commit adultery." But I say to you that whosoever shall look on a woman to lust after her hath already committed adultery with her in his heart;' Matth 5, 27-28), he said in a general audience on 8 October 1980: 'Adultery in your heart is committed not only when you look with concupiscence on a woman who is not your wife but also if you look in the same manner at your wife.' That assertion not only sounded extreme but also contradicted the common opinion of moral theologians that between married people. all 'natural' internal and external acts referable to marital relations are licit and that also irrespective of intercourse, sexual acts between married partners are allowed if they do not lead to self-satisfaction. But to all acts between spouses the caveat applies that they should not be done with sinful (for example, adulterous or sodomitic) intent.

　　Pope John Paul II's comment on lust can be understood if it is put into the context of his doctrine on love and chastity which he set forth twenty years before becoming pope (Karol Wojtyla, *Liebe und Verantwortung — Eine ethische Studie*). He starts from the old distinction between '*amor benevolentiae*' and '*amor concupiscentiae*' (love of benevolence and love of concupiscence). If the love of concupiscence prevails in the relations between husband and wife, the love of benevolence will be reduced to second place. Love of benevolence means the desire for the well-being of the beloved, the affirmation of the beloved's own lovableness, self-surrender for the happiness of the beloved irrespective of him or her being a source of good to oneself. Marriage, Karol Wojtyla said, means 'total mutual self-giving.' Selfless love demands the mutual affirmation of the value of the person. This love is different from love life. In love, the dominant aspect is the responsibility of one person to the other; in love life, sensual desires and the affectionateness of concupiscence predominate which, as the author put it, bring the 'tastiness' of more intense feelings but are not true love because they imply egoism. The emotional excitement stimulated by the senses involves an attitude of enjoyment which indicates a disposition to 'sinful' love. The apparent love covers the subjectivity of values which leads to the egoism of emotion and the senses. The virtue of chastity has the rôle to keep love free from such dispositions and control not only sensuality and the concupiscence of the body but also the inner centres where the attitude of delectation originates and grows. Chastity demands the subjugation of all forms of subjectivism and egoism.

In the relation to a person of the opposite sex, chastity means a pure attitude. Chastity does not demand the suppression of the values of the body and sex into the subconscience nor the blockage of sensuality and carnal desires but the rejection of the attitude of delectation. Chastity does not negate the values of the body and sex but requires that the person should be affirmed therein and that they should not be separated from personal values. Chastity ordains a 'personalistic' norm: 'Thou shalt love the person; thou shalt not use it.'

Every human being is burdened with the concupiscence of the flesh and inclined to seek the 'tastiness' of love, particularly in the satisfaction of concupiscence. Chastity demands the 'humility of the body.' Humility means the right attitude towards genuine greatness. For man, personality constitutes the true and final greatness so that the human body must be humble towards the person. It must be humble towards the greatness of love and to accomplish this subordination is the task of chastity. If the carnal enjoyment in which the values of sex become a common experience arrogates to itself the decisive rôle in personal love, it offends against chastity.

Happiness can only be found in the permanent union of persons. The pleasure sought from the body and sex in the relations between man and woman is not the same as happiness. Only if the 'humility of the body' subordinates the delectability of pleasure to personality can happiness grow.

Personalistic Interpretation of Marriage

The personalistic interpretation of marriage and sex is by no means the private opinion of Karol Wojtyla but is also expressed in official Church documents. In the Constitution *'Gaudium et Spes,'* the Second Vatican Council said of marital love: 'Indeed by its generous activity, it grows better and grows greater. Therefore, it far excels mere erotic inclination which, selfishly pursued, soon enough fades wretchedly away. This love is uniquely expressed and perfected through the marital act. ... Sealed by mutual faithfulness and hallowed above all by Christ's sacrament, this love remains steadfastly true in body and mind, in bright days and dark. It will never be profaned by adultery and divorce. Firmly established by the Lord, the unity of marriage will radiate from the equal personal dignity of wife and husband, a dignity acknowledged by mutual and true love' (The Church Today, Nr. 49).

The Council also finds a relation between conjugal love and its condemnation of birth control and abortion: 'Therefore, from the moment of its conception life must be guarded with the greatest care, while abortion and infanticide are unspeakable crimes. The sexual characteristics of man and the human faculty of procreation wonderfully exceed the dispositions of lower forms of life. Hence the acts themselves which are proper to conjugal love and which are exercised with genuine human dignity must be honoured with great reverence.

'Therefore when there is a question of harmonising conjugal love with the responsible transmission of human life, the moral aspect of any procedure does not depend solely on sincere intentions or on an evaluation of motives. It must be determined by objective standards. These, based on the nature of the human person and his acts, preserve the full sense of mutual self-giving and human procreation in the context of true love. Such a goal cannot be achieved unless the virtue of conjugal chastity is sincerely practised. Relying on these principles, sons of the Church may not undertake methods of regulating procreation which are found blameworthy by the teaching authority of the Church in its unfolding of the divine law' (Ibid. Nr. 51).

In short, whatever violates the dignity of the human person cannot be love, and love can only be right and genuine if it means an unfolding of human personality. Love as such implies ethical postulates. T. Styczén, the successor of Karol Wojtyla on the chair of ethics at the Catholic university of Lublin, writes: 'Experience prohibits to separate love from obligation and obligation from love. On the contrary, it reveals that the ethical ought is an obligatory demand to love and that love of a person regarding a person is an ought.'

A comprehensive statement of the Church's teaching on sexuality was issued on 10 March 1987. The document, entitled 'Instruction on Respect for Human Life in its Origin and on the Dignity of Procreation — Replies to Certain Questions of the Day,' was prepared by the Congregation for the Doctrine of Faith (headed by Cardinal Ratzinger) and approved by Pope John Paul II. Basic to the instruction's pronouncements is the Catholic view of man as the substantial union of a spiritual soul with the human body which, the document says, 'cannot be considered a mere complex of tissues, organs and functions, nor can it be evaluated in the same way as the body of animals.' The image of man is supplemented by two principles underlying the Church's position on sexual morality, that the life of every human being must be respected from the moment of conception and that the only acceptable way to procreate a child is through natural sexual acts between married spouses.

Traditional morality is threatened by new biomedical techniques which, if left unchecked, could lead to a 'system of radical eugenics' or the attempt to improve the human species through the control of hereditary factors in mating. The document condemns all forms of test-tube procreation, artificial insemination and surrogate motherhood, restating the view that marriage does not give an absolute right to offspring. Also rejected are experimentation on living embryos, cloning, attempts to fashion animal–human hybrids, freezing of embryos and the planting of human embryos in artificial and animal uteri. The instruction calls on governments to outlaw sperm and embryo banks and surrogate motherhood.

Pre-natal diagnosis is permissible if the method used safeguards the life and integrity of the embryo and the mother but is immoral when it is done with the thought of possibly inducing an abortion depending on the results. 'A diagnosis which shows the existence of a malformation or a hereditary illness must not be the equivalent of a death sentence.'

Rejecting the excursions of scientists into the realm of philosophy or ethics, the instruction states: 'No biologist or doctor can reasonably claim, by virtue of his scientific competence, to be able to decide on people's origin and destiny.' Scientific research and its applications are not morally neutral. 'Science without conscience can only lead to man's ruin.'

Kant on Sexual Morality

Kant's views on sexual morality are more or less identical with the position of the Catholic Church. He distinguishes the natural and the unnatural use of sexual organs and faculties. The unnatural use may be either with a person of the same sex or with an animal, and as violations of humanity in one's own person, these infractions must be condemned without qualification or exception. The natural union of the sexes must be based on a contract between man and woman for the mutual use of the sexual faculties but the procreation of offspring, although a purpose of nature, is not necessarily the purpose of marriage (*Metaphysik der Sitten*, 1-2-3, Par. 24). Only monogamy safeguards the equality of possession, and concubinage or prostitution cannot be the objects of a legally binding contract (Par. 26). Kant castigates masturbation as an abominable misuse of the sexual faculties and calls it unnatural lust because it is directed not towards the purpose of nature but towards an object created by imagination. Man degrades his own person below an animal. Kant concedes that it is difficult to demonstrate the illicitness of the unnatural or casual use of the sexual faculties as a violation of man's duties against himself but he thinks that man throws away his personality if he uses himself for the satisfaction of animal instincts (ibid., II-I-Par. 7). He states that the purpose of nature in copulation is procreation, the preservation of the species, and that at least nothing should be done against this purpose (ibid.).

Affirmation of Sexuality

The opposite of the Catholic doctrine on the morality of sex is the position that every expression and activation of sexuality is good or at least morally indifferent, and that all restrictions are imposed by social taboos, good manners, custom and education. Basically, this opinion assumes that sexuality has nothing to do with morality. Sexuality, it is said, has its purpose in itself, and two people who love each other have the right to complete sexual union. The procreation of children is an addition to love life which can be renounced if it is unwanted (Poul Henningsen). In its consequences, such an opinion leads to the negation of all restrictions on sex and to 'licentious hedonism.' This point of view, which has been asserted for the entire field of sexuality or for certain actions (masturbation, birth control) disregards the principle that all voluntary actions must be in conformity with man's personalness.

People may not know the rationale of sexual taboos and prohibitions but they experience embarrassment, shame and an intense feeling of guilt when they violate moral norms or even social inhibitions. Practising Catholics go to confession but in some circles, the psychiatrist has replaced the father confessor. There is little evidence to show which method helps people better to get over their sexual hang-ups.

It cannot be denied that sexual lust belongs to man's highest sensual pleasures (cf. the original text of Eccles 2,8). The question is whether man has a right to the enjoyment of sexual pleasure and if so, whether this right is absolute or subject to limitations.

Since respect for the dignity of the human person constitutes the basic norm of morality, all sexual acts (including inner acts such as fantasies or desires) are immoral if they imply a violation or degradation of human personality, offend against the right order in man or man's development as a free rational being. This means that sexual activity should never be degrading. Human nature and the right order in man do not change but the image of man and the consciousness of human dignity can be influenced by cultural and social factors. This means that the moral consciousness of a given society and the moral norms that it recognises do not necessarily agree with the concept of personality and human dignity in another culture. What is commonly considered decent or custom in a society may be closely related to human dignity (note

Lenin's example that 'good manners' forbid man from drinking from a puddle in the road) but the perception of the personal value of man is not always and everywhere the same.

Generally speaking, sexuality ought to be treated less as a problem of morality and more as a matter of manners, self-respect and education. From the point of view of a personalistic concept of marriage, polygamy is morally wrong and objectionable, but it seems somewhat presumptuous to declare that people living in other cultures may be subjectively inculpable but that the norms of these cultures objectively authorise immorality. We consider the image of man from which we deduce our personalistic concept of marriage as objectively right and universally valid, but the validity of our image of man is not so categorical as to convict every deviation as a flagrant error. This does not mean that truth is relative but that our knowledge of truth is not absolute. There can be no doubt that the human intellect is by nature ordained towards the apprehension of the truth and necessarily seeks and affirms what appears to be true, but all human knowledge is subject to the principle already mentioned above: *Quidquid recipitur, per modum recipientis recipitur.* In this sense, our knowledge is influenced by our experience and our image of man reflects our culture. Insofar as our moral norms are based on our image of man, they are subject to these limitations.

In dealing with sexual morality, it is important to distinguish solitary acts of the individual and interpersonal conduct. Sexuality is essentially bound to the difference between man and woman and ordained to their union, but each human being is a sexual being and capable of using his sexual faculties independently and irrespective of another sexual being. Moral problems, therefore, can arise with regard to solitary acts as well as conduct involving more than one person.

'Natural' and 'Instinctive'

A special difficulty is presented by actions described as 'natural' and which, on account of their 'naturalness,' have given rise to conflicting assertions. On the one hand, 'natural' has been identified with 'instinctive' which, as mentioned above, has prompted the assertion that man has a right to satisfy his instincts because this is 'natural.' On the other hand, nature has been represented as a norm prohibiting wilful interference. This applies particularly to the act of copulation whose biological structure has been considered as an ethical norm by Catholic moralists. It is clear that, biologically, the sexual union of man and woman is directed to the procreation of offspring but it is not so clear that every other use of sexuality offends against the personal dignity of man and represents a misuse. Sexual intercourse as an expression of love and mutual surrender (which, of course, is a completely different dimension from the physiological action) does not depend on the possibility of conception, and for women who are not or no longer capable of conceiving and for sterile men, infertility does not make marital intercourse immoral. Only if the biological process involves a moral obligation can birth control by 'interference' with the 'natural' act and, in reverse, conception outside the 'natural' act (test-tube babies) be considered immoral.

Human propagation is not a necessary natural event and the procreation of children depends on the free will of the parents who want children and are able to educate them. Man is not bound to bow before the necessity of natural phenomena and to let physical or biological occurrences take their course. The conquest of physical limitations is not immoral so long as it does not imply a negation of personal values. Marriage does not include the obligation to produce children (but the express exclusion of the right to sexual intercourse makes the consent to marriage invalid) and the consummation of the marriage is not required for its validity. If there is a reasonable danger that children will suffer from serious deformations, or if would-be parents are unable to bring up children in an appropriate way, they have an obligation not to produce children and to bring children into the world would be irresponsible.

Conception as a Natural Process and Birth Control

According to traditional Catholic moral theology, spouses who do not want or should not have children must either abstain from marital intercourse or regulate intercourse in such a way that conception is 'naturally' impossible (that is, limit intercourse to the so-called 'safe' periods). Every interference with the natural course of copulation which impedes the primary end of the sex act is immoral. Procreation is the ultimate purpose of marital intercourse while proximate effects such as the physical expression of mutual love, fostering of affection and sexual satisfaction are subordinate to the final end and cannot be procured in themselves if the primary purpose is intentionally frustrated.

The Church rejects birth control not only if 'artificial means' are used but also if the couple practices natural family planning without just reasons. The use of the rhythm method for avoiding procreation is only justified if the couple has a sufficient reason for not wanting (more) children. The ordinary burden involved in having children (including the physical and mental demands on both parents as well as the material disadvantages) does not constitute such a reason.

Pope Paul John II spoke on the subject of marriage and sexuality for four months in his Wednesday audiences expressing the view that birth control meant interference with the rights of God who alone had the power to decide on the creation of life. He also stated that the marital act ceased to be an act of love if the spouses practised birth control. Even in a theistic view, God as First Cause does not replace the causality of created beings, and birth control is no obstacle to making the marital act a manifestation of genuine affection.

In an address commemorating the anniversary of Paul VI's 1968 encyclical *Humanae Vitae,* Pope John Paul II declared that the ban on artificial birth control was part of natural law and applied to all men and women. 'Every matrimonial act must remain open to the transmission of life.' This point of view presupposes that the biological process involves the obligation to have this process take its natural course. Such a precept or principle cannot be proven and it is hard to understand that the sex act should be subject to a restriction that obviously does not apply to other biological processes. The Committee of Morals of the Church of Scotland decided in 1960 that birth control should no longer be considered as an 'act against nature.'

Copulation as a human act concerns mating, not fertilisation. Neither the sexual desire of the male nor female responsiveness to sexual excitation is directly related to fertilisation. In both sexes, the sex instinct leads to mating which means the union of a male and a female sex partner, not the fusion of a spermatozoon with an ovum. In itself, coitus is not a reproductive process. Reproduction is the possible but not necessary consequence of mating. The question, therefore, is whether all biological effects of human acts must be allowed to take their 'natural' course. Man interferes in a variety of ways with natural processes such as digestion or blood circulation; even using glasses is an interference with the natural course of vision. To a large extent, medical art consists in the interference with biological processes, suppressing natural effects or redirecting natural processes to results not 'intended' by nature. Interference with a natural process is not immoral unless this process is necessary for fulfilling a moral duty. As mentioned above, usually, there is no moral duty to produce offspring.

In a broader context, the problem is whether the 'natural' functions of an organism involve an ethical duty to use the organism only in accordance with the functions given by the organism's organisation, structure, dispositions or inclinations. Such a general principle is not self-evident and there are no arguments to prove it. The sex act in itself is not immoral, otherwise, it would not be allowed even in marriage, and the same holds true for other deliberate sexual activities. The morality of sexual acts, therefore, is not determined by their object but depends on the circumstances and purposes of the acts.

The marital act is teleologically ordained to the procreation of offspring, but the only valid inference from this ordainment seems to me that the procreation of offspring is the natural result of sexual relations and in harmony with the purpose of marriage. The sex function serves for the continuation of the species and in this sense, its purpose is the *bonum speciei* (the good of the species), not the *bonum individui* (the good of the individual). The *bonum speciei* does not require that every sexual act must actually or on principle lead to conception. As an expression of personal togetherness and the experience of sexual lust and satisfaction, intercourse can have a human value irrespective of fertilisation (which it obviously does not have in situations like rape).

The morality of artificial insemination and other procedures related to test-tube babies has been discussed in Ch. 3 of Vol. 3. The Church considers artificial insemination immoral chiefly because it dissociates fertilisation from the conjugal union and negates the 'natural' act of conception. There are moralists who apply the term adultery to the use of semen or eggs of a person other than one's lawful spouse as well as surrogate mothers.

The prohibition of the pill cannot be based on the ground that artificial birth control constitutes an interference with the natural course of copulation. The efficiency of the pill depends on the prevention of ovulation and its use does not affect intercourse.

According to some authors, the idea of the Church that every sexual engagement should retain the potency of engendering new life originated from an erroneous view of sexual propagation. Until the discovery of the female egg cells by von Baer in 1827, the man's semen was thought to contain the entire new human being with all its faculties. The mother's womb was merely the soil into which the seed was planted, just as the peasant sows the seed in the field where it finds the possibility to grow. ('In perfect animals, generated by coition, the active force is the semen of the male, as the Philosopher says; but the foetal matter is provided by the female.' St Thomas Acquinas, Sum. theol., I, q. 118, a.2, ad 4). From an ethical point of view, therefore, the dissipation of the seed, for instance, by the interruption of intercourse, came close to abortion.

Towards the end of the seventeenth and the beginning of the eighteenth century, the discovery of spermatozoa in the semen of men and animals gave rise to the preformation theory. The animalculists believed that the sperms created in the beginning of the world contained in miniature all future generations so that the semen of Adam incorporated the entire future human race. The ovists contended that the female ova enclosed all subsequent generations and that the semen only served to stimulate the reproductive process.

In my opinion, the problem whether every activation of the sex organs and every sexual arousal is morally relevant has not been convincingly solved. Compared with other instincts, the sex instinct has been considered too much *a priori* as sinful. In the satisfaction of the appetite for food, traditional morality considers the intake of food in an amount sufficient to maintain health as part of the obligation of self-preservation while gluttony is immoral as an impairment of health and drunkenness condemned as incompatible with human dignity. The sex instinct is felt more strongly than the instinct of self-preservation although the latter is undoubtedly stronger than the instinct of preserving the species. Because people usually satisfy the requirements of self-preservation, this instinct is seldom felt in its full force whereas the satisfaction of the sex instinct is subject to numerous restraints which greatly increases the attention given to this instinct. Moreover, sex is often experienced as a threat to the harmony and balance of human personality which creates the tendency to view sex as something of a sinister and evil force. This, of course, is entirely groundless. Sex and the experience of the sex instinct belong essentially to man's nature and the satisfaction of the sex instinct must be seen in connection with man's total personality.

According to an American survey, a considerable number of priests who theoretically agree with the teaching of the Church on sexual morality regard its literal application impossible and do not follow it in counselling and guiding their penitents. This deviation was admitted by 87 per cent of the priests with regard to birth control, by 78 per cent for masturbation, by 38 per cent for pre-marital sex, by 21 per cent for extra-marital sex and by 46 per cent for homosexuality. In the recent Church statement on sex education, masturbation is called a grave moral disorder, but the qualification is added that it is necessary to be cautious in evaluating its subjective side.

Disciplinary Action Against Father Curran

On 18 August 1986 Father Charles E. Curran, professor of moral theology at the Catholic University of America, was summoned to the Archbishop of Washington (who is chancellor of the University) and informed that the Sacred Congregation for the Doctrine of Faith had rescinded his canonical licence to teach theology. Father Curran's refusal to recant his dissenting views on questions of sexual morality made him no longer 'suitable or eligible to teach Catholic theology.' The measure had been personally approved by Pope John Paul II on 10 July.

Already in 1967, Father Curran had been dismissed from his post for his opposition to the encyclical of Pope Paul VI reaffirming the ban on artificial birth control but he had been reinstated following a campus-wide strike of faculty and students. Father Curran asserted that couples were justified in following their own conscience in the question of artificial birth control, that abortion might not be censurable in extreme cases, that there might be just grounds for sterilisation, that under some circumstances, pre-marital sex might be acceptable, and that homosexual acts could be morally licit in the context of a permanent commitment. Father Curran also thinks that the Church should allow divorce and remarriage after divorce and holds that under certain circumstances, euthanasia should be permitted.

In 1979, the Vatican sent Father Curran a list of 16 principal errors and ambiguities which he was asked to repudiate. He refused and contended that the traditional teachings on sexual morality had not been defined infallibly and that, although they were taught by the ecclesiastical magisterium, dissent could be justified. He might hold such views privately, Vatican theologians declared, but could not teach them. Father Curran considers his position 'mainstream' and accepted by the majority of Catholic theologians. Nine former presidents of the Catholic Theological Society agreed with him and circulated a petition in his support.

Vatican officials said that the action against Father Curran should be seen as a warning to all theologians who question traditional Church teaching, and in an Apostolic Letter dated 28 August 1986, on the occasion of the 1,600th anniversary of the conversion of St Augustine, Pope John Paul II issued a stern call for full obedience to Church teachings.

Enjoyment of Sexual Pleasure

It has often been asserted that the unrestrained gratification of sexual desires makes man the slave of his lust. In this respect, the enjoyment of sexual pleasure is not different from the craving for drugs or alcohol. Self-control is one of the unconditional demands of personality so that, also apart from possible consequences (for example, impairment of health, social disgrace, marital trouble), being dominated by the instinct would be immoral. But this does not mean that every conscious and deliberate satisfaction of the sex instinct constitutes a violation of personality and an impairment of the dignity of man. Father Stephen Pfürtner, O.P., of the University of Fribourg (who was barred from teaching at the behest of the Sacred Congregation for the Doctrine of the Faith) stated: 'Sexual pleasure is a basic human right to be enjoyed in accordance with individual conscience rather than a moral code,' but this formulation is unsatisfactory. Conscience must be formed after the moral law and constitutes neither an independent nor an infallible norm. But it can be maintained that the satisfaction of the sexual desire also for the mere purpose of enjoying sexual pleasure is not in itself immoral and becomes immoral only on account of an evil purpose or circumstances. Such a condition is, for example, marriage. In a personalistic conception of marriage, the spouses form a community of life which involves an exclusive sexual relationship so that extra-marital sex is an injustice against the marriage partner. In a monogamous marriage, the personal dignity of the spouse, requires the exclusiveness of sex relations and the express or silent consent of the partner to extra-marital sex does not change the immorality of adultery. Luther's animosity against the Catholic view of the sacramental character of marriage led him to assert that adultery is permissible in cases where the physiological aim of marriage cannot be fulfilled (as in the case when the husband is impotent). The prohibition of extra-marital sex does not make masturbation, either solitary or mutual, illicit. Although marital sex ideally means the mutual surrender of the spouses, it is not immoral if each partner seeks the satisfaction of his or her sexual appetite by masturbation. Catholic moralists were aware of the fact that orgasm does not always occur simultaneously in marital intercourse and that women fail to experience organism during coitus. They considered it licit if the wife's orgasm preceded that of the husband, and despite the general condemnation of masturbation held that the wife could procure satisfaction manually after the husband's ejaculation.

Traditional moral theology considers the voluntary activation of sexuality by unmarried people or consent in involuntary arousal as infringements of the right moral order. The mere thought or imagination of things related to sex is morally indifferent and can have a just reason or purpose, for example, information. But thoughts or fantasies indulged in voluntarily in order to feel sexual pleasure, desires deliberately intending acts against the right use of sexuality, or delight in sexual arousal intentionally procured or unintentionally occurring are sins.

According to this position, internal acts against chastity are sinful. For unmarried people, thoughts, desires, emotions, fantasies and imaginations leading to sexual arousal (usually referred to as 'bad thoughts') deliberately sought are morally reprehensible and have to be 'put away' (repressed and disavowed) if they arise involuntarily. For married people, such internal acts are only licit if related to one's spouse and, if apart from marital intercourse, they do not create the proximate danger of self-satisfaction.

Critical Evaluation

Basically, the criterion for the morality of sexual acts is the same as that for all human acts, the conformity with the right order implied in man's personal nature. A sexual act in accordance with the teleological ordainment of man's sexuality is good if the other conditions for moral rightousness (intent, circumstances) are fulfilled. Sexual acts not conducive to procreation are morally indifferent if they are not degrading, for example, if they are not in conflict with man's dignity as a personal being.

As shown above, the teleological ordainment of sexuality does not constitute a moral norm. The satisfaction of the sex instinct without relation to the propagation of the species does not negate the inner teleological ordainment of sexuality. In itself, the potential of sexual enjoyment is not limited to marriage. The analogy of the satisfaction of the sex instinct with the satisfaction of the instinct of self-preservation is not quite convincing. Different from eating and drinking, sex may involve another person and may have consequences beyond the single act (pregnancy). Furthermore, the sex instinct is only one aspect of the sexual desire and the attainment of sexual pleasure may involve the union with another person, normally of the opposite sex. There are no such personal elements in eating and drinking, and in masturbation, the satisfaction of the impulse is usually dissociated from the desire for personal union. But there is no reason why the sex instinct should be activated only in the context of a sexual relation with another person.

Eating and drinking merely for the sake of enjoyment are not immoral as long as this is done with moderation. But immoderation in sexual enjoyment is different from immoderation in eating and drinking where immoderation results from a coherent chain of actions which hardly applies to immoderation in the satisfaction of sexual lust. Immoderation, however, is not only a question of action but also a question of attitude. The term gluttony and drunkenness may signify a somewhat permanent disposition or attitude which the Scholastics called habit. Habit is a pivotal concept in the Aristotelian-Scholastic doctrine of virtues and vices. Virtues and vices are qualities or properties of a person's character, constituting his distinctive psychic configuration. The vice of unchastity is primarily a question of attitude which dominates sexual activity. The quest of sexual lust seems incompatible with human dignity if it becomes a controlling determinant of man's behaviour to which all other considerations are subordinate, in other words, if it is made the highest value in human life. The single act is immoral in as much as it is a manifestation of the basic immoral attitude and the warped scale of human values. Don Juan was possessed by his passion to seduce every woman he met without the slightest commitment to the victims of his lust and the boast of *Playboy* founder, Hugh Hefner, that until his 60th birthday, he had been in bed with about a thousand women — most of them young although not necessarily innocent — illustrates a perverted view of sexual enjoyment which regards sexual lust as the main objective of human life.

Sexual Fantasies

A particular problem is presented by sexual fantasies unrelated to one's partner during coitus. As a matter of fact, people frequently indulge in sexual fantasies and daydreams while masturbating and during intercourse. Often, the imagination of the naked body of somebody of the opposite or the same sex stimulates sexual desire but fantasies may also involve fornication, incest, adultery and all kinds of sexual deviations from homosexuality and lesbianism to bestiality and sadomasochism. A favourite fantasy represents one's sexual conduct being observed by others (see, for example, Nancy Friday, *My Secret Garden — Women's Sexual Fantasies;* a third party watching sexual acts appears frequently in erotic pictures). Many people apparently find it impossible to achieve orgasm without imagining themselves having intercourse with somebody else, being engaged in a sexual orgy, or imagining breasts, genitals or other parts of the body of someone other than the partner. These fantasies often involve feelings of shame or guilt, and although the thought of deceiving or betraying one's partner may cause pain, few people are ready to confess their fantasies to their mates.

An American psychologist who studied the sexual attitudes of 5,000 men and women over a period of 26 years reported that women's sexual fantasies have gone from romance to obscenity. In the 1950s and 1960s, women looked on sex as an emotional, sentimental and tender experience; they now reduce it to its physical dimension, expect a sense of bodily release while maintaining their psychological freedom and indulging in pornographic imagery.

From the point of view that the enjoyment of sex is legitimate if it does not offend against the dignity of man, there is no reason why man should not use his senses or imagination for procuring sexual pleasure. The same applies to external acts, including intercourse. The imagination of morally reprehensible acts such as adultery, incest or bestiality is not the same as committing or approving such conduct, even if pleasure is derived from such fantasies.

Mental Adultery

Theologians have generally condemned as incompatible with marital fidelity thoughts or desires directed towards somebody (or something) other than the spouse, and imagined situations during marital intercourse in which somebody different from the spouse is pictured as the sex partner have been branded as 'mental adultery.' The selflessness of the love of benevolence mentioned above certainly demands the wholehearted affirmation of the beloved in which the thought of a third party would be a shrill dissonance. The perfect inner devotedness to the marriage partner constitutes a goal to be desired and is uniquely in harmony with the spiritual unity of the spouses. But the ideal love can hardly be imposed as a moral duty on all married people.

Sexual fantasies do not necessarily destroy the inner faithfulness to one's spouse. They do not mean a breach of the marriage bond, a denial or repudiation of the union of soul, heart and body. Sexual fantasies may make a man or woman sexually more receptive and a better partner in marital relations. They may contribute to the actualisation of an individual's sexual potential, and among married people, too, are men and women who are able to achieve orgasm only by imagining having sex with somebody different from their partner, indulging in the reverie of the sexually exciting body of a particular person or a phantom lover. This does not necessarily diminish the love of the partner or the respect for his or her dignity.

Sexual Conduct Outside Marriage

Since the morality of sexual conduct often depends on circumstances, it may become a problem of situational ethics, that is to say, it is impossible to judge it in terms of a general norm valid in all cases. As in other questions of morality, it is not always a question of black and white. There are many gray areas in general as well as in particular cases. One can take the view that sexual relations betwen two unmarried (or divorced) and independent adults should be left to the discretion of these individuals. But this general point of view is subject to certain qualifications. By its nature, intercourse is the outward expression of mutual inner personal surrender and this is hardly the case in promiscuous, impulsive or frivolous relationships. Moreover, there is a possibility that undisciplined sexual behaviour will damage the personal or social position of the individual. For the woman, in particular, the possibility of pregnancy is an aspect that makes shallow sex relations at least undesirable, and in communities with strong traditional views, such conduct will meet with disapproval (which does not necessarily imply what has been called 'moral turpitude').

Pre-Marital Sex

Parents and educators have been at a loss to define the moral norms adolescents should observe. Japanese society never experienced the contradiction between a puritanical sex ethic and a life-style allowing unrestrained sexual gratification. While pre-war Japan kept sexual permissiveness within strictly circumscribed limits, today's adolescents are exposed to ubiquitous erotic stimulants and enjoy almost limitless opportunities for engaging in sex. With a growing number of married women holding part-time jobs, many children are free from parental supervision after school, and some adolescents have enough money to check in at love hotels or motels. As everywhere else in the world, the car provides a convenient shelter for sex play. Contraceptives (except the pill) are readily available in Japan — although many adolescents do not use them — and abortion is only a question of money. Often, when a girl's boyfriend doesn't have the money to pay for an abortion or if she doesn't know which of her boyfriends is the father of the child, her schoolmates organise a 'campaign' to raise the necessary funds.

More than any rules on conduct, the young generation needs to understand the importance of approaching sex with reverence and develop the conviction that sex involves not only man's body but also his personality. Sex must be recognised as a fully human activity which entails personal responsibility. The problem of pre-marital sex cannot be solved by telling young people that bodily intimacy will more often than not lead to coitus and that they have to draw the line somewhere before it is too late. Young people engaged in petting, especially heavy petting, will seldom want to draw a line.

For the unmarried woman, pre-marital sex often leads to fear, disappointment and unhappiness. The attitude that social relations with men necessarily involve sex is basically wrong. Even if relations with a particular man advance from 'dating' to 'going steady,' neither long discussions on sex nor bodily intimacies are required. The experience of the sex act is unnecessary for personal maturity and is not needed as a preparation for marriage. Usually, newlyweds can achieve a satisfactory physical relationship also without pre-marital intercourse. It is natural that both partners feel tensions during their engagement but sexual relations are neither psychologically nor physically necessary for overcoming these tensions. The idea of binding the partner and making marriage certain by sexual concessions is basically wrong. In many cases in which a man has married a woman who has given herself to him, marriage is endangered right from the start because pity, the sense of responsibility or chivalrousness are no substitute for love.

In 1976, the Holy Office condemned the opinion that pre-marital sex was morally justifiable because it represented an external expression of the affection which, in the psychology of the partners, was already in some way matrimonial.

But for people who have to put off marriage until their economic circumstances allow them to start a home, pre-marital sex is not just a question of how much fun they miss but of keeping alive their mutual affection. The traditional morality stressed the necessity of preserving the reverence for each other but failed to recognise the at least equal necessity of saving the attraction and fondness essential to their union. They may not only want but also need to reaffirm that they belong to each other which justifies pre-marital sex.

Acceptance of sexual impulses is the basic tenet of humanist psychology. The mature man trusts the directives of his inner organic processes in his sexual self-determination. Personal relations are not confined to marriage; extra-marital experiences which Carl Rogers calls 'satellite relations,' bring growth experiences and serve the realisation of one's inner nature. The new man as envisaged by humanist psychology is ready to enter quickly into personal relations and to create proximity, but he also can sever relationships without deep conflicts and painful separations.

It should be noted that the moral and sometimes the legal responsibility extends not only to the particular act but also to its natural and foreseeable consequences. A man who seduces an innocent girl (this sounds very corny but it still happens) is morally bound to take care of the girl and, in case a child is born, of the offspring — which, depending on the circumstances, means that he must marry the girl and legitimate the child. If a man commits adultery, he may have to assume responsibility for the woman if she is repudiated by her husband and will in any case be responsible for the child born out of the illicit union. He may have a moral duty to protect the woman if the adultery puts her in danger or deprives her of her means of subsistence. Somebody suffering from a venereal disease who infects an unsuspecting person is liable for the medical expenses. But in these and similar situations, there are innumerable variations and the rights and duties of the parties may vary depending on the circumstances of the case.

Prostitution

There can be no doubt that prostitution constitutes a degradation of sex and a denial of its personal character. Sex becomes a merchandise, a service which can be bought by the hour or even by the minute. The same is true for the sexual 'services' available in Turkish baths, massage parlours, bars and nightclubs.

The exhibition of the naked body is often branded as a kind of prostitution but such a condemnation is not always justified. Even apart from artistic merit, the general denunciation of nude representations is based on the identification of naked with immoral which as such is unwarranted. Traditional morality disapproves of such presentations also because spectators will be sexually aroused which means that the performers will become an occasion for others to sin. This view is founded on the premise that voluntary sexual arousal outside marriage and without reference to the marriage partner is sinful but such an assumption seems unprovable. In this respect, nude representations do not seem different from the presentation of nakedness and sexuality in art, literature and pornography. Whether somebody reads a book in order to stimulate sexual desires, masturbates in front of a picture of a nude woman or sees a pornographic movie does not change the morality or immorality of masturbation.

Abuse of Female Nudity

However, it should not be overlooked that nude representations usually exhibit the female body and that the profanation of the female figure is hardly conducive to cultivate esteem for woman and respect for her as wife and mother. 'Topless' or 'bottomless' waitresses certainly constitute an abuse of female sex appeal. Some time ago, a Swiss women's association protested against the use of figures of nude women as figures for rifle practice by a company of Swiss soldiers. In another case, soldiers used the 'vital statistics' of the waitresses in the restaurants and bars of the town for communication exercises.

The use of female nakedness in advertising is less a moral problem and concerns more the image of woman, respect, dignity and rôle assignment. Women are represented as sex objects, erotic symbols, intent on being seduced. Women appear as empty-headed and silly housewives getting ecstatic at the sight, smell or taste of trivial products. A problem peculiar to Japan is the use of western models for advertising and the impression created by the mass media that western females are the willing recipients of aggressive sexual advances.

The Consumer Association of Penang recently published a book entitled *Abuse of Women in the Media,* and a Danish court ruled that representations of scantily-clad or nude women cannot be used to attract attention to products and that such advertising constitutes discrimination.

Even government agencies succumb to the tendency to regard women as promotional props. Inspired by an American magazine article, Japan's Posts and Telecommunication Ministry stated in a pamphlet distributed to some 180,000 postal employees in 1983 that attractive young women in 'cute' uniforms positioned behind 'smart' counters would result in more business. The women's section of the Japan Postal Workers' Union found this discriminatory because women were considered as objects to look at and treated as pieces of merchandise.

Respect for women is essential to the spiritual and moral health of society, but such respect cannot be created by law and enforced by the police. It is a question of education and social manners.

Homosexuality

As long as an individual seeks the satisfaction of his sexual desires alone, his personal dignity is not necessarily in jeopardy, but sexual relations with somebody else create the problem of personal integrity. In antiquity, homosexual relations between men were generally approved, and this approval included sexual relations with minors (the original meaning of 'paederasty'). But under the influence of Jewish tradition, the Christian Occident regarded homosexuality as a perversion and in many countries, homosexuality was punished as a crime. In recent years, the endeavour for greater psychological, medical and sociological understanding of so-called deviational sexuality has resulted in greater tolerance of homosexuality, but understanding and tolerance do not mean moral approval. The reprobation of homosexuality may appear as a particularly glaring example of elevating biological facts to moral norms; actually, however, homosexuality as an interpersonal relationship amounts to a denial of the basic meaning of sexual differentiation and the constitutional ordainment to heterosexual relations. The evilness of homosexuality does not lie in the sexual activities as such but in the corruption of interpersonal relations which contradict the personal being and natural ordainment of the individual.

Homosexual behaviour may be the outcome of a 'natural' inclination but the assertion that man can follow any and every natural inclination is fundamentally wrong. Man has the ability and the duty of controlling his impulses and if the impulse clashes with a moral duty, he is bound to repress it.

A special problem is involved in the homosexual relations of married people. Although such behaviour does not constitute adultery in the usual sense, it is incompatible with the personal bond and the intimacy of the sexual relations between spouses.

The denial of human dignity and the violation of the right order in man is also obvious in other deviational forms of sexual behaviour, particularly in sodomy, sadism, masochism, necrophilia and fetishism. Between spouses, fellatio and cunnilingus are not essentially different from other forms of masturbation, and the morality of such acts between other persons depends on the approval or disapproval of sexual intimacy between such persons.

Incest

A difficult problem is the moral qualification of incest. In all known cultures, some kind of taboo is observed with regard to sexual relations between near relatives, but the extent of this prohibition varies from society to society and the reasons for these restrictions are not very clear. Particularly uncertain is the extension to relatives by marriage. Pyrrho of Elis (ca. 365 — ca. 275 BC), commonly regarded as the founder of scepticism, is said to have pointed out the different appraisal of marriage between parents and children, marriage between brothers and sisters, community of wives, theft and lying among different peoples in order to illustrate the variance in the moral evaluation of human activities.

The most categorical prohibition bans sexual relations between mother and son and father and daughter. While incest between father and daughter is typical of the West, sexual relations between mother and son seem more prevalent in Japan. Actually, sexual relations between mother and a grown-up son occur relatively seldom, but in Japan, the concern of over-protective mothers for their sons are said to have led to a considerable increase in this kind of incest. Cases in which mothers seek sexual arousal by fondling or kissing the genitals of small or growing boys are not rare. A Tennessee woman married her son because she did not want any other woman to have him. They lived together as man and wife for six years before their true relationship came to light.

Relatively frequent is incest between father and daughter or daughters. It happens that a wife who loathes intercourse with her husband induces, at least indirectly, sex between father and daughter; but in most cases, the sexual attractiveness of the young body and the opportunity to seduce or rape the girl are the main reasons. It happens that the daughter seeks sexual contact with her father (for example, the story of the two daughters of Lot, Gen 19, 30-39), but Freud's Oedipus and Electra complexes can hardly claim universal validity. In Japan, most cases of incest in which the Family Planning Counselling Office was asked for advice involved sex between brother and sister.

Sociologists have found no convincing explanation of the origin of the incest taboo. It has often been asserted that there is an instinctive aversion against sex relations with near relatives, but this proposition cannot be substantiated and lacks any physiological foundation. The dysgenic effects of inbreeding are neither universal nor immediately apparent. The assertion that people growing up in the same household do not develop mutual sexual affections is unproven and hardly unconditionally valid.

There can be no doubt that sexual relations between mother and son or father and daughter destroy the structure of the family and are irreconcilable with the social order and the social rôles of the members of the family. Seen from the side of the parents, such a relation is incompatible with the biological ordainment of the family to produce the next generation and it also clashes with the respect and obedience demanded by the position of the children. The claim of some American authors that the prohibition of incest is an antiquated prejudice and that 'consensual incest' (as distinguished from 'abusive incest') should be encouraged is horrendous.

Marriage Between Brother and Sister

Marriage between brother and sister is not unknown. In Egyptian mythology, Isis was the sister and wife of Osiris. They were said to have been attracted by incestuous love and had intercourse already in the womb of their mother. Osiris was slain and dismembered by his brother Set when he copulated with another sister. The Greeks of Homeric times regarded Hera, the daughter of the Titan Cronus and Rhea, as the sister and wife of Zeus, and the Romans took over this representation for Jupiter and Juno. Okeanos and Tethys, according to Hesiod the children of Uranos and Geia, were the ancestors of all gods. Solon's legislation permitted marriage between half brother and half sister if they had different mothers. Marriages between brothers and sisters have been reported for Sumer and Elam. Egyptian pharaos, the Inkas of Peru and the old royal family of Hawaii adopted the marriage of brothers and sisters in order to preserve the purity of the royal blood, but the evidence is not clear. The adherents of matriarchal evolution assert that the pharao could only exercise authority over the children if he was also their uncle.

The custom of marriages between brothers and sisters seems to have existed at one time or another in Persia and Siam, in Burma, among the Dravidians in southern India and the Singhalese, in south-east China and on Java and Bali. The custom was not uncommon in Africa, in the region of the Upper Nile, in Uganda and among the Yoruba. Thousands of years after the Old Kingdom of Egypt, the ruler of an African state south of the Zambezi married his 'Queen Sister.' In South America, such marriages were practised among the aborigines of Brazil and Tierra del Fuego.

When she was 17, the famous Cleopatra VII, the last queen of the Macedonian dynasty in Egypt, was married to her younger brother Ptolemy XIII, who was then nine, and they became co-dynasts of Egypt. Cleopatra was not the only woman of the dynasty who, although not Egyptian, followed the Pharaonic tradition of marriage between brother and sister. Ptolemy VIII forced his sister, Cleopatra II, to become his wife, and also married her daughter from a previous marriage.

Incestuous relations appear in some of the myths on the origin of the world, the gods or mankind. A Nigerian myth has the god Aganja marry his sister Yemaja producing Oringa, the god of the atmosphere. Oringa has incestuous relations with his mother, Yemaja, which result in the birth of a number of gods. The same kind of incest between mother and son is also found in Iranian mythology in which the god Hormizd produced with his mother the sun as well as animals such as dogs, donkeys and pigs. In some Iranian societies, marriages between near-blood relatives (father-daughter, mother-son, brother-sister) actually occurred.

According to an old Finnish custom, a daughter was entrusted for a long time to relatives living far away and upon her return, she was married to her brother (W. L. Thomas, *Primitive Behaviour,* p. 194).

'Open Sexuality'

A denial of the traditional morality is the 'open sexuality' described by Gay Talese in his book *Thy Neighbour's Wife.* The basic tenet of this movement derived from the ideas of the Austrian psychiatrist Wilhelm Reich which included the abolition of the 'double' morality for man and woman and the creation of 'a sexually free and open trusting atmosphere in which there would be no need for possessiveness, jealousy, guilt, or lying.' The movement regards sexual relations with somebody other than the spouse with the knowledge and consent of the partner as a deepening of marital love and a demolition of the romantic illusions concerning sex and sensual pleasure. Although the movement appeared similar to 'wife swapping,' open sexuality was to achieve a permanent transformation of society, 'altering the socio-political system through sexual experimentation and thus creating a healthier, more sex-affirmative and open society.'

Wilhelm Reich was a follower of Freud and espoused Freud's theory of libido and the sexual origin of neuroses (Freud himself never believed that all neuroses were sex-induced). Reich, who tried the amalgamation of psychoanalysis and Marxism, was more interested in sex than in neuroses which brought him into conflict with the American authorities so that he died in prison. He glorified orgasm as the highest expression of life (one of his works was *The Function of Orgasm,* 1927).

Group Nudity

Some of the ideas propounded by Reich, his followers and successors are justifiable. Sexuality is a fundamental fact of human existence and the denial of sex in the public order, exemplified by the prohibition of pornography, creates an atmosphere of hypocrisy and falsehood which imparts to sex the aura of the forbidden fruit. In itself, group nudity is just as little reprehensible as the affirmation of lust in marital intercourse. 'Sex is to be enjoyed, not to be repressed,' brings out a legitimate point, but the tendency to make sex an independent value unrelated to and separate from all other human concerns offends against the personal structure of man and social norms protecting the intimacy of sex relations. The view that 'the overriding purposes of sex are self-discovery, self-assertion, and self-gratification' disregards the basic significance of sex as a social factor. 'Healthy adultery' is a negation of the personal meaning of marriage and the preeminance of the spiritual over the animal in man.

Cohabitation

Cohabitation without formal marriage cannot be termed immoral without certain qualifications. The formal religious or civil wedding is an institution of positive law. On the basis of natural law, the agreement of the two partners to live together as man and wife is sufficient to contract a marriage, and this agreement need not necessarily be put into words or fixed in writing. There are, however, good and valid reasons why church or state prescribe the formal conclusion of marriage (certainty of social relations, regulation of property rights, inheritance), and circumstances may make the formal celebration of marriage a moral duty. In the old 'closed' societies in which everybody knew everybody, cohabitation without the solemnisation of marriage was a 'public scandal' and often entailed considerable disadvantages, particularly for the woman. In today's atomised society of the large cities and the atmosphere of 'open sexuality,' cohabitation without formal marriage has become so common that it can hardly be considered as 'scandalous.' But this does not mean that a formal marriage has become superfluous or a matter of preference. Many of the people living together do not regard their relationship as a marriage, but if the partners intend more than a temporary diversion or a 'trial marriage' and want to live together as man and wife, their cohabitation is morally not different from the old common-law marriage.

Legal Restraints on Sexuality

The variety of the actions prohibited as sexual offenses and the disparity in the punishment of sex crimes show that there is no universal standard for determining to what extent the law should regulate sexual conduct. In many instances, the law enforced the moral norms prevalent in a given community so that the same actions were considered immoral as well as unlawful. Adultery, incest, homosexuality, bestiality, transvestism, prostitution, voyeurism and sexual techniques such as oral and anal sex are some of the sins proscribed by Christian morality which the secular legislator transformed into crimes. In Europe, the Code Napoléon initiated a departure from traditional morality but in England and the United States, public opinion generally backed legal control of sexual behaviour.

The purpose of the law is not to make people virtuous but to institute and protect the public order. The law prohibits certain external actions not because they are bad but because they are unjust, that is, injurious to the common good. The protection of life and liberty constitutes an essential task of the state but the actions of individuals or groups of individuals which are irrelevant to the public order should not be prohibited by law let alone made punishable. There are valid reasons for some of the legal prohibitions in the sphere of sexuality. Directly concerned with the public order are proscriptions forbidding rape (including statutory rape: sexual abuse of minors, the mentally retarded and the insane), forcing into prostitution (white slavery), procurement, solicitation and exhibitionism. The protection of minors is a valid concern for pertinent curbs in prostitution and pornography but there is no reason for their blanket criminalisation. Both have been treated as crimes not because they deprave the individual but because they were considered disturbances of the public order and threats to the well-being of society (which includes the spiritual and moral health of the community) but there is no direct influence of prostitution or pornography on matters of public interest. While adultery should entitle the innocent party to a divorce, there is no reason to make it a crime.

Upholding 'public morality' was one of the many functions the state took over from the Church in the Christian Occident where Christian morality constituted an integral part of the public order. But in a pluralistic society, it becomes increasingly difficult to enforce the moral convictions of Christianity by legal rules. Nevertheless, there remain numerous legal provisions punishing certain kinds of sexual behaviour. Recently, the US House of Representatives, under pressure from fundamentalist religious groups, overruled a District of Columbia law that would have legalised most sexual acts between consenting adults. This keeps in force statutes permitting sex only between married partners in a face-to-face position. Needless to say, such a regulation of private sexual behaviour is outside the scope of public authority. In the Federal Republic of Germany, punishment of adultery and homosexual acts between men over 18 years of age was abolished. Adultery was deleted from Japan's Criminal Code already in 1947, and adultery as well as concubinage are no longer punishable in Spain. In many American states, 'criminal conversation' (enticement to adultery) constitutes a ground for damages, but the

Washington State Court of Appeals turned down a suit for damages stemming from adultery and rejected the common-law action for criminal conversation on the grounds that it was based on the notion of the husband's ownership of his wife. Said the court: 'Neither wives nor husbands are property. The love and affection of a human being is not susceptible to theft.'

Emperor Augustus already tried to counter the licentiousness of Roman society by prohibiting adultery — to no avail. But adultery is still treated as a crime in many countries. In Greece, adultery is punishable by up to a year's imprisonment and a couple convicted of adultery is barred from marrying each other (a prohibition taken over from Canon Law). The Greek government wanted to delete these provisions but the Greek Orthodox Church is opposed to the decriminalisation of adultery. The Greek Supreme Court ruled that a husband has the legal right to repossess gifts he has given to his wife if he discovers that she has had an extra-marital affair. He may take presents, including property, away from his spouse irrespective of the circumstances leading to the infidelity. In Turkey, the present (1984) law provides a jail term of six months to three years for a woman who commits adultery. The man involved can escape conviction if he claims that he did not know the woman was married or if he can prove that the act was committed only once. A bill submitted by a woman member of parliament would make adultery equally illegal for men as well as women.

In South Korea, adultery is prosecuted as a crime upon the complaint of the aggrieved party. In Africa, adultery is often dealt with on the basis of tribal law. In Zimbabwe, where African customary law was reintroduced for rural areas, adultery is not a criminal offence but provides grounds for a civil case by the injured husband seeking damages. Among the Afghan tribes, the tribal elders impose the death penalty on men and women guilty of 'fornication.'

In Jewish and Roman law, extra-marital sexual relations were regarded as adultery only if the woman was married to a third party; if the partner was an unmarried woman, the man's conduct was not punishable. Often, a distinction is made between 'simple' adultery (if only one of the adulterers is married to a third party) and 'double' adultery (if both are married to third parties). The moral evaluation of adultery ranges from unconditional condemnation of all extra-marital sex in Christianity to approval of any kind of sexual behaviour freely agreed to by the parties.

The Saudi government protested against the broadcasting of 'Death of a Princess,' a dramatised account of the execution in July 1979 of a Saudi princess for adultery with her commoner lover. In 1983, the US Supreme Court upheld a ruling by an appeals court that Alabama's public television commission acted properly when it refused to broadcast the programme.

Some European countries retain punishment for homosexuality (for example, Spain, France, Switzerland, Czechoslovakia). In Switzerland, proposals of a government-appointed panel of experts for lowering the age of consent to 14, decriminalising certain forms of incest and liberalising the pornography laws ran into vehement opposition in most of Switzerland's 26 cantons. Reducing the age of consent from 16 to 14 (the age of sexual majority in Italy, West Germany and Austria; it is 15 in France) would make homosexuality at that age unpunishable (it would remain prohibited in the army). Asserting that genetic damage through incest could not be scientifically proven, the commission proposed to legalise incest between brothers and sisters over 18. The commission also favoured to make rape within marriage a crime, to scrap the provision of the Swiss Criminal Code punishing adultery as a crime, and to allow 'eros centres' for prostitution and pornography in private clubs.

At common law, indecent exposure was an indictable offense. It meant the baring to sight of the private parts in a lewd or indecent manner in a public place. In many American states, indecent exposure is prohibited by statute and it is regarded as a crime or a misdemeanor in many countries. Recently, a French woman was fined for accepting the challenge of an orchestra conductor to appear naked with him on the stage. Another French court upheld the dismissal of 24-year-old woman who refused to wear a bra to work. She had worn a transparent blouse with nothing underneath in the office and had been dismissed when she disregarded the order of her boss (a woman) to wear a bra. Modern trends allow women to bare their breasts on the beach but this tolerance does not extend to the workplace except in the case of cabaret artistes, the court decided.

Another term, public indecency, has been used by courts in England and the United States for a variety of offenses, including the public display of the naked body and the publication, sale, or exhibition of obscene books or prints. The term means indecency in conduct and does not extend to indecent words.

Under a Greek law passed in September 1983, nudists will be prosecuted only if a citizen is really upset by the appearance of a nudist and files suit against him. Naturist hotels and camp-sites can be established in isolated areas with the approval of the local authorities and the state tourist organisation. In the past, nudists were arrested for 'provoking a public scandal through immoral action' and faced fines or jail terms of up to six months.

Japanese Law

The Japanese Criminal Code provides punishment for nine sexual offenses. They include: 1. Indecent public acts (Art. 174). 2. Distribution, sale, and exhibition of indecent writings, pictures, etc. (Art. 175). 3.

Indecent assault on males or females (if over 13 years of age, by violence or threats) (Art. 176). 4. Rape of a female (if over 13 years of age, by violence or threats) (Art 177). 5. Indecent assault or rape if the person is unconscious or unable to resist (Art. 178). 6. Attempt of the actions enumerated under 3 to 5 (Art. 179). 7. Indecent assault or rape connected with homicide or the infliction of injuries (Art. 181). 8. Pandering (enticement of a respectable woman to commit indecent acts) (Art. 182). 9. Bigamy (Art. 184). The prohibition of bigamy is largely ineffective because it supposes the official registration of the marriage. The Criminal Code does not prohibit incest, homosexuality and bestiality. The Child Welfare Law forbids the enticement of minors to perform obscene acts (Art. 34, Par. 1, Nr. 6; punishment Art. 60, Par. 1).

In a split decision, the Japanese Supreme Court upheld the constitutionality of a prefectural ordinance punishing obscene acts with minors under 18 years of age. The Kokura Summary Court had found a 30-year-old man who had sex with a 16-year-old high-school student in a love hotel guilty of violating an ordinance of Fukuoka Prefecture prohibiting 'obscene acts' *(inkō)* with minors under 18 and fined him ¥50,000. Such ordinances have been enacted by 44 of Japan's 47 prefectures and while the main provisions are more or less the same, the exact wording and the penalties for their violation reveal some differences. The defence appealed but the Fukuoka High Court rejected the appeal and the case came before the Supreme Court.

The defence argued that the expression 'obscene act' was too broad and vague and therefore in conflict with Article 31 of the Constitution ('No person shall be deprived of life or liberty, nor shall any other criminal penalty be imposed, except according to procedure established by law'). It also claimed that the differences in the ordinances offended against the principle of equality laid down in Article 14 and that sex based on mutual consent should be protected as a basic right guaranteed by Article 11. The provision of the Child Welfare Law prohibiting obscene acts has been applied only to acts to which the minor did not consent, the defence contended. Furthermore, it seemed unreasonable to fix the legal age for marriage at 16 and forbid sexual conduct for minors under 18.

The majority opinion interpreted the expression 'obscene acts' (which is used in most of the ordinances) to mean sexual conduct for which improper means such as seduction or coercion relying on the immaturity of minors are used, then acts using minors solely as objects for satisfying one's own sexual lust. This, the majority said, could be readily understood from this expression.

Three of the fifteen judges dissented holding that the ordinance violated Article 31 because the expression 'obscene act' was vague, provided no clear standard of conduct and invited abuse by the law-enforcing authorities.

According to the National Police Agency, 8,210 people were arrested in 1984 for violating prefectural ordinances and 4,678 of the violators were charged with committing obscene acts.

The exposure of certain parts of the body in public is punishable under the Minor Offenses Law (Art. 1, Nr. 20). Actions that can be punished under the Prostitution Prevention Law comprise solicitation if done in public, pimping, procurement, provision of rooms for prostitution and prostitution as a commercial undertaking. The law also provides detailed measures for the rehabilitation of prostitutes (supervision, compulsory institutionalisation). The clients of prostitutes cannot be punished. Moreover, the definition of prostitution and solicitation are so ambiguous that it is relatively easy to circumvent the provisions and difficult to prove the facts necessary for conviction. The police, therefore, have adopted the strategy of suppressing the organised white slave trade as much as possible. In comparison with the Federal Republic of Germany where public prostitution is legalised and England where prostitution is allowed but solicitation in public places prohibited (brothels are illegal but a prostitute can have a place where she engages in her profession), the Japanese law is much stricter but it provides less control over venereal disease and makes it easier for organised crime to use prostitution for money-making, intimidation and extortion. It can hardly be said that the legal prohibition of prostitution is very effective. In France, Italy and those of the American states in which it is punishable, prostitution has certainly not been eradicated.

Since the promulgation of the 1978 liberal constitution, Spain has relaxed laws on divorce, contraception, abortion, civil marriage and pornography. Each day, the country's leading newspaper carries numerous classified ads for call girls and massage parlours.

A Swedish commission proposed the decriminalisation of incest and indecent exposure but the proposal drew heavy fire and these points were dropped from a new sexual offences code.

Sexual Offences in Islamic Law

Contrary to the development in the West, the Islamic world tends to enforce religious restrictions on sex by legal prohibitions. Islamic law punishes extra-marital sex relations with death by stoning if the offender is a married person and by 100 lashes for unmarried offenders. On the other hand, an unproven accusation of unchastity is punished by 80 lashes (these punishments are based on Sura 4,19f and 24,2-5 of the Qur'an). In Pakistan, the federal Shariat, the country's highest Islamic court, issued guidelines on flogging which provide that males should cover their bodies from below the belt to the knees while women should cover their entire body except their faces and hands. Male criminals will be flogged while standing but women will be flogged while sitting. The stripes should be spread over the body but head, face, stomach, chest and 'delicate parts

SEL-E

of the body' are not to be hit. The guidelines also provide for pauses if the lashes are numerous.

In Pakistan, death sentences have not been carried out under the martial law régime but Islamic courts have imposed prison sentences together with lashings. A provincial Islamic court sentenced an unmarried pregnant girl to 100 lashes and two years in prison on the charge of being the prospective mother of an illegitimate child. The girl was to be flogged publicly after giving birth to the child but the sentence was overturned by the Federal Shariat (Islamic court) in Islamabad following protests by the women's action forum and letters from outraged Pakistanis to the newspapers.

Iran has outlawed kissing for sexual pleasure and homosexuality (together with the drinking of alcohol). First-time offenders against the kissing ban are to be punished with 100 lashes and persistent homosexuality will bring execution. The stoning of adulterers has so far been relatively rare in post-revolutionary Iran.

A sex manual, written by Imam Ali Riza Demircan entitled *Sexual Life According to Islam* explains how Muslims should choose a mate, perform in bed and avoid sexual sins. The book, published in Ankara, is based on the *Qur'an*, the *Hadis* (statements attributed to the prophet Mohammed) and *Sunnet* (practices). It advocates a return to the customs of pre-republic days, supports female circumcision and exhorts women to shun male company. Even in front of fathers and brothers, a woman should only show face and hands. Women should not go to beauty parlours and similar places where they would run the risk of lesbianism. Islam is not against masturbation, the author says, but homosexuality, adultery, birth control and nudity are sins. A deputy denounced the book in Parliament as an attempt to bring the social life as practised in the Islamic Republic of Iran to Turkey, and women called it an anachronism in a country where the constitution guarantees the rights of women.

Demircan was put on trial, charged with advocating the return to Islam in social life but also with defaming and insulting Islam and the prophet Mohammed. The book, which had become a best-seller, was withdrawn from circulation and the imam dismissed from his position as a state-employed preacher at an Istanbul mosque. The subject of sex remains largely taboo in Islamic countries and Turkish authorities are wary of the upsurge in Muslim fundamentalism threatening the secular republic instituted by Kemal Ataturk.

Saudi Arabia and the other members of the Gulf Cooperation Council (Kuwait, Bahrain, Oman, Qatar and the United Arab Emirates) agreed on a five-year plan under which they will implement Islamic law. A committee of three Ulema (religious scholars) will study how existing laws can be adapted to the *Sharia*. Their recommendations will be examined by a committee of six Ulema, one from each of the six countries, and submitted to the justice ministers for decision by the heads of state.

Some of the problems are the prohibition of interest on money, the ban on alcohol and the punishment of crimes. Islamic banks do not charge interest on loans but take commissions instead, but most banks follow capitalistic principles. Consumption of alcohol is strictly forbidden in Saudi Arabia, Kuwait and the UAE but allowed in Bahrain. Saudi Arabia, home of the puritanical Wahhabist movement, enforces complete separation of the sexes in public and a halt to all business activities during prayer periods. Some of the punishments provided for in the *Sharia* are carried out in public. Bahrain applies *Sharia* law to civil matters such as marriage, divorce and inheritance but is considerably more liberal than other Gulf states. Legally, adulterers are stoned to death in the UAE but the execution of these sentences has been blocked by the rulers. Instead of being stoned to death, adulterers are flogged in Qatar but the flogging is not carried out in public. Thieves are punished by imprisonment, not by amputation of the hand.

Kuwait's General Organisation for Koranic Interpretation, the country's highest religious authority, decreed that husbands and wives may resort to test-tube baby fertilisation but cautioned that 'strict precautions should be taken against descent mix-ups.'

A court in Abu Dhabi sentenced an unmarried couple to ten days in prison for kissing on the cheek. They were found guilty of committing an action that could be harmful to the general public.

The trend to incorporate moral standards into legislation also appeared in Malaysia. The law covers all aspects of 'public morality' such as prostitution, indecent exposure and obscene acts. Necking and kissing in public are punishable. Recently, four couples were fined by the Muslim religious court for what is termed *khalwat* (translated as 'close proximity'). Unmarried couples caught cuddling or embracing each other in a private place can be arrested and charged with this offence even if they have no sex.

Clash of Sexual Mores

A difficult situation arises from the clash of the sexual mores of one culture with the norms of another. A typical example is the practice of polygamy in a monogamous society, another the conduct of foreigners residing in Saudi Arabia and other Muslim countries. Recently, the Saudi Interior Ministry sent a directive to foreign companies operating in the country warning that all foreigners are obliged to respect the country's Islamic traditions and that the harsh punishment stipulated by Islamic law on violations would be enforced without discrimination. The companies having their own residential compounds were ordered to segregate the quarters of single employees from those of married people as well as those of single men from single women and not to allow opportunities for mixing. Segregation must also be maintained in recreational facilities, and swimming pools and gymnasiums for women are to be 'isolated' from the presence of men. The directive further stated that alcohol and drugs as well as sexy photographs and artwork were strictly forbidden and made the importation of printed material by the companies subject to prior approval by the Information Ministry.

Defying orders to dress in accordance with Islamic law, the female staff at the London branch of the Bank Melli Iran turned up for work as usual in short skirts and make-up. The 50 women, most of them British, had been told by the managers of the state-controlled bank to cover their heads, wear long, dark clothing and shun cosmetics, otherwise, they would be sent home. Their union, however, advised them to ignore the instructions and sent a letter of protest to the bank.

Japan yielded to the demand of the Iranians that the girls working at the Iranian pavilion of the 1985 Tsukuba Science and Technology Exposition conform to the Iranian dress code. The uniform originally designed for the 'companions' was discarded and replaced by an outfit covering head, arms and legs.

In a move designed to turn the country into an Islamic republic, Sudan's former President Jaafar Nimeiry decreed that Islamic law should be observed in the whole country, including the largely Christian and animist south. He also contravened the peace treaty of 1972 that ended the civil war between the north and the south by repartitioning the south into its three original provinces. A case in which an Islamic court in Khartoum sentenced an Italian religious, Brother Joseph Manara, procurator of the Catholic Sudan Bishops Conference, to 25 lashes, 30 days in jail and a $300 fine for possessing a bottle of whiskey, 16 bottles of wine and a case of beer attracted much attention in the West. The flogging was carried out minutes after the sentence was passed. But this case was only a small episode in the relapse into barbarism in which robbers and thieves have had their hands chopped off in public, adulterers stoned to death and consumption of alcohol outlawed not only for Muslims but for everybody. Worse than the violation of personal freedom by Islamic fanaticism was the rekindling of the civil war in the Sudan.

2

Birth Control

Infanticide in Old Japan

THE PROBLEM OF BIRTH CONTROL is not new. In Japan, the limitations on resources during the age of civil war *(sengoku jidai,* 1490-1600) and during the Edo period induced the peasants to kill their newborn children (called *mabiki,* thinning out), whereas in the cities, abortions induced by abortifacients were common and a certain class of midwives specialised in abortions. In the countryside, the standard of living rarely surpassed the starvation level, and not only infanticide but also the abandonment of old people — *abasute,* dramatised in Shohei Shimomura's film *Narayamabushi-kô* — was used to reduce the mouths to be fed. A similar custom was reported to exist among the Sierapaluk, the only surviving Eskimos in the north-west corner of Greenland. When the food runs out, the old women go off into the snow to die so that the rest of their families can live. The Catholic missionaries working in Japan during the *Kirishitan* period already denounced the custom of *mabiki* and the clans issued prohibitions as well as instructions on child care but the custom persisted until the Meiji era.

Malthusianism

The modern birth-control movement goes back to Thomas Robert Malthus who, in his *Essay on the Principle of Population* (1798) propounded the thesis that population grows in geometrical ratio while food supply increases only in arithmetical proportion. He recommended late marriages and the reduction of births by moral restraint so as to prevent poverty. Malthus rejected all artificial and unnatural methods of birth control as immoral and as removing the necessary stimulus to industry. Neomalthusianism which was largely inspired by the poverty caused by industrialisation and the housing conditions in the urban slums placed the main emphasis on birth control by contraceptives. The term 'birth control' was coined by Margaret Sanger and means all methods of fertility control, including abortion and sterilisation. In later years, the terms family planning and planned parenthood came into use (the latter term also includes treatment of infertility) besides voluntary parenthood and family limitation.

Prominent in Japan's birth control movement was Baroness Shizue Ishimoto who met Margaret Sanger in New York. She opened a birth control clinic in Tokyo in 1934 but was arrested in 1937 and her clinic closed. She later married Kanju Kato, a leading Socialist, and became president of the Japan Family Planning Federation (*Nihon Kazoku Keikaku Renmei*).

In recent times, birth control has been advocated mainly from three points of view: the danger of overpopulation, rational family planning, and a woman's rights over her body. From a different point of view, quantitative and qualitative birth control can be distinguished; the first is concerned with the number of births, the latter with the health of the offspring, including eugenic considerations. Both forms can be advocated for individual or social reasons.

The ideology behind birth control was sometimes elitist and hedonistic. Restraints on the poorer classes, enforced, if necessary, by coercive sterilisation and baby licenses but made palatable by the possibility of sexual gratification without the burden of children, would result in a preponderance of the offspring of the more successful minority.

Overpopulation and Birth Rates

Today, the central problem of overpopulation lies in the high birth rates in the developing countries. The actual increase in population depends on many factors of which the number of marriages, the age (of the woman) at the time of marriage and the birth of the first child, infant mortality and the ratio of childbirth deaths are of particular importance. In Japan, the number of marriages dropped from a high of 1,099,984 in 1972 to 762,553 in 1983 and 717,000 in 1986. The relative number of marriages (per 1,000 of population) reached a high of 12.0 in 1947 (post-war marriage boom), was down to 6.4 in 1983 and fell to a low of 5.9 in 1986. Births had numbered 2,696,638 in 1949, the peak of the first post-war baby boom; they fell to 1,378,000 in 1986, the lowest number since 1966 (the year *hinoe uma,* the unlucky year for baby girls). The birth-rate per 1,000 which has been declining continuously since 1974 (1973: 19.4) dropped to a record low of 11.4. The decrease has been attributed to a smaller number of women between the ages of 20 and 34. In 1983, the average age of women was 26.5 years at the birth of the first child, 29.0 years at the birth of the second and 31.2 years at the birth of the third child.

Whereas the birthrate has declined almost without exception in the industrialised countries, it is still rising in most developing countries. The reduction of infant mortality contributed even more to an accelerated growth of the world population than the high birth rates. Infant mortality had been the most important factor in keeping the population increase down in past centuries, and the higher survival rate of children was of decisive importance for the growth of the world population in the nineteenth and twentieth centuries. The reduction of infant mortality was closely related to the progress in the education of women. In Latin America, the probability of infant deaths up to two years of age declined almost linearly with the increase in the mothers' education. Children of illiterate women had a risk 3.5 times that of children whose mothers had ten or more years of education. Nevertheless, 10 per cent of all infants born in the Third World die before their first birthday. In Africa, West Asia and South-East Asia, half a million women die annually from causes related to pregnancy and childbirth, leaving behind at least one million motherless children. Five million infants under 5 years old die of diarrhoea every year.

A study published by the private research organisation Worldwatch reported that about 17 million children die each year from the combined effects of poor nutrition, diarrhoea, pneumonia, measles, whooping cough and tetanus. More children die because they are improperly weaned than because of famine, and more children die because their parents do not know how to manage diarrhoea than because of epidemics. More children die because their mothers did not space births far enough than because of drought. Women have not learned that breast feeding must be supplemented with other foods after a baby is six or seven months old; that small children cannot digest all adult foods; that diarrhoea can be effectively treated with a solution of salt and sugar; and that clean water is essential.

Generally speaking, the high birth rates have doubled the population in the countries in Asia, Africa and Latin America about every 20 years. Estimates of the world population put the total at 545 million around 1650, 730 million in 1750, and 1,075 million in 1850, when the number of people first exceeded 1 billion. The world population doubled to 2 billion in the next 80 years, reached 3 billion in 1960 and 4 billion in 1974. As of June 30, 1983, the world's population totalled 4.7 billion and the Population Institute announced that the 5 billion mark had been reached in July 1986. But the Population Reference Bureau said that this occurred in March 1987. The growth rate peaked at 2.2 per cent in 1964-65 but declined to about 1.8 per cent in the mid-1970s. In real numbers, the world population grew by over 80 million from mid-1982 to mid-1983. Demographic prognoses anticipate an increase in the world population until the year 2010 when it will stabilise at 10.5 billion. During the coming 30 years, the strongest growth is expected in Africa (from 400 million in 1980 to 2.1 billion in 2010, an expansion of 5.3 times). For the other continents, the predictions are as follows: Latin America from 400 million to 1.7 billion (3.0 times), South Asia from 1.4 billion to 4.1 billion (2.9 times), Oceania from 23 million to 41 million (1.8 times), East Asia from 1.4 billion to 1.7 billion (1.4 times), Soviet Union from 265 million to 380 million (1.4 times), North America from 248 million to 320 million (1.3 times), and Europe from 450 million to 500 million (1.1 times). The prognosis of the United Nations was the reassuring prediction that the increase in the production of food will keep pace with the growth of population and that existing technology will be able to feed a population of 20 billion. While Malthus was mainly concerned with the food supply, today's population policies consider not only the parameters of survival but also the political, economic and social implications of the country's demographic development.

A study of the World Bank entitled 'Population Growth and Policies in Sub-Saharan Africa' stated that Africa is the only region that has not experienced a fall in population growth rates and predicted that the population south of the Sahara would rise from 470 million in 1985 to 700 million by the year 2000. Africa's average growth rate increased from an average of 2.8 per cent in the years from 1970 to 1982 to 3.1 per cent a year in 1985 and is now the highest in the world. Population growth rates vary for individual African states, but about half fall in the 2.7 to 3.5 per cent range. A few have much higher rates (Kenya 4.0 per cent) while several countries (Chad, Guinea, Sierra Leone and Somalia) have lower growth rates not because fertility is lower but because the mortality rate is high. Before the 1970s, the newly independent African states showed little interest in population movements but now more than three-quarters officially support family planning.

Robert McNamara sharply criticised the complacency about population control. He argued that the decline in the annual growth rate of the world population from 2 per cent to 1.7 per cent in the past decade has created a false sense of security. The slow-down, he maintained, had come almost exclusively in the developed world while birth rates in most of the Third World, above all in the poorest regions, were as high as ever.

The Population Reports International organisation warned that population growth in the world as a whole had risen to a yearly rate of 1.8 per cent from the 1.7 per cent level maintained over the past decade. Population growth in the Third World, excluding China, had increased to 2.5 per cent after holding at 2.4 per cent between 1960 and 1977.

According to the World Health Organisation, about 270 million couples around the world practise some form of birth control; the shares of the methods are roughly as follows: sterilisation 30 per cent, the pill 20 per cent, condoms 10 per cent, intra-uterine devices 15 per cent, others 25 per cent. The WHO estimates that a 2.4 percentage points increase in the use of contraceptives results in a one percentage point drop in the crude birth rate.

The experience with population control in the post-war era seems to show that changes in the birth rate are not so much the effect of progress in the methods of birth control than of changes in attitudes. This is particularly true for developed countries but also applies to developing countries. Birth control pills and abortion are just the tools for limiting births but the real reasons for high or low birth-rates lie in attitudes. The failure of many attempts to curb population growth can be ascribed to the one-sided emphasis on the mechanism of contraception without creating the attitudes necessary for the successful implementation of family planning.

Birth Control in China

Although ideological indoctrination has been used in some countries, the carrot-and-stick approach has been relied upon in countries as different as the People's Republic of China, India and Singapore. China's population policy is based on the goal to keep the increase in the country's population until the end of the century to 1.2 billion, and in order to attain this goal, the family planning measures have become increasingly stricter. The one-couple, one-child rule was adopted in 1980. It was relaxed in 1984 to let couples who were themselves only children have a second child. Couples whose first child is handicapped can also have another child as can workers in hazardous occupations. The members of China's 55 ethnic minorities are also exempt from the one-child rule.

The enforcement policy has become more difficult because, in 1981, the minimum marriage age was reduced to 22 years for men and 20 for women, about five years lower than was the practice under Mao. One of Mao's most fatal errors was his encouragement of China's population explosion. In three decades of Communist rule, the population nearly doubled. This increase of 450 million equalled the combined population of the United States and Europe. According to the preliminary results of China's nationwide census, the population of the Chinese mainland as of 1 July 1982, stood at 1,008,175,288. Since the last census, in 1964, the Chinese population had grown by 314 million, corresponding to an average yearly growth rate of 2.1 per cent. The actual growth rate has dropped from 2.85 per cent in 1965 to 1.57 per cent in 1975 and 1.15 per cent in 1983. It was 1.08l per cent in 1984, near the target of 0.95 per cent the authorities deem necessary to reach the goal of a population of 1.2 billion in the year 2000.

In spite of the drastic one-child policy, China's population seems likely to grow beyond the planned target and may reach 1.25 billion by the end of the century even under the most favourable conditions. Out of a total of 150 million couples in which the woman is of child-bearing age, 130 million practise some kind of birth control. Sterilisation of one of the partners seems to be the preference of about half of the couples and about 40 per cent rely on intra-uterine devices. Only 5.3 per cent use the pill and 2.4 per cent condoms. Government figures put abortions in 1984 at 8.89 million, about one-third of all pregnancies.

China's population represents over one-fifth of the world population but the country's agricultural area comprises only one-seventh of the world's farmland. Because of the large deserts or semi-desert areas, notably Sinkiang and the Tibetan plateau, 78 per cent of the population live on 32 per cent of the country's land surface. Early marriages have been discouraged or prohibited by advocating late marriages (men 27 years, women 25 years), penalties or disincentives for having more than one child which may include reduction in salaries of government employees, income-tax concessions only for the officially-allowed number of children, stiff maternity charges, educational handicaps for children exceeding the official limit, low housing priorities or reduction of living space and even compulsory sterilisation. The pill is distributed gratis to married women and abortions are performed free of charge.

The US Congress has cut off funding to international agencies that support abortions. Senator Jesse Helms wanted to have the American financial commitment to the United Nations Fund for Population Activities rescinded because the agency helps family planning in China where, the Senator charged, birth-control policies included forced abortions.

The strict requirement that families have only one child has exacerbated the antagonism and bitterness caused by the birth of a girl. Failure to produce a son and heir who will carry on the family name and support the parents in their old age is regarded as a cause of shame, and so far the authorities have not succeeded in persuading Chinese families that a daughter should be just as welcome as a son. Female infanticide has become rampant, mothers who gave birth to girls have been mistreated, chased out of the house or even killed. Some mothers have committed suicide after having been beaten and insulted for having born a girl. In some villages, a bucket full of water is kept by the mother's bed as she is giving birth. If the screaming infant turns out to be a girl, she is immediately drowned. Girl babies are abandoned in caves or thrown into streams and ponds. The authorities have been telling the men that they are the ones who determine a baby's sex but this scientific education has had no influence on people's behaviour.

The national census put the ratio of men to women (including children) at 51.5 to 48.5 (519 million males, 489 million females) which means that there are 106 men to every 100 women. The present policy is bound to worsen this ratio. In some villages, new-born boys outnumber girls by up to nine to one. Advertisements offering 'artificial sex control' claimed that their methods would allow parents to ensure that their baby would be a boy.

In 1970, the late Dr Herman Kahn predicted that a pill which would enable a father to preselect the sex of his offspring would be available in ten years. Fortunately, such a pill is not yet on the market but the possibility of such a pill remains extremely disturbing. The imbalance in the sex ratio likely to appear from such an agent in countries such as China or India would create a social catastrophe.

The Chinese authorities declare that the country's policy of one child per family is an emergency measure, but they admit that it will take 70 years to reduce the population to the ideal level of 650 to 700 million even if the policy is effective. The population policy can be enforced to a certain extent in the cities but it is in trouble in the countryside where tradition and the partial restoration of private farming favour large families. In 1984, only children constituted 83 per cent of all new-born babies in the cities but only 62.3 per cent in rural areas. One-child families accounted for 21.2 per cent of all families with children and only children numbered 35 million.

Although the family planning programme is supposed to be voluntary, there have been numerous reports of compulsory measures. Mothers of two or more children have been forced to undergo sterilisation and mothers who became pregnant a second time were ordered to have an abortion and submit to sterilisation. The State Family Planning Commission decided that either husband or wife must be sterilised if the couple has two children.

Birth Control in Vietnam

A situation similar to that in the People's Republic of China exists in Vietnam. The government, alarmed by the high population growth, launched a family planning programme in 1963. In order to bring the population increase down to 1.7 per cent, couples were advised to limit their offspring to two. Faster promotions and larger rice rations were among the incentives promised to women following the policy. The country's population doubled from 24 million in 1955 to 50 million in 1977, and although in 1985, the growth rate was down to 2.2 per cent as against 3.8 per cent in 1960 and 3.3 per cent in 1970, it still added a million babies to a population of 60 million. According to government figures, 712,000 women of child-bearing age were using IUDs in 1984; pill users numbered 50,000, condoms were used by 542,000 and 26,900 underwent sterilisation. Altogether, 34 per cent of Vietnamese couples relied on some form of contraceptives in mid-1985.

Birth Control in the Philippines

A serious confrontation occurred between the former government under President Ferdinand E. Marcos and the Catholic Church over the implementation of the country's family planning programme. The government wanted to reduce the birth rate from 2.4 per cent to 2 per cent by 1987 and promoted a 'cafeteria-style' programme, offering a wide range of contraceptive services, except abortion. Jaime Cardinal L. Sin, the archbishop of Manila, complained that the government was pushing the use of artificial contraceptive methods although the country is predominantly and overwhelmingly Catholic, and utterly neglected the natural family planning programme which was supposed to receive at least equal support. Church leaders charged that some foreign donors, particularly the US Agency for International Development, threatened to withhold funds unless the government promoted contraceptive methods like IUDs or the highly controversial Depo-Provera.

Indonesia

Indonesia's family planners have used peasant volunteers to distribute contraceptives and spread birth-control information. The country, with a population of almost 168 million, making it the world's fifth most populous nation, has succeeded in reducing the birth rate from a high but unknown percentage in the past to an estimated 2.23 per cent in 1984. On Bali, one of the most crowded of the Indonesian islands, the average births per woman declined from 5.8 in 1971 to 3.8 in 1976. Users of contraceptives went up from practically nil 15 years ago to about 14 million people, with the pill the most popular method. The government opposes abortion on religious grounds (Indonesia is one of the world's leading Islamic nations).

In February 1985, the Irish Parliament approved a bill legalising the sale of contraceptives to anyone over the age of 18. The measure, dubbed the 'Pill Bill,' had been strongly opposed by the Catholic hierarchy but was passed by a vote of 83 to 80.

Birth-Control Methods

From the point of view of the individual, the basic requirements for birth-control methods are reliability, effectiveness, and physical as well as aesthetic acceptability. Sex partners have to agree not only on the question whether to use birth control or not, but also on the method. No method should be used which might physically or psychologically hurt one or the other, and birth control should not diminish the attractiveness or joy of sexual relations. For their social use, birth-control methods should be effective, but this requirement also includes that their use does not involve undesirable side effects or dangers.

Basically, two kinds of birth-control methods can be distinguished, appliance and non-appliance techniques, but all methods currently in use have some drawback. They may be too difficult to use, too unreliable, too expensive or not available in a particular country or region. Among the methods not using artificial means, withdrawal of the penis has been the most successful in history, but it is unsatisfactory to both partners. On account of the story in Gen 38, 9, this method of contraception is called onanism (the word is also used for masturbation). Exegetically, as noted earlier, it can be maintained that the condemnation of Onan's action and its punishment was not because of the interruption of the copula but because he refused to beget children who would be born in his brother's name. Other forms of avoiding ejaculation into the vagina are *coitus obstructus* which means the suppression of ejaculation by depressing the base of the urethra and forcing the semen into the bladder, and *coitus reservatus* in which ejaculation is intentionally withheld.

Rhythm Method

Since the discovery of the relation between ovulation and the menstrual cycle by Dr Herman Knaus of Prague (1929) and Dr Kyūsaku Ogino of Japan (1931), the 'rhythm method' has been widely used. These two scientists did not collaborate but their findings were practically identical. The period in which conception is possible is the time of ovulation, the five days from the 16th to the 12th day prior to the next menstruation. Since spermatozoa can stay alive for a period of three days and an ovum remains fertilisable for a day, the front-end of the five-day period must be extended by three days and another day must be added at the end so that the period of possible conception becomes nine days. The time from menstruation to the beginning of the fertile period is relatively 'safe,' but not as safe as the period from the end of ovulation to menstruation. The calculation of the period of ovulation requires a rather extended observation of the menstrual cycle and it is impossible to exclude sudden changes. Other methods of ascertaining ovulation are measuring basal temperature in the morning or checking changes in the hormone levels in urine. A method first developed by Drs John and Evelyn Billings in Australia determines the fertile days by charting the secretion of a certain type of mucus from the cervix which always accompanies ovulation. This method avoids the uncertainties of the rhythm method arising from the changing cycles of women.

A device developed in Britain measures vaginal temperature to a fraction of a degree. Inserted into the vagina, the device lights up red if the woman is in the fertile time of the month and green if she isn't. A Swiss architect invented a device consisting of a thermometer attached to a microcomputer. Based on her temperature curve, each woman can programme the computer for her fertility cycle, and when she takes her temperature, the device (called 'Bioself') indicates the fertility level (green for infertile days, on average 46 per cent of the cycle, red for slightly fertile days, on average 23 per cent, and a flashing red light for the highly fertile days, 31 per cent). A similar 'fertility clock' incorporating a high-precision thermometer and a microcomputer to interpret daily fluctuations on body temperature (taken each morning orally) indicates the periods of fertility and infertility and thereby the time when it is 'safe' for a woman to engage in unprotected sexual intercourse.

Natural Family Planning

A growing number of women stop taking the pill and turn to 'natural family planning' (NFP). While many doctors and the pharma industry consider NFP unreliable, feminist groups denounce the pill not only because it requires women to swallow chemicals which have undesirable side effects but also because it puts the entire burden of birth control on the women who, therefore, feel themselves manipulated and exploited by men.

NFP has come a long way from the traditional Knaus-Ogino method. Exact and honest self-observation is the key to the success of NFP. The basis of NFP is the determination of the period of ovulation by taking the morning temperature, examining the cervical mucus (whether it is still or again thickish, whitish and clumpy or clear, ductile and fluent) and observing the individual symptoms of the fertile period (breast pains, vulva pains, swelling, and so on). With some experience, women can dispense with one or the other of the observations. NFP requires periodic abstinence from intercourse for seven to thirteen days but it is inexpensive, without harm to health and it can be terminated at any time. Above all, NFP involves both partners and can make them discover and appreciate forms of tenderness only fleetingly experienced in foreplay.

Even among illiterate slum-dwellers, NFP has had success rates of 90 to 95 per cent but it demands the conscientious cooperation of both partners and could hardly be recommended to young and inexperienced newlyweds.

An Australian researcher reported that saliva tests give a clearer indication of the fertile time after ovulation than other methods. Dr Peter Hartmann, a specialist on lactation, said he had found sharp changes in the composition of breast milk and the amount of glucose in saliva five to six days before ovulation and six to seven days after. Saliva tests could also help to ascertain the return to fertility of a breast-feeding mother.

Potentially promising, perhaps, is a method that would detect an increase in temperature in a ripening ovary relative to a quiescent one, but the work on this method is at a very preliminary stage. At present, the failure rate of the rhythm method is high, 10-25 per cent.

Birth Control in Antiquity

Birth control by artificial means includes the application of mechanical devices and the use of chemical substances. Soranus of Ephesus already explained the difference between contraceptives and abortifacients in the second century AD, and the Islamic physicians transmitted what knowledge there was on this matter to medieval Europe. The Egyptians and Jews used substances considered spermicides and for centuries, the use of some kind of fat or butter, although ineffective, has been a popular practice. The Greeks used vinegar and the Romans oil and soft wool. Indian tribes in Brazil and Peru are said to use herbs that act as contraceptives. The Ifugaos, a tribe in the northern Philippines, were reported to conduct their own family planning programme and also a scheme to reduce the size of rival tribes with a potion made from cassava roots. In small doses, the potion will make a woman sterile for four years; if taken in large amounts, the sterility will be for life. A survey team of a local census department noticed that women always had their children four years apart.

The crudest methods of mechanical birth control include devices preventing access to the vagina, such as chastity belts, much used in the Middle Ages, or infibulation, the tying together of the prepuce or the labia with clasps or stitches (already used in Rome). Modern barrier methods intend to prevent the penetration of the semen into the vulva. Intra-uterine devices come in many forms, coils, loops and rings, but no one quite knows how they work. They are inserted into the uterine cavity and must be put in place by a physician to be effective and to avoid injuries. Caps to cover the uterine cervix were first made of metal or crepe rubber and later of latex. Diaphragms or pessaries are larger in size; they are made of latex or soft rubber and mounted on a spring metal rim. A barrier contraceptive under trial is a moulded rubber cap to be fitted over the cervix. One model has a valve to permit menstrual flow so that it can be worn for months. A new disposable diaphragm can remain in place for 24 hours. During this time, the device releases nonoxynol-9, the spermicide most commonly used with vaginal contraception.

Mechanical means also include vaginal tampons or sponges. A sponge contraceptive uses nonoxynol-9 and is comparable to the diaphragm in safety and effectiveness. It lasts 24 hours; the failure rate is 18 per cent during the first year and 10 per cent thereafter. Barrier methods interfere with the sex act and are not absolutely effective. They are more popular in developed than in developing countries (though the condom is widely used in India). Condoms offer some protection against venereal disease; sometimes, their use is combined with that of a spermicide jelly.

Some years ago, the sale of intra-uterine devices was temporarily suspended in the United States and Britain on account of a possible link with septicemia (pathogenic bacteria in the bloodstream) and septic abortions. In 1978, the California Court of Appeals held that when it was found that an intra-uterine device (Dalkon shield) could be dangerous, the doctor was obliged to inform his patient of the risk. The court ruled that a doctor had an obligation to inform his patients of any newly-discovered dangers in drugs or devices that the doctor had prescribed in previous years. Sales of the Dalkon shield were discontinued in 1974 and its manufacturer, A. R. Robins Co. of Richmond, Virginia, started a worldwide campaign to get women still using the device to have it removed. The company faced thousands of lawsuits and payments to women who suffered infections, miscarriages or sterility amounted to $378 million. In August 1985, the company filed a bankruptcy petition.

Copper 7, an intra-uterine device used by about a million women in the United States was taken off the market at the end of January 1986 because its manufacturer, S. D. Seale & Co., could no longer afford the costs of defending product litigation. Although approved by the government's health regulators and considered safe and useful, the device has been the target of 775 lawsuits alleging that it can perforate the uterus and cause ectopic pregnancies or pelvic inflammatory disease. The company had won eight out of ten lawsuits which had been tried so far but said that product liability insurance for its domestic IUD business had become virtually unobtainable.

Some women find IUDs painful, and the devices are said to increase blood loss during menstruation by 20 per cent and up to as much as 120 per cent. There is also suspicion that IUD-users face a higher risk of ectopic or tubular pregnancies. An IUD that can last 20 years has undergone nine years of testing in Belgium.

A report in the *Journal of the American Medical Association* in August 1983 stated that all intrauterine devices, not just the discredited Dalkon shield, can cause infection and infertility, and that the risk of pelvic inflammation is nine times greater among current IUD users than among women who rely on other contraceptives although sexually-transmitted diseases are the leading cause of pelvic disease.

Chemical contraceptives include spermicidal jellies and creams, vaginal suppositories and above all the pill.

The Pill

The most popular pill combines two steroid sex hormones, estrogen and progesterone. It prevents pregnancy by suppressing ovulation. Theoretically, the pill is 99 per cent effective; in practice, the failure rate may be 2-3 per cent. However, the pill is not without risks, the most serious of which are cardiovascular, particularly cerebral thrombosis and deep vein thrombosis of the leg. Pill-related heart attacks occur in an estimated one in 14,000 users between the ages of 30 and 39. The risk increases for women aged 40 to 45 with one case in 1,500 users. Strokes occur in about one in 2,700 women on the pill. Blood clots affect one in 500 previously healthy women on the pill.

A pill for use after unprotected coitus, called Tetragynon, combines the two hormones gestagen and estrogen. Each package contains four tablets of which two must be taken 48 hours after intercourse at the latest and the other two 12 hours later. If conception is to be prevented, the drug must be consumed within 60 hours after coitus. Since the pill represents a heavy dose of hormones, it should not be taken twice within the same monthly cycle. The drug is not classified as an abortifacient because it is ineffective once nidation has taken place. Possible side effects include nausea, vomiting and menstrual disturbances but clinical tests in the United States and Canada have confirmed a better than 90 per cent effectiveness.

According to one opinion, women under 25 years of age get maximum benefit from the pill and are at minimum risk. A woman's safest course would be to start with the pill and use it for four years to get the maximum protection against ovarian cancer, have the number of children she desires by her mid-20s and then persuade her husband to have a vasectomy. Women suffer greater risk from contraception than from childbirth only if they take the pill when they are over 40, or use the pill and smoke when they are older than 35.

Some 500 of the 10 million pill-users in the United States die each year from causes related to pill use, mainly strokes and heart attacks, compared with nearly 30 from complications of tubal sterilisation, 30 from intra-uterine devices and 15 from abortion complications. But the pill use prevents approximately 850 ovarian cancer deaths. For women under 35, the risks from the use of the pill are negligible. This opinion asserts that there is no evidence to link the pill with cancer of the ovaries, uterus or breasts though it has been connected with a rare benign cancer of the liver, and some cases of damage to brain vessels, headaches, and skin and hair disorders have been reported.

Studies conducted by the US Centres for Disease Control concluded that no association appears to exist between the use of oral contraceptives and breast cancer and that the use of the pill seems to lower the incidence of endometrial (womb lining) and ovarian cancer. But researchers at the University of Southern California School of Medicine reported in October 1983 that the relative risk of developing breast cancer for women who started on the pill while young is directly related to the progestin potency of the pill they used and the length of time they were on it. The risk is six times greater for women who began using the high-progestin pill at age 19 or earlier and continued taking it for six years than for women the same age who took a low-progestin pill or did not use the pill. The risk is 1.4 times greater for women on the pill for one to two years, 2.4 times greater for two to four years of use, and 4.1 times greater for four to six years. There is no greater risk for women between 25 and 40 using a high-progestin pill. Professor Martin Vessey of the University Department of Community Medicine at Oxford suggested that there was a link between long-term use of the pill and cancer of the cervix.

It has been assumed that the side effects of the pill would cease when the use of the pill was discontinued but they actually persist for about a decade after discontinuation. According to an American researcher, the risk of heart attack from past use of the pill is concentrated among older women who smoke and who were in their 30s when taking oral contraceptives. But there is no evidence of a residual risk of heart attack among women who had used the pill when they were young (under 30) and then stopped. Medical experts disagree on the effects of the pill on adolescent girls. Some doctors maintain that the pill is always injurious to girls around 14 while other researchers assert that there is no permanent effect on the harmony of the endocrinal systems. A study of 2,000 mothers of twins in the United States, Britain, Australia and South Africa who became pregnant within three months after going off the pill showed an increased chance of having twins.

Dr Davies Grimes of the Centres for Disease Control told a 1985 conference of gynaecologists that fewer women used the pill than ten years ago because of fear of complications, fear which, according to Dr Grimes, was unfounded. The result has been a sharp increase in unplanned and unwanted pregnancies which often plunge unmarried and teenage mothers into poverty. More than half of all pregnancies in the United States, an estimated 3 million, were unplanned, Dr Grimes said, and more than a quarter end in abortion.

In Japan, the over-the-counter sale of the pill has not been approved. The Ministry of Health and Welfare maintains that the possibility of adverse side effects has not yet been sufficiently studied and recently appointed a 12-member committee of experts to establish the safety of oral contraceptives. A report is expected to be completed in three or four years. Officially, doctors can dispense the pill for the treatment of dysmenorrhea (painful menstruation), and according to an estimate some 700,000 women actually take the pill for the purpose of birth control. But the forms of the pill now available in Japan do not include pills with a low hormone content so that the danger of untoward side effects cannot be ruled out. Rumour has it that the real reason for the 20-year foot-dragging of the ministry taking steps for the approval of the pill was the lobbying of gynaecologists and obstetricians who wanted to protect their lucrative practice of artificial interruption of pregnancy. This was also said to have been behind the government's prohibition of IUDs in 1936 under the Injurious Medical Treatment Instrument Control Law.

In December 1983, the Japanese Consumers League asked the Ministry of Health and Welfare to suspend the sale of a spermicide in the form of a jelly or film containing a surface-active agent because of possible carcinogenic effects. The ministry, however, replied that the spermicide had long been used in many countries and that its safety had been confirmed.

Other Contraceptives

In the United States, the Population Council developed a contraceptive called the Norplant subdermal implant system which consists of six small rods containing 35 mg of the progestin levonorgestrel. The rods are implanted under the skin, usually in the upper arm, and are said to be effective for five years. In addition to inhibiting ovulation, the hormone also thickens the cervical mucus, impeding the passage of sperm into the uterus. Because of the minimal daily dose of progestin — 30 micrograms as compared with 150 micrograms of many brands of the pill — and the absence of estrogen, Norplant should pose less health risks such as strokes and blood clots than other contraceptives.

Levonorgestrel is also contained in a T-shaped IUD developed by the Population Council which also sponsored a vaginal ring containing both a progestin and a natural estrogen. The ring is worn for three weeks and removed one week in conformity with the woman's regular cycle. The World Health Organisation supported the development of a vaginal ring which can be worn continuously and slowly releases a progestational agent which thickens the cervical mucus and stops sperm transport.

A new non-steroid contraceptive for women is based on LHRF (luteinising hormone-releasing factor). This substance, secreted by the hypothalamus, stimulates the pituitary gland to release hormones that activate the ovaries. It was first considered as an aid to fertility but it was discovered that analogues could prevent ovulation. An LHRF pill seems impossible because the substance is broken down in the stomach but trials using nasal sprays and injections look promising.

A French-Swiss research team has developed what it claims to be a safer birth-control pill which is free of harmful side effects but also acts as an abortifacient. The drug, an anti-progesterone called RU-486, produces an entirely opposite effect to the old pill. Whereas the pill interrupts the female hormone cycle and suppresses ovulation, the new drug causes menstruation (and thereby abortion). The new substance has to be taken only a few days a month compared with three out of four weeks each month for the old pill. In a new approach to contraception, researchers are trying to develop a drug that will inhibit ovulation by controlling the signals sent by the pituitary gland to the reproductive system.

A process on which a researcher at the Ohio State University worked for 12 years involves a hormone called human chorionic gonadotropin which will not affect fertilisation but prevent sustained pregnancies. A single injection will provide immunity for a year. Tests are due to be conducted in Australia and the process may only be ready for public use in 1992.

A single injection of a synthetic female hormone called Depo Provera prevents pregnancy for three months. The drug's active ingredient is a synthetic progestogen hormone that suppresses the pituitary hormones normally effecting ovulation. The drug is approved for the treatment of certain kinds of kidney and uterine cancer. Researchers at the US Centres for Disease Control at Atlanta could not find a strong association between

Depo Provera injections and cancer of the breast, uterus or ovaries. Due to the opposition of women activists and consumer groups, its use in the United States as a contraceptive was banned by the US Food and Drug Administration in 1978 after it had been on the market for five years. The government admits that the drug's benefits outweigh the risk of cancer but refuses to clear it for general use. There is no evidence of an increased risk of cancer or birth defects but critics contend that the drug has not been used long enough to tell how risky it is for humans.

A three-member public inquiry panel formed by the US Food and Drug Administration in 1981 recommended after three years of study that the US government continue to withhold approval of Depo Provera. The manufacturer, Upjohn Co., has indicated that it would file an 'exception' to the board's findings.

Minimal clinical side effects have been claimed for a pill that contains the lowest possible dose of estrogen. A slow-release steroid that can be implanted under a woman's skin can prevent pregnancy for six years. Researchers at Northwestern University developed a vaccine that, they said, could preclude conception for up to six months at a time. The vaccine which can be manufactured from readily available chemicals stimulates the production of antibodies which react against sperm. Conception becomes possible again after the vaccine wears off.

The drug DES (diethylstilbestrol) operates in a different way. It is a synthetic estrogen and is usually effective if taken twice a day for five days after intercourse. A similar effect is claimed for a suppository, ONO 802, a prostaglandin extract which essentially is an abortifacient.

The Chinese news agency Xinhua reported that a single injection of a hormone derivative developed by the Family Planning Institute of the Zhejiang Academy of Medical Science near Shanghai prevented pregnancy for an entire month. Tests of the contraceptive, a compound of norethisterone enanthate and estradiol valerate, were said to have shown no side effects.

Researchers at Northwestern University have been studying a synthetically-produced steroid called anordin which has proved to be 100 per cent effective in preventing pregnancy in monkeys. The drug has been used in China as a so-called 'honeymoon pill' which, when used after unprotected intercourse, prevents a fertilised egg from implanting in the uterus. Low doses of the hormone also prevent egg production in monkeys when administered four days after the start of the cycle. Injected monthly thereafter, anordin prevents both ovulation and menstruation. Dr Robert Chatterton, who reported on the research, expected the hormone to be equally effective in humans although some women may dislike not having menstrual periods.

Some investigators have expressed misgivings about the side effects of contraceptives and human feelings and behaviour. A contraceptive that works by inhibiting ovulation also suppresses menstruation. The reaction of women to the lack of menses is ambiguous. Some women welcome it, others feel uneasy. Women on the pill do not experience the mid-cycle surge in sexual activity that other women do. Actually, the long time of menstrual cycles now common in the West may be partly due to the decrease in breast-feeding. Research into breast-feeding patterns and the length of time a lactating woman does not ovulate suggests that the most decisive factor is the frequency of suckling. If breast-feeding is not limited to a few long sessions but given more or less on demand and weaning is postponed, ovulation could be avoided for at least one or two years and as long as three.

The least reliable methods of birth control are the interruption of coitus, the rhythm method, rinsing of the vagina or the injection of chemicals into the vagina after coitus.

Male Contraceptives

A male contraceptive in the form of nosedrops developed in the United States reduces the sperm count to 25 per cent of the 250 million spermatozoa normally found in a healthy ejaculation. The active ingredient is a synthetic substitute of LHRF. But the drug has severe side effects, such as hot flushes similar to those suffered by women during the menopause. It can also result in impotence from which recovery may take up to three months which makes its use as a contraceptive meaningless. Similar contraceptives administered as nasal sprays or injections have the same drawbacks.

A male contraceptive in the form of a salve rubbed on the skin was reported ready for testing on humans in August 1983. The salve works on the same principle as birth control pills used by women, by raising the level of sex hormones in the bloodstream. The hormones affect the pituitary gland's control of sperm and ovum production.

Scientists at the West German Max Planck Institute in Munich discovered a chemical which stops sperm production without causing harmful side effects. The only snag is that the synthetic steroid shrinks the testes to half their normal size, but the sex drive is not affected.

The developer of the birth-control pill, Professor Carl Djerassi, deplores the slowness with which new drugs are approved. The American legal system, he thinks, encourages the suing of drug companies while discouraging risk-taking research. Media coverage blows up the genetic defects caused by a drug in rats without discussing the application to humans. Every chemical starting with sugar and salt has undesirable side effects, Dr Djerassi says. He thinks that except for the prevention of nuclear war, effective human fertility control will be the most important social task affecting the quality of life on earth during the rest of this century.

Sterilisation

A fundamentally different form of birth control is sterilisation. Usually, sterilisation is irreversible so that the decision not to have children cannot be undone. Formerly, sterilisation was performed by castration, the removal of the testicles in men, and hysterectomy, salpingectomy or ovariectomy in women. These methods have been replaced by surgery that leaves the sex glands intact but severs or obstructs the tubes or ducts through which sperm or ova pass to accomplish fertilisation, which means vasectomy in men and tubal sterilisation in women. These operations impair neither sexual appetite nor performance but are generally irreversible.

Chinese doctors, however, have developed a method of blocking the Fallopian tubes by the injection of mucilage from natural substances. The same effect can be obtained by using methylcyanoacrylate ('superglue'). The Chinese have also devised a technique of sterilising men by injecting a very small quantity of 'superglue' into the vas deferens (the duct that transports the sperm from the epididymis to the penis). Theoretically, it should be easy to reverse this form of sterilisation.

Researchers in Britain and the United States found that, unlike monkeys, men who have vasectomies do not run the risk of having a stroke or a heart attack in the short term. Satisfactory pharmacological means of sterilisation have not yet been found.

Castration not only prevents reproduction but also greatly modifies sexual characteristics. In the male, the voice may become high as in childhood and the growth of hair on face and body may become weak or cease altogether. In women, ovariectomy produces the same effects as the menopause.

In Italy, boy singers were castrated to preserve their treble voices; the custom was finally abolished by Leo XIII in 1878. In eastern countries, the eunuchs originally served as bedchamber or harem attendants but often ascended to high state offices in China, India and Persia. Eunuchs are still found in oriental, especially Islamic countries. Until its condemnation by Pope Benedict XIV (1740-58), castration for preserving the voices of boy singers was held morally licit by some Catholic moralists (notably St Alphonsus Liguori) but is now considered illicit except for lawful medical reasons.

The Catholic bishops in the United States have forbidden Catholic hospitals from sterilising women for contraceptive purposes by cutting or tying the Fallopian tubes. The National Conference of Catholic Bishops, in a directive issued in July 1980, ruled that such an operation was totally alien to the mission of Catholic hospitals, and immoral, even for medical reasons.

Compulsory Sterilisation

Laws providing for voluntary or compulsory sterilisation exist in many countries, above all in India, the People's Republic of China, Thailand and many American states. Compulsory sterilisation has been decreed for the purposes of population control, but especially for eugenic or social reasons (for example, in the case when families are already too large) or as a preventive measure for sex criminals. Eugenic reasons include hereditary diseases such as feeble-mindedness but also syphilis, and the sterilisation of criminals sometimes extends to habitual or violent criminals. A judge in San Antonio, Texas, ordered a defendant found guilty of two charges of burglary with intent to rape to undergo treatment with Depo Provera for ten years as part of probation. Experts had testified that, as a child, the defendant had received 'more sexual stimulation than he could handle.'

In Britain, the law lords of the House of Lords ruled that a mentally retarded girl identified only as Jeanette could be sterilised. The girl's mother and social workers concerned with the case had brought the problem to the attention of the authorities. The sterilisation had been approved by the lower courts and the issue was submitted to the House of Lords in a speedy test appeal to beat the deadline of Jeanette's 18th birthday, 20 May 1987, when she would legally become an adult and would have to give her 'informed consent' to sterilisation. The girl, with a mental age of 5, was held incapable of making such a decision although she had, as Lord Chancellor Quintin Hailsham said in his judgement, 'all the physical sexual drive and inclination of a mature young woman of 17.' According to the Lord Chancellor, the girl has shown that she is vulnerable to sexual approaches and there is significant danger of pregnancy resulting from casual sexual intercourse.

The law lords and the government's official solicitor gave assurances that the ruling did not involve public policy or sterilisation for social purposes.

As part of a programme of racial purification, Sweden adopted a law providing for compulsory sterilisation of mentally retarded, dangerous criminals and men with abnormal or excessive sex urges. Prisoners could either submit to castration or stay in jail. Between 1935 and 1948, 12,108 women and 3,378 men were sterilised and another 26,619 women and 1,251 men were sterilised between 1949 and 1964 when the law was partially amended. The law, however, is still on the statute books and there have been castrations on 'humanitarian' grounds.

Compulsory sterilisation is a serious interference with personal freedom. Bertrand Russell once speculated that the ruling party might one day decide to sterilise its political opponents, thus hoping to guarantee the perpetuity of its own power. The sterilisation of criminals can be defended on the grounds of public policy (not only as part of the punishment) if it is confined to recidivistic sex offenders. It would appear that in many cases, sterilisation might be desirable for the sake of the individual himself, since it protects him against the responsibilities of parenthood which he is unable to acquit properly. But this decision should be left to the individual himself or his guardian. The use of compulsory sterilisation for the purposes of population control or for eliminating the biologically unfit constitutes an abuse of public power.

In a report published in 1981, the Johns Hopkins Medical Institutions stated that voluntary sterilisation has become the world's most common method of birth control, used by at least 100 million men and women, including 40 million in China, 25 million in India, 13 million in the United States and 4.5 million in Latin America. The report attributed the popularity of sterilisation to its success rate of about 99 per cent, few side effects in connection with surgery and virtually none afterwards. But this assessment may be too optimistic. Some researchers have expressed concerns that vasectomy does not eliminate the production of sperm, and since the testes have a limited capacity to reabsorb sperm, some get into the tissues where they trigger the production of antibodies against them. Because nature never intended sperm to enter the tissues, they are perceived as foreign invaders of man's immune system. Nevertheless, according to the *Shere Hite Report,* many men have found vasectomy very satisfactory.

A 1983 study on contraceptives stated that male and female sterilisation had become the leading birth-control method in the United States. Sterilisation was the most common choice for couples who had completed their families. Of the 11.6 million sterilisations among these couples, 4.9 million were vasectomies. The pill was used by 10 million women, the condom was third with about 4.5 million users. The number of users of other birth-control methods were: IUDs 2.3 million, diaphragm 1.9 million and vaginal spermicides 1.5 million. Withdrawal was practised by 900,000 and the rhythm method by 600,000. More than 3 million married and unmarried women aged between 18 and 44 used no birth control at all. About half the number of unmarried women questioned said they would have an abortion if they had an unwanted pregnancy.

Reliability

The reliability of the various birth-control methods is still uncertain. The diaphragm and condom, while relatively complication-free, may not be as effective as has been thought. In the United States, almost 10 per cent of the women who rely on their husbands' use of condoms in the first year of marriage get pregnant and more than 18 per cent of the women using diaphragms become pregnant during the first year of marriage. Other failure rates for this period are: vasectomy or tubal sterilisation

0.4 per cent, the pill 2.4 per cent, IUDs 4.6 per cent, spermicides 17.9 per cent, and rhythm 23.7 per cent.

Complications

Complications each year result in the hospitalisation of 0.4 per cent of the IUD users (mainly by causing or spreading pelvic inflammatory disease), 4.5 per cent of those who have tubal sterilisation, 0.3 per cent of those who have legal abortions, and 0.1 per cent of the pill users.

Overall, 56,000 or 0.3 per cent of the 14.6 million women in the United States who use the riskiest methods of birth control — the pill, IUDs, tubal sterilisation and abortion — suffer major complications each year while 60,000 or 2.0 per cent of the 3 million sexually-active women who use no birth control have either Caesarian sections or ectopic pregnancies — only two of the many major complications of pregnancy and birth. It is difficult to name the most recommendable birth-control method. One of the leading experts, Dr Sidney Wolfe, director of the Public Citizen Health Research Group, stated: 'Carefully used, the diaphragm is very effective. I wouldn't recommend the pill as first choice.'

Morality of Birth Control

As explained above (Ch. 1), the rejection of the use of 'artificial means' for preventing conception is based on the assumption that the biological structure of the sex act implicates an ethical norm. This principle is not asserted for other biological functions for which the illicitness of interference is predicated on the injury to health and bodily integrity. That the sex act 'by its nature' is capable of procreating new life is a generalisation which is only conditionally valid in physical reality. In itself, the sex act is an act of mating and fertilisation does not enter into the constitution of this act. It only occurs if other conditions, above all ovulation, are fulfilled. The sexual act of men and women who are capable of coitus but infertile is, 'by its nature,' impotent to generate new life but, as far as the actions of the partners are concerned, indistinguishable from acts which can result in conception. By its nature, the sex act can include the possibility of fertilisation but this possibility does not constitute a condition for the performance of the sex act. Nor can the possibility of fertilisation be regarded as a necessary condition for making the sex act a human act, that is to say, an act compatible with the dignity of man.

Morality depends on the relation of man's free action to the individual and social order implied in man's nature. The sex act and, generally speaking, the satisfaction of sexual desire within and outside marriage is only immoral if it offends against the right order given with human nature. Just as man can intervene in other life functions in order to control them and adapt them to the total requirements of man, he can also interfere in the process of conception in order to adjust it to other legitimate concerns.

From a broader point of view, the separation of sexual enjoyment from reproduction implies a change not only in moral but also in social value systems. Sex has become recreational rather than institutional and the dissociation of sexual activity from personal responsibility, formerly the prerogative of the male, can now also be enjoyed by the female. This problem cannot be solved by restricting sexual freedom but by safeguarding the rôle of the family and making family life more attractive. Above all, it requires sex education that brings out the personal engagement in sex. It is not a question of compensatory gratification for inconvenience in sexuality but of motivation.

Court Decisions

While birth control now is being encouraged in many countries, it initially met with sometimes vehement political opposition. It was very much an anti-establishment issue and in the United States, the cases in which the Supreme Court became involved turned on the right to privacy. In its 1965 decisions of Griswold v. Connecticut, the court ruled that Connecticut could not prohibit married couples from using birth-control devices. In Eisenstadt v. Baird (1972), the court overturned the conviction of a birth-control activist for distributing birth-control devices without a license. The court's position was that the right to privacy certainly included the right of the individual, married or single, to be free from unwarranted government intrusion into matters so fundamentally affecting a person as the decision whether to bear or beget a child. This position greatly influenced the court's decisions on abortions.

A sharp controversy arose when the Reagan administration tried to rein in teenage sex by ordering clinics receiving federal funds under the Family Planning Law to inform parents within 10 working days when their daughters aged 17 or younger received prescriptions for birth-control pills, diaphragms or intrauterine devices. The regulation — branded as the 'squeal rule' by its opponents — was attacked by a number of family-planning and medical groups. A federal judge enjoined the US Department of Health and Human Services from enforcing the rule until a trial were held. 'The parental notice requirement is invalid because it contradicts and subverts the intent of Congress,' US District Judge Henry F. Werker said. 'Common sense dictates but one conclusion: the deterrent effect of the regulation will cause increased adolescent pregnancies.' In July 1983, the federal US Court of Appeals upheld the decisions of two lower federal courts prohibiting enforcement of the rule of the Department of Health and Human Services. 'Because we agree that the regulations are fundamentally inconsistent with Congress' intent and purpose ... and are therefore beyond the limit of the secretary's delegated authority, we affirm the decision below,' the court said.

Opinions Based on Religious Convictions

Surveys by the National Opinion Research Centre at the University of Chicago going back to 1972 show only small differences on reproductive attitudes and behaviour of Catholics and Protestants. On some issues, Catholics may be more liberal than Protestants. In a 1983 survey, 86 per cent of the Protestants and 85.5 per cent of the Catholics favoured giving birth-control information to teenagers, 66 per cent of the Protestants and 80 per cent of the Catholics thought that pre-marital sex was not always wrong, and 85 per cent of the Protestants and 88 per cent of the Catholics approved of sex education in public schools.

In Britain, Mrs Victoria Gillick, a Catholic mother of ten children, including five daughters aged one to thirteen when she started her action, wanted a court declaration to the effect that her daughters could not be given contraceptives without her consent. She also asked the court to ban a Health Department circular instructing doctors that they have the right to give contraceptives and advice to girls under the age of 16 if they consider it appropriate. Sexual intercourse with girls under 16 is illegal in Britain. The court turned down Mrs Gillick's request but the case finally reached the House of Lords.

In October 1985, the House of Lords ruled that physicians could prescribe the pill to girls under 16 without their parents' knowledge in exceptional circumstances. In a 3-2 vote, the Law Lords upheld a Health Department appeal, quashing an earlier court ruling in favour of Mrs Gillick.

Protestants generally do not object to artificial birth control. A study of the University of Kerala produced in 1963 describing the Protestant position stated that abstinence, although an obvious means of family planning, had no exclusive or basically higher ethical value than the means allowing sexual union without wishing a child. Abortion, of course, was strictly rejected as a method of birth control.

Desirability of Birth Control

It is difficult to make a general judgement on the value or desirability of artificial birth control. Disregarding any moral qualification and limiting the evaluation to its social usefulness (an approach which is condemned in some moral systems), a distinction must be made between its possible function from a public and a private or individual point of view. While birth control gets a positive rating as an instrument of population policy, above all of the developing countries, it is detrimental to the social order of at least some industrial countries. To bring the population explosion under control is an urgent policy goal for the developing countries in Asia, Africa and Latin America. For these countries, it is crucial to reduce birth rates to levels that permit a balance between population growth and the increase in economic resources, above all, food supplies and employment opportunities. The improvement in the standard of living in these countries depends on reducing the rate of population increase below the rate of economic growth. The magnitude of the human problems involved can be seen in the slums of cities such as Calcutta, Cairo or Rio de Janeiro where the lack of housing and other infrastructural facilities together with under-nourishment produces disease and untold human misery. Artificial birth control is definitely preferable to the growth of a population for which human living conditions cannot be secured.

The situation is entirely different in some industrial countries where the aging of the population is creating difficult problems. It is not the aging of society as such but its effects on the particular form of welfare state created in those countries which causes the problems. Because old-age pensions are not based on the actuarial principles of traditional insurance systems (that is, payments financed by the previous accumulation of capital) but on what is euphemistically called a 'pact between generations' (that is, payments financed by the contributions of the succeeding age classes), the aging of society leads to an impasse. The growth of the older age groups combined with the shrinkage of the younger age groups will necessitate a confiscatory level of taxes and social security contributions, if the level of social benefits is to be maintained. Such a situation has already appeared in Sweden and will develop in West Germany and Japan if the present trends continue. In Japan, people under 14 years of age accounted for 26.1 per cent of the population in 1985 and people over 65 years of age for 10.2 per cent, but in 2020, these ratios will come to 19.15 per cent and 23.6 per cent. The number of people entering the labour force will become proportionally (and eventually also absolutely) smaller while the number of people to be maintained by the work of others will grow. Taxes and contributions to social security would rise to 60 per cent and more of the average worker's wages, a burden nobody would be willing to shoulder.

Birth control should be available to individuals and families irrespective of their motives and marital status. In countries wanting to reduce their birth rates, birth-control devices might be given free of charge to those who cannot afford to pay for them but there is no reason why this should be extended to everybody everywhere. The warning that the availability of the means of birth control might lead to sexual promiscuity is not without foundation but it seems much better that teenagers should use the pill rather than to have unmarried teenage mothers and teenage abortions.

The basic problem is the creation of a social order which makes the affirmation of life possible. The destruction of nature, the precariousness of peace, the disregard of basic human values in living conditions, the despair created by the chronic unemployment of large numbers of healthy and skilled people and the bleak prospect of an old age spent in the ghettos of heartless institutions make life a crushing burden. The systems to ensure safety, prosperity and progress have failed and their failure has created deep-seated insecurity. Despite the amazing advances in technology, the intricate relations of the world economy, the ruthless exploitation of natural resources and the enormous sums spent on social security, people have no hope, no joy, no enthusiasm and no optimism. Only confidence in one's own future and the future of one's children will assure that birth control will remain a means subordinate to the meaning of marriage and the family.

3

Abortion

Perils of Pregnancy

WHEN A WOMAN IS PREGNANT she is often asked whether she expects a boy or a girl. To most expectant mothers, however, the health of her child and the safety of delivery are of much greater concern. The rates of still-births vary greatly; they lie between 2 per cent and 20 per cent of all births, depending on the age of the mother (lowest for women in their mid-twenties), the sequence of birth (lowest for the second child), and the interval between births (lowest for moderate intervals). Ectopic pregnancies constitute a danger for the foetus as well as the mother, and up to 3 per cent of all babies may begin life with major defects. The causes of 70 per cent of all birth defects are unknown, and about 20 per cent can be attributed to genetic factors. The agents responsible for birth defects, called teratogens, may be divided into three types: microorganisms, such as the rubella virus; physical agents, such as heat or blows; and chemicals, including drugs.

Genetic Defects

About 3,000 diseases are related to genetic changes which may be caused by many factors but particularly by chemicals. Two broad classes of genetic disorders are biochemical deficiencies and structural anomalies. Biochemical deficiencies are linked to conditions such as sickle-cell anaemia, Tay-Sachs disease, some forms of muscular dystrophy and probably cystic fibrosis. These disorders usually involve the faulty production of some crucial protein. Structural defects include congenital abnormities of the heart or other organs, neurological deformities such as spina bifida (failure of the spinal column to close properly), and malformations of the limbs, head or face. Another class of defects results from mutations in the genes themselves.

There are between 50,000 and 100,000 human genes, and the average person has from four to eight defective genes. If a gene is recessive, there is usually no problem, because its function will be taken over by the complementary gene from the other parent, but if the defective gene is dominant (as is the case for Huntingdon's disease), the disease occurs even if the other gene is normal.

Common defects are called those that occur in one birth out of 1,000.

In the United States, these include major cardiovascular defects, clubfoot, hypospadias, cleft of lip and/or palate, neural tube defects (spina bifida, anencephaly), deformed limbs (shortened or missing arms, legs, fingers or toes) and Down's syndrome.

Researchers at the Massachusetts General Hospital developed a technique for determining the carrier of the defective gene that causes Huntingdon's disease. This disorder which affects the nervous system begins with the loss of muscular control, causing jerky, involuntary movements, and ends with mental deterioration, dementia and death. The symptoms of the disease do not appear until mid-life, and children of victims run a 50 per cent risk of inheriting the disease.

Hereditary factors may be involved in some cases of club-foot and torticollis, and the congenital dislocation of the hip may be due to polygenetic factors. Fusion and webbing together of the digits of hands and feet (syndactyly) or the presence of extra digits (polydactyly) are often inherited but their form may vary even among the same kindred.

Due to inbreeding, about 1.6 million of the 20 million children born each year in China, or roughly 8 per cent of all Chinese babies, have congenital defects or suffer from mental retardation. The problem is greatest in remote areas where the gene pool is limited and custom allows marriages between cousins.

Researchers at the US National Cancer Institute claimed to have found evidence that some people are born carrying cancer genes-related bits of genetic material that predispose them to cancer. Studying a patient with bladder cancer, they discovered cancer genes in normal tissues as well as in the cancer tumours.

A number of genetic defects are sex-linked. Haemophilia is a disorder carried only on one of the two female X-chromosomes. Girls with the defective chromosome are carriers but normally do not have the condition because the genes on the other X-chromosome compensate for it. Boys acquiring the defective X-chromosome have the disease because there is no compensating gene on the Y-chromosome. Male children of a haemophilia carrier run a 50 per cent risk of being stricken and female children have the same chance of being carriers. Another sex-linked condition is red-green colour blindness. This defect which is transmitted through a seemingly normal mother is found in 4 to 5 per cent of all males but affects only 0.2 to 0.3 per cent of all females.

Down's Syndrome

Down's syndrome (mongolism) is caused by a chromosomal abnormality (an extra 21st chromosome). Characteristic of this defect which is often linked with idiocy are narrow, slanted eyes, a broad nose base and a wide, flattened skull. In this, as in some other malformations, the prospects at birth are uncertain; the only certainty is that the handicaps of mongoloid babies are formidable. Some will be incapable of speech (and apparently of thought), of walking, feeding themselves or being continent. Others will be intelligent and resilient enough to overcome appalling physical disabilities. In between these two extremes is a wide range of ability eventually achieved by babies born with Down's syndrome with the help of competent therapy, but above all the devoted care of a loving mother under the direction of a specialist. The probability of Down's syndrome is one in 600, but it is high for women over 35. The chance of having a second child with the same disorder is less than 1 per cent but the risk is 30 to 40 per cent in a certain form of mongolism. Overall, this disorder accounts for one-fifth of all actual cases of genetic defects.

According to a Japanese survey, 0.81 per cent of all newborn babies are deformed. About 17.03 per cent of all deformed children were born to mothers aged 40 and over and had Down's syndrome. The ratio was 1.6 per cent of all deformed babies for children suffering from Down's syndrome if born to mothers aged 34 and under.

Sickle-cell anaemia is prevalent among blacks. The red blood cells assume a sickle shape and cling together, thus obstructing small blood vessels and reducing oxygen supply to tissues. It results in swelling of the joints and jaundice. Each child of parents who carry the gene for sickle-cell anaemia runs a 25 per cent risk of having the disease and a 50 per cent chance of being born a carrier. Thalassemia involves faulty haemoglobin (red blood cells) production and causes the death of unborn children.

Neural tube defects occur in one or two out of every 1,000 births. The most common are anencephaly (part of the brain is missing) and spina bifida (part of the spine is missing or lies exposed outside the body). Anencephalic babies die shortly after birth but spina bifida victims may live with many disabilities, including retardation, paralysis and lack of bladder and bowel control. Formerly, paralysed children with spina bifida survived in only five out of a hundred cases; today, thanks to the progress in medical science, every second child stays alive but their survival requires enormous human efforts as well as extraordinary expenses.

Babies suffering from Tay-Sachs disorder slowly lose muscle control and become blind and deaf, usually by the age of five. Paralysis and retardation sets in. This disorder occurs mostly among Ashkenazim (Jews from Central and Eastern Europe). One in 25 carries the recessive gene responsible for the defect for which no cure exists. A blood test (for the foetus amniocentosis) can detect the lack of an enzyme called 'Hex A' which causes the disorder.

A genetic defect found mainly in whites and never in Down's syndrome children is cystic fibrosis (mucoviscidose). The pancreas and lungs become clogged with thick mucus, interfering with respiration and digestion, and even with special care, about 90 per cent of the children die by the age of ten. The disorder is caused by the deficiency of an enzyme linked to a regressive gene. Although the number of patients is relatively small, cystic fibrosis is carried by about one in twenty.

A hereditary defect, propion acidemy, in which the waste products of the amino acid metabolism accumulate, used to cause the death of a newborn child within a few days or weeks because dietary treatment usually was too late. Now a risky but successful treatment, peritoneal dialysis, can save these infants.

In the oro-facio-digital syndrome, the baby has small hands and feet and a small face; males who inherit this defect die before birth. Anomalies such as hare-lips and cleft palate can be surgically corrected.

Researchers discovered that dwarfism results from the lack of a basic growth gene, the first time that a defect other than blood diseases was found attributable to the lack of a gene. The ailment keeps the average adult height to 1.2 metres and can also cause mental retardation. Genetic factors are also involved in elephantiasis.

Defects in the circulatory system are not readily diagnosed, and mental deficiencies often only appear in the course of development and are sometimes only detected with the beginning of schooling.

Based on the examination of children whose parents were heavily irradiated at Hiroshima and Nagasaki, scientists have come to the conclusion that genetic damage has been over-estimated. This applies to high-dose nuclear radiation as well as chronic low-level radiation.

Drug-Related Malformations

The best-known examples of malformations caused by drugs are the thalidomide babies. Used as a tranquiliser, thalidomide, when taken during pregnancy, has been responsible for foetal abnormalities. Women who were given the drug, Duogen, as a pregnancy test soon after becoming pregnant had children with various congenital defects (hydrocephalus, hare lips, cleft palate, clubfoot and deformed hands). Some daughters of women who had taken the drug DES (diethylstilbestrol, a synthetic hormone prescribed for pregnant women to prevent miscarriage) had abnormal pre-cancerous cells, and others had already developed a rare form of vaginal cancer called clear-cell adenocarcinoma.

Doctors at Massachusetts General Hospital estimated that women who take the drug Accutane either during or shortly before their pregnancy are 26 times more likely to have a child with serious birth defects. The prescription-only drug used against acne carries risks similar to those of Thalidomide and can cause cranial, facial, heart and central nervous system abnormalities. The manufacturer, Hoffman-Laroche, has always warned that pregnant women should not take the drug but some women denied to their doctors that they were pregnant or likely to to become pregnant.

In 1980, the US Food and Drug Administration advised pregnant women to avoid caffeine but a later study of Harvard Medical School showed that heavy coffee drinkers were likely to be heavy smokers and that the poorer pregnancy outcomes (premature births, smaller babies) were attributable to smoking.

Heavy drinking during pregnancy may cause a set of defects known collectively as foetal alcohol syndrome. The infants are underdeveloped, their heads are too small, they have drooping eyelids and a receding chin, the ridge of the nose is shortened, they have heart defects and are mentally retarded. These defects which seem unrelated to the genes, have been found in 30 to 45 per cent of the children born to women who drink upwards of 3 ounces of pure alcohol daily (equivalent to six or more cocktails). Mostly affected are babies born to older women who drink heavily. Similar problems occur in about 10 per cent of the offspring born to women who consume 1 to 2 ounces of alcohol a day, but the effects have not been firmly established. One ounce of alcohol a day may result in a low birth weight and 2 ounces increase the risk of spontaneous abortion. Small amounts of alcohol such as a glass of wine with the evening meal are harmless and relaxing. The foetal alcohol syndrome is most frequent among Canadian Indians (one child in a 100) and in Sweden (one child in 600).

Apart from the effects on the offspring, alcohol has a particularly deleterious effect on women. According to an American study, women drinking beer, wine or liquour were 1.4 to 1.9 times more likely to develop breast cancer than those who were teetotal.

In the United States, the number of 'cocaine babies' has been growing rapidly in the last years. Mothers who are cocaine addicts have a very high incidence of miscarriage (one study reported a rate of 38 per cent) and premature labour. The drug-produced fluctuations in blood pressure can deprive the foetal brain of oxygen or cause blood vessels to burst, causing the pre-natal equivalent of a stroke and permanent physical and mental damage in the infant. Cocaine babies begin life with a two-to-three-week-long state of withdrawal, have a high rate of respiratory and kidney trouble and an increased risk of sudden death. They may suffer from visual problems, lack of coordination and developmental retardation. Some pregnant women use a variety of drugs and bear infants with multiple addictions. One of the dangerous substances is pentachlorophenol (PCP, commonly referred to as phencyclidine); infants suffer from disorientation — they don't seem to recognise where their hands and feet are.

Another threat to babies comes from AIDS. By the middle of January 1986, 231 cases of AIDS in infants had been reported to the National Centres for Disease Control of which 103 cases occurred in New York City. Most of the mothers had no outward signs of the disease, and most of the children with AIDS were born to mothers who were intravenous drug abusers. For every child who had AIDS in New York, there were three to five children who had AIDS-related complex which may or may not progress to become AIDS.

Rubella affects up to 50 per cent of the children of women who contract German measles during pregnancy. Babies may be born with cataracts, mental retardation and heart defects if the mother's sickness happens during the first two months of pregnancy. Brain damage, hearing disorders and deformities of the liver, spleen and lungs may result from cytomegalovirus, an infection often transmitted sexually.

Untreated chlamydis often moves to the uterus lining and the Fallopian tubes and causes pelvic inflammatory disease. This condition which can also be caused by gonorrhea is responsible for a large number of ectopic pregnancies. Chlamydis can cause lung and eye infections in newborn babies and every year, hundreds of babies are born with neo-natal herpes. Without treatment, many of them die, and survivors often suffer permanent neurological damage.

Exogenous influences may have acted as releasing factors in 8 per cent of congenital malformations. Radiation can cause children to be born with small heads and brains. Anencephalic children may be the result if the mother develops high fever between the 18th and the 30th day of pregnancy.

Fatyam Semyonova, chief doctor of Moscow's Maternity Hospital told the newspaper, *Komsomolskaya Pravda,* that one-quarter of the women who smoke half a pack of cigarettes a day while pregnant give birth to dead babies.

Intra-Uterine Diagnosis

The progress in medical technology has made it possible to diagnose the condition of the foetus inside the uterus with increasing reliability. Among the methods used is ultrasonic sounding in which an ultrasonic picture is obtained by bouncing sound waves off the foetus; fetoscopy, in which a tube is introduced through the uterus and the foetus examined directly through a lens; and amniocentosis in which a needle is inserted through the abdomen of the mother to take a sample of the amniotic fluid. Because the fluid contains cells shed by the foetus, it allows the examination of the chromosomes. In a new procedure called chorion biopsy, a needle is inserted into the womb and a tiny sample of tissue is snipped from the chorion, the precursor of the placenta. Chromosomes from the tissue are analysed to check for possible birth defects. Chorion biopsy can be used as early as the seventh week of pregnancy while amniocentesis cannot be performed until the 16th week. Moreover, the results of chorion biopsy are available over night but an amniocentesis test takes a week to process.

A team of scientists and engineers from Georgetown University Medical Centre has developed an automatic genetic analyser which separates genetic material from tissue samples, washes, dries and analyses it and prints out the results. With these probes, doctors can determine whether a patient has a gene for a number of genetically-transmitted diseases, such as Huntington's disease, phenylketonuria (PKU) syndrome, haemophilia, sickle cell anaemia and muscular dystrophy.

A kind of genetic probe developed by British and American doctors makes it possible for women to find out whether they are carriers of haemophilia before deciding to have children. A woman can also be told as early as the 10th week of pregnancy whether her baby will suffer from the disease.

New genetic tests rely on special DNA (deoxyribonucleic acid) probes to identify specific genes. This technology allows scientists to discover before birth about 15 genetic diseases with greater than 90 per cent accuracy. They include blood disorders such as sickel-cell anaemia, haemophilia and thalassemia, muscular dystrophy, Lesch–Nyhan disease (a gradually fatal disorder that causes severe mental retardation and self-mutilation), cystic fibrosis, adult polycystic kidney disease, Huntingdon's disease and a rare but fatal eye cancer known as retinablastoma. Biochemical tests are now available for some 100 genetic diseases.

The ethical implications of such tests have not yet been fully explored. Can the results of genetic tests justify the termination of pregnancy if they show that the unborn child will suffer from severe genetic disorders? When is the carrier of a genetic disease obliged to inform others of his condition? Employers could decline to hire someone if tests indicate the likely occurrence of a chronic disease years later that could lead to expensive health care and disability payments. Insurance companies might use the results of genetic tests to refuse medical coverage and employers who have expensive insurance packages might be unwilling to increase their risks. Tests could be used to put pressure on those carrying genetic diseases to avoid or abort pregnancies.

Scientists are thinking of treating severe genetic disorders resulting from a single gene by replacing the defective gene by an intact gene during the one-cell stage of the embryo. Whereas a gene transfer into somatic cells would ethically not be different from an organ transplant, the transfer into a gamete or zygote, which at present is not technically feasible, is rejected by Catholic moralists because it would constitute a manipulation of human individuality and would lead to the destruction of embryos in which the genetic transfer would not be successful. The method could be used not only to remedy genetic defects but also for 'positive eugenics.'

Genetic Counselling

In case of the possibility of hereditary diseases, a survey of the ancestors and the medical history of the parents and the family may be helpful. Based on these data, genetic counselling can be undertaken. Genetic counselling involves serious medical as well as legal risks. A geneticist is often asked for an assessment of the possibility that a genetically-handicapped child will be born. The variety of the problems that come up in such inquiries is endless and no geneticist in the world is competent to solve all of them. As already noted, there are hundreds of diseases and malformations in which genetic variables play a part, but all too often, the mode of inheritance of these defects (that is, dominance, recessivity, sex linkage, penetrance, and so on) is not precisely known. In some instances, reasonably clear answers can be given, if for example, the parent himself or herself is a carrier of a dominant genetic defect.

The aim of genetic counselling, therefore, should be to inform the prospective parents as clearly as possible of the situation, the risks involved in pregnancy and birth. The chances of survival, the means that can be used to help mother and child, and to leave the decision to the parents themselves. One of the most important tasks of genetic counselling is to dispel the fear of deformed offspring.

In West Germany, a court ruled that a doctor must pay for the upbringing of a handicapped child because he had told the mother that pregnancy tests for ascertaining Down's syndrome were unnecessary. The woman, who was 39 at the time, said she gave birth to the child only on the doctor's advice. The court's reason for holding the doctor liable for all the child's maintenance costs was that it was born so badly handicapped that an abortion would have been allowed if its condition had been anticipated.

Positive eugenics seems hopelessly complex — it is not easy to decide what artificial selection should select, but negative eugenics is sufficiently practical. In an address to an international medical conference held in December 1982, Pope John Paul II condemned as morally inadmissible scientific research for detecting abnormal foetuses that leads to abortion. 'Equally unacceptable,' the Pontiff said, 'is any form of experimentation that leads to abortion.'

In the United States, religious leaders adopted a resolution urging scientists never to conduct experiments to alter human heredity. 'Once we decide to begin the process of human genetic engineering, there is no logical place to stop,' said Jeremy Rifkin, one of the organisers of the group. But scientists criticised the resolution as too broad, opposing both the 'improving' of the race and curing genetic diseases. Moreover, techniques to alter defective human genes are years, or even decades, away.

In India, amniocentosis is used as a sex test, and if the foetus is a female, abortion is usually the sequence of the test. The traditional discrimination against women has reduced India's sex ratio to 935 females per 1,000 males.

Intra-Uterine Treatment

With better means of diagnosis, doctors have begun to treat foetuses inside the womb of the mother. In the United States in April 1981, five operations were carried out on the brain of a foetus in the Brigham Maternal Hospital. The mother was in the sixth month of pregnancy and the foetus showed signs of hydrocephalus. Altogether, 0.95 ounces of fluid were extracted from the brain of the foetus. To prepare for the operations, an ultrasonic picture of the uterus was projected on a screen. A hollow needle was inserted through the abdomen of the mother and the wall of the uterus into the skull of the foetus and the water sucked up. Each operation required about 20 minutes.

In an unprecedented operation, doctors at the University of California at San Francisco removed the foetus from the mother, cleared a urinary tract obstruction that would have killed it, and successfully replaced the foetus. The mother who at the time of the operation was about 24 weeks pregnant carried the baby to term but it died after birth from underdeveloped lungs, a complication unrelated to the surgery. The same team of doctors had earlier performed another foetal surgery first. They inserted a needle through the mother's abdomen into the bladder of the foetus, the male of a pair of twins, drained the urine to prevent damage to the kidneys and lungs and corrected a life-threatening blockage of the urinary tract. In another case involving twins, doctors, guided by ultrasound, pierced the heart of a foetus suffering from Down's syndrome with a needle and withdrew blood, causing cardiac arrest. The mother who was then in the 20th week of pregnancy carried both foetuses to term when the healthy twin was born normally. The parents had secured an order from the New York State Supreme Court confirming their right to consent to the procedure on behalf of the normal foetus. This construction, though ingenious, is without legal basis, and the case raises the problem of abortion and the rôle of the state in abortion.

Partial abortions have been carried out also in the Netherlands and in Belgium. In Japan, a woman who had an infertility problem, took fertility drugs and conceived quadruplets. She and her husband told her doctor that they would be financially unable to take care of the babies and wanted the pregnancy terminated. The doctor persuaded the woman to give birth to two of the quadruplets after aborting two. In February 1986, two foetuses were aborted with the aid of an ultrasonograph and the woman was delivered of two baby boys in August.

What Is Abortion?

Abortion is the termination of pregnancy before the foetus can survive outside the uterus. There is no complete agreement on when exactly a foetus can be considered viable. The minimum requirement is either a pregnancy of 21 weeks or a birth weight of 400-500 gms but, generally speaking, a foetus has almost no chance of survival if it weighs less than 1,000 gms and if the pregnancy is of less than 28 weeks of duration. Usually, the expulsion or extraction of all (complete) or any part (incomplete) of the foetus, the placenta of the membranes before the 20th week (134 days) of gestation is considered an abortion. It is an early abortion if it occurs before the 12th week (84 days) of gestation, and a late abortion if it is performed after the 12th complete week but before the beginning of the 20th week (85-134 days) of pregnancy. In common language, the term miscarriage is used for any spontaneous or accidental expulsion. A spontaneous abortion is the ejection of the foetus before the 20th week and an induced abortion the deliberate interruption of pregnancy before the 20th week. If the removal of the unviable foetus is intended, the induced abortion is direct; if the expulsion of the foetus results from an action for some other purpose or as a secondary and unintentional consequence from the use of means directed towards some other objective, the abortion is indirect.

A therapeutic abortion is the termination of pregnancy for legally-acceptable and medically-approved indications, if, for example, the pregnancy endangers the life or health of the mother or a complication threatens the life of the foetus. If the foetus dies and is retained in the uterus for eight weeks or longer, it is called a missed abortion; if the abortion is associated with an infection of the genital organs, it is an infected abortion. A septic abortion is caused by septicemia (pathogenic bacteria in the bloodstream).

The majority of fertilised eggs never take hold in the uterus and about 10 per cent of all pregnancies terminate in spontaneous abortions, mostly between the 6th and the 12th week after conception. Spontaneous abortions are generally inevitable because the fertilised egg is abnormal. These abortions are beyond medical control. Induced abortions are carried out by curettage, that is, the scraping of the uterus lining with a curet, or by suction evacuation which is possible up to the 10th week of pregnancy. Both methods involve the risk of perforating the uterus and of excessive bleeding. After the first 12 weeks, the size of the foetus and the placenta usually requires vaginal or abdominal hysterotomy (surgical incision into the uterus).

Abortifacients

There are many other methods, particularly in developing countries which involve enormous dangers for the mother. Abortifacient herbs or potions have been used since time immemorial and are still in use. Even cruder methods such as beating are not uncommon. In India, for example, a stick coated with phosphorous or arsenic is inserted into the uterus. At present, research is under way for the development of an abortion pill. In Sweden, the abortive effect of the hormone group of prostaglandins was noticed when prostaglandin was used in the form of injections to start delivery. Prostaglandin F 2 Alpha is found in human seminal fluid. In Japan, Ono Pharmaceutical Ltd developed a contraceptive labelled ONO 802 which was clinically tested as an abortifacient for treating toxaemia of pregnancy. In the form of a suppository, it can be used as an abortifacient because it prevents the implantation of the blastocyst or separates it from the uterine lining and softens the uterus. The suppository, marketed under the trade name, Preglandin, is effective by five vaginal insertions at three-hour intervals and induces safe abortion in the early and medium terms of pregnancy. Side effects of the drug are diarrhea, stomach ache, nausea and fever. Some reports stress the risk of serious complications, including miscarriage in subsequent pregnancies.

With such a pill, abortion will become a question beyond the reach of the penal code, a practice wholly in the personal private realm which laws can only affect by prohibiting the pill.

A drug developed by the French firm Roussel-Uclaf causes the expulsion of the fertilised egg from the womb even after implantation by inducing menstruation. The drug, called Mifepristone and labelled RU-486, blocks the body's use of progesterone, a hormone essential for maintaining the lining of the uterus. When the drug is taken, the uterus sheds its lining and any fertilised egg attached to it.

In clinical tests in the Hôpital de Bicètre (France), the drug was effective in 85 out of 100 cases. The drug seems to work best if taken during the first half of the first three months. Because it is effective if taken within a few days after a missed period, it is different from the 'morning after' pill which must be taken shortly after intercourse before the fertilised egg is embedded in the uterus. The main danger seems to be an incomplete abortion if the pill is taken too late.

Professor Marc Bygdeman of Stockholm's Karolinska Hospital combined an anti-hormone called anti-progesteron (developed by Professor Etienne Baulieu of the University Paris Sud) with a Swedish-developed hormone called prostagladin analogue into a new abortion pill. The drug must be administered over three days within the first three weeks after a missed period. Tests of the drug on 600 pregnant women showed a success rate of 95 per cent; in the remaining 5 per cent of the cases, the foetuses were aborted surgically for fear that the medication. might cause deformities. Side effects were said to be no more serious than those brought about by a natural miscarriage.

Infanticide: the Alexandra Case

In addition to abortion, birth defects may occasion recourse to euthanasia or outright infanticide. When a mongoloid baby was born to a professional couple in Britain (the husband an engineer, the wife a dentist), the parents refused to let doctors perform an emergency operation to remove an intestinal blockage which would have killed the infant within weeks. The doctors, however, informed the local authorities and the Hammersmith Social Services Department invoked the Children's Act, had the girl called Alexandra made a ward of the court, obtained legal care and control of the baby and authorised the operation. But the surgeons at the Great Ormond Street Hospital where Alexandra was moved for the operation refused to perform it when they learned of the parents' objection. The local authority went back to the judge who had issued the care and control order. This time, upon hearing the parents' case, he changed his mind and denied permission for the operation. So the local authorities appealed.

The court of appeal decided that the judge was wrong because he had been influenced by the parents instead of deciding what were the best interests of the child. It was wrong, the court seems to have reasoned, that advantage should be taken of the mongoloid baby's potentially fatal but curable disability to allow her to die, whereas without the disability she would live. A successful operation was performed and Alexandra gained a good chance of living 20 to 30 years although handicapped by her mongoloid conditions. The extent may only be fully understood when she is 3 to 5 years old.

The case created a considerable controversy, particularly because it occurred shortly after another case in which a paediatrician, at the request of the parents, ordered the hospital staff to give a baby born with Down's syndrome only 'nursing care' — meaning that it was not to be fed. The baby died after living 69 hours. The doctor contended that apart from mongolism, the infant also suffered from major physical defects that gave her little or no chance of survival. The doctor was first charged with murder but the charge was reduced to attempted murder during the trial because the prosecution's medical case was incomplete, and a jury of six men and six women acquitted the doctor.

Some years ago, in 1975, a Boston doctor was found guilty of manslaughter for killing a 20- to 24-week-old foetus he aborted at a hospital, but the verdict was later overturned. A public opinion poll during the trial of the doctor for attempted murder showed that 59 per cent of those questioned thought handicapped babies rejected by their parents should be allowed to die, and in answer to another question which included no reference to the parents' view, 60 per cent of those questioned said the decision to let a baby live or die should depend on the severity of the handicap. A poll before the trial had shown that 40 per cent of the respondents thought everything should be done to save a child's life, no matter how severe its handicap.

Of the 280 doctors who answered a questionnaire sent to 1,500 paediatricians by the BBC after the Alexandra case, 70 per cent said they thought a spina bifida baby rejected by its parents was better dead.

In a case similar to the Alexandra case, the parents of a mongoloid baby suffering also from birth defects that prevented him from eating (his esophagus was not properly formed and food could not reach his stomach) decided that the infant should not be given food, water and medical aid. When the doctors remonstrated, the parents (who lived in Bloomington, Indiana), pleading the infant's 'right to die,' appealed to the Indiana Supreme Court. The court, in a 3-1 ruling, refused to order surgery or nourishment for the baby who died on the sixth day after his birth. Spurred by this case, President Reagan ordered the Department of Health and Human Services to prevent deliberate neglect of newborn babies.

On the premise that discriminatory denial of care to handicapped children was illegal (Section 504 of the Rehabilitation Act of 1973 forbids discrimination solely on the basis of handicap), the department issued regulations requiring child protection agencies to police federally-assisted hospitals and examine medical records to prevent wilful neglect. A revision of the regulations obliged hospitals and doctors treating severely deformed newborn babies whose defects made survival uncertain to report if the parents refused to allow medical treatment and permitted the government to conduct on-the-spot investigations. Hospitals contravening the regulations were to be denied federal aid.

'Baby Jane Doe'

The role of the state in the treatment of defective children became the central issue in the 1983 case of baby Jane Doe of Port Jefferson, New York. The infant was born with three major birth defects: an abnormally small head, excess fluid in the brain, and spina bifida. Her parents decided against corrective surgery for the spina bifida when the doctors told them that the infant would die within two years without the operation while with it, she might live for two decades — severely handicapped and mentally retarded. But the parents agreed to a programme of antibiotics. A Vermont right-to-life activist sued to force the surgery, but the New York courts turned down the demand. Then, the federal government stepped in and, arguing that withholding surgery might violate the infant's civil rights, asked the hospital to hand over her medical records. The hospital refused, and the Justice Department went to court. The judge dismissed the hospital's claim that the constitutional right of privacy and doctor-patient confidentiality shielded the files from scrutiny but ruled that the hospital had not violated the law forbidding discrimination against the handicapped because the hospital had been willing to perform the operation if the parents would consent. But the parents, the judge said, had made a reasonable choice based on medical options and a genuine concern for the interests of the child. The Justice Department appealed the decision, but the Supreme Court refused to intervene.

A ruling of the Supreme Court on the issue came through a suit brought by the American Hospital Association and the American Medical Association to have the regulations which they considered harassment declared invalid. They lost in the first instance but the Circuit Court of Appeals ruled that the federal government could not force lawful medical institutions to give medical treatment and that a hospital was under no obligation to report to the federal government if the parents did not consent to medical treatment. On 9 June 1986, the US Supreme Court upheld this decision of the Circuit Court of Appeals and ruled that the enforcement of medical treatment for handicapped children was a misinterpretation of the 1973 Rehabilitation Act. The government could not cut off federal aid to hospitals for failure to give such treatment. There was no evidence that hospitals had refused treatment sought by parents or mandated by state courts. Federal law does not authorise the government to give unsolicited advice either to parents, to hospitals or to state officials faced with difficult treatment decisions concerning handicapped children. Hospitals need parental consent to treat a minor, handicapped or not. Since parents are not compelled by law to consent to treatment, federal regulation is intrusive.

As a result of the decision, the situation returned to what it had been before the Baby Joe regulation. The parents have a right to decide on the treatment of handicapped babies. If the doctors disagree, they can appeal to the state courts but the parents' decision will be upheld if based on competent medical opinion.

'Baby Jane Doe,' whose real name was Kerri-Lynn, was discharged from the hospital after surgeons drained excess fluid from the brain to relieve pressure on her head.

A German doctor decided to remove a foetus from a 33-week pregnant woman after ultrasonic scanning suggested that the baby had an underdeveloped head and would not survive. The parents believing that their baby would be deformed (it actually was not) wanted an abortion. But the baby was alive after delivery by Caesarean section and the doctor instructed his assistant, a woman doctor, to fill a syringe with a lethal injection (Luccinyl, a drug which acts on the respiratory system) but she refused to administer the injection and the doctor made the injection himself.

Right to Die: Karen Anne Quinlan

These cases have raised more questions than they have answered. In countries in which the law recognises eugenic or medical indication, a foetus may be destroyed if the chromosomal abnormality that causes Down's syndrome is detected before birth. Alexandra's mother who was in her mid-thirties, a time, therefore, at which the danger of having a mongoloid baby is particularly great, had the necessary test but it was inconclusive. The law does not allow 'passive infanticide' or so it seems. The legality of 'passive euthanasia,' that is, not intervening to stop the natural process of dying, has been recognised in a number of cases involving terminally-ill patients. The most famous case is that of Karen Anne Quinlan, the New Jersey girl who lapsed into a coma on 14 April 1975 from a combination of drugs and alcohol. Her parents, having been reassured that Catholic doctrine did not require keeping her daughter alive by extraordinary means, asked the doctors to disconnect their daughter's respirator in July 1975. When the doctors demurred, the Quinlans went to court and the New Jersey Supreme Court ruled that Miss Quinlan had a constitutional right to die, based on the right to privacy. Although the respirator was removed, Miss Quinlan remained alive; she was able to breathe without a mechanical respirator and her brain showed electrical activity. She lay motionless in a foetal position on a waterbed, received daily injections of antibiotics to ward off infections and was fed through a nasal tube. Nurses changed her body position every two hours to prevent bed sores. Karen Anne Quinlan died on 11 June 1985 at the age of 31.

Elizabeth Bouvia

Elizabeth Bouvia, a 26-year-old quadriplegic cerebral palsy victim and a patient in the Riverside General Hospital, California, asked that the hospital be required to provide her with pain-killers and hygienic care while she starved herself to death. She considered her life hopeless and sought death because she was suffering unendurable pain and did not want to be dependent on others. In a decision announced in December 1983, Superior Court Judge John H. Hews conceded that Miss Bouvia had the fundamental right to terminate her own life but ruled that she could not do so with the aid of society and that the hospital could force-feed her to keep her alive. The California Supreme Court refused to hear an emergency appeal seeking to stop the hospital from force-feeding her and to block the hospital from discharging her. In January 1984, the court denied a request to overturn the lower court's decision. Miss Bouvia continued her fight against force-feeding and in January 1986 sued to have the Desert Hospital in Lancaster, California, where she was being cared for, to remove the nose-to-stomach feeding tubes. She said that she no longer wanted to starve herself to death and was willing to take liquid food — she cannot hold down solids. Superior Court Judge Warren Deering sided with the hospital officials who claimed that their patient was losing weight and was in danger of dying. Although Miss Bouvia had an absolute right to refuse medical treatment such as force-feeding, the judge said, she could only exercise this right if the medical staff believed that the refusal would not endanger her life — a very controversial decision because it subordinates the individual's decision to the opinion of the doctors. But in April of the same year, Miss Bouvia, for the first time in two years, was freed from her feeding tube. A California State Appeals Court ruled that she had a right to halt the forced feeding and instructed the lower court in Los Angeles to immediately grant Miss Bouvia's request for a preliminary injunction, to order the doctors to remove the feeding tube and to prohibit them from replacing it without her consent. State policy should not demand that 'all and every life must be preserved against the will of the sufferer,' Associate Justice Lynn D. Compton wrote in his opinion. 'If there is ever a time when we want to be able to get the "government off our backs" it is when we face death either by choice or otherwise.' The public prosecutor, however, seemed to disagree with this view and appealed to the California Supreme Court but his appeal was turned down. Another California judge held that a terminally-ill patient can refuse to be connected to life-supporting equipment and that doctors carrying out the patient's wishes are not guilty of any wrongdoing. A New York Supreme Court justice upheld the right of an 85-year-old retired college president to commit suicide by fasting and advised a nursing home that it had neither the right nor the duty to feed the man against his will. The justice based his decision on the First Amendment to the US Constitution (right to privacy) and a state law permitting patients to refuse medical treatment.

Probate Judge David H. Kopelman of Dedham, Massachusetts, decided that a comatose fireman had to be kept alive despite his wife's wish that he be allowed to starve to death. He permanently enjoined the hospital's physicians 'from either removing or clamping Paul E. Brophy's gastrotomy tube for the purpose of denying Brophy hydration or nutrition required to sustain his life.' Brophy, 48, lapsed into a coma in March 1983, 10 days after suffering an eneurysm, a swollen blood vessel in the brain. He underwent surgery at a medical centre in Boston but never regained consciousness. Brophy was later transferred to New England Sinai Hospital where he was given food and water through a tube inserted into his stomach. In November 1984, Mrs Brophy requested the hospital to remove the tube and all life-support systems but she failed to get the court's permission.

Brophy died in October 1986 following his transfer to another hospital after the Massachusetts Supreme Court had granted his wife's request that he no longer be fed artificially. A court-appointed attorney appealed the ruling to the Supreme Court but three justices refused to consider it. Brophy had been kept alive for 3½ years although the technical

advances which sustained his bodily functions offered no hope of a cure
or improvement.

After two years of deliberations, the Council of Ethical and Judicial
Affairs of the American Medical Association adopted guidelines affirming
that the wishes of the patient concerning medical treatment should be
respected and the patient's dignity maintained. The council ruled that it
was not unethical for doctors to discontinue all life support for patients
who were in irreversible comas even if death was not imminent and
included food and water on the list of treatments that could be withheld.
While the precedent created by the Quinlan case has made the decision
to shut off a respirator or discontinue kidney dialysis for terminally ill
or comatose patients more acceptable, to stop food and water remains a
much harder step to take for doctors and the family

In the 4-to-3 Brophy decision, the majority of the Massachusetts
Supreme Court deemed feeding tubes too 'intrusive' and declared that a
distinction was required between death as traditionally understood and
death in which the body lives in some fashion but the brain (or a significant
part of it) does not. Of the minority judges, one accused his colleagues
of condemning Brophy to a 'gruesome' death and another thought that
the court was endorsing mercy killing and suicide.

A meeting sponsored by the Catholic Hospital Association attended
by health administrators and scholars from 28 American states and Canada
in February 1987 discussed the morality of removing feeding tubes. The
traditional Catholic position that nobody is obliged to preserve his life
by extraordinary means (which formed the foundation of the Karen Anne
Quinlan case) was interpreted by Pope Pius XII to include that life-
sustaining methods are morally required only when they do not involve
any grave burdens for oneself or others. Many Americans have come to
regard kidney dialysis, cancer chemotherapy and the use of respirators
as treatments that can be halted if they become too burdensome physically,
emotionally and financially. But New Jersey's Catholic bishops, in a brief
filed with the New Jersey Supreme Court in the case of Nancy Ellen
Jobes (whose family had asked for the removal of a feeding tube from
the 31-year-old comatose woman) took the position that medical
treatment is entirely different from food and fluids which are basic to
human life. Nutrition, in their view, must always be provided to a
patient. This standpoint is not the traditional Catholic view but that of
strict right-to-lifers who oppose killing by 'starvation.' Catholic tradition
allows an end to feeding in medically hopeless cases.

The removal of life-support systems (as well as the adoption of brain
death as the end of human life) is increasingly connected with organ
transplants (which tends to make decisions to end medical treatment look
suspicious). The father of a comatose 15-month-old girl who had suffered
a blood clot that cut off the blood supply to the brain agreed to let doctors
at California Hospital Medical Centre in Los Angeles disconnect the

life-support system so her heart could be given to another critically-ill infant. The doctors, therefore, asked a court to allow them to turn off the respirator and when the child died, gave her heart to a sick baby in another hospital.

Mercy Killing

Active euthanasia, that is, termination of the dying process by active interference based on the choice of the dying or of third parties, is advocated by organisations in 27 countries. The oldest was established in the United States in 1934, a British organisation dates from 1938. Some moral theologians think that there are situations in which the general norm that a man has no right to dispose of his own life may seem doubtful. There are situations in which different human values have to be balanced and the principle *minus malum est eligendum* (choosing the lesser of two evils) has to be applied. In such a case, respect for the free choice of the patient may not justify cooperation with suicide but may excuse it.

German law prohibits active euthanasia but passive euthanasia is a murky subject. 'Killing on demand' is prohibited by Article 216 of the Penal Code which also makes the attempt punishable. Somebody who fails to give help in case of danger or need although this was required and demandable (*zumutbar*) under the circumstances is also punishable (Art. 323c). But a doctor can inform a patient on the means to end his life and procure these means although he cannot apply them (cooperation to suicide is not punishable). According to the decisions of the German Federal Court, to start or continue medical treatment without or against the will of the patient is prohibited and punishable.

A Krefeld Superior Court (Landgericht) found a doctor not guilty of 'killing on demand by omission.' The doctor respected the wish of a 77-year-old widow who was suffering from a severe heart disease and arthrosis and did not want to be taken to a hospital and connected to a life-sustaining machine. She wanted to join her husband in death. The prosecution has appealed to the Federal Court. In another case which created much publicity, Professor Julius Hackethal procured 4 grammes of potassium cyanide for a patient whose lips, cheeks, upper jaw and right eye had been destroyed by cancer and who had been unable to take any solid food for months. The patient's other organs were not affected and her intelligence was not impaired, but the tumour made it impossible to relieve her pain by drugs. Asked by the patient on the best method to end her life, the doctor explained that it could be done with 40 sleeping pills but more effectively with potassium cyanide. She chose the potassium cyanide. The doctor instructed her how to take the poison and a friend of the patient gave her the cup which she drank herself. The doctor was not present when she died but was called after her death and noted on the death certificate 'Unnatural death. Poisoning by potassium cyanide.' This alarmed the police and the case became public.

The doctor's action triggered another round of heated debates on the right to die and the physician's rôle in the gray zone between life and death. On the one hand there are the doctors, clergymen and jurists who maintain that even in the case of incurable sickness, the physician's task is to prolong life as much as possible. On principle, the physician should not help people to die. 'To give a cup of poison conflicts with all the basic norms of medical action,' declared the president of Germany's Federal Chamber of Physicians. On the other hand, some physicians agreed that a doctor should not try to prolong life at any price. Professor Hackethal thinks that the law should be changed and active euthanasia not only be allowed but even made the duty of the physician in certain cases. In many situations, the treatment of patients with brain damage in an irreversible coma is not the prolongation of life but the prolongation of the process of dying. Intensive care should not have the task of sustaining life which consists merely of a few functions.

The legal distinction between the punishable 'killing on demand' and the permissible 'cooperation to suicide' depends on the action leading to death. If this action is taken by the suicidee freely and without coercion, on his own responsibility and by his own determination, cooperation (such as the procurement of poison) is not punishable under German law. Nevertheless, Professor Hackethal was later indicted for manslaughter.

The religious implications of the views on human life became the main issue of a debate provoked by remarks of the president of West Germany's Federal Constitutional Court, Wolfgang Zeidler, in a discussion on 'Biotechnology and Law' which was the theme of the 16th 'Bitburger Gespräche' organised by the Gesellschaft für Rechtspolitik. The German jurist charged that the influence of the churches and religious convictions constituted an obstacle to humanity and progress and might impede the application of new technology. The authority of religion had been reduced in recent years, President Zeidler said, but the prohibition of 'killing on demand' (Penal Code, Art. 216) represented 'an island of inhumanity as the result of ecclesiastical influence on our legal order.' His remarks on abortion directly challenged the 25 February 1975 decision of the Federal Constitutional Court affirming the duty of the state to protect unborn human life. President Zeidler, a Social Democrat who left the Protestant Church, seems to labour under the hoary 'religion — opium' ideology of classical Marxism and his anti-religious bias made him overlook the fact that centuries before the Christian churches, the reverence for human life found expression in the 'oath of Hippocrates' in which the practitioners of the art of healing vowed not to perform abortions and not to provide means for terminating life.

Cardinal Höffner of Cologne sharply rebuked the jurist for his intemperate attacks on ecclesiastical influence, religious convictions and the unconditional protection of unborn life and the life of the aged.

In 1986, the assembly of German jurists *(Deutscher Juristentag)* adopted a resolution which practically endorsed active euthanasia. In case of 'killing by demand,' the resolution stated, the possibility that the courts could forgo punishment if the killing was carried out for terminating unbearable suffering should be taken into account. The responsibility of the doctor to save life is limited by a contrary free decision of the patient. Failure to stop somebody from killing himself is not punishable if the decision to commit suicide is based on the free and clearly expressed will of the suicidee. But German courts have held doctors and relatives responsible if the suicidee became unconscious in the execution of his design.

In the United States, the controversy has been about the 'right to die' which need not necessarily be restricted to terminal illness and the process of dying. In Germany, however, a distinction is made between *'Sterbehilfe'* and *'Beihilfe zur Selbsttötung.'* Professor Hackethal's patient, as Manfred Seitz, professor of Protestant pastoral theology at the university of Erlangen animadverted, was not in the process of dying and Hackethal's action constituted cooperation to suicide.

Dr Joseph Hassman injected Demerol, a painkiller, and Vistiral, a tranquiliser, into the intravenous tubing system of his terminally-ill mother-in-law. A nurse found the death of the 80-year-old woman suffering from Alzheimer's disease suspicious and reported the death to the authorities. The doctor pleaded guilty to a charge of manslaughter but the prosecutor for New Jersey's Atlantic County did not want to send the doctor to jail. Following the prosecutor's recommendation, Superior Court Judge Paul R. Porreca did not sentence the doctor to prison but ordered him to perform 400 hours of community service and pay a US$10,000 fine.

In the Maidstone crown court, the parents of a 22-year-old road accident victim were cleared of a murder charge but found guilty of manslaughter by the jury and placed on two years' probation. English law does not permit mercy killing, the prosecutor had told the jury. For five years, the couple had cared for their son 24 hours a day but the son, whose intellect was not impaired, was tired of living and repeatedly asked his parents to end his misery. They mixed a drink of various drugs and placed a plastic bag over his head.

In a Japanese case, a woman suffering from rheumatoid arthritis and facing the amputation of some fingers asked a woman friend to kill her because she could no longer endure the pain. Under the pretext of arranging for her operation, she returned home from the hospital and anaesthetised herself by swallowing sleeping pills. Her friend then strangled her.

Article 202 of Japan's Criminal Code punishes participation in suicide. It reads: 'A person who, by instigating or aiding and abetting causes somebody to commit suicide or kills somebody by accepting the victim's request or obtaining his consent is punishable by penal servitude or imprisonment above six months and under seven years.' According to Japanese jurisprudence, euthanasia is punishable under this article but the action may not be deemed criminal depending on the following four factors:

1. If the time of death was near or death certain. 2. If the patient suffered from intolerable physical pain which could only be relieved by death. 3. If the action was done at the request or with the consent of the patient or his near relatives. 4. If the means were appropriate. Should one of these factors be absent, the action, though not exempt from criminality, will often be punished lightly or not at all for want of or diminished responsibility and probation may be granted.

Morality of Euthanasia

Theistic morality asserts that man cannot dispose of human life because it is created by God and to dispose of human life would infringe on the right of the Creator. But human life is no absolute value and there are situations in which a man can risk his own life, or in which physicians balance the risk to life against the possibility of saving the patient. Despite the commandment 'Thou shalt not kill,' killing in self-defence (if this is necessary to repulse an 'unjust aggressor'), capital punishment and killing in a 'just' war have been held not to contradict this commandment. While Catholic moral theology considers it man's duty to preserve his life, it has qualified this duty by the assertion that man need not use 'extraordinary' means for preserving his existence.

In an address to scientists attending a meeting on 'The Artificial Prolongation of Life and the Determination of the Exact Moment of Death' held in October 1985, Pope Paul John II stated that doctors and families must ensure the right of the incurably ill to 'die with dignity.' He repeated the condemnation of mercy killing, calling euthanasia a crime to which cooperation and consent are inadmissible but noted the position of the Church set forth in a 1980 document which said that when inevitable death was imminent in spite of the means used, it was permitted in conscience to make a decision to refuse forms of treatment that would only secure a precarious and burdensome prolongation of life.

Man is not obliged to save his life at any price and under all circumstances because the task imposed on him by his existence and the meaning of life is not life but human life. If according to ordinary human standards, a further existence no longer appears as meaningful, the preservation of man's life may be inhuman and man should no longer be obliged to preserve his life. But, as Norbert Hoerster, professor at the University of Mainz explains, such a decision would have to be the strictly personal decision of the individual and suppose his free determination that, under such circumstances, he would prefer the end to his life. Nobody has the right to pronounce a judgement on the value of somebody else's life. Man has the right not to have his life curtailed by other people even under the most painful circumstances. But just as it would be unacceptable to destroy another life because it appears to be valueless according to the standards of one's own *Weltanschauung,* Professor Hoerster argues, a humane consideration must find it equally unacceptable to enforce the prolongation of another human life because the standards of one's own *Weltanschauung* regard human life beyond man's disposition.

The Dilemma of Defective Babies

The number of children born with spina bifida, without brain or without a functioning gastro-intestinal tract and who, with the consent of the parents, are left to die, has been estimated at 1,200 a year in Germany. Such children could be kept alive for days, months or even years if all modern means were used, but could their life be called a human life?

Enormous progress has been made in the treatment of neonates, but diagnosis as well as therapy remains risky. Underweight newborn babies (weight at birth 1-1.5 kg) require intensive care which may not be available everywhere. Newborn babies weighing less than 750 grammes seem beyond salvation. A premature infant with a birth weight of 450 grammes may be kept alive for a few hours in an incubator but its survival is hopeless. In such cases, the biological limits are also ethical limits to medical intervention: a doctor should not try something that cannot help the patient. A newborn baby with multiple defects should not be operated upon if the operation is technically feasible but cannot relieve the defects.

The birth of a defective child is an enormously difficult experience not only for its parents but also for other members of the family, friends and acquaintances. After the initial shock, parents may be assailed by feelings of guilt. The mother, in particular, will be inclined to review her conduct during pregnancy and look for things she did wrong. She may blame herself for actions or omissions entirely irrelevant to the condition of the child but which she considers responsible for the misfortune. On the other hand, parents may revolt against the unjust fate and religious believers may feel their trust in God sorely tried. In a regrettable development, husband and wife may blame each other and their recriminations only increase anguish and remorse. What parents need is a realistic assessment of the situation created by the birth of a defective child and the changes required in their daily routine.

In consideration of the English cases, the Board for Social Responsibility of the Church of England discussed the treatment of severely handicapped children and issued the following interim statement:

'The Church of England upholds the Christian moral tradition that all human life is sacred. There are, however, two positions which should be distinguished.

'It can be morally legitimate not to seek to preserve life at all costs, as if existence were the main or only end to be achieved. On the other hand, a deliberate intention to kill must be condemned.

'There is an overriding responsibility to relieve pain and distress, even though this may shorten life, as well as to provide proper nursing and care.'

Catholic moralists would say that every effort must be made to save life, but that there is no obligation to use extraordinary means. There is no doubt that in the cases mentioned above, the actions of parents and doctors were quite different from not taking what was referred to as 'extraordinary' means in the Quinlan case and were, to all intents and purposes, infanticide. In each of these cases, the victim was no longer a foetus, but, philosophically and juridically, a person.

At the 1984 General Synod of the United Evangelical-Lutheran Church of Germany, the presiding bishop, Karlheinz Stoll, opposed a rigid application of the commandment 'Thou shalt not kill' in cases of euthanasia. The commandment's validity is absolute, he declared, but in practice, love requires moderation.

'Living Will' Laws

In California, a 'Right-to-Die' bill was passed in 1976. The law allows adult terminal patients to order their physicians through a signed 'living will' to disconnect life-sustaining equipment when the 'procedures would serve only to prolong' death.

The signing of the 'will' must be witnessed by two persons other than a relative or doctor. The doctor cannot be held criminally or civilly liable for following the patient's directive. Insurance companies cannot claim that such a death is suicide.

In the beginning of 1985, 22 states and the District of Columbia had 'living will' laws permitting mentally competent adults to declare that they don't want their lives prolonged artificially.

These laws leave many questions unanswered. When is a patient 'terminally ill?' Miss Quinlan's doctors were sure that she could not live if she were taken off the respirator. And what constitutes 'extraordinary means?' Should a patient be denied antibiotics? Feeding by tube? There are no guarantees that people cannot be tricked into signing a 'will' or that such a will cannot be forged.

Although most 'living will' laws grant immunity to doctors and hospitals acceding to a patient's request to allow him to die, a comatose patient is unable to make a decision or, as happened in a California case, the hospital may contend that the patient is not competent to make a choice. On the other hand, the refusal to disconnect a patient from a life-support system may also cause trouble. In Ohio, the survivors of a patient whom doctors declined to unplug even after the family obtained a court order brought suit against the doctors.

The courts can have recourse to expert opinion or rely on the opinion of ethics committees but patients, families, doctors and hospitals are facing life-and-death decisions for which the principle that the patient should have the last say on a problem that concerns his own life is of little help.

Defining Death

Modern medicine has made it difficult to ascertain the moment of death. Said Dr Harvey Wolinsky, a cardiologist: 'With the artificial heart, you don't have the end point of knowing when a heart stops, and if you have artificial respiration, you don't have the end point of knowing when the lung stops. Even when you are using the brain as end point, you have to be very specific that there is nothing else going on that could give the appearance of brain death.'

A commission appointed by President Carter in 1978 prepared a series of reports including 'Defining Death' and 'Deciding to Forgo Life-Sustaining Treatment.' It recommended that the law regard death as the irreversible loss of all brain functions and not merely as the permanent cessation of heart and lung function, the traditional definition. About 36 states have 'brain death' laws that allow the disconnection of life-support equipment when a patient no longer shows any sign of brain activity.

Legislation recognising brain death as official death has been passed in 12 countries, including Canada, Australia, France, Italy, Finland and Czechoslovakia. In Britain, Ireland, West Germany, Switzerland and South Korea, medical authority has established brain death as a criterion of death but there are different definitions of brain death. Britain uses the standard of brain stem death which implies the destruction of brain functions responsible for consciousness and respiration while in the United States, brain-death is defined as the destruction of the total brain functions. Both are different from the comatose state in which the brain-stem damage may be reversible although there may not be reasonable hope of recovery (the now classical example is Karin Anne Quinlan).

In heart-failure death, the heart stops and there is no pulse. In the case of brain death, the heart is still beating, the colour of the face may still be good and there is still an appearance of life. However, there is no recovery and death due to heart failure will come in one or two weeks. Sweden retains the cessation of the heartbeat as the sole criterion of death. So when Bjarne Semb, the Chief of the Thorax Clinic of Stockholm's Karolinska Institute replaced the heart of Leif Stenberg with a Jarvik artificial heart, the patient was legally dead but Sweden's public prosecutor continued pressing criminal proceedings against Stenberg for tax fraud.

There is no statutory definition of death in Japan but most jurists maintain that death should be defined as the cessation of pulsation. However, the cessation of brain waves and the functions of the brain stem have also been proposed as evidence of death. A team of doctors at Tsukuba University Hospital who had removed organs for transplants from a woman who had ceased breathing and whose brain waves had levelled out were accused by colleagues and a citizens' group of having murdered the woman because her heartbeat had not yet stopped. Some members of the Diet (parliament) intend introducing legislation for having brain death accepted as the legal definition of death.

A panel selected by the Japanese Ministry of Health and Welfare investigated the standards used by 713 of the country's medical institutitons for determining brain death and compared them with the standards developed 11 years ago by the Japan Electroencephalogram Studies Society. These standards listed six symptoms including deep coma, flattening of brain waves, dilation of pupils, stoppage of spontaneous breathing and a rapid decrease in blood pressure. The last condition was dropped because of the development of drugs which keep blood pressure high. The panel reported that of 718 cases chosen for study, 288 (32 per cent) met the remaining conditions; in another 188 cases, the dilation of the pupils was smaller than standard (usually, a person is considered dead if the diameter of the pupils is 6mm or more; in the cases not conforming to this rule, diameters were as small as 4mm). In 302 cases, the panel found greater discrepancies from the standards, and in 52 of these cases, brain death appeared doubtful.

Excluding 142 cases in which life support systems were disconnected, heart death came in 74 per cent (409 out of 552) cases in a maximum of four days after the brain death, in 47 cases, the heart continued to beat for 10 days or more, in 20 cases, for 15 days or more, and in one case, the heart continued to beat for 83 days.

Let Babies Die?

The patient's will, of course, is irrelevant when it comes to babies. They cannot decide whether they want to be saved and be kept alive despite their deformities. In the appeal court's judgement in the Alexandra case, the court suggested that a court might decide not to interfere if a child's life was going to be so demonstrably awful that it should be condemned to die.

The degree of handicap, therefore, may be taken into account in other cases. This seems to amount to a confirmation that society has no clear view on the rights and wrongs of medical intervention in decisions about the severely handicapped. When parents, because of their religious beliefs, refuse to consent to a blood transfusion for a child needing one, doctors disregard their objections because their professional ethics do not allow them to withhold life-saving treatment from a child whose life should not be put in jeopardy on account of what 'society at large' (that's the usual term) thinks mistaken beliefs.

Some American experts were of the opinion that parents and doctors should not deny life-sustaining therapy to infants born with Down's syndrome. Mental retardation in infants, they said, was not sufficient reason to withhold treatment. While some doctors and lawyers maintain unconditionally that the withholding of medical treatment amounts to killing, others are equally sure that rearing a severely handicapped child is too great a burden to impose on parents and siblings, especially if the child is likely to survive to adulthood. The decision to treat or not to treat a deformed child with an additional disability may be beyond the competence of many parents. Some parents would have no hesitation and would consent to the treatment aware that the consequence would be a mentally and physically handicapped child whose prospects are unknowable. Because of the uncertainty created by the fear that their child may have to suffer unnecessarily and the prospect that they will have to take care of a severely-handicapped child for its entire life, many others would find themselves quite unable to make a decision and would want their doctors to do so. Still others would feel that it would be in the best interest of the child that it should be allowed to die. Aging parents, in particular, would be faced with fearful anxiety about a handicapped child's future. Even if they bring up a child willingly and lovingly, they do not know what will happen after their death.

An American doctor, Michael Harrison, proposed to use organs from unborn babies doomed to die from brain defects for transplants to save other children. There was a serious shortage of organs to transplant and most infants needing transplants died waiting for donors. Foetuses with defects so hopeless that they met the requirements for abortion at any gestational age would be ideal donors, the doctor said.

Zoologists have been intrigued by what is called infanticide in the animal world. It has been observed in mammals (including rodents such as hamsters and gerbils but also cats) as well as in birds, and the killer can be a male, a female other than the mother, and siblings. It seems to occur most often among animals living in troops consisting of one adult male and several females (monkeys such as langurs, lions) when a new male usurps the leadership. One of the reasons given for the killing is that a lactating female cannot conceive but that she will go into estrus soon after losing her offspring. There is no evidence to link infanticide among animals to human infanticide which is attributable to social, economic or psychological factors. Although it may have been 'common' in some primitive societies, it can hardly be called 'normal.'

As mentioned above, infanticide was widely practised in feudal Japan. Today, it is committed frequently by unwed mothers who feel unable to cope with the complications an unwanted child will bring. Recently, police arrested a divorced marriage-parlour employee who had choked her newborn baby girl to death and kept the body in the freezer because she did not find an opportunity to dispose of it. A 34-year-old mother, who already had eight children, choked her ninth baby immediately after birth because she felt unable to take care of the additional child. In China, the government's population policy has caused a sharp increase in the killing of baby girls. An unprecedented wave of infanticide and abandonment of newborn infants has been reported to have swept Zimbabwe.

When Does Life Begin?

For the moral evaluation of abortion, the time when human life starts is of decisive importance. *Time* magazine called this 'The Unsolvable Question.' There are at least seven different opinions on the beginning of biological human life: 1. Fertilisation. 2. Implantation. 3. When the heart of the embryo starts beating (around the fourth week of pregnancy). 4. When the central nervous system has developed to a stage where simple reflexes are evident (around the sixth week). 5. At the time of the transition from embryo to foetus (recognisable as human being, around the eighth week). 6. At the first appearance of brain waves (twelfth week; however, the nervous system is not fully connected until the 24th week). 7. When the foetus has become viable (sufficiently developed to live outside the mother's womb. This stage is placed between the 24th and the 28th week, but doctors have been able to keep premature babies alive as young as 20 weeks and weighing 500 gms).

While Catholic doctrine holds that life begins at conception many Protestant moralists maintained that true human life does not begin until the foetus 'quickens,' that is, the stage of pregnancy at which the child gives indications of life, about 12 weeks after conception. Some Jewish scholars were of the opinion that an embryo is a 'mere fluid' until 40 days after conception and thereafter at least a 'partial person.'

If the view is adopted that at the moment of conception a human soul is created, human life starts with conception. Naturally, in such a view, the beginning of human life has no connection with the emergence of a human form. The problem, however, is whether it can be regarded as human life. The soul is considered the directive principle of life formation, the principle of physiological, sensitive and spiritual life. Sensitive life, if possible at all, is very restricted and spiritual life impossible in the mother's womb. It would, therefore, be more correct to say that the life of the unborn is potential human life, human life *in fieri*, the formation for human life.

The Soul and the Start of Life

The theory of the soul creates a difficult problem for artificial fertilisation. If an egg is extracted from the mother and fertilised *in vitro,* this fertilisation would imply the origin of a human soul. It is essentially the same as the start of human life by intercourse. But at the present stage of biogenetic technology, fertilisation *in vitro* cannot lead to the development of a human being unless the fertilised egg is implanted in a human being where it can grow. The egg fertilised *in vitro* is potential human life only conditionally, but the existence or non-existence of a human soul constitutes the basic philosophical and ethical question in the present process of *in vitro* fertilisation. Although several eggs are fertilised, nidation is usually limited to only one and the other fertilised eggs perish. The same problem also complicates the freezing of embryos, the possible research use of spare (presumably non-viable) embryos, the development of cloning techniques, and genetic engineering in the case of genetic faults. Since from the very beginning, the development of any fertilised egg is directed from within and in conformity with the prospective potential, that is, a human being, the presence of some kind of principle capable of this kind of direction seems necessary. Nevertheless, the destruction of a fertilised ovum can hardly be termed 'killing' and even less 'murder' and to call the disappearance of life at such a stage 'death' seems inappropriate, just as a fertilised egg incapable of development and absorbed by the mother cannot be said to die.

The opinions of scientists and the legal terminology on the nature of embryo or foetus vary greatly. As stated above, it is only through birth that the child becomes an independent being, and although it still lacks some of the functions proper to man as 'animal rationale,' it is capable of an independently directed development towards the unfolding of these functions. There is, however, no unanimity on the meaning of 'birth.' The common view holds that birth is 'a process which causes the emergence of a new individual from inside its mother'; once outside the body of the mother, the child has been born in the commonly-accepted meaning of this word. Another opinion, however, asserts that birth means the 'separation of the foetus from the mother's life-support system,' regardless of whether removed from her body.

Roe v. Wade

The US Supreme Court has decided that the term 'person' in the 14th Amendment does not include the unborn, and in the case of Roe v. Wade (1973), in which the court, in a 7 to 2 decision, held that the states could not interfere with a woman's right to an elective abortion before the point at which the foetus could survive outside the mother, Justice Blackmun wrote: 'When those trained in the respective disciplines of medicine, philosophy and theology are unable to arrive at any consensus, the judiciary, at this point of the development of man's knowledge, is not in a position to speculate as to the answer.' The court conceded that if the foetus were indeed a 'person,' which it ruled was not the case, its right to life would have to be guaranteed.

The case arose from a Texas law which prohibited abortions also in instances of rape or incest. The Supreme Court tried to balance the woman's right to control her own body, the states' rights over their citizens, and the professional judgement of a physician. Since the states could not assert any interests before the foetus became viable, state regulation was prohibited until viability, that is, the third trimester of pregnancy. The decision, therefore, divided a pregnant woman's rights into thirds. During the first three months, the court said, the decision to have an abortion was up to the woman and her doctor, and government could not restrict abortion. Abortion was also legal, the court held, during the second trimester, but medical restrictions could be imposed to protect the mother's health. The government could enforce restrictions on abortions for the last three months in order to safeguard the foetus as well as the mother.

The decision was greeted with approval by many feminists but raised a storm of protest from churches. Much of the opposition stemmed from the confusion between morality and law. Churches may take a moral position on the issue but this is not the business of the state. As far as the state is concerned, legality (as distinct from morality) of allowing abortion hinges on the right and duty of the state of protecting unborn human life. If the meaning of human life were extended to the time of conception and its protection based on a 'right to life' of the embryo or foetus, the state would be bound to respect this right and not tolerate abortion. A conflict between the right to life of the foetus and the right of the mother would sometimes be unavoidable. But it is possible to deny a 'right to life' of the embryo (foetus) and consider unborn human life as some kind of 'good' or 'value' which the state should protect. On such a premise, this value could be balanced against different values and sacrificed for some higher value.

Protection of Unborn Life

In the case of the Boston doctor charged with manslaughter in the death of a 20-24-week-old foetus he aborted, the judge said that a manslaughter charge would not apply to death within the womb. 'A foetus is not a person and therefore not a subject for an indictment for manslaughter.'

A Kentucky court held that abortion was murder if the foetus was viable and that a viable foetus came under the constitutional protection of human life. In Connecticut, a federal judge ruled that a viable foetus has independent legal rights. A boy who was injured as a 5½-month-old foetus when his mother was manhandled by police can claim damages on his own, the judge decided. A Yale law professor reasoned that this decision recognised the foetus as a human person which would prevent the mother from having an abortion.

The California Supreme Court rejected a request by the Catholic League for Civil and Religious Rights that the state should hold a public memorial and burial service for 16,500 foetuses recovered from a dump when the firm responsible for their incineration went bankrupt. The foetuses had come from the Feminist Women's Health Centre which operates an abortion clinic in Los Angeles. In the court's view, to permit such a burial would show a preference by the state for a belief not universally held — that foetuses were human beings. The Catholic League intended to file an appeal with the US Supreme Court.

In a decision in which the Constitutional Court of the German Federal Republic held the unrestricted legalisation of abortion during the first three months of pregnancy sanctioned by the 1974 revision of the Penal Code unconstitutional (the decision will be discussed below), the court declared that, on principle, the protection of the unborn child must take precedence over the right of self-determination of the mother. In view of the barbarism of the Hitler era, the protection of human life constitutes a highly explosive issue in Germany. In its decision, the court followed the implantation theory: 'On the basis of certain biological-physiological knowledge, life in the sense of a human individual unquestionably exists starting with the 14th day after conception (implantation, individuation). ... The right to life is guaranteed to everyone who lives; no difference can be made between the various phases of the developing life prior to birth or between unborn and born life.'

The choice of the implantation theory is dictated by German criminal law which provides that actions whose effect takes place prior to the completion of the implantation of the fertilised ovum do not constitute termination of pregnancy (Penal Code, Art. 219 d). Implantation is completed 11 days after fertilisation; in German legal practice, the required time is assumed to be 13 days. The defenders of the implantation theory contend that the time for the moral and legal protection of the unborn child should start with implantation because an extension of the time back to fertilisation would create insolvable difficulties. Theoretically, the protection would have to cover a fertilised ovum rejected by the mother's body. Ordinarily, severe numerical or structural chromosomal deficiencies impede the implantation of the blastocyte. In the first weeks following fertilisation, about 80 per cent of all fertilised eggs are spontaneously discharged.

The exemption of punishment from actions prior to the implantation makes contraception possible. If a spiral is placed into the uterus, the spermatozoa can migrate into the uterus and fertilisation can occur, but implantation is impossible and the ovum is discharged.

The discussion of the protection of human life contains expressions which are inconsistent with the actual development of life. The German Constitutional Court based its decision on the protection of human life in Germany's Fundamental Law ('Everybody has the right to life and corporal integrity;' Art. 2, Par. 2). The court obviously assumes that an embryo is covered by the term 'everybody.' But the dictum 'nasciturus (is) an independent human being' is an assertion which has never been proven. Although the Irish Constitution acknowledges the right to life of the unborn child, only a person can be the subject of rights. The German Civil Code says 'Man's legal capacity starts with the completion of birth' (Art. 1). The Convention for the Protection of Human and Fundamental Rights does not contain the slighest indication that the legal protection of the right to life of every human being (Art. 2, Par. 1) is to be extended to unborn life.

At the end of a discussion on Germany's abortion legislation, the Central Committe of German Catholics adopted the view that 'the unborn child is a human being from the start and therefore has an inviolable right to life.' 'From the start' would mean from the moment of fertilisation, but neither physiologically nor philosophically can an embryo be called a human being. The statement that the fusion of the two gametes creates a 'new human individual' (Prof. Franz Bücher, Freiburg) is incorrect, just as the assertion that 'the embryo is a human being' and is 'a human being from the start' (Prof. Blechschmidt) or that 'man begins with fertilisation' (Prof. Lejeune, Paris). It can only be said that with fertilisation, the entire genetic inheritance of a being that some day will be a human being is fixed. I also find the view of Professor Dr Gerhard Müller, President of the Federal Labour Court at Kassel, incompatible with the actual process of human development. He maintains that the fertilised egg, the embryo, is 'a complete human being in all phases of development.' He concedes that the embryo depends on the mother as its environment but asserts that 'this does not change the fact that it exists in its highly individual spiritual and physical peculiarity constituting its concrete personality in every respect.' The embryo is ordained to become a person but it is no person, no matter whether its dependence on the mother is regarded as an intrinsic or extrinsic dependence. In an unborn child, the self-possession of the person exists only *in potentia*. not *in actu*.

While it makes sense to require that the protection of human life should include the protection of unborn life, it is impossible to base this protection on the right to life of the foetus as a human being. It is also meaningless to qualify the abortion of an unviable foetus as 'anticipated murder.'

Some scientists have proposed to consider the beginning of brain activity — which can be recorded by electroencephalogram — as the beginning of a human being. This corresponds to the position that human life ends with the cessation of brain activity.

In a book with the title *Tagebuch eines ungeborenen Kindes* (Diary of an Unborn Child), the first entry says: 'Today, my life has begun. My parents do not yet know it. I am smaller than a pin-head but I am nevertheless already an independent being.' This assertion is certainly erroneous. By the way, the last entry into the diary reads: 'Today, my mother has killed me.'

Legal Status of the Unborn Child

The difficulty of giving a precise legal status to the unborn child is apparent in the language of the American courts. 'The Constitution does not confer or require legal personality for the unborn.' — '... that a foetus has an independent genetic package with potential to become a fully-fledged human being and that it has an autonomy of development and character although it is for the period of gestation dependent upon the mother,' — 'But unborn children have never been recognised as persons in the whole sense.'

Nevertheless, the question of 'foetal rights' has become a controversial topic in the United States. Morally, there can be no doubt that a woman must do for her foetus what can be reasonably demanded of her once she has decided to have a child and has become pregnant. But the assertion that a foetus gains rights as a mother cedes them is wrong. Moral responsibility does not automatically involve legal duties. In the United States, 16 states have passed 'foeticide' laws making it a crime to cause the death of an unborn child. In 1984, an Illinois judge ruled that a pregnant heroin-user was abusing her foetus, made it a ward of the state and committed the mother to a drug-rehabilitation centre. Courts in at least five states have ordered women to undergo Caesarian sections against their will.

A San Diego woman has been charged with criminally contributing to the death of her baby by ignoring her doctor's advice. The woman, Pamela Rae Stewart, had placenta previa, a condition in which the placenta totally or partially covers the opening of the cervix so that the foetus cannot descend without rupturing the placenta which involves maternal hemorrhage and cuts off oxygen supply to the foetus. Her doctor had warned Mrs Stewart to refrain from drugs and sex and seek medical care as soon as she started bleeding. According to the prosecution, the woman took amphetamines and had sex with her husband the day she delivered and didn't call paramedics until 12 hours after bleeding began. Her baby was born brain dead and with amphetamines in his system. But the court ruled that the law relied on by the prosecution did not apply to the case and dismissed the charge.

In Arkansas, a proposed constitutional amendment which would have made it a state responsibility to protect 'every unborn child from conception to birth' was narrowly defeated in the November 1986 poll.

In February 1987, Britain's Court of Appeal turned down the plea of a 23-year-old Oxford student to stop his ex-girlfriend from aborting his unborn child. High Court Judge Rose Heilbron had ruled that in law a foetus had no legal standing to bring an action to keep itself alive. The father's claim that an abortion would be an offence under Britain's 1929 Infant Life Preservation Act was inadmissible because there was no certainty that the foetus of 18 weeks would be born alive. The father could not sue in his own name because a 1978 case had decided that a man has no legal rights over a foetus he has fathered. When three appeal judges rejected the appeal, the student took his case to the House of Lords but the Lords in turn upheld the original High Court ruling and the ex-girlfriend was free to continue with her plans for an abortion.

The rationale for state action is the relation to the common good. The state can command what is necessary for the common good and prohibit what is against it. But the state cannot lawfully override individual rights. The assertion of 'foetal rights' may collide with a woman's right over her own body. If a woman can be prosecuted for 'foetal abuse,' it will be necessary to draw a line where a pregnant woman's use of alcohol, tobacco or drugs, dancing, gymnastics or other exercise becomes criminal. How will such a line be drawn and who will draw it? There is no moral obligation to employ extraordinary means for preserving one's own life, let alone for saving that of somebody else; how can a woman be ordered to undergo a Caesarian section if this would put her own life in jeopardy? Basically, the criminal law is hardly the proper way of protecting unborn life.

A foetus is not a part or an organ of the mother. Though dependent on the mother, the foetus is a separate organism; 'it is human in the sense that it is of human origin and in the process of becoming a human being if nothing interferes' (Leon Klass). A foetus is not a human individual and not a person but it is growing human life. 'The foetus is live enough not to be dead, not yet mature enough to be an infant, yet human enough to deserve protection' (Paul Ramsay).

It is the question of how far this protection should extend which is at the bottom of the abortion controversy. In the United States, the problem of the protection to be given to unborn life has split public opinion and particularly the women's movements into two hostile camps, fighting each other under the slogans 'Pro Life' and 'Pro Choice.' The anti-abortionists want to make the protection of unborn life absolute, the abortionists contend that human life in fieri can be subordinated or sacrificed to other values. The anti-abortionists maintain that, except where the mother's life is at stake, there is no rational basis for distinguishing between the foetus and the newborn infant. The infant is only a potential member of society, just as the foetus is. The proponents of abortion contend that prior to the fourth month of pregnancy, the foetus has acquired very few of the characteristics commonly identified as human.

The Pro-Natalist Position

In what might be called the philosophy of abortion, the pro-natalists appeal to the sacredness of human life, all human life, and maintain that the unborn child has a right to life just as other human beings. They consider abortion as murder and describe the present situation as 'the carnage of the innocent.' Human-life advocates point out that laws legalising abortion for genetically-defective children result in the destruction of healthy foetuses. If the law allows the interruption of pregnancy up to the 22nd week, doctors usually perform an abortion if there is, for example, a 25 per cent risk of severe metabolic disorders. This means that there is a 75 per cent probability that healthy offspring will be aborted.

The sanctioning of abortion invites a general decline in the respect for human life. From a theological point of view, the Catholic Church and many other Christians think that the Fifth Commandment, 'Thou shalt not kill,' applies also to unborn life. Demographic considerations are involved in both abortionist and anti-abortionist arguments. Where the decline of the birth-rate threatens a shrinkage of the population and a shift in the population structure to a large bulge in the older age groups, abortion is thought of as a threat to the nation's existence. In countries where over-population is acute, abortion is regarded as one of the means of population control.

The fight against abortion has led to the bombing of abortion clinics. Since 1982, there have been 30 cases of bombing or arson directed at abortion clinics across the United States. In 1984, 24 cases, including three in Pensacola, Florida, on Christmas Day and the eighth such bombing in Washington, DC, in two years on New Year's Day 1985. One of the suspects arrested in the Florida bombings told federal agents that he and a companion planted the bombs because of a 'call from God.'

The Abortionist Position

The anti-natalist position ranges from the assertion of a woman's unrestricted right to an abortion to the view that in a more or less limited number of cases, abortion should be exempt from legal punishment. The feminist movement asserts that a woman's body belongs to her, not to the Church, not to the state, not to her father or her husband. Their real point is that a foetus is part of a woman's body until it is born. Anti-abortion laws give foetuses rights that living people do not enjoy. No human's right to life includes the use of another being's body or life-support system against that individual's will. No woman, therefore, should be forced to bear a child against her will. 'We believe there is no greater tyranny over an individual than the power to control child-bearing.' The late Justice William O. Douglas held that personal freedom includes not only control over the development of ones personality but also freedom of choice in the basic decisions on marriage, divorce, procreation, contraception, and the education and upbringing of children.

The right to choose an abortion has been linked to the right to privacy. The right 'to the privacy of their bodies' is said to include the right to decide within an appropriate period of time after conception whether or not the woman wishes to bear the child. The California Supreme Court adopted this view: 'The decision whether to bear a child or to have an abortion is so private and so intimate that each woman in this state — rich or poor — is guaranteed the constitutional right to make that decision as an individual.' Generally, the right of the woman or the parents to choose is considered to outweigh the right to life of the foetus. In the abortionists' view, every foetus is replaceable. The right to abortion, they assert, is based on the right of married couples to make their judgements by themselves. Unmarried mothers, in particular, are said to have the right to decide whether they want a baby out of wedlock. The consulting office Pro Familia in Bremen propounds two principles: 1. Every child has the right to be wanted. 2. The woman's will is decisive. The first sentence is mere propaganda, the second is the rule for the agency's actual work.

To the assertion of the freedom of choice, a Letter to the Editor which appeared in the 27 April 1981 issue of *Time* gave the following answer: 'Yes, a woman has the right to choose what happens to her body. ... She makes that choice when she decides to have intercourse and when she does or does not use birth control. Pregnancy is the result of her choice' (Nancy Bohm, Germansville, Pennsylvania). This is certainly true but in today's society, intercourse has so much become a means of personal satisfaction that the possibility of conception is almost overlooked and birth control is neglected.

The Decision to Abort

A reason which is often cited for making abortion legal is that prohibition will not reduce the number of abortions but will increase the risk of injuries to the mother.

According to Dr Corinne Shear Wood, professor of anthropology at California State University, to abort or not to abort is not the question. Women have had recourse to abortion at all times and in practically all societies when they found pregnancy or childbirth unacceptable. In many cases, the reasons for terminating pregnancy are economic, but other personal or social conditions may leave a woman no other choice but to abort. The option left to her, Dr Wood maintains, is not whether but how to accomplish the abortion. In some poor countries, she must find someone who will 'assist' her by rolling logs over her abdomen, pounding her body with heavy objects until the conceptus is expelled, wrapping increasingly tighter cords over her abdomen or inserting an unbelievable variety of objects into the uterus. The methods frequently terminate the life of the mother as well as that of the foetus.

A report on the health effects of abortion written by Dr William Cates Jr for the Centres of Disease Control in Atlanta credited the legalisation of abortion with a decrease in maternal deaths, improved training in pregnancy termination, increased use of low-cost out-patient gynaecological services and a decline in out-of-wedlock births. On the other hand, questions such as the connection between abortion and complications in later pregnancies and possible increased risk of breast cancer remain unsolved.

The American College of Obstetricians and Gynaecologists released a report based on the observation of more than 1,200 women who had undergone abortions at three Massachusetts clinics. The report asserted that women who have abortions do not experience a decrease in fertility. The evidence that abortion produces infertility, the report states, came from Europe, Japan and Greece, where many women underwent illegal abortions. The methods used in those countries, usually dilation and sharp curettage, were more dangerous and traumatic than vacuum curettage common in the United States where major complications that might require hysterectomy occurred at most once in 20,000 cases of abortion.

Up to the twentieth century, abortion was usually prohibited and punishable by severe criminal sanctions. It was very exceptionally permitted or tolerated to save the life of the mother. Abortion at the request of the mother was first legalised in the Soviet Union in 1920; the availability of abortion was restricted in 1935 but freedom was restored in 1955. At present, liberal laws for abortion exist in Japan, in most of the Eastern European countries and in Cuba where abortions are provided free by the state in the first three months of pregnancy. The right to seek an abortion gives women an element of freedom and control over their lives that women never had before but men have always had. In Eastern Europe, abortions are restricted to hospitals but in Japan, they can be performed in doctors' offices.

Japanese Law

In Japan, the Civil Code states: 'The enjoyment of private rights starts with birth' (Art. 1-3) which decides nothing about the constitutional and legal protection of human life. It seems difficult to extend the constitutional protection of life (Art. 13) to unborn children. Japan's legislation has created the somewhat paradoxical situation that abortion *(datai)* remains punishable under the Penal Code (Art. 212-216; the Code does not provide a definition of abortion) but that interruption of pregnancy *(ninshin chūzetsu)* is practically available upon request under the Eugenic Protection Law *(Yūsei Hogo-hō)*. In Japanese criminal law, the child is regarded as a human being as soon as part of its body is exposed; in such a case, its destruction would be murder and not abortion (there is no special punishment for infanticide). Although the Eugenic Protection Law was enacted after the war (1948), it strongly reflects the influence of the eugenic (and racist) theories of Nazi Germany and actually copies some of the provisions of the Nazi sterilisation law *(Gesetz zum Schutz der Volksgesundheit)*. The statement of the purpose of the law emphasises the priority of eugenics: 'This law aims at protecting, from a eugenic point of view, the life and health of the mother together with the prevention of the birth of inferior offspring' (Art. 1). The law allows sterilisation (Art. 3-13) and artificial interruption of pregnancy (Art. 14). Both measures can be taken for eugenic, medical and social reasons. Eugenic reasons are given: 1. If the pregnant woman or her spouse is afflicted with insanity, feeble-mindedness, a hereditary physical disorder or a hereditary deformity. 2. If the parents or relatives up to the fourth degree of kinship of the pregnant wife or her spouse suffer from such afflictions. 3. If the pregnant woman or her spouse suffers from leprosy (Art. 14, Par. 1, Nr. 1-3). Interruption of pregnancy is also permissible if the pregnancy has resulted from rape or intercourse through violence or threat (ibid., Nr. 5) and in case of 'risk that the continuation of pregnancy or birth will severely impair the health of the mother for physical (literally, 'bodily') or economic reasons' (ibid., Nr. 4). The term 'economic' was added in 1949, and in 1972 and 1973, the government planned to eliminate this word, but resistance was so strong that this plan was abandoned. When the economic indication was added, living conditions were actually difficult. In the meantime, the standard of living has improved but the economic situation of many families remains precarious, not so much on account of the costs of daily necessities (which certainly are high) but because of the financial burden assumed out of the desire to have their own house and to give their children a better education.

The Ministry of Health and Welfare resumed the consideration of a revision of the Eugenic Protection Law in March 1981 when Masakuni Murakami, a member of the House of Councillors belonging to the Liberal-Democratic Party, wanted to have 'economic' reasons struck from Article 14. Family planning organisations and women's groups oppose the revision arguing that it should be left to the women themselves to decide whether they want to give birth or not. In January 1983, members of the Dietwomen's Association submitted a request to the Minister of Health and Welfare opposing the amendment of the law. They pointed out that common contraceptives such as the pill and IUDs are still banned in Japan and that 99.7 per cent of the 596,000 abortions reported for 1981 were on economic grounds.

In the implementation of the law, abortion was allowed up to the eighth month of pregnancy but the period was shortened to seven months in 1976. In practice, the legal restrictions are not always observed and the number of unreported abortions may be double the number of officially reported cases.

The government of Prime Minister Nakasone which wanted to restrict abortions adopted a programme 'affirming the family base.' Some leading politicians of the Liberal-Democratic Party support the 'respect for life' campaign of *Seichō no Ie* (House of Growth), a right-wing religious sect established in the militaristic pre-war era. A sub-committe of the party proposed a basic review of the Eugenic Protection Law in order to adapt it to the changes in social conditions. So far, Japanese politicians have failed to see that the solution of the problems involved in the economic indication of the law does not lie in the restriction of abortions but in improved birth control.

American Abortion Law

In the United States, abortion is one of the political issues on which the country is deeply divided, together with the Equal Rights Amendment, school busing, sex education in public schools, gun-control laws and foreign aid to leftist régimes. According to opinion polls, 80 per cent favour abortion in cases of rape or incest and when pregnancy is a threat to the woman's life, only 40 per cent for other reasons. The so-called Pro-Life movement, whose supporters are dubbed the 'new abolitionists,' calls for a constitutional amendment but its advocates are divided on its exact wording. Catholics propose an absolute ban on all abortions and want the amendment to read: 'Every human being possesses the inalienable right to life from the moment of fertilisation, irrespective of age, health and mode of dependency.' But the National Committee Right to Life wants to make an exception if the mother's life is endangered and others propose to sanction abortion also in case of rape and incest.

The legality of abortions depends on state legislation and many states have made abortions easier. In 1970, New York permitted abortion for many reasons during the first six months of pregnancy. A bill to repeal this law was vetoed by then Governor Nelson Rockefeller in 1972. In the same year, in Connecticut, an anti-abortion law passed in the 1860s was challenged in a suit 'Women v. Connecticut.' Two judges of the three-judge panel held the law unconstitutional because 'due process of law' requires 'the women to be given the power to determine within an appropriate period after conception whether or not she wishes to bear a child.'

As mentioned above, the US Supreme Court, in Roe v. Wade, held that in the light of the woman's 'right to privacy,' a state may not prohibit abortions within the first three months of pregnancy if the woman and her doctor decide that pregnancy should be terminated, and the judgement may be effected by an abortion free of interference by the state. If the foetus can be presumed viable (that is, if it can be reasonably expected to survive in an incubator, normally about the 28th week of pregnancy), the state can protect the rights of the child-to-be, including laws forbidding abortion; but abortion cannot be prohibited if the mother's life would be endangered by continuing the pregnancy. For the mother's safety, a state may regulate the medical practice of abortion and ensure that it is properly done.

In 1976, the Supreme Court decided that the states may not require a woman to obtain the consent of her husband, or a girl under 18 to receive permission from a parent to get an abortion. On the other hand, the court held that the states may oblige a doctor to notify the parents of a minor seeking an abortion but they cannot veto an abortion. The decision does not apply to 'emancipated' minors, such as those who support themselves, or 'mature' minors capable of making informed decisions about their own health and welfare.

On the conflict between a teenage girl's right to have an abortion and her parents' right to protect their child's best interest, the Supreme Court has ruled that parents have no absolute veto over their daughter's abortion but, in some circumstances, have a right to be informed of her intention to seek an abortion. One of the unsettled issues is whether a child who does not want to discuss her pregnancy with her parents and instead seeks a court-ordered abortion, must first inform her parents that she is going to court to request an abortion.

In an appeal from a decision of a three-judge panel invalidating Florida's spouse and parental consent requirements, the Supreme Court declined to decide whether husbands can veto abortions sought by their wives and whether a daughter under age needs the consent of her parents for having an abortion.

Following the Supreme Court's suggestion in Roe v. Wade, 21 states made hospitalisation mandatory for abortions after the third month, but lower federal courts have split on the legality of these restrictions. An appeal panel overturned Missouri's regulations while another upheld those of Akron, Ohio. The 1978 Akron ordinance required minors under 15 years of age to obtain parental or judicial consent for abortion, obliged doctors to tell their patients that life begins at conception, and forced the patient to wait 24 hours before going ahead with an abortion.

In an affirmation of its 1973 decision in Roe v. Wade, the Supreme Court struck down a number of state and local regulations limiting abortions in three 6 to 3 decisions announced on 15 June 1983. The court invalidated regulations that would have required women to receive abortions in a 'full-service hospital' after the third month of their pregnancy; doctors to tell women seeking abortions about possible alternatives and inform them that the foetus is a 'human life;' doctors to wait at least 24 hours after a woman signs an abortion consent form before performing the operation. States and communities may require that abortions on women more than three months pregnant be performed in licensed abortion clinics or 'out-patient hospitals.' The court also upheld portions of a Missouri law requiring the presence of a second physician during abortions on women in the last three months of pregnancy; requiring minors to obtain the consent of a parent or a judge prior to an abortion; and prescribing a pathology report for every abortion performed. Justice Sarah O'Connor was one of the three dissenting justices and President Reagan denounced the decisions.

In a 5 to 4 decision announced on 11 June 1986 the Supreme Court struck down a Pennsylvania law imposing tough restrictions on abortions. The law required printed information to be given to each woman wanting an abortion on the dangers of abortion and possible alternatives, the presence of a second doctor to help save the foetus and the use of an abortion method most likely to produce a live birth unless it posed a significant medical risk to the woman. Doctors were also required to file a detailed report on each abortion. The court held that the law was an unconstitutional attempt to intimidate women and restrict their freedom to avail themselves of their constitutional right to have an abortion. The majority opinion written by Justice Harry Blackmun who also wrote the court's 1973 majority opinion, stated: 'Few decisions are more personal and intimate, more properly private or more basic to individual dignity and autonomy than a woman's decision to end her pregnancy.' — 'The states are not free, under the guise of protecting maternal health or potential life, to intimidate women into continuing pregnancies.' The decision was a defeat for President Reagan who had the Solicitor General argue for the constitutionality of the Pennsylvania law.

While some pro-life activists have waged a campaign of violence by bombing abortion clinics, pro-abortion groups charge that regulations in some states are attempts to intimidate patients and that the in-hospital rule blocks access to abortion because many hospitals refuse to perform them. Many physicians believe that abortion techniques (dilation and evacuation) have advanced to the point where abortion can be performed safely in clinics well on after the third month.

In a case involving an 11-year-old girl, a court denied abortion, and in a case which attracted much attention, the mother of a 12-year-old girl who had been raped by three young men and was suffering from venereal disease because of the rape did not permit an abortion. The mother, a member of the Holiness Church, contended that God would cause a miscarriage if He wanted the pregnancy to terminate.

Anti-Abortion Movement

In order to nullify the effect of the Roe v. Wade decision, Senator Jesse Helms and Congressman Henry Hyde co-sponsored a bill known as the Human Life Statute which stated: 'For the purpose of enforcing the obligations of the states under the 14th Amendment not to deprive persons of life without due process of law, human life shall be deemed to exist from conception.' — 'Each human life exists from conception, without regard to race, sex, age, health defect or condition of dependency.' The effect of such a law would be to allow the states to pass laws defining abortion as murder.

The anti-abortion forces launched the so-called 'human life movement' with the goal of passing a constitutional amendment guaranteeing the right to life to the unborn from the moment of conception. Naturally, such an amendment would nullify the Roe v. Wade decision. The 'human life federalism' amendment proposed by Senator Orrin Hatch and approved by the Senate Judiciary Committee said: 'A right to abortion is not secured by this Constitution. The Congress and the several states shall have the concurrent power to restrict and prohibit abortion: provided that a provision of a law of a state which is more restrictive than a conflicting provision of a law of Congress shall govern.' But in June 1983, the US Senate rejected this amendment by a vote of 50:49 (67 votes would have been necessary for adoption).

The import of the Hatch amendment would have been to establish that the constitution does not protect the right to abortion so that the federal government as well as the individual states could prohibit or limit abortion. The conference of American bishops decided to support the Hatch amendment as an acceptable solution for doing away with abortion on demand although it did not give unconditional protection to unborn life.

The abortion battle has become one of the most controversial political issues in the United States and both sides try to muster organised support. The pro-abortion groups include the National Abortion Rights Action League, the National Organisation for Women and the National Women's Political Caucus. The leading anti-abortion organisation is the National Pro-Life Political Action Committee, and most churches campaign vigorously for the prohibition of abortion. Many women who are in favour of the Equal Rights Amendment also defend the right to abortion and these two issues have created an unbridgeable split in the American women's movement.

Dr Bernard Nathanson, a New York gynaecologist who had been the head of the country's largest abortion clinic but became an anti-abortionist when the first sonograms of abortions were developed, produced a documentary entitled *The Silent Scream*. The film greatly impressed President Reagan but critics charged that the narrative provided a biased interpretation of the jerks and kicks appearing in the sonograms. They maintained that brain and nervous system of a foetus were not sufficiently developed to feel pain and that the convulsions were nothing more than animal reflexes.

The US government prohibits using US foreign aid funds for abortions in poor countries. The reason given by the government is that of the 40 to 60 million abortions performed annually worldwide, most of those in poor countries are performed under unsanitary conditions and by unqualified personnel.

In order to prevent US Medicaid funds being used to pay for abortions, Senator Jesse Helms attached a rider to another bill which eliminated incest and rape as grounds for abortion and allowed the government to pay for the operation only if the mother's life was threatened. The Supreme Court upheld the constitutionality of the Helms amendment in a 5 to 4 decision in 1980. The majority of the court was of the opinion that the question concerned the authority of Congress to allocate money and that the judiciary had no right to redirect the allocation of federal funds. In dissent, Justice Brennan declared that the Helms amendment caused a 'discriminatory distribution of the government's largesse,' Justice Marshall thought that the 'denial of Medicaid-funded abortions is equivalent to denial of legal abortion altogether,' and Justice Stevens called it a 'breach of the government's duty to treat citizens impartially.'

Led by Senator Orrin Hatch and Representative Jack Kemp, conservatives wanted to eliminate federal funds for family-planning clinics which inform their clients that abortion is an alternative to unwanted pregnancy. Clinics receiving grants under Title X of the Public Health Services Act are prohibited from funding abortions but have routinely counselled women on abortion as a legal right and referred them to other clinics and hospitals. Kemp says that Title X clinics should not counsel pregnant women and that abortion is not a method of birth control.

The legalisation of abortion in case of rape is a controversial policy in the United States because of the alleged widespread misuse of such provisions. It seems to me that the possibility of misuse is a poor reason for not allowing or discontinuing something which, in itself, is right.

Abortion Law:

Britain

Britain was one of the first European countries to liberalise abortion. Under the Abortion Act of 1968, abortions are legal for women who would suffer mental or physical auguish if they had their child. Two doctors must certify that a woman's physical or mental health would be impaired without an abortion. Because abortion was available under the country's nationalised health service, abortions became rather numerous and many women came to Britain from countries where abortions were more restricted. Britain was also one of the countries in which a growing number of teenage abortions was noticeable. In 1969, two 11-year-old girls had abortions; in 1971, three 11-year-olds were among the 2,290 girls under 15 years of age who had legal abortions, and some girls of 15 were coming for their second or third abortion.

Canada

Since 1969, the Canadian Criminal Code has permitted abortion but only if a committee of doctors at an accredited hospital certifies that the woman's life or health is in danger. As a result of court battles, abortion is freely available in Quebec and the issue is fiercely debated all over Canada. The government-run health insurance programme which pays nearly all bills for doctors, hospitals and drugs, covers abortion like any other medical expense.

   As in other areas of vital importance to women, the laws concerning abortion have been made by legislatures dominated by men, and the decisions on abortion are handed down by courts on which women are seldom represented. In Ireland, however, the issue has been decided by the entire electorate. About 67 per cent of the people who voted in a nationwide referendum in September 1983 approved the eighth amendment to the Irish Constitution which reads: 'The state acknowledges the right to life of the unborn and, with due regard to the equal right to life of the mother, guarantees in its laws to respect and, as far as practicable, by its laws to defend and vindicate that right.' Abortion has been illegal in Ireland since 1861 and can be punished by life imprisonment. Together with the legal ban on divorce the amendment has deepened the rift with Northern Ireland. The theoretical problems concerning the right to life of the foetus and the conciliation of this right with the rights of the mother has been left unsolved. It remains to be seen how the amendment will affect the current practice that sanctions terminating a pregnancy to save the life of the mother.

West Germany

The situation is confused in the Federal Republic of Germany. The present form of Article 218 of the Penal Code which punishes abortion is the result of a series of revisions. In 1972, a draft prepared by the administrative agencies involved with the cooperation of nongovernmental groups which provided exemption from punishment for certain emergency situations (medical, ethical and eugenic indications) was scrapped in favour of a revision sponsored by the majority parties in the Bundestag (Social Democrats and Free Democrats) sanctioning unrestricted abortion in the first three months of pregnancy. This so-called *Fristenlösung* (term regulation) was incorporated in the revision adopted by the Bundestag in 1974. But a decision of the German Federal Constitutional Court on 25 February 1975 held this amendment unconstitutional. The protection of human life laid down in the Fundamental Law, the court ruled, could not be unconditionally suspended for a certain period of time. The revision necessitated by this decision passed by the Bundestag in 1976 went back to the indication model but added the so-called 'social' indication which has become the centre of a bitter controversy.

The Penal Code protects human life against murder (Art. 211) and manslaughter (Art. 212) only with the beginning of birth and neither article applies to abortion. Already, prior to the latest amendment, abortion was considered permissible if it was the only means of saving the life of the mother. This regulation has been incorporated in the amendment adopted in 1976 in the form of the medical indication. The present law (Art. 218) lays down the principle that termination of pregnancy is punishable (up to 5 years imprisonment for the mother and up to 10 years for the person performing the abortion) and then defines four cases in which abortion, if performed by a doctor with the consent of the pregnant mother is not punishable. These four cases are: 1. If in consideration of the present and future living conditions of the pregnant woman, the doctor deems termination of pregnancy indicated in order to prevent a serious impairment of the physical or mental health of the woman and this threat cannot be prevented in any other way which can be reasonably demanded of the woman (medical or therapeutical indication; Art. 218 a, Par. 1). 2. If there are serious reasons for the assumption that on account of hereditary factors or harmful influences before birth, the child would suffer from an incurable impairment of its health so serious that a continuation of the pregnancy cannot be demanded of the woman (eugenic or genetic indication; Art. 218 a, Par. 2 Nr. 1). 3. If the pregnant woman has been the victim of rape or similar crimes and serious reasons suggest that the pregnancy is the result of this action (criminological or ethical indication; Par. 2 Nr. 2). 4. If the termination of pregnancy is indicated in order to avoid the danger of an emergency so serious that the continuation of the pregnancy cannot be asked of the pregnant woman and the danger cannot be averted in any other way which can be reasonably demanded of the pregnant woman (Par. 2 Nr. 3). In case No. 1, no more than 22 weeks should have been elapsed since conception, in cases Nos. 3 and 4, no more than 12 weeks.

The law requires consultation at least three days prior to abortion (except in case of the medical indication) in which the pregnant woman is to be informed of public and private help available to pregnant women, mothers and children and particularly the means for continuing the pregnancy. Moreover, the pregnant woman must be instructed by a doctor on the medical implications of abortion. For the consultation, the woman can call on any publicly-recognised consultation centre or on a doctor who does not perform the abortion. Abortion without prior consultation or the certificate of a doctor stating that the requirements for one of the legally recognised indications are fulfilled is punishable (Art. 218 b; 219).

The Penal Code also punishes infanticide (Art. 217), promotion of abortion (Art. 219 b), the distribution of abortifacients (Art. 219 c) and abandonment (Art. 221).

The Social Indication

The vague definition of the social indication has made it into a pretext for abortion on demand. In 1980, over 63,000 of the 87,000 abortions reported, equivalent to 72 per cent, were performed on the basis of the social indication. Of these, 30,000 abortions were sought by married women, the others by unmarried or divorced women. Of the total number of women who underwent abortions, 51 per cent were aged from 18 to 30 years, 33 per cent from 30 to under 40, 9 per cent 40 and older, and 5 per cent under 18 years.

Doctors are obliged by law to report abortions but in 1980, the health insurance agencies paid for 212,000 abortions while only 87,000 cases were officially reported. The latest estimate of the Federal Medical Chamber put the number of births at 600,000 and that of abortions at 230,000 of which about 80 per cent were based on the social indication.

The Constitutional Court based its 1975 decision not on the Penal Code but on Art. 2, Par 2 of the Fundamental Law guaranteeing the right to life. In the view of the court, therefore, abortion does not become illegal by the prohibition of the Penal Code but is unlawful because it is incompatible with the constitutional protection of human life and therefore would remain unlawful even if the article of the Penal Code prohibiting abortion would be deleted. Hence, the provision in the Penal Code exempting certain kinds of abortion from punishment does not make these abortions 'legal.' The state has no right to authorise the destruction of a foetus. In the opinion of the court, the legislator can forego to punish certain kinds of abortion if they constitute serious cases of conflict, but the conditions for exempting such cases must be equally weighty in all exemptions. The operating word in evaluating the seriousness of the conditions is *unzumutbar* (what cannot reasonably be demanded), and the social indication should only apply if the burden imposed by the birth of the child would be just as unreasonable as in the case of the medical, eugenic or ethical indication.

The government draft of 1972 contained the following explanation of the social indication: (a) The pregnant woman is already burdened with the task of rearing several children or of taking care of a sick or handicapped child to such an extent that the woman cannot possibly fulfil this task and rear an additional child so that serious harm such as a disruption of development or a recrudescence of the illness would result. (b) The condition of the pregnant woman's husband imposes such a burden on the family that the woman will not be able to take sufficient care of the infant. This may be the case if the husband suffers from a psychosis or drug addiction or is otherwise mentally defective. (c) The pregnant woman will be unable to take sufficient care of the child on account of her own condition (such as epilepsy, severe depression, blindness).

The burden ordinarily associated with pregnancy does not constitute a sufficient reason for abortion. Financial disadvantages, deterioration of the standard of living, postponement of planned acquisitions, temporary interruption of employment, or professional drawbacks such as decreased chances of promotion do not constitute burdens which cannot be reasonably demanded of the woman. The limit of reasonable impositions is reached if conditions threaten the indispensable living conditions of the woman or her family.

West Germany's present abortion legislation has led to some juridically correct but somehow unpalatable decisions by the country's highest court (Bundesgericht). Unsuccessful abortions can constitute a violation of a legal duty. A doctor who undertakes an abortion is obliged to perform this service to the best of his medical ability. If the abortion is unsuccessful and a child is born, the doctor may be liable for 'damage.' In case an abortion is based on the social indication, the doctor will have to pay for the upbringing of the child and pay a solatium to the mother for the physical and mental pain caused by pregnancy and childbirth. But in a case involving an unsuccessful abortion based on the medical indication in which the mother had to bear the child to term and a healthy child was born, the court ruled that the doctor was not liable for the costs of rearing the child. The purpose of the agreement for an abortion was to avert the danger to the life of mother and child and since the danger did not materialise, the failure of the abortion did not cause any damage. But the doctor had to pay a solatium to the mother for the physical and psychic burden of pregnancy and birth.

In a case in which a doctor had discontinued an abortion because he feared that he had perforated the uterus and the mother eventually bore a healthy child, the court decided that the doctor was not liable for paying the costs of upbringing. The distress which would have supported the social indication did not exist and the economic situation of the family did not make the rearing of the child an unreasonable burden.

In connection with the social indication, the payments of the health insurance agencies for abortions have become the subject of a fierce debate in West Germany. Birth and abortion are not diseases but both events give the insured a legal claim to health insurance payments. But in the case of the social indication, mother and child show no symptoms of sickness when they appear before the doctors and the 'sickness' on which the claim to insurance is based results from the termination of pregnancy. The health insurance agencies, therefore, maintain that other than medical indications should not establish claims to insurance payments. In view of the exemption of certain cases of abortion from punishment, the insurance law provides that 'not illegal' termination of pregnancy establishes a claim to the usual health insurance payments.

Financing of Abortion by Health Insurance

In a 1981 verdict that directly involved the financing of abortions based on the social indication but also discussed the constitutionality of such abortions, the Social Court at Dortmund asserted that the payments for abortions other than those based on a medical indication by the health insurance agencies in which membership is compulsory are unconstitutional. The court reasoned that in a number of cases in which the pregnant woman could not reasonably be expected to carry the child to term, the legislator exempted the termination of pregnancy from punishment, but the absence of punitive sanctions does not establish the legitimacy of financing abortions as a public task. In the social indication, abortion is relied on as a means for shaping personal life and social conditions, but the killing of human life is not a means for the formation of the social state. Therefore, the financing of abortion by the contributions to health insurance cannot be a part of the constitutional order.

From the point of view of the insurance law, abortion, except in case of medical indications, is neither a disease nor one of the typical contingencies of human existence against which insurance is relied on for protection.

The court disagreed with the opinion that the exemption from punishment of a wide range of abortions contributed to the protection of the health of women by making it unnecessary to have recourse to quacks. Such a view assumed that abortion as such was unproblematic and that the prevention of injury to the mother was sufficient reason for allowing abortion.

The court held that the financing of abortion was not merely an administrative question. Collaboration in abortion was a question involving beliefs and conscience whose freedom is guaranteed by Art. 4, Par. 1 of the Fundamental Law. Financing of abortion also implies collaboration and a policy of encouraging abortions is incompatible with the constitutionally guaranteed freedom of belief and conscience. But the Constitutional Court, in an obvious attempt to evade a decision on the substantive merits of the case, quashed the verdict on the merely formal ground that there was no legal basis for bringing the complaint before the Social Court. The German bishops have appealed to the politicians to abolish the compulsory financing of abortions by the health insurance organisations but the Christian Democratic Union has been unable to agree on a way to change the existing legislation. Members of the Free Democratic Party consider the present regulation the only feasible compromise between the postulates of Christian ethics and West Germany's social and political reality.

Public Opinion on Abortion

As in the United States, public opinion in West Germany is divided into two diametrically-opposed camps. The 'Pro-abortion' point of view is mainly supported by the Socialists and left-wing organisations. They identify the 'unpunishable' of the Penal Code with 'not illegal' and intend to change the present exemption from punishment into a right to abortion. They regard the obligatory consultation as a measure for preventing the emancipation of women and an obstacle to their right to self-determination.

In conformity with their position upholding the unqualified protection of human life, the Christian churches generally want to strengthen the rôle of the consultative procedure (which can be performed by private agencies) and use it to dissuade women from abortion by arranging for help with the household chores, employment, etc. The ambiguous definition of the social indication has lead to arbitrary interpretations. The consulting office 'Pro Familia' in Bremen, for example, considers as social emergency everything detrimental to the woman's needs and life expectations, everything threatening the woman's future or the emotionally stable education of her children.

Polls by the Allensbach Institute for Opinion Reseach taken in 1982 and 1983 discovered a shift against the liberalisation of abortion compared with earlier polls. In April 1973, 38 per cent supported the unrestricted right of a woman to have an abortion in the first three months of pregnancy, but only 28 per cent held this view in July 1983. Nevertheless, in the latter poll, 55 per cent favoured abortion for certain specified reasons as against 46 per cent in 1973. In 1979, 52 per cent disagreed with Cardinal Hoeffner who had called abortion in the Federal Republic mass murder and only 27 per cent agreed; in 1984, the ratio of opponents had declined to 42 per cent and that of supporters had risen to 35 per cent. Abortion in the case of pregnancy resulting from rape was approved by 74 per cent (men 76 per cent, women 72 per cent) and rejected by 12 per cent (men 9 per cent, women 14 per cent). Abortion in case of congenital disease was endorsed by 84 per cent (men 81 per cent, women 86 per cent) and condemned by 5 per cent (men 6 per cent, women 4 per cent). But less than half of the respondents were in favour of the so-called social indication (in case of a woman living on welfare: for abortion 39 per cent — men 42 per cent, women 36 per cent; against abortion 41 per cent — men 36 per cent, women 45 per cent; in case of a woman with two children: for abortion 19 per cent — men 21 per cent, women 17 per cent; against 56 per cent — men 52 per cent, women 60 per cent). While 48 per cent expressed horror at the killing of young seals in Canada (men 46 per cent, women 49 per cent — 57 per cent of the women between the ages of 16 and 29), only 34 per cent felt disgusted if a healthy woman had an abortion (men 31 per cent, women 37 per cent — 25 per cent of the women between 16 and 29, 53 per cent of the women aged 60 years and older).

In a survey conducted in November 1985, the Allensbach Institute found little change from the results of July 1983. Overall, 54 per cent of the pollees were in favour of allowing abortion in specified cases (men 53 per cent, women 55 per cent) and 29 per cent would approve unrestricted abortions in the first three months of pregnancy (men 31 per cent, women 28 per cent) while 11 per cent wanted restoration of the absolute ban on abortions (men 9 per cent, women 12 per cent; 6 per cent were undecided). By denomination, unrestricted freedom for abortion in the first three months of pregnancy was the choice of 31 per cent of the Protestants, 24 per cent of the Catholics and 47 per cent of those not belonging to these two denominations; 57 per cent of the Protestants, 54 per cent of the Catholics and 39 per cent of others agreed with the regulation permitting abortion in specified cases; and 7 per cent of the Protestants, 16 per cent of the Catholics and 7 per cent of others were against the legalisation of abortion.

The differences in religious and moral persuasions also appeared in the difference of opinions by political preferences. Freedom of abortion in the first three months of pregnancy was advocated by 19 per cent of those who voted for the Christian Democratic Union (CDU) or the Christian Social Union (CSU), 37 per cent of the supporters of the Social Democratic Party (SDP), 34 per cent of the adherents of the Free Democratic Party (FDP) and 61 per cent of the 'Greens.' For abortion limited to specific cases were 56 per cent of CDU/CSU voters, 54 per cent of SDP, 60 per cent of FDP and 36 per cent of the 'Greens'; total prohibition was affirmed by 20 per cent of CDU/CSU, 5 per cent of SDP, 4 per cent of FDP and 1 per cent of the 'Greens.'

The 1985 survey included the question whether the abuse of the social indication should be tolerated or stopped. Overall, 24 per cent of the pollees thought that it could not be helped (men 28 per cent, women 21 per cent), 66 per cent said that something should be done about it (men 61 per cent, women 71 per cent) and 10 per cent were undecided (men 11 per cent, women 8 per cent). The percentage of those who wanted the abuse corrected rose with age (16-29 years: 58 per cent, 30-44 years: 65 per cent, 45-59 years: 68 per cent, 60 years and older: 76 per cent). This opinion found greater support from conservative voters (CDU/CSU: 75 per cent, SDP: 63 per cent, FDP: 64 per cent, 'Greens': 54 per cent) and by church members (Protestants 64 per cent, Catholics 71 per cent, others 55 per cent). The view that no reform was called for found its most numerous supporters among the 'Greens' and those not belonging to one of the established churches (both groups 34 per cent).

In order to accommodate religious and ethical objections against abortions, the law provides that nobody is obliged to cooperate in such operations. This right of refusal creates serious difficulties for women seeking abortions because in many locations, the only hospital is managed by a religious organisation and in public hospitals, doctors and other personnel can decline cooperation in abortions. According to Professor Hans Brox, justice at the Constitutional Court, the right to refusal implies: 1. An employment contract does not oblige an employee to cooperate in a legally permissible abortion. To this extent, the employee is entitled to refuse work. No reason is required for the refusal to cooperate in abortions. 2. There is no legal claim against doctors, hospital employees, and the director or management of a hospital to perform a legally permissible abortion. 3. The employees of a hospital are not allowed to cooperate in abortions if the management of the hospital has decided not to perform abortions. 4. Communes are not allowed to deny subsidies to recognised consultation centres because this would contribute to the prevention of abortions.

France

In France, the Law Simone Veil enacted in 1975 allows the termination of pregnancy in hospitals and clinics up to ten weeks after fertilisation. The damage to the health of women from widespread illegal abortions was one of the reasons for the very liberal provisions of the law.

Spain

Spain legalised the sale of contraceptives in 1978 but abortions remained prohibited. Nevertheless, about 300,000 women had abortions each year, and since most were performed in back-alley clinics, about 3,000 women died yearly from illegal operations. Those who could afford it went to London on special abortion charter flights each weekend (in 1983, 23,000 women, cost of the package deal, 60,000 pesetas, over $300). Some years ago, in a trial in Bilboa on charges of receiving or abetting abortion, the accused were either acquitted or given only token sentences. The judge justified his lenient verdicts by citing the extreme poverty of the defendants and pointed out that existing legislation — written in the late 1930s — was in open conflict with the privacy guaranteed in Spain's 1976 'democratic' constitution. But in 1983, a Barcelona court sentenced a medical assistant, his aid, six women who underwent abortions and four men who accompanied their wives or girl-friends to prison terms. In the same year, the Socialist government of Prime Minister Felipe Gonzalez sponsored a law amending the penal code to legalise abortions in the first three months of pregnancy in cases of rape or incest, malformation of the foetus or danger to the mother's life. After an unsuccessful challenge to the constitutionality of the law, it was passed second time round by the Spanish parliament in June 1985.

Portugal

In January 1984, the Portuguese parliament adopted a bill which waived prosecution of abortion in cases of foetal deformity, pregnancy resulting from rape and when the mother's life is in danger. A Communist proposal to allow abortion for socio-economic reasons was defeated.

Italy

Under a law passed in 1978, abortion is free on demand in Italy for a woman of 18 or over during the first three months of pregnancy but a waiting period of seven days is required except in emergency cases. In 1980, there were 800,000 abortions, approximately the same number of live births, but the actual number of abortions probably was much higher. A referendum in 1981 rejected a ban on abortions except in cases of extreme danger to a woman's health by a 68.0 per cent majority but a proposal to remove restrictions and allow abortions for women under 18 without parental consent was turned down by 88.5 per cent of the votes.

Switzerland

In Switzerland, a referendum in 1977 rejected a proposal to lift all restrictions on abortions within 12 weeks of pregnancy, but in a referendum in June 1985, Swiss voters turned down a proposed constitutional amendment that would have required the federal authorities to enact legislation for the protection of the 'right to life,' banning all abortions except those necessary for saving a mother's life and prohibiting 'abortive' contraceptives. The amendment, defeated in 19 cantons and endorsed in seven, intended to clamp down on what abortion opponents considered too liberal abortion practices in some cantons.

Austria

In Austria, the General Civil Code of 1811 still in force provides in Art. 11 that from the time of conception, unborn children are entitled to the protection of the law but a law passed in 1975 makes abortion during the first three months of pregnancy unpunishable. A consultation with a doctor is required but the doctor who performs the abortion can conduct the consultation.

Holland, Belgium

In Holland, the doctor and the pregnant woman must agree that the abortion is justified by social or health reasons, and a period of five days must intervene between consultation and operation. This interval was made obligatory in 1980 in order to stop the inflow from abroad, particularly from Belgium. In Belgium, a law dating from 1867 makes it a criminal offence both to carry out a deliberate termination of pregnancy and to obtain one. Actually, however, abortions were rarely prosecuted. There exist special abortion clinics and abortions are estimated at between 16,000 and 20,000 a year, half in Belgium and half abroad. (Abortions can also be prosecuted if they are performed abroad.) In 1977, the government arranged with the public prosecutor not to enforce the ban on abortions for two years because the government was working on an amendment to the law. But when the government failed to amend the law, the public prosecutor for Brussels gave the green light to prosecute in order to force the government into action. A number of doctors and other persons involved in abortions were brought to trial and most were given suspended prison terms of two months. Among the 21 doctors was the head of the Gynaecology Department of the Brussels University Hospital. He received a suspended sentence of 18 months in jail. Among the five cases of abortion for which he was tried was that of a 14-year-old girl, who was in the 21st week of pregnancy. The court stressed that abortion laws had been changed in most neighbouring countries and that a revision of the law was overdue in Belgium.

A mass trial involving a total of 30 defendants, including 14 doctors, 16 medical workers and 30 women who had abortions and/or their partners opened in November 1986 in Ghent but was postponed to February 1987 because of legal technicalities. A bill before parliament would allow abortions during the first 15 weeks of pregnancy but there seems to be little chance for its adoption.

Norway, Denmark

In Norway, abortion is allowed without restrictions in the first two months of pregnancy but the medical personnel in hospitals has the right to refuse cooperation in abortion cases. In Denmark, abortion is permitted in the first 12 weeks of pregnancy for medical and social reasons; for later abortions, the consent of public agencies supervising abortions must be obtained.

Greece

In Greece, a law passed in 1984 legalised abortions in the first three months of pregnancy. Married women, however, have to obtain their husband's consent. The law replaced a 1978 law allowing abortion in cases of rape, incest, abnormality in the foetus, or if the birth would endanger the life of the mother. The law left the medical profession considerable freedom and maternity clinics, gynaecologists and family doctors terminated unwanted pregnancies without fear of prosecution. Actually, abortion became the most popular form of birth control, mainly because other methods of contraception were viewed with suspicion and birth control pills and other contraceptives remained illegal. Doctors estimated that two abortions were performed for every birth in Greece so that the minister of justice could say: 'We are simply legalising a public reality.' Both public and private health insurance systems cover the costs of abortion.

Turkey

Turkey's military rulers submitted to the consultative assembly a draft bill which would make abortion legal and accessible up to the 12th week of pregnancy. Married women would have to obtain the consent of their husbands and minors would need parental approval. Untrained practitioners performing abortions would be punished with prison sentences of up to seven years; in case of death or bodily injury to the patient, a minimum sentence of 15 years would be imposed. The draft also permitted sterilisation of any adult upon demand.

Legislation approving abortion has been proposed before but has not been enacted. Illegal abortions are said to amount to 300,000 a year, resulting in 10,000 to 15,000 deaths. The scarcity of doctors in rural areas will make it difficult to get abortions even if they are legalised. The government is promoting family planning and family planning units visiting rural areas recommend IUDs.

Israel

In Israel, abortions are permitted in case of danger to the mother's physical or mental health, pregnancy from rape or incest, in case birth defects seem likely and for unwed mothers. Final approval from a committee of two doctors and a social worker is required.

Kuwait

In a step that constituted a basic reinterpretation of the Islamic *Sharia* (law based on the *Qur'an*), the Kuwaiti parliament voted in January 1982 to permit abortions if the continuation of pregnancy would result in 'gross physical harm' to the mother or if the foetus is determined to suffer from brain damage 'beyond the hope of any treatment' and the parents consent to the abortion.

India, Singapore, South Korea, Taiwan

Among other reasons, abortion is allowed in India in case contraception fails. Although the abortion law was liberalised in 1972, illegal abortions are estimated at 4-6 million a year, and 15-25 per cent of the maternal deaths in Indian hospitals result from illegal abortions. In Thailand, abortions were restricted to cases of rape or if the pregnancy was hazardous to the mother's health but the law has been revised to include economic difficulties and babies that are susceptible to physical or mental problems. In Singapore, abortion had to be approved by an official pregnancy board but this requirement was lifted in 1974. In South Korea, a Maternity and Child Law passed in 1973 allows abortion in cases of risk to maternal health, rape, incest and possible foetal deformity. A ten-year debate on the legalisation of abortion came to an end in Taiwan with the adoption of a law that, aside from health reasons, permits abortion if the child would have undesirable effects on family life which, practically, legalised abortions on demand.

The State's Right and Duty

As this survey shows, there are great differences in what is considered permissible or unlawful, and the existing laws offer no clue to what the law should be. Apart from the fact that the morality of abortion is also a very controversial subject, the task of the state, as remarked above, is not to legislate morality but to enforce and protect the public order. The proper object of the state is not the good but the just, that is, what is conducive to and required by the common good. In this sense, not everything that is good is also just although nothing that is bad can be just. The right to life is a basic human right which man possesses because he is a human being and which, therefore, is a natural right. The state has the duty and the right to protect human life but in the traditional view, the state can take a man's life for protecting the common good (for example, as punishment) and can demand from its citizens to lay down their lives for the defense of the country. Both postulates have been attacked and even if they are affirmed, neither the right to inflict capital punishment nor the right to demand military service is absolute.

In the case of abortion, the question is complicated by the difficulty discussed above of deciding when human life starts. The belief that human life begins at the moment of conception is not unreasonable and in this sense, it can be made the basis of legislation. But it is a minority view and its foundation, the existence of a human soul and its creation at the moment of conception is hard to prove. Only a person is the subject of rights and duties, and the opinion that a foetus becomes a person at birth seems to be more reasonable. Therefore, although human life is a value that the state must protect, it is impossible to demand, as a general rule, that this protection must start at the moment of conception. In this sense, a law allowing abortion (or not punishing it) up to a certain point of time is not unjust. The demand for absolute protection of all human life disregards the theoretical as well as the practical difficulties of this position. Apart from the uncertainty of the beginning of human life, the problems of the possible danger to the life of the mother and of genetic defects cannot be solved merely by invoking the sacredness of human life. The pro-life party stresses that an embryo is more than an agglomeration of cells while the defenders of the decriminalisation of abortion contend that ethical problems cannot be solved by punishing controversial actions. Moral crusades make bad law, and if the moral principle is doubtful, the rationality of the law will also be doubtful.

Infanticide was very common in many countries and it is perhaps less the result of law enforcement and rather the greater availability of medical services that abortion and birth control have reduced infanticide. Nevertheless, illegal abortions still endanger the life of the mother and many women are crippled for life. Such situations suggest the question whether the exemption of abortion up to a certain point of time from punishment would not be the lesser evil.

Moreover, as in many other cases, prohibition alone does not solve the problem. It would be necessary to take positive measures to help women contemplating abortion to carry their unwanted babies to term and have them adopted. There are private organisations engaged in this work but in order to make this choice a valid alternative, a network of agencies acting as intermediaries would be necessary. They would have to assure women beforehand that their babies would be accepted, help to pay delivery expenses, take temporary custody of the babies until adoption and assume responsibility for the babies who do not find foster parents. The worldwide organisation of such a scheme seems to be an impossible dream.

Christian View on Abortion

Although Christianity stresses the eternal destiny of man, it also inculcates the value and dignity of human life. Some of the earliest Christian writings explicitly condemned abortion, as, for example, in the second century, the *Didache*, the so-called Epistle of Barnabas, Tertullian, Minucius Felix, Athenagoras and Clement of Alexandria. The Catholic Church has always maintained that abortion is a grievous sin against the Fifth Commandment. The new Code of Canon Law retained the automatic excommunication of those procuring an abortion (can. 1398) and also kept the designation of abortion as one of the crimes entailing irregularity, that is to say, blocking all cooperators from receiving or exercising holy orders (can. 1041, nr. 4; can. 1044, par. 1, nr. 3). Abortion, however, is also reprobated by many evangelical Protestants, orthodox Jews and Mormons. The Church has often reiterated her condemnation of abortion, and in an address in January 1983, Pope John Paul II lumped together genetic engineering, abortion and pollution as threats to the existence of mankind. In her opposition to abortion, the Church disapproves not only every form of direct cooperation but also every activity indirectly promoting abortion. In 1983, Archbishop Edmund Szorka of Detroit advised a nun, sister Agnes Mary Mansour, to resign her $58,300-a-year job as a departmental director with the Michigan Social Services Department because the agency provided funds for abortion under Medicaid. The 52-year-old sister who had been a member of the Sisters of Mercy for 30 years and held a degree in biochemistry was presented with the choice of quitting her job or leaving the congregation. She asked to be released of her vows. While she opposed abortion, the sister said, she considered it unjust to deprive the poor of this option.

In the diocese of Mainz, church authorities appealed publicly to the director of an abortion clinic to repent and excommunicated him when he continued his practice.

Opposition to the Church's prohibition of abortion is less widespread than the dissent from the ban on birth control but there is considerable disagreement. A British survey of more than 1,000 people of all religious denominations conducted in 1982 found Catholics slightly more restrictive than other religious groups but more than 80 per cent of Catholics favoured abortion to protect a woman's health and 69 per cent supported a woman's right to choose abortion in consultation with her doctor.

In the American 1984 presidential election, the Catholic hierarchy severely criticised Geraldine Ferraro for her position on abortion. She was personally against abortion, the democratic vice-presidential candidate said, but she opposed anti-abortion legislation and supported freedom of choice. The Right Reverend James Timlin, Catholic bishop of Scranton, Pennsylvania, likened Mrs Ferraro's view to saying, 'I'm personally opposed to slavery, but I don't care if the people down the street want to own slaves.' There are two points where the simile is wrong. First, Mrs Ferraro didn't say that she didn't care if other people supported abortion but that she didn't want to force her belief on everybody else. As Senator Edward Kennedy declared: 'People of faith should not evoke the power of the state to decide what everyone can believe or think or read or do.'

Moral Evaluation of Abortion

The second disparity is that, in the western world, slavery is now generally regarded as incompatible with human dignity while there is no unanimity on the morality of abortion. The bishop unwittingly touched on the crux of the controversy when he remarked that Ferraro should 'do all that she can ... to stop the slaughter of innocent human beings.' Whether foetuses are human beings is just one of the unsettled issues which underly the polemics.

In view of the condemnation of abortion, the opposition of the Church to birth control appears even more unreasonable than it is in itself (because it is based on a biased interpretation of the sex act). Is birth control not more humane and less repulsive than abortion?

The Mother's Position

The point of view that unborn life is morally just as valuable as the life of an adult is unconvincing. It seems to me that in the case of conflict of values, unborn life may be regarded as the lesser value. This is the case if the choice is between saving the life of the mother and protecting a possibly viable foetus. If the foetus is not viable, it would perish anyhow with the death of the mother.

It would be presumptious to lay down any rule on abortion of genetically-defective foetuses (abortion does not include infanticide by the denial of care to newborn defective infants). More than in any other context, it is necessary to stress that life is no absolute value. The question is what can be 'reasonably demanded' (the *zumutbar* of German law) of the mother or the family. In many cases, the child will be not only physically but also mentally defective and will never be able to live what is usually called a 'normal' human life. Sometimes, the issue is obscured by arguing from handicapped children who have been born and raised and become capable of living a satisfactory human life. The trouble is that nobody can predict the outcome when a genetically-defective child is born. The human and moral values occasioned by the care for handicapped children do not compensate for the human suffering, the physical and spiritual pain of the child and its parents, particularly its mother, if the child's handicaps cannot be overcome. In the Christian view of suffering, its supernatural meaning, its value as a sacrifice, the merit of trusting in God's providence and submitting to God's will can motivate a person with strong religious convictions to endure the enormous hardships imposed on the family by the birth of a genetically-defective child, but this is no reason to create opportunities for such sacrifices. The Christian faith provides the motivation for bearing the suffering but no solution of the problem. The spiritual value seen by Christians in suffering is no reason to increase human pain or not to prevent it. The alternatives in the genetic indication are not the preservation of human life and its destruction but the saving of potential human life with the possibility (or probability) of untold suffering and early death and the destruction of potential human life.

The social indication involves more difficult problems. In many cases, the question is one of material hardships or the unwillingness of having a child, but many women have abortions under the pressure of circumstances from which they see no escape: husband or lover refuses to share the responsibility for the child, the family threatens to break off all relations if the child is born, an unwed mother would find it impossible to go on working, a young woman would have to discontinue her professional training. For unwed women or married women having an affair, abortion seems an easy way out to avoid not just embarrassment but a derailment of their entire lives. The sacredness of human life becomes a very abstract value when people face very real difficulties. Moral exhortations only aggravate the mental and emotional perplexities of the women. There is little sense of arguing what people should have done or should not have done. A foetus is not a human person, and a woman cannot possibly feel the same obligation towards a foetus that she would feel towards a child. (I use the word 'feel' on purpose because it is not a theoretical but an emotional issue.) Many moralists point out that, if once an exception is made, the principle will be eroded and that, therefore, unborn life should be protected absolutely and abortion prohibited under all circumstances. This reasoning supposes that unborn life is entitled to such an absolute protection which is unproven and, I think, unprovable. This does not mean that unborn life should not be protected or that abortion does not involve moral problems. But it is not only a problem of the value of unborn life in itself but also of the value that the mother or the parents attach to the expected child. It is unrealistic to consider the good of the child without taking into account the conditions under which it will be born. An unwanted child can grow up to become a good human being but there is no guarantee of a happy ending in every case and instead there may be human tragedy. In short, it is impossible to lay down a definite rule for deciding what will be in the best interest of the child. There are enough cases in which one can say, 'It is better for the child not to be born than to be born under these circumstances.' The solution of the problems involved in the social indication is not prohibition of abortion and punishment but more effective birth control and better information about the organisations to which women can go for help and advice.

The intricacy of the problem appeared in an opinion poll conducted by the magazine *Life* in November 1981. A majority of the women polled (56 per cent) considered abortion morally wrong but two-thirds were of the opinion that a woman who wanted an abortion should have the legal right to terminate pregnancy. A large minority, 39 per cent, thought that abortion was not a moral problem. The same ambivalence was notable in a poll taken in August 1982 by Associated Press — NBC News. Of 1,594 adults, 49 per cent believed that abortion was wrong, 44 per cent approved of abortion and 7 per cent were not sure. Of those who thought that abortion was not wrong, 88 per cent supported its legalisation; of those who considered abortion wrong, 53 per cent were for and 40 per cent against legalisation. Altogether, 62 per cent said that abortion should be legal, 31 per cent wanted it prohibited and 7 per cent were not sure. 77 per cent agreed with the view that the decision to have an abortion should be left to the woman and her doctor, 20 per cent disagreed with this view and 3 per cent were uncertain.

In Malaysia, a poll of young people found that 52 per cent considered abortion always bad but 51 per cent thought that abortion was acceptable as a method of birth control.

It seems to me that abortion is morally right if pregnancy results from rape. The right of the woman not to bear a child against her will is higher than the value of unborn life. The case of incest is less clear. If incest is carried out by force or threat or abuse of authority, it should be treated the same as rape; otherwise, the same considerations apply as in the case of the social indication.

Treatment of Embryos

The question of experimentation on human embryos is first of all a question of decency. To treat human embryos in the same way as animals are treated reveals a basic lack of reverence for human life. Of course, this sounds rather ridiculous given the way aborted foetuses are actually discarded but there should be more decent methods of disposing of the remains of human foetuses than burning them in city incinerators together with trash and the cadavers of cats and dogs. The 500 human foetuses recently found in Los Angeles preserved in formaldehyde in plastic bags packed in cardboard boxes and stored in a large metal container were a gruesome reminder that society still has a long way to go to solve the problems linked to the operation of 'abortion factories' all over the world.

Two French authors, Claude Jacquinot and Jacques Delaye, have investigated the trade in human embryos. Their account gives frightening examples of what is done in the name of scientific progress and under the cover of professional secrecy. An American doctor declared that abortions served two purposes. In the case of viable foetuses, the mother is told that the baby had died but it is actually sold for adoption. If foetuses are not viable, they are used for all kinds of experiments. Among the cases cited by the authors is the research of a doctor who decapitated 12- to 21-week-old foetuses and connected their heads with machines to study certain metabolic processes. Foetuses have been used to obtain human organs, such as the pancreas, for medical research. For such use, the foetus must be intact which can only be assured if the pregnant mother agrees to a Caesarian section. The French medical association considers a Caesarian section for the sole purpose of obtaining an intact foetus as improper and also rejects abortions for procuring organs.

Tissue from human foetuses is used as material for the production of cosmetics, drugs and vaccines. The Salk vaccine against poliomyelitis and the vaccine against rabies required such tissue, and some kinds of interferon are produced from embryonic connective tissue. Embryos have also been used for testing bacteriological weapons. For at least six years, the authors report, South Korea supplied over 4,000 foetuses a year at a unit price of $25 for such research. An Italian doctor interested in developing an artificial placenta cultivated 18- to 24-week-old foetuses removed by Caesarian section and grew some of these foetuses to a length of 30 cm. He had to terminate some of his experiments because the foetuses were reaching maturity.

The whole question concerning the disposal of aborted foetuses, experiments on such foetuses, the treatment of test-tube embryos and the trade in human foetuses is without legal regulation and the self-policing of the medical profession and research institutions leaves large loopholes.

Undoubtedly, science and practical medicine can achieve progress through experiments on embryos but the inescapable dilemma characteristic of many abortion situations is not there. It is not a choice affecting directly one or more human beings but a question of obtaining results by a method which promises quicker success. For those believing in a human soul created at the moment of fertilisation, experiments on embryos are just as much anathema as artificial insemination and test-tube babies.

Similar considerations apply to the manipulation of sex. It certainly constitutes interference with the natural process of reproduction but biological conditions as such do not represent moral norms. Nevertheless, even aside from the question of genetic damage, there is no reason to recommend its general application.

Extent of Abortion

A study published by the Allan Guttmacher Institute in 1986 estimated the number of legal abortions at 30 million to 40 million a year. No reliable data are available on illegal abortions and estimates range from 10 million to 25 million. The world's rate for legal and illegal abortions is between 37 and 55 abortions per 100,000 women in the 15 to 44 age group. Abortions are outlawed or permitted only to save a mother's life in countries that comprise about 24 per cent of the world's 4.9 billion people. Most Muslim countries in Asia, two-thirds of the Latin-American countries, about half of the countries in Africa and three European countries (Belgium, Ireland and Malta) fall into this category. A few of these countries allow abortion also for foetal defects or for pregnancies resulting from rape.

Abortion based on broader grounds, such as danger to the mother's health, are permitted in countries accounting for 13 per cent of the world's population. Social factors may provide grounds for abortion in countries with 24 per cent of the world's population. India, Japan, the United Kingdom and West Germany belong to this category. Abortion on request, generally in the first trimester of pregnancy, is available in countries comprising 34 per cent of the world's population. They include Austria, Cuba, Denmark, France, Italy, Sweden, the Soviet Union and the United States.

Of legal abortions, a high percentage involves married women while a large number of illegal abortions are carried out on very young women, unmarried women, previous abortees and wives pregnant at marriage. About 85,000 women die each year from abortion complications.

Abortions are as common in some countries in which they are illegal as in countries in which they are allowed. This is particularly the case in South-East Asia. The Soviet Union has the highest abortion rate, followed by Romania, Cuba, the United States, Japan, Sweden, Italy, Great Britain, Canada and West Germany. In the USSR, abortions are more numerous than births; the average woman has six abortions during the course of her life. One of the reasons for the high abortion rate in the Soviet Union is the high percentage of women in the labour force. Women do not want to have children and have recourse to abortion rather than to contraceptives.

Very alarming has been the increase in abortions performed on young girls. As mentioned above, girls of 11 and 12 years of age have had abortions, and among the girls seeking abortions were some who already had children. A girl of 17 who had an abortion already had four children, a girl of 16 had two and several girls of 14 had one child.

In Japan, officially notified abortions amounted to 567,539 in 1983. Since births numbered 1,508,687, the ratio of abortions to births came to 37.6 to 100. In 1985, abortions performed on teenagers numbered 28,038. This figure, however, refers only to officially notified cases and the actual number may be twice as high. Among teenagers, high school and university students are numerous, but they also include office employees. Some of the teenagers have had three or four abortions. In many cases, failure of birth control led to pregnancy. Teenage abortions constitute an important source of income for some clinics since these abortions are usually not reported and the income is not entered on the tax returns. The money for student abortions is often raised by their classmates through collections (called *kampa* — campaign) and the young man responsible for the pregnancy sometimes takes on part-time work (*'bait'* — *Arbeit*) to help pay for the operation.

Among the reasons for the teenage pregnancies is first the early maturity of girls who have their first menstruation at the age of 12; before the war, the average used to be 14.7 years. Other reasons are the changes in the views of sexuality, the failure of sex education to create proper attitudes towards sex and the dissociation of sex from procreation.

In many instances, abortions create feelings of guilt and psychologically-induced illnesses. Sometimes, they disturb sex relations. Abortion doubles the risk of later miscarriages and triples the danger of premature births. Legal abortions in the first 12 weeks of pregnancy are nearly nine times safer than carrying the pregnancy to term but the death rate of mothers is twice as high if the abortion is performed in the 16th week or later. The mortality rate is the lowest for legal abortions performed in the first eight weeks of pregnancy with 0.4 deaths per 100,000 pregnancies; it is 3.9 for all legal abortions and 14.8 for childbirths. Another estimate put the mortality rate in criminal abortions at 35 to 94 per 100,000 pregnancies, the death rate for legal but non-medical abortions performed in the first three months at 1.2 and for all legal abortions at 4.0 per 100,000 pregnancies.

In the United States, 1.55 million abortions were performed in 1980. This was more than double the number of legal abortions carried out in 1973, the first year of legalised abortions. The Alan Guttmacher Institute which reported these figures, expressed the opinion that a shift from the pill and intra-uterine devices to abortions was a significant factor in the increase. Adverse effects linked to birth-control methods, strokes caused by the pill in susceptible women and perforation of the uterus by IUDs played a rôle in this shift.

4

Sexual Deviations

Sexual Anomalies

DEVIATION means the departure from a standard or norm. Sexual deviation, therefore, refers to sexual behaviour not in accord with what is considered the normal pattern of sexual conduct. Such abnormal conduct has sometimes been called sexual perversion but nowadays this term is avoided because it conveys disapproval or censure. The expression sexual anomalies covers a wide range of phenomena and includes, in addition to behaviour usually classified as deviation, sexual hyperaesthesia (erotomania), sexual anaethesia (frigidity), and so on. Intersexuality which is listed among sexual deviations is not, in the first place, a problem of behaviour but of morphology. As indicated by the terms hermaphroditism and gynandromorphism, an individual is called intersexual if he or she exhibits morphological characteristics of both sexes. If psychologically conditioned, excessive or exaggerated sexual lust and activity are termed satyriasis in males and nymphomania in females. If biological factors (for example, brain lesions, hormonal imbalances) cause intense sexual desires and frequent spontaneous erections of penis or clitoris, the condition is called hypersexuality. Deviant behaviour in the sense of conduct occurs in sexual acts performed by the individual alone (transvestism, fetishism, exhibitionism and voyeurism), in the objects of the sexual acts (incest, paedophilia, bestiality and necrophilia), and in the manner in which the sex act is performed (rape, sadism, masochism). Homosexuality is usually included in sexual deviations but homosexuals claim that it constitutes an alternative and legitimate form of sexual behaviour.

Because in today's world, there are no universally accepted standards of 'normal,' 'good' or 'right,' some authors are content to regard as normal whatever is legally permissible and as perverse what is legally forbidden. This means, of course, that perversity differs from country to country and from state to state and that there are no universally valid norms of sexual normality. But the inhumanness of certain forms of conduct are beyond doubt. The psychic deviant who does not indulge in sadistic practices may be unaware of the sexual component of his or her maltreatment of children, pupils, maids or subordinates nor recognise the abuse of power in order to humiliate, mortify, harass or intimidate as a sexual surrogate. There is no uncertainty about the anomaly of sexual sadism or the perversity of acts in which violence and the infliction of pain take the place of coitus in the procurement of sexual lust. The perversity of the conduct is unquestionable whether the perversion takes the form of slitting the victim's dress or slitting her throat.

Outside the sphere of sex, congenital malformations, diseases and dysfunctions do not *per se* involve psychological disturbances although they may cause depression and other mental and particularly emotional distress. But psychic problems are common in sexual deviations and some of the sexual deviations are characterised by gender identity problems which have received wide publicity on account of the 'gender reassignment operations,' commonly referred to as sex change, performed on transsexuals.

Transsexualism

Transsexualism is a condition in which males feel they are females trapped in a male body, and females feel they are males trapped in a female body. Biologically, these individuals are normal and have no hormonal or congenital deformities but their sexual orientation is at variance with their sexual constitution. Psychologically, they identify with the opposite sex and experience an overwhelming desire to be members of the other sex. A transsexual does not simply imitate members of the opposite sex in clothing or behaviour but the individual's interest is centred on the life-style of the other sex. Different from transvestites, transsexuals do not gain sexual excitement from cross-dressing because it is in accord with their sex consciousness.

The sex reassignment procedure can only change the visible sex organs and secondary sex characteristics and usually combines hormonal treatment with surgery. The male is given estrogen to develop female secondary sex characteristics, especially breasts. In addition to surgical thinning of the larynx, genital surgery attempts to make that area look and function somewhat like that of the 'assigned sex' through the removal of the testes, amputation of the penis, and the creation of an artificial vagina from retained penile skin or intestinal grafts and scrotal tissue. Female transsexuals use testosterone to produce facial and body hair, lower the voice and enlarge the clitoris. Breasts, ovaries, tubes and the uterus are removed and the vagina is closed. Only rarely is skin grafting used to create a non-functioning phallus. Transsexuals have experienced difficulties when they tried to return to their old jobs after the sex change.

Intersexualism

Different from transsexuals, intersexuals show congenital anomalies responsible for gender disorientation. An intersexual individual may have external or internal features of both sexes, the external genitals of one sex and the gonads (testes or ovaries) of the other. In a true hermaphrodite, both ovarian and testicular tissues are present on either one or both sides but the arrangement of other genital structures is extremely variable. (In Greek mythology, Hermaphroditus was the son of Hermes and Aphrodite. He spurned the nymph Salmakis who had fallen in love with him. When he was bathing, she clung to him and asked the gods to be indissolubly joined with him. The two became a single bisexual being.) In pseudo-hermaphrodites, the sex organs appear not to correspond to the individual's gonads. In female infants, the production of adrenal hydrocortisone may be disturbed by an inherited recessive defect already present before birth which results in overproduction of the male sex hormone. The clitoris, therefore, enlarges and at birth may resemble a penis with hypospadias (in which the urethra opens on the underside of the penis). The vagina which is not visible seems connected with the urethra and the labial folds look like the scrotum. Male pseudo-hermaphrodites include individuals with hypospadias and undescended testes, persons with a clitoris and vagina ending in a mass connected to testes and others with an imperfect uterus, a single Fallopian tube and no sex gland on that side.

Operations on intersexuals, therefore, do not intend a sex change but attempt to correct the congenital malformations which cause the sexual uncertainties.

Related to intersexuality are Turner's syndrome and Klinefelter's syndrome. Turner's syndrome is a form of monosomy. Usually, only one female chromosome (X-chromosome) is present although more complex forms can occur. The external genitalia are feminine but remain infantile also after puberty. The ovaries are rudimentary and do not contain eggs. Body growth is impaired, the neck shows a distinctive webbing and there is a characteristic deformation of the face. In Klinefelter's syndrome, the number of female chromosomes is higher, usually in the XXY pattern, but other combinations such as XXXY, XXXXY or XXYY, although very rare, also occur. The genitals are normal and masculine before puberty. Later, development is usually retarded; the testes are without sperm. By the 20th year, the breasts often enlarge and mental retardation increases.

There are numerous cases in which children brought up as girls were discovered to be boys (by a sex chromosome study). They were turned completely into boys by operations and were able to father children.

Sex Change Operations

In 1979, Johns Hopkins Hospital stopped performing sex change operations because research failed to show that the surgery improved the lives of transsexuals. Male to female patients are generally more satisfied than individuals who have undergone female to male operations. The medical profession has always emphasised that the effects of the gender reassignment operations are psychological rather than biological. The hormone balance existing at birth cannot be changed but the patient who loathes his or her own sex can obtain an appearance more in harmony with his (her) wishes.

One of the difficulties connected with sex change operations is the legal status of the individual. In Japan, such operations are said to be forbidden under the provisions of the Civil Code, the Medical Practice Act and the Eugenic Law. Actually, there are no provisions expressly covering this subject. If the required documentation is submitted, a family court can authorise changes in the family register. A man who had worked as a male prostitute and had become a transvestite employed as a 'hostess' in various night clubs went to the United States in 1974 for a sex change operation at the Stanford Medical Centre. The Centre issued a certificate to the effect that this individual's gender should be considered as being female and that she should be accorded a change of all legal documents to that effect. The family court ordered a medical examination and based on the medical report, the court sanctioned the change to female in the family register.

In 1982, the Italian parliament passed a law permitting a change of sex in a person's civil status. In the United States, a New Jersey court accepted a medical affidavit stating that a neuroendocrinal condition existing from birth had been responsible for a gender rôle disorientation and that the sex of the individual was female. The court, thereupon, declared the person physically and legally a female. There have been other cases in which people who underwent sex change operations officially changed their names.

Unnatural Vice

The grey zones of sex imply difficult moral problems. Traditional Christian morality generally condemns deviant sexual conduct as 'unnatural' vices. As noted in Chapter 1, Catholic moral theology distinguishes between sins 'in accordance with nature' (such as fornication or adultery) and sins 'against nature' (masturbation, sodomy, bestiality). The censure of unnatural vice also applies to sadism and masochism in as much as sexual satisfaction is not derived from 'regular' intercourse but from circumstances extraneous to the sex act proper. Fetishism, transvestism, exhibitionism, voyeurism and necrophilia also belong to the category of unnatural vices. The qualification is doubtful for rape which can be considered a deviant form of sexual behaviour if the man achieves excitement only in the awareness that he is harming the victim who is resisting. Rape involves an injustice against the woman who is subjected to forcible sexual intercourse but the act as such is not unnatural. There are forms of sexual deviation which injure the victim but involve no sexual abuse. In Scotland, a former hospital worker was sent to jail because he had scalped a woman in her living room. 'I get sexual satisfaction from cutting and stroking women's hair,' the offender told the police. Small consolation to the victim who is permanently disfigured and must wear a wig.

The morality of sex change is rather complex. Operations merely correcting biological abnormalities pose no moral problems but the gender reassignment operation seems to offend against the obligation of self-preservation which includes the preservation of bodily integrity. Man cannot cut off a limb or organ without sufficient cause which usually means some kind of malady requiring amputation or removal. But it may be argued that mental health is no less important than bodily health. To cure the mental dichotomy of transsexuals, relieve their tensions, ensure their emotional balance and give them tranquility of mind may seem sufficient reason for the impairment of bodily integrity by a sex change operation if the purpose cannot be achieved by any other morally unobjectionable means. This latter condition is somewhat difficult to verify but it is said that psychotherapy has so far been unsuccessful. On the other hand, the effectiveness of gender reassignment operations is also doubtful.

Sadomasochism

In the United States, and particularly in California, the greater sexual openness or permissiveness has encouraged an increase in private and commercial deviant sex — above all homosexuality and sadomasochism. Bondage boutiques offer corsets, whips, shackles, handcuffs and other paraphernalia which are also available through mail-order services. Bondage parlours enable their customers to live out their violent sexual fantasies in dungeons elaborately equipped with mirrors, whipping posts, pillories and wooden crosses. In 1983 Los Angeles police estimated the number of prostitutes earning a living in the sadomasochistic trade at about 100, but men outnumber women in the bondage culture and sexual rôle reversal is common. Bondage activities usually lead to some form of sexual gratification but participants assert that bloodshed is uncommon and physical injury rare. Experts estimate that sadomasochism experiences are 90 per cent fantasy and 10 per cent physical and are much more sensual than sexual. There are sadomasochism organisations, and a number of sadomasochistic periodicals carry advertising of bondage parlours as well as of individuals looking for partners.

Recently, a California court sentenced a man to 104 years in prison for kidnapping a young hitch-hiker and holding her as his sex slave for seven years. The man's estranged wife told jurors that she had engaged in bondage practices with her former husband for years but found some of the acts painful and wanted to stop. She therefore agreed that he could take a sex slave. He abducted the young woman at knife-point in 1977 and held her captive until 1984. She was bound, hung from rafters, locked in wooden boxes, raped and trained to cater to her captor's wishes.

Psychologists disagree about the causes of sexual deviations in general and those of sadomasochism in particular. Dr Wardell Pomeroy of San Francisco who assisted Dr Alfred Kinsey in his sex research contended that everyone has some propensity for sadomasochism and that the occasional experience of pain connected with pleasure can expand into more ritualised behaviour. Sex researchers estimate that about 10 per cent of the population has sadomasochistic inclinations.

Transvestism

Transvestite behaviour can take on many forms. In the paederastic establishments of Tokyo's Yoshiwara, the boys had to wear the hair-style of unmarried girls. A Greek wedding custom required the bridegroom to wear women's clothes and the bride male attire. For transvestism as a sexual deviation, the excitement created by the wearing of clothing of the opposite sex is essential. Besides the complete outfits of regular transvestites, men often ask their lovers for some piece of clothing, preferably panties or something else with sexual connotations which they can wear. Here transvestism fuses with fetishism. Men involved in accidents and taken to a hospital are often found wearing women's underclothes. The usual purpose of men who steal women's underwear from clothes-lines is masturbation. Women dressing as men seem to experience little sexual titilation themselves although they may appear more sexy to men.

Some years ago, a US Senate sub-committee charged that the federal government, through a number of departments and agencies, administered behaviour modification projects without a review structure fully adequate to protect the constitutional rights of the subjects. Behaviour control technology tries to cure child molestors, homosexuals, drug addicts, alcoholics, shop-lifters, hyperactive children and other 'anti-social' persons through such techniques as psycho-surgery — a type of brain surgery called 'murder of the mind' by its critics.

5

Masturbation

MASTURBATION, the manipulation or stimulation of one's own or another's genitals to achieve orgasm may be the most common form of experiencing sexual pleasure. Even if not carried on to full orgasm, the pleasant sensation from fondling the genitals provides an instant uplift. To use the genitals, particularly the penis or clitoris, as playthings seems to have an almost irresistible fascination. Once young people have tasted this pleasure, they find it difficult to resist this urge, all the more so if it relieves tension. But masturbation is by no means limited to the young or unmarried. Depending on his mood, a man may perceive the sight of his penis as an invitation to caress it. Older men who can no longer achieve an erection at will readily indulge in the lustful delight of fondling their penis. Women find just as much gratification in self-stimulation as men.

There may be a narcissistic element in masturbation but, especially in young years, the gratification of the instinctive urge seems to be the prevalent if not the only motive for masturbation.

Medical Evaluation of Masturbation

The psychological and medical evaluation of masturbation has undergone a radical change. The old psychology considered masturbation mainly as a threat to will-power and self-control. A Chinese booklet entitled *Sex Knowledge* warns that masturbation is a bad habit which 'not only can easily tire the brain and stop one from getting a proper rest but can also easily result in nervous debility.' — 'It can also block other interests, adversely affect work and study and in the long term naturally affect one's development.' Masturbation was censured as self-abuse and habitual masturbation was thought to cause neurasthenia, lead to nervous prostration and even to a nervous breakdown. Blindness and mental illness up to insanity were listed as possible consequences.

Modern psychology denies that masturbation involves medical or psychiatric problems. It is considered a normal and appropriate form of sexual activity at any age or stage of development. Experience of pleasure with one's own body is acceptable whether a person is single or married, heterosexual or homosexual. The enjoyment of one's own body is a precursor to the enjoyment of love-making with a partner and an important aspect of the affirmation of sexuality as an integral part of the human being.

Feeling of Guilt

Although the experts maintain that masturbation does not do any physical or psychological harm, many people experience feelings of guilt, shame or at least uneasiness about sexual self-gratification. These feelings have been attributed to the childhood taboo proscribing the genital area as impure. Babies around six or seven months discover their genitals in much the same way that they discover their fingers or toes. Parents usually discourage children from touching those parts just as they teach them, at least in western society, to keep the private parts covered. Children, therefore, learn that touching the genitals is bad which implants the notion that the genitals are bad and that anything connected with them is also bad. When children become older, the repression of genital play may increase curiosity and preoccupation and give it added fascination.

The view that the feeling of impropriety or anxiety results from the belief that masturbation is bad may be illustrated by a story Shere Hite was told by a Japanese woman when she visited Japan. 'In Japanese,' the woman said, 'the word "masturbate" usually refers only to men. So until I was 15 years old, I didn't realise I was doing that awful thing I'd been told not to do. I just thought I'd found a great pleasure.'

Mutual masturbation has greatly increased among adolescents through petting. Although masturbation is called the solitary vice, some men as well as women like to masturbate with their partners. Men masturbating in front of the picture of a naked woman derive excitement from the imagination that the woman is looking at them. A favourite ploy of masturbators is to dial a number at random. If a female voice answers the phone, they say: 'I'm just at it,' if a man answers, the dialers remain silent and hang up.

Extent of Masturbation

In her book *The Hite Report. A Nationwide Study in Female Sexuality,* Shere Hite states that of 3,000 women in the United States covered by the survey, 70 per cent could not achieve orgasm by intercourse alone while 81 per cent of the women masturbated and easily achieved orgasm. The *More Report* relates similar findings for Japan. The second survey contained in this report which elicited 348 answers showed that 92 per cent of the respondents practised masturbation. To the question 'At what age did you start to masturbate?' 13.4 per cent answered that, as far as they could remember, they did so in infancy (before the age of 7), but adolescence was the time when most women took up the habit (26.6 per cent: 13 to 15, 13.4 per cent: 16 to 18). Girls begin masturbating earlier than boys. According to the *Hite Report,* three-quarters of the boys start to masturbate between the ages of 10 and 15, with one-half having their first masturbation in the years from 11 to 13. Some women first felt guilt or shame and almost all kept it secret but later modified their opinion and thought it natural to use their own bodies for procuring sexual pleasure. Some women quoted in the *More Report* relate that they considered masturbation bad in their young days but nevertheless did it because they liked the pleasure. They changed their minds and thought that masturbation was a good thing when they grew up and learned that 'everybody was doing it.' Obviously, the assertion that masturbation cannot be wrong because everybody is doing it constitutes a *non sequitur.* While most women achieve orgasm readily through the excitation of the clitoris, they are also aroused by stimulating the vulva or other parts of the genitals and fondling the breasts, particularly the nipples. In the United States, about 80 per cent of all college women masturbate and 82 per cent agreed with the statement that masturbation is acceptable if the objective is simply the attainment of sensory enjoyment.

Motives for Masturbation

While the immediate motive, incentive or occasion may vary, the general intention for resorting to masturbation is the procurement of sexual pleasure. Children may discover masturbation accidentally by the contact of their genitals with some object. A girl first experienced sexual pleasure when climbing a pole in a gymnastics class. Boys often learn it from other boys, but girls seldom speak about it to other girls. Adolescents practise masturbation before they engage in sex with a partner, and the lack or absence of a sex partner is frequently the reason for masturbating. The relief of tension is often mentioned as motivation, and sexual arousal by reading or erotic representations as well as depression or boredom may provide the occasion for self-gratification. As mentioned above, women may procure orgasm by masturbation if intercourse leaves them unsatisfied, and partners may practise mutual masturbation if they want to avoid intercourse or change their usual sex habits. The *Hite Report* suggests that masturbation gives a pleasure of its own. But while some value it as the most satisfying sexual experience, others find it empty and desolate. Over three-quarters of the men who have sex every day masturbate at least once a week, with 5 per cent masturbating daily. Many men, however, feel that it somehow is an injustice to their wives.

Moral Evaluation

The Church has consistently condemned masturbation as a grievous sin against chastity, and this position has inspired heroic efforts to achieve self-control and repression of the sex instinct but also caused immeasurable anxiety, despair and a warped attitude towards sex. To the priest in the confessional, the fight against the solitary sin against chastity creates the same sense of frustration and futility as the attempt to dissuade married people from birth control.

The reason for the condemnation of masturbation as wrong and sinful by the old morality was the dissociation of pleasure from the 'natural' purpose of sexual activity. (Catholic moralists allow the wife to procure orgasm by masturbation in connection with marital intercourse if she fails to achieve it by the act itself.)

Morality of Sexual Pleasure

Sexual activity is largely controlled by man's free decision (there are exceptions such as the spontaneous reaction to unsought external or internal stimulations or nocturnal emissions). In these decisions, man must observe the right order, his own personal dignity and that of others. This means that, as in the enjoyment of all other pleasures, he must observe moderation, not be dominated by but dominate his instincts. Following Aristotle's doctrine of virtues, the Scholastics considered temperance as the habit (dominant disposition) restraining the concupiscible appetite, that is, keeping the pursuit of sensual pleasures within the bounds of reason. The sensual pleasures to be controlled by temperance are the pleasures connected with the appetite for food and drink and venereal pleasure. Gluttony (excess in food), insobriety (excess in drink) and unchastity (excess in sexual pleasure) are vices opposed to temperance. The offence against temperance does not lie in the satisfaction of the instincts unrelated to their purpose but in immoderation, the disregard of a reasonable measure. In itself, to eat or drink even if it is not required for preserving one's life and to enjoy the pleasure connected with it is not immoral. But to get drunk to such an extent as to lose the use of reason is considered a grave sin. There is nothing wrong with enjoying the pleasure associated with eating but to induce vomiting so as to be able to continue eating is unprincipled. Catholic moralists maintain that to seek sexual pleasure unconnected with the natural purpose of sex, the procreation of life, is sinful. There can be no doubt of the objective linkage between sexual pleasure and the preservation of the species but, as explained in Chapter 1, the problem is whether the natural teleology involves a moral obligation, that is, whether it is morally wrong to seek sexual pleasure when the sexual activity does not serve the purpose of procreation.

In the case of drunkenness, the inordinateness of the behaviour does not consist in the pursuit of pleasure but in the over-indulgence in drink (without which the pleasure cannot be had) which is contrary to the right order. (Excess in food and drink involves no moral turpitude if it results from illness.) To engage in sexual activity and to gratify one's sexual lust is not immoral if it does not contravene other duties although the sexual act may be unrelated to reproduction. This may sound hedonistic but it isn't. Hedonism maintains that pleasure or happiness is man's highest good and ultimate end which is quite different from the assertion that man can enjoy sex as long as this enjoyment is not in conflict with the dignity of man and man's rational nature.

Roger Scruton distinguishes between a 'normal' and a 'perverted' form of masturbation. The former is guided by a fantasy of copulation, the latter uses images as a substitute for the real thing. The masturbator seeks sexual gratification without the trouble of the human encounter, his imaginings 'are not personal but corporeal, perhaps explicitly phallic' (*Sexual Desire,* p. 319). But Scruton seems to agree with Kant that masturbation is the archetype of all preversion, and that even in the 'normal' case it is obscene.

Ascetic Ideals

That something is not immoral does not mean that it is the most desirable or recommendable course of action. In his book *Marriage and the Sex Problem,* Friedrich Wilhelm Foerster (who was a Protestant) has a remarkable chapter on the indispensability of the ascetic ideal and the importance of celibacy as institutionalised in the Catholic orders and the clergy. Asceticism, he wrote, should be regarded not as an attempt to extirpate natural forces, but as practice in the art of self-discipline. Natural life does not flourish unless the spirit retains the upper hand, and asceticism serves as an encouraging example of the conquest of the spirit over the animal self. In the face of the immense suggestive power of wealth, of ambition and of every kind of sensuous temptation, humanity cannot dispense with the counteracting suggestion of a life which has made itself absolutely independent of all these things. More important than the question of external freedom is that of inner freedom and the central question is: 'How shall I become free from myself?'

Foerster regards ascetic ideals as a necessary counteracting factor for guarding the inner health of western civilisation against the increasing brutality of the aimless and meaningless struggle for life, the disintegration of will-power through the ever increasing multiplication of demands upon it, the disturbance of the nervous equilibrium and the deadening of spiritual power by the creation of artificial needs and the breathless pace of life.

The feeling of guilt often connected with masturbation may arise from the overwhelming passion involved in the experience. Once engaged in genital play, it is difficult to stop and all self-control is lost, which means that genital preoccupation is felt as a lack of will-power. Children who habitually masturbate may do so in public or with friends. But in children, masturbation may be a symptom of difficulties and a sign of distress and unsolved problems — which may also be the case in adults. The important thing, therefore, is to find out what is troubling the child and to understand the reason for his anxiety. Scolding without going to the root of the problem may only create greater misery. The situation is different for adolescents who need specific motivation for self-control without building up a guilt complex which is formed when masturbation is treated as something unconditionally bad and sinful.

6

Homosexuality

Definitions

HOMOSEXUALITY means sexual desire or activity directed towards a person or persons of one's own sex. The term homosexuality is used for both sexes but homosexual relations between women are often referred to as lesbianism. In legal texts, the word sodomy denotes unnatural, especially anal copulation by man with man, or, in the same unnatural manner, with woman or a beast. Strictly speaking, sodomy is the equivalent of paederasty, the sexual act as performed by a man on the person of another man or a boy by penetration of the anus, but paederasty usually implies that one of the males (generally the passive partner) is a minor. The term sodomy has sometimes been applied to other non-conventional sexual conduct, including hand-genital contacts with minors and mouth-genital contacts between persons of the opposite sex. Some courts have held that sodomy does not include oral sex which is properly called fellatio if the penis is inserted into the mouth of the partner but a greater number of jurisdictions has taken the opposite view. Cunnilingus, the oral stimulation of the female genitals, is not regarded as sodomy. The carnal copulation of a human being with a beast is properly called bestiality and should be distinguished from sodomy. Occasionally, the term buggery appears in legal texts. It means a carnal copulation against nature, either by the confusion of species — a man or woman with a brute beast — or by the confusion of sexes, a man with a man, or a man unnaturally with a woman. Anglo-American sodomy laws have been applied even to married couples and voluntary homosexual acts between consenting adults have sometimes been punished with life imprisonment.

Rejection and Acceptance

The above definitions ante-date the modern 'gay' movement and its claim for recognition of homosexuality as an 'alternative' life-style. Historically, homosexuality has usually been regarded as a deviation even if, as in ancient Greece and Rome or in Tokugawa Japan, some kind of homosexual behaviour was socially acceptable. The attitude of Christian Europe was determined by the biblical reprobation of homosexuality in the Old as well as the New Testament. Christian tradition not only condemned homosexuality but also branded it as a vice against nature.

The sinfulness for which Sodom and Gomorrha were destroyed was generally interpreted as homosexuality (Gen 19,5), and this interpretation is adopted in the New Testament (Jude 7). The Pentateuch links the prohibition and punishment of homosexuality and bestiality (Lev 18, 22-23; 20, 13 15-16) but while it condemns bestiality committed by women, it does not mention lesbianism. St Paul represents homosexuality as the worst of the vices to which idolatry has led the pagan world and his condemnation lives on in the reprobation of homosexuality by Christianity. 'For this cause (that is idolatry), God gave them up to unto vile affections; for even their women did change the natural use into that which is against nature: and likewise also the men, leaving the natural use of the woman, burned in their lust one towards another; men with men working that which is unseemingly, and receiving in themselves that recompense of their error which was meet' (Rom 1, 26-27).

Homosexuality was generally practised in ancient Greece, particularly in the form of paederasty which was considered as part of a young man's education. The older man was friend and mentor. Homosexuality was not unknown in high places. Louis XIII of France was a homosexual himself and his court was greatly influenced by his example (it is a matter of speculation whether his domineering mother, Maria de Medicis, had something to do with the king's sexual orientation). Homosexuality has been widespread in the English establishment and some of the people in high places who spied for Soviet Russia were homosexuals. But official intolerance of homosexuality in leading positions, especially in the armed forces, is a fact of life in most western nations. Generally, however, the proscription of homosexuality in Christian Europe has vanished in today's society. Homosexuality flourishes in one-sex communities. It has been a problem in boarding schools and army barracks, in monasteries and sports clubs, in prisons and on board ships. In the United States, not even a proximate estimate of the gay population seems possible and guesses go as high as 10 per cent of the population. A 1984 survey based on 500 interviews concluded that almost 10 per cent of San Francisco's 706,900 residents were homosexuals, accounting for about 40 per cent of the city's single adult men. The survey found that 57 per cent of the gay men had completed university courses, that 87 per cent were white and 66 per cent under the age of 40.

In the Federal Republic of Germany, manifest homosexuals number about 3 million out of a population of 61 million. By comparison, Japan's gay population, estimated at 2 million, is small. Japan has a long history of homosexuality, and particularly paederasty. Accounts of homosexuality among Buddhist monks date from the early Heian period (794-1192) and in the latter part of this era, homosexuality had spread to the warrior class and the aristocracy. In 1687, the novelist Ihara Saikaku published a collection of essays entitled *Nanshoku Okagami* (Great Mirror of Homosexuality) which extolled the beauty and benefits of homosexual love among *samurai*. Homosexuality was no obstacle to heterosexual relations. Oda Nobunaga, whose involvement with his page, Mori Ranmaru, was one of the famous examples of homosexuality of the period, had 11 sons and 12 daughters.

The all-male *kabuki* theatre and the all-female Takarazuka theatre are often cited as symbols of Japan's homosexual world, but the homosexual bars, clubs, hotels and magazines are a more solid indication of the presence of homosexuality in Japan than the reputation of those groups. In Tokyo's Shinjuku 2-chome district alone, there were about 900 bars and other establishments catering to homosexuals in 1981. Of the homosexual bars, 30-50 were said to be engaged in pandering. Advertisements in newspapers seeking 'hosts' were common; wanted were athletic-looking types or clean-looking 'pretty boys.' One bar was said to have had a stable of 16 minors. The hosts were paid a ¥2,000 retainer for making themselves available to customers who wanted to engage in sodomy. Fees were ¥6,000-8,000 for two hours and ¥10,000 for an all-night tryst. The clientèle, mainly between the ages of 30 and 50, comprised company executives, journalists, performing artists and physicians; gynaecologists were said to be particularly numerous.

Gay Movement

The gay movement has encouraged homosexuals 'to come out of the closet' and homosexuality has gained considerable notoriety by the demonstrations and counter-demonstrations. In places like San Francisco and New York, there are gay communities making homosexuality a particular life-style but most homosexuals are ordinary people employed in virtually every sector of the economy. Many keep their private lives entirely separate from their careers.

The film, *Making Love,* the story of a young doctor leaving his wife for a homosexual lover, was intended for gay audiences, and *Personal Best,* a film depicting a lesbian relationship between two women athletes, was hardly surprising after the real-life episode of tennis star Billie Jean King being sued for property division by her former secretary because they had lived together and had a lesbian relationship in the 1970s. In the Marvin case which gave rise to the palimony doctrine, Michelle Triola Marvin based her claim on something analogous to marriage. The claim against Mrs King was purely for sexual partnership. Mrs King hinted that the practice had become widespread among professional tennis players on the women's circuit who may fear that heterosexual relations will interfere with their work.

The United Church of Christ claims to have been the first church to ordain a known gay and the first to have voted in favour of gay rights. Most Christian denominations maintain that homosexuals should have the right 'to let God be their judge.' Without prejudice to the morality of homosexual conduct, Christian denominations have gay rights organisations, mainly for pastoral purposes, the Episcopalians 'Integrity' and the Catholics 'Dignity.' In addition to the 'Methodist Gays,' there are gay organisations of Mennonites, Pentecostals, Mormons, Christian Scientists, Seventh-Day Adventists and Jews.

Condemnation by Catholic Church

The 1975 Vatican Declaration on Sexual Ethics maintained the basic principle that homosexual acts are intrinsically disordered but stressed the pastoral care to be shown to individuals. In a pastoral letter on homosexuality (1976), the American Catholic bishops declared that 'homosexuals, like everyone else, should not suffer from prejudice against their basic rights, they have a right to respect, friendship and justice. They should have an active rôle in the Christian community.' The letter does not recognise homosexuality as an alternative life-style and does not spell out what the 'active rôle' of homosexuals in the Christian community should be. In 1980, San Francisco's Archbishop John R. Quinn stated that normalising public homosexual behaviour would erode the meaning of the family. In response to the criticism of the archbishop's pastoral letter, the archdiocese commissioned a 14-member task force including gays and lesbians to write a report on homosexuality.

The report, published in 1982, contained 54 recommendations, many of them critical of the Church. It demanded that the Church should minister fully to homosexual followers and stop condemning as immoral those who were sexually active. It rejected the Catholic position that homosexual orientation, in itself, was not sinful as long as one remained celibate but sinful if one engaged in intimate sexual behaviour. The Church should work towards a 'viable sexual theology,' the report said and remedy the oppressed relationship to the Church of divorced Catholics in second marriages, couples who use artificial contraceptives and unmarried couples living together. It further demanded that the Church welcome gay men into the priesthood, upgrade services to the gay community and recognise the unique spiritual experience of devout homosexual Catholics.

As a response to these recommendations, a report entitled 'Ministry and Homosexuality in the Archdiocese of San Francisco' stated: 'Homosexual orientation is not held to be a sinful condition. As with heterosexuality, it represents the situation in which one finds oneself, the starting point for one's response to Christ's call for perfection.' — 'Responding to this call does not mean one must change this orientation. Rather, it entails living out the demands of chastity within it.' Which means that it is not a sin to be a homosexual but this does not sanction the decision to act as one.

A document entitled 'Letter to the Bishops of the Catholic Church on the Pastoral Care of Homosexual Persons' approved by Pope John Paul II and issued by the Sacred Congregation for the Doctrine of the Faith on 30 October 1986, restated the Church's traditional teaching that homosexual activity is morally unacceptable. Although homosexual tendencies are not in and by themselves sinful, they are ordered towards an intrinsic moral evil, and thus the inclination itself must be seen as an objective disorder.

The document was accompanied by a letter of Joseph Cardinal Ratzinger containing pastoral guidelines. It urged Church leaders to minister to gay Catholics and condemned violence committed against them but ordered to withdraw all support from any organisation seeking to undermine the teaching of the Church regarding homosexuality. Pastoral care must not give the impression that the Church approves or condones homosexual conduct. The practice of scheduling religious services or permitting the use of Church buildings or Catholic schools by gay rights groups seems just and charitable but contradicts the purpose for which these institutions were founded, is misleading and often scandalous. No pastoral programme should include organisations in which homosexual persons associate with each other without clearly stating that homosexual activity is immoral.

Partly as a result of the AIDS crisis, homosexuality among the clergy and in religious communities has received increased attention. The extent of clerical homosexuality is largely a matter of conjecture. Estimates of about 20 per cent of the 57,000 US Catholic priests or even up to 40 per cent seem somewhat high, as is the guess that one-third of the Anglican clergy and up to 50 per cent of the churchmen of the Episcopal Church in urban dioceses such as San Francisco and New York are gay. Homosexuality and paederasty used to be lesser problems than alcoholism and heterosexual liaisons but the situation has changed. Because the Catholic Church maintains her strict prohibition of homosexuality, priests and nuns who recognise the authority of the Church usually pay with a bad conscience for practising homosexuality. Economic and social considerations keep priests and nuns from leaving the Church but gay priests, if found out, are removed from pastoral duties and open advocacy of homosexuality is not tolerated.

Other Christian Denominations

Homosexuality is a controversial issue in Protestant churches. The most 'progressive' churches or groups recognise homosexuality as a legitimate life-style. Some denominations have ordained homosexual or lesbian ministers and organised homosexual communities. Clergymen of denominations sympathetic to homosexuals have conducted services blessing homosexual unions. Such services may include a promise of fidelity or permanency, a commitment for love and support, and the blessing of rings. In many American cities, gays have organised their own churches or synagogues, and the Universal Fellowship of Metropolitan Community Churches, the first gay Christian denomination, has applied for membership in the National Council of Churches.

The Church of England does not ban homosexuals from its priesthood or its congregations and a 1981 report declared that it is not incompatible to be Christian and gay. But the Presbyterian Church, Methodists and Lutherans do not ordain self-professed practising homosexuals as ministers, elders or deacons.

The opposition to the gay movement has led to the excommunication of ministers professing homosexuality and the vandalisation, including the burning, of homosexual churches.

A report called 'Homosexual Relationships' published in 1979 by a working party of the Board of Social Responsibility of the Church of England stated that homosexual love could be justified if it were conducted under circumstances similar to those of marriage. But a recognition of homosexual relations that implied an analogy with marriage was fundamentally wrong. The board, however, neither adopted nor endorsed the conclusions of the report and some members regarded the report's attempt to justify homosexual love as a denial of both scripture and tradition. An Anglican clergyman blessed two homosexuals in a special service including hymns, prayers and communion. Although the ceremony was not called a wedding and the men did not exchange vows, the bishop of Manchester ordered that such a ceremony should not be repeated without prior approval of the Church of England.

In the United States, a minority of the 1979 conference of bishops of the Episcopal Church issued a statement in favour of the ordination of homosexuals although the conference as a whole had rejected the proposal.

Judaism upholds the biblical condemnation of homosexuality despite the attempts of some scholars to obscure the meaning of the Old Testament texts and dissent in the American Jewish intelligentsia. Muslim countries have executed homosexuals.

The traditional Christian and Jewish teaching confronted homosexuals with the alternative of repressing their sexual preference or violating moral rules. Now homosexuals assert that their sexuality is part of their natural endowment. In every generation, they contend, God creates some men and women who are drawn to members of the same sex, and since God created them the way they are, homosexuals have a right to live according to their inclination. The problem, therefore, whether homosexuality is a 'natural' or 'normal' form of sexuality concerns not only biology and psychology, but also morality and law.

Analysis of Homosexuality

In their study, 'Homosexualities,' Alan Bell and Martin Weinberg distinguish five types of homosexual behaviour: 1. Those who live stable lives as close couples (10 per cent). 2. Those who live together as open couples and have sex outside as well (18 per cent). 3. The functionals who roam freely and like it (15 per cent). 4. The dysfunctionals who are active but have problems with their sexuality and image (12 per cent). 5. The asexuals who are loners, have little sex and have a hard time with their lives (12 per cent). The rest (33 per cent) did not fit into any of these five categories. This large residue makes the typology somewhat unsatisfactory but in view of the inherent difficulties in determining the sexual inclinations of an individual, sexual ambivalence and sexual faking, it seems unlikely that a classification can be devised that will accommodate all forms of homosexual behaviour.

Male homosexuality has often been described in a dichotomous way, active and passive, masculine and feminine, insertor and insertee. The most effeminate restrict their behaviour to a feminine rôle, they dislike to act as insertor, prefer to assume a woman's receptivity in sexual acts, enjoy being seduced and overpowered by their partner, dress flamboyantly and effeminately, even put on women's clothes (drag balls). But homosexuality cannot be reduced to standardised behaviour. Between men, the passive partner as well as the active one may experience pleasure. Many homosexuals alternate in masculine and feminine rôles; they can be habitually effeminate, intermittently so, or habitually masculine. The Kinsey seven-point scale avoided a dichotomy by rating people from exclusively heterosexual to exclusively homosexual in their choice of sexual partners throughout life.

Female homosexuals can be very masculine ('butch'), always feminine ('femme'), or alternatively masculine or feminine. In sexual relations, those who play a masculine and seductive rôle may use artificial penile devices but lesbians hate maleness although they sometimes get along well with effeminate men. The imitation of a man-woman relation is common but lesbians may also comport themselves as mother and daughter and this relationship can vary from affectionate behaviour to ferocious sado-masochistic rôles.

It seems that lesbians find it easier than male homosexuals to combine marriage with their sexual preference. It sometimes happens that lesbians abhor sex with men but want to have children. In her book, *The Marrying Kind. Homosexuality and Marriage,* Brenda Maddox, a staffer of the London *Economist,* describes the homosexual relations of two married men. After their initial anguish, the two wives decided to keep up the appearances of a convential marriage but let the two husbands have their 'freedom' several times a week. Mrs Maddox considers homosexuals as a minority whose condition must invite pity if only because of their extra sense of anxiety which sometimes takes the form of excessive secrecy but has also led to excessive publicity. The life of a lesbian, in particular, is filled with pain, ostracism and feelings of guilt. But almost no female homosexuals want to change and the course of wisdom should be not to make them change.

Genesis

There are about as many opinions on the genesis of homosexuality as there are therapists. In a later study, *Sexual Preference: Its Development Among Men and Women,* the authors of *Homosexualities* together with Sue Hammersmith assert that their research has disproved earlier theories on the origin of homosexuality. In the past, the psychiatric explanation was dominant but it was proposed in partly contradictory variants. The possessive theory stressed the psychological influence of the early environment, a strong, possessive mother and a weak father; the rôle failure theory blamed the failure of either parent to offer a strong model for masculine or feminine identity while another explanation derived homosexual tendencies from the strong attachment to either parent, especially the mother, fostered by excessive coddling and protection. The psychological theories note that shock-like negative impressions of heterosexual models in infancy may prepare a deviationist sex identification that remains latent but is made manifest by corresponding experiences in puberty or early adulthood. The seduction theory maintains that male and female homosexuality is caused by juvenile seduction experience. Seduction may be the trigger by which latent homosexual tendencies are actuated. Early experiences predisposing to homosexuality can remain dormant and may even be extinguished by other experiences. Latent inclinations may not result in overt homosexuality but such behaviour possibly appears if youths are seduced. Early 'gender nonconformity' is also cited as a reason: little boys like girl games and little girls like boy games. But here, the question arises: is this cause or effect? Is there not some early factor responsible for forming sexual identity?

All these influences may be contributory factors but it seems difficult to attribute homosexuality to any of these experiences because they go together with later heterosexual development as well as with homosexuality. There is no reason to postulate that all homosexuality goes back to the age of around 7.

Biological Basis?

Taking a clue from the research that discovered the rôle of hormonal and chemical imbalances in many forms of mental illness, a team of the British Medical Research Council under Dr J. A. Loraine, director of the clinical endocrinology unit in Edinburgh, came to the conclusion that analogous defects may be involved in the origin of homosexuality. The fixing of the homosexual tendency, Dr Loraine inferred, takes place as a result of abnormal endocrine activity during the late pre-natal period, the very early post-natal period, or at the time of puberty. The pattern would thereafter be stamped for life.

Dr Loraine still considered homosexuality as a deviation which, he said, was 'multifactorial,' that is, due to a variety of influences, psychological as well as physiological. Researchers found a deficiency in the androgen (male sex hormones) secretion in male homosexuals and an abnormally high daily secretion of androgens together with an abnormally low production of estrogens (female sex hormones) in lesbians.

The hormonal theory of homosexuality was further elaborated by Professor Günther Dörner, head of the Endocrinology Department of the Charité University Hospital in East Berlin. Professor Dörner thinks that homosexual inclinations are established long before puberty. The level of the male hormone testosterone in the foetus has a permanent influence on the brain. If the level is too low in a male, he will develop a predominantly feminine brain, reacting later to sexual stimuli in a way similar to a woman. If the level of the male hormone is too high in a female, she will be predisposed to lesbian behaviour later in life.

The cause of the pre-natal hormone imbalance remains unclear. Maternal stress is said to be involved because the mothers of a considerable number of homosexuals had suffered severe or moderate stress during pregnancy.

Researchers at the State University of New York claimed to have found clear laboratory evidence of biological differences between homosexual and heterosexual men. The patterns of response after the hormone estrogen was injected into a group of homosexual men were between those of heterosexual men and women. The response, a higher level of luteinising hormone (LH) was observed in nine of the 14 homosexual men tested while no LH elevations occurred in a group of 17 heterosexual men. There were also differences in the response patterns when the male hormone testosterone was injected, the LH levels remaining lower for a longer period in the homosexual group than in the heterosexual men. The hormone response of female homosexuals was not tested because of difficulties in finding test subjects.

According to Dr Brian A. Gladue who directed the study, there might be a biological basis to homosexuality in some homosexual men, but this association does not necessarily indicate a cause. The biological changes could possibly be linked to hormone exposure in the womb or inherited factors but either would be difficult to prove.

Alfred C. Kinsey maintained that there is no sexual predisposition at birth and that homosexuality is entirely learned. He considered the physiological capacity of all mammals to react to any sexual stimulus if it is strong enough as the decisive factor. Kinsey stressed the importance of the first sexual experience as a determinant of the later sex life. The emphasis on sexual stimulation may be too narrow. 'The most important aspect is not so much about sex, *per se,* but about with whom you fall in love.'

William H. Masters and Virginia E. Johnson also concluded that there is no evidence that homosexual preferences are genetically determined. They regard homosexuality in males and females as completely natural and particularly dispute the theory that it is a disease. In their opinion, there is no 'disease' in any form of consenting adult sexuality. There are only 'dysfunctions' that can be set right by therapy. Homosexuality does not mean gender confusion. The homosexual is first a man, then a homosexual; the lesbian is first a woman, then a lesbian, regardless of whether or not they are active or passive partners. Therapy is possible for those who want to break away from homosexual behaviour and also for those who want therapy for their inadequacies as homosexuals. If homosexuality were a physical matter, which would be the case if it were due to a pronounced endocrinal factor, it would be possible to correct it medicinally and attempts to reorient homosexuals would be futile. But the Masters were dissatisfied with the high failure rate of their therapy because 35 per cent of the homosexual men and women who wanted to function as heterosexuals failed to achieve a lasting reversal of their homosexuality during their treatment.

In a rather unique theory of paederasty. Schopenhauer found in it an eminently teleological meaning because nature deflects old men whose generative potential is depraved from begetting weak offspring and also blocks the use of the immature semen of adolescents.

Legitimate Form of Sexuality?

At the present stage of research, there seems to be no definitive explanation of the origin and nature of homosexuality. A solution of these problems would be of major importance for settling the controversy whether heterosexuality and homosexuality are equally valid forms of sex relations, in other words, whether homosexuality is a legitimate form of sexuality or a deviation, and whether the choice of a homosexual mate is the same as that of a heterosexual mate. Answers to these questions would also be decisive for solving the problem whether one-sex marriages should be recognised or homosexual couples should be allowed to adopt children.

Those who contend that homosexuality represents a legitimate form of sex relations define it as a deep-seated, inborn gender non-conformity, a powerful set of needs and feelings, attachment and orientation; a state over which a person has no control, not something that one chooses to be or not to be. But homosexuality, whether a biologically caused inclination or an acquired sex preference, does not mean 'automatic' or 'natural' sex relations.

Defenders of homosexuality have argued that nature is no moral institution and that sexual 'perversity' is the attempt of nature to overcome the difficulties opposing the satisfaction of the sex instinct. But man's duty to control his impulses applies also to homosexual inclinations. Actual sex relations depend on free choice and decision in homosexual behaviour no less than in heterosexual conduct, and personal choice involves personal responsibility. This is the reason why comparisons with the homosexual behaviour of monkeys and other animals are irrelevant.

A four-year study by a team of 31 natural and social scientists published in 1981 stated that homosexuality is as healthy and biologically normal as heterosexuality and that attempts to 'cure' gay people are 'ethically questionable.' One of the originators of the study, Professor William Paul, claimed that homosexuality is biologically natural since it appears spontaneously all over the world. 'Among some animal groups it leads to bonding by cutting down on aggression among males and helps the gene pool survive simply because they are not killing each other.'

The position that homosexuality is biologically as normal as heterosexuality amounts to a denial of the natural ordainment inherent in human sexuality and of all criteria of normalcy. The divergence of heterosexuality and homosexuality is not the same as, for example, the difference between right-handedness and left-handedness. The contention that something is normal because it is a fact is not just erroneous but silly. Nobody would say that near-sightedness is normal because near-sighted people are found all over the world, nor can it be claimed that homosexuality is 'in the natural order of things' or 'part of the natural order' because 'humankind is diversified.'

The basic question is not whether homosexuality is a sin or a crime, that is, against the moral or legal order, but whether it is one of equally valid and possible forms of sexuality or a deviation. This is not the same as the question whether homosexuality is a disease. That the World Health Organisation has dropped the classification of homosexuality as a malady does not mean that homosexuality is normal. Heterosexual behaviour needs no explanation but homosexuality always prompts the question 'why?' Many researchers deny that homosexual conduct is something unnatural, perverse, morbid or the consequence of some personality disorder, but there is an immense literature on the therapy of homosexuality.

The basic fact is that homosexual relations do not involve sexual activities conforming to the natural differentiation of male and female and the teleological ordainment of this differentiation. Such relations do not imply a common task and a community of life but serve for the purely individualistic satisfaction of sexual desire. A homosexual relationship possesses no institutional significance but is just something two people do together

Homosexuality: a Special Status?

One of the reasons for today's acrimonious debate surrounding homosexuality is the claim of the gay movement to have a homosexual relationship recognised as a special status. It is no such thing. While a homosexual relationship may be important to the individuals involved, it cannot take the place of marriage and the family in society. Socially, homosexual couples are not treated as spouses but as friends, and they are not listed among the legal survivors when one dies. But as long as homosexuals do not disturb the public order (even now, some laws regard the existence of a homosexual relationship as such or a homosexual act as a disturbance of the public order) they can demand tolerance.

The city council of West Hollywood passed an ordinance giving gay couples and live-in lovers who have registered with the city as 'domestic partners' the same hospital and jail visitation rights as married couples. An estimated 10,000 homosexuals live in the city of 30,000 inhabitants and homosexuals form the majority on the city council. The effect of the ordinance is less objectionable than the reason given by a city spokeswoman: 'It's symbolic, the seed to the idea that couples living together, whether they are homosexual or heterosexual, deserve the same rights married couples enjoy.'

The recognition of homosexuality as a 'legitimate form of sexual relations' is not the only demand of the gay movement. Other goals are the removal of legal restraints on homosexuality and social equality of homosexuals. In 1981, the Social Affairs and Health Committee of the Council of Europe asserted that all individuals having attained the age of majority have the right to determine their own sexual preference; it condemned discrimination against homosexuals and demanded measures to eliminate discrimination. The measures proposed by the committee were: 1. Reform of legislation in all member countries where homosexual acts between consenting adults are subject to prosecution. 2. Destruction of police files kept on homosexuals. 3. Equality of treatment for homosexuals with regard to employment, salary and job security. 4. End of all medical treatment aimed at modifying the sexual leanings of adults. 5. Abolition of the World Health Organisation's classification of homosexuality as a malady.

As mentioned above, the last demand has already been complied with. The other proposals are based on the unqualified acceptance of the claim that homosexuality is a legitimate form of sexuality which it is not. The American homophile organisation appealed for recognition of civil and legal rights of homosexuals in all countries and to fight for pride, dignity, identity and social and legal justice. The same issue underlies a resolution adopted by the third international conference of the International Gay Association in 1981 calling on the United Nations to designate a year for homosexuals. Such a measure would undoubtedly amount to a public recognition of the legitimacy of homosexuality.

The assertion of the 'right' to homosexual relationships relies on the ethics of self-fulfilment, meaning that everybody is entitled to do whatever he thinks conducive to 'self-actualisation.' While the private sex life of an individual is his own business, recognition of homosexuality as an alternative life-style would imply legal protection of such a relationship. Because homosexuality is no status or relationship entitled to legal protection, it is misleading to speak of homosexual rights. Homosexuals have rights as human beings and citizens of their respective country but not as homosexuals.

What homosexuals regard as discrimination is, in many cases, the reaction of people who do not accept the premise that homosexuality is a 'natural' and 'valid' form of sexual behaviour. There is no reason why people who retain traditional moral values should accept the theories of some psychologists or sociologists as guidelines for their judgements on homosexuality. Every human being has the right to be respected as a person but this does not mean that everybody must agree with the ideas, preferences or values of the other.

According to a *Newsweek* poll on homosexuality (July 1983), the majority of Americans thinks that homosexuals should have equal rights in terms of job opportunities but does not consider homosexuality as an accepted alternative life-style.

Tolerance is compatible with the ban on sexual advances not only to minors but also to adults. The necessity of protecting minors is sufficient reason to reject an unqualified endorsement of homosexuality.

Decriminalisation

In 1969, a US government task-force recommended that homosexual behaviour between adults should no longer be a crime. The confusion in the thinking about this issue appears in the reasons given for the recommendations, namely, that the repeal of the laws against homosexuals would reduce their emotional stress and improve their mental health. This is complete hogwash: the repeal of the laws against burglary would reduce the emotional stress of burglars. If homosexuality does not constitute a threat to the public order, the sodomy laws should be repealed, but there seems to be no agreement on the extent to which homosexuality can be considered legally irrelevant. The prohibition of seduction seems entirely appropriate although it certainly implies some kind of censure. This reservation may influence employment of homosexuals. Problems related to this issue have arisen most frequently in connection with teaching, government service, and the armed forces.

Sodomy is still outlawed in 24 American states, and in a 5 to 4 decision, the US Supreme Court, on 30 June 1986, upheld the constitutionality of a Georgia law that defines sodomy as 'any sexual act involving the sex organs of one person and the mouth or anus of another.' It makes consensual sodomy — even between heterosexuals — a felony punishable by up to 20 years in prison.

The case was the unintentional outcome of the attempt of an Atlanta policeman to serve a warrant for publicly carrying an open container of alcohol on Michael Hardwick, a bartender then 29. When the officer called on Hardwick, a house guest told him that Hardwick was in his bedroom. Peering through the half-open door, the policeman saw Hardwick and another man engaged in oral sex and arrested him. The lower court held that sexual activity 'is quintessentially private and lies at the heart of the intimate association beyond proper reach of state regulation.' Although Georgia dropped the criminal charges against Hardwick, his attorneys decided to challenge the law in federal court. An appeals court equated oral sex between homosexuals with sexual activity in marriages and ruled that the law could stand only if a 'compelling state interest' demanded the prohibition of sodomy.

In Georgia's appeal to the Supreme Court, the state's Senior Assistant Attorney General, Michael E. Hobbs, argued that the Supreme Court never intended the right to privacy to extend to an activity which for hundreds of years, if not thousands, has been uniformly condemned as immoral. 'No basis exists for adding the crime of sodomy to the list of fundamental rights,' he said.

The Supreme Court agreed. Not any kind of sexual conduct between consenting adults was protected by the constitutional right of privacy, the Court held, only sexual conduct between a married couple. The decision caused an uproar in some liberal circles but, as evidenced by the ruling of the US Circuit Court of Appeals for the District of Columbia referred to below, it affirmed an old position. The case appears to support the constitutionality of state fornication laws making it a crime for two unmarried persons to have sex and may be important for outlawing homosexuality if it involves the danger of transferring a contagious disease, like AIDS.

Homosexuality in the Military

In Britain, homosexual acts by servicemen are still officially serious crimes which, under military law, could lead to court martial, imprisonment and dishonourable discharge. Actually, if a serviceman is discovered to be gay, he is usually encouraged to resign quietly in a way which will not hurt a future civilian career. Because homosexuality is forbidden by military law, it is unnecessary to rely on the possibility of blackmail for removing a man from the service. Outside the armed forces, homosexuals are generally tolerated but not in leading positions. Security clearance would be denied to civil servants, diplomats or policemen known to be homosexuals. The 1982 report of the security commission, while emphasising the danger from blackmail, clearly recommended that homosexuality should no longer be an absolute bar to security clearance in the home civil service.

In one of the cases involving high-placed British officials in homosexual relationships, Commander Michael Trestrail, Queen Elizabeth's personal police officer and head of the Royal protection squad at Buckingham Palace, confessed to a homosexual relationship with a male prostitute and resigned in July 1982, ten days after an intruder had entered the Queen's bedroom and had chatted with the Queen for ten minutes.

Homosexuals are not tolerated in Ireland's military establishment and they would be unable to remain in a leading position in civilian life.

A case which caused an outbreak of political furore was the dismissal of four-star General Günter Kiessling from his post as deputy commander of NATO forces by West German Defense Minister Manfred Wörner because the officer's alleged homosexuality made him a security risk. A military counter-intelligence report had informed the minister that four witnesses had identified the general as a frequent visitor of pubs frequented by homosexuals. The minister refused to accept the general's statement under oath and his word of honour that he was not a homosexual. But Cologne police discovered that a well-known patron of homosexual establishments, a former army officer, bore a striking resemblance to General Kiessling, and three of the four witnesses expressed doubts about their testimony. Prime Minister Kohl thereupon ordered the reinstatement of General Kiessling which could hardly alleviate the bitterness felt by the general.

The West German Defence Ministry says that homosexuality is no bar to recruitment. But when a soldier is found to be gay, security clearance is withheld or withdrawn and promotion is ruled out. The official justification is that the individual's authority could be reduced and that he could be exposed to blackmail. Sweden, Norway, Denmark and the Netherlands are officially tolerant of homosexuality in the armed forces but in Belgium, homosexuals may face disciplinary measures and dismissal.

In Spain, the socialist government has decriminalised homosexuality but it is still punishable in the armed forces. There are no regulations forbidding homosexuality in the Italian armed forces. Although the social taboo is very strong, homosexuality was said to be widespread.

Official policy in the United States is that homosexuality is incompatible with military service and known homosexuals are not allowed to enlist or be commissioned as officers. The rule applies regardless of rank and in 1983, 1,706 people were discharged from the US forces on grounds of homosexuality. Discipline, order, morale and the prevention of breaches of security are given as reasons for this policy.

In December 1983, a 19-year veteran navy commander was convicted of having an homosexual affair with a crew member and sentenced to be dismissed from the service and fined $1,200. In 1981, the US Supreme Court rejected a challenge to navy regulations that require the discharge of sailors who engage in homosexual acts. An avowed lesbian who was dismissed from a Reserve Officer Training Corps programme at the University of Maine after she admitted to being gay filed suit in a US district court claiming the army regulations against homosexuality were unconstitutional.

In a decision that upheld the right of the navy to the mandatory dismissal of a serviceman who had engaged in homosexual acts with another sailor, the US circuit court of appeals for the District of Columbia ruled in August 1984 that homosexuals have no constitutional right to privacy in their sexual affairs. In its unanimous decision, the court declared that homosexuality had been 'traditionally condemned' in American society and could not claim constitutional protection from government intrusion.

Homosexuality is forbidden in the Israeli army, and homosexuals are exempt from the draft in France and Greece.

Legal Prohibitions

There are sodomy laws in Denmark, Sweden, France, Italy, Switzerland and Mexico. In 1967, acting on a proposal of the Wolfenden committee (Report of the Committee on Homosexual Offences and Prostitution), England and Wales abolished the criminal provisions against homosexuality except in cases involving violence, children or public solicitation to commercial vice. The committee also proposed to lower the age of consent for homosexuals from 21 to 18; 18-year-olds, the committee said, were mature enough to take responsibility for their sexual preferences.

Female homosexuality was never banned in Britain, but male homosexuality remained punishable in Scotland until 1980 and is still outlawed in Northern Ireland. Homosexual relationships are denied legal status for the purpose of inheritance and housing. The charities commission, which decides which organisations deserve tax relief, will not register any homosexual charity. An amendment to Canada's Criminal Code passed in 1969 removed the prohibition of private homosexual acts between consenting adults. In the Soviet Union, homosexuality is punishable by up to five years in prison.

In the Federal Republic of Germany, homosexual acts between consenting adults are not forbidden but seduction of a minor (under 18 years of age) to commit homosexual acts is punishable as are all sexual acts involving children (under 14 years of age).

A Belgian court acquitted a university professor of charges that his private clubs, called 'Le Macho,' where male homosexuals can dine, bathe or take a sauna together, were an incitement to debauchery and prostitution. Under Belgian law, homosexual intercourse under the age of 18 is prohibited although heterosexual intercourse is allowed from 16.

A commission of Swedish legislators proposed to change Swedish law and offer asylum to homosexuals abroad who are persecuted for their sexual preferences. The same commission recommended a constitutional amendment safeguarding homosexual rights and placing homosexual couples on a par with heterosexual ones for social benefits. It failed, however, to agree with the demands of Sweden's gay rights movement that homosexuals should be given the right to marry and to adopt children.

In Japan, the Prostitution Prevention Law (*Baishun Bôshi-hô*) cannot be used against male homosexuals because the term *'baishun'* is not applicable to men and the provisions of the law dealing with prostitution as such (that is, not those related to pandering, knowingly providing premises for prostitution, and so on) obviously refer to female prostitution. Police raids on gay bars because of suspicion of paederasty are based on the Child Welfare Law (*Jidô Fukushi-hô*).

Laws against sodomy and oral sex between consenting adults in private have been repealed in many states in the United States. But in 1976, the US Supreme Court upheld Virginia's sodomy laws and the North Carolina conviction of a man on a charge of committing 'oral sex' in his home with a willing male partner. The North Carolina statute makes it a felony to commit the 'crime against nature.' The American Civil Liberties Union contended that the state laws involved an unconstitutional invasion of privacy and were discriminatory against homosexuals. The Supreme Court held that a state's prohibition of private homosexual acts between consenting adults was constitutional.

Compatibility with Public Office

In the United States, federal civil service guidelines provide that a government worker cannot be fired solely because that person is a homosexual or has engaged in homosexual acts. Federal courts in a number of states and the District of Columbia have held that homosexuality in itself is not sufficient cause for dismissal from public employment. But in the 1950s, 1960s and the early 1970s, the Federal Bureau of Investigation (FBI) and the Pentagon routinely spied on organisations promoting homosexual rights and compiled voluminous lists of homosexuals. The FBI automatically reported federal employees discovered to be homosexuals on grounds they might pose a security risk. Another reason was to protect homosexuals from blackmail by common criminals.

The question of the compatibility of homosexuality with public office came to the fore in the United States in 1982 when charges were made that congressmen were involved sexually with their messenger boys. After a highly publicised investigation, two congressmen were cited by the ethics committee for censure by the House. There is no law making it illegal for an elected official to be homosexual and, as one of the congressmen said, he did not violate his oath of office. However, many people do not consider homosexuality morally indifferent and the moral blemish impairs an official's authority and credibility. Moreover, the fact that the young people involved were messenger boys gave the impression of an abuse of trust and authority.

Homosexual Teachers

Can a teacher be dismissed merely because he is a homosexual? The refusal of employment solely on that basis seems to constitute discrimination. In 1973, a US federal court decided that a teacher's homosexuality did not constitute immorality and afforded no ground for dismisssal. The court ordered all references to immorality to be removed from the record.

But those who oppose the right of homosexuals to pursue the teaching profession cite the potential impact of homosexual teachers in the classroom. Since teachers are also leaders and models, students may conclude that homosexuality is all right if an identified homosexual serves as teacher. The contrary view argues that a teacher's homosexuality as any other individual's sex life is his own private business. In a widely discussed case, the Washington Supreme Court in a split decision upheld the dismissal of a teacher from Tacoma, Washington state, from his position in a public high school. James M. Gaylord had kept his homosexuality secret for 20 years but when he joined a local homosexual organisation, he was dismissed. The majority of the court thought that students could interpret retention by the school board as adult approval of homosexuality. The dissent contended that dismissal merely for being homosexual without sufficient evidence that it affected his teaching was unconstitutional: 'To base dismissal on the proof of a status, with no showing of an actual detrimental effect on teaching efficiency violates the constitutional due process rights to which Mr Gaylord is entitled.'

In 1969, the California Supreme Court ruled that the state cannot revoke the teaching credentials of a homosexual unless there is proof his homosexuality makes him unfit to teach.

An episode which brought the question of discrimination against homosexuals into the limelight was the campaign led by singer Anita

Bryant which resulted in the voter repeal of a Dade County, Florida (Miami) ordinance prohibiting discrimination against homosexuals. Their employment as teachers was a major issue in the campaign.

The question seems not to have arisen in Japan but then it is difficult to imagine a Japanese teacher imitating the stupidity or brazenness of an American teacher by bringing his homosexual partner into the classroom and introducing him to the class as his 'wife.'

Homosexual 'Marriages'

A controversial subject are the so-called homosexual marriages. There have been several cases in the United States in which homosexuals obtained marriage licences and were married by ministers, but in Texas, where one such marriage took place, the attorney general ruled that county clerks were not authorised to issue marriage licences to two persons of the same sex — although anyone who has a licence can marry. In 1972, the US Supreme Court turned down an appeal designed to sanction homosexual marriages 'for want of a substantial federal question.'

In a panel discussion on 'Women's Liberation and the Constitution,' Mrs Rita E. Hauser, a New York lawyer and US representative to the United Nations Human Rights Commission, asserted: 'Legal distinction on the basis of sex is no longer reasonable, and I am willing to apply that view to any and all sets of circumstances the mind may conceive.' The lady applied that view to state laws that required marriage partners to be of opposite sexes. These laws, she said, predicate reproduction as the legal consideration of marriage and that view was no longer consistent with fact. If limiting reproduction had become the social goal, there was no better way of accomplishing that than marriage between persons of the same sex.

The lady's assertion reveals a basic misunderstanding of marriage as an institution. As such, marriage is not an arrangement for individual convenience to be adjusted to individual wishes. It is up to the individual to enter marriage but an individual cannot arbitrarily form some kind of liaison with another individual and call it marriage. If two persons of the same sex want to live together, that is their own affair, but there is no reason why this kind of cohabitation should be called marriage or be entitled to the legal status of marriage. Marriage between a man and a woman is not an arbitrary form of union but a basic fact of human nature. And although reproduction is not the only reason for marriage, it is essential for both individuals and society. The lady's cavalier dismissal of legal distinctions on the basis of sex does certainly not accord with the existing legal order. Sex is irrelevant for human rights to which every human being is entitled but it is hard to see how, for example, the rights of a mother can be dissociated from sex.

American courts have passed on the validity of weddings between homosexuals in immigration cases. Two homosexuals, one of them an Australian, got 'married' in Colorado with the help of an accommodating clergyman but the government contended that a same-sex 'marriage' was invalid for immigration purposes. The lawyer for the Australian argued that Colorado law did not specifically prohibit same-sex 'marriages' so that, by inference, such marriages were permitted, but the court refused to accept this argument. 'The basic structure of society and social values rely upon the historical man-woman marital relationship,' the court said. 'There can be no doubt that there exists a rational basis for the state to limit the definition of marriage to exclude same-sex relationships.'

The Unitarian Universalist Assocation, a liberal Protestant denomination, voted in June 1984 to affirm the growing practice of some of its ministers to conduct services of union of gay and lesbian couples.

A Protestant pastor in Hamburg who blessed a lesbian 'marriage' asked the church authorities to investigate the case. The media had called his action a 'wedding,' but the pastor's superior explained that this may not necessarily have been the intention of the pastor. While a wedding of two people of the same sex is, theologically and legally, impossible, it is possible to 'bless' many things if there is a demand for a blessing. Nevertheless, the women were given a 'wedding' certificate stating that they had been united 'in the name of the triune God' according to the words of the Bible, 'Receive ye one another, as Christ also received us to the Glory of God' (Rom 15, 7).

In the Dutch city of Groningen, a Catholic priest conducted a wedding ceremony for two women, but the diocesan authorities at once denounced it as incompatible with Canon Law.

Homosexuals complain that this discrimination denies them the legal benefits (such as preferential tax treatment) and other advantages (such as 'societal respectability') of state-sanctioned marriages. This discrimination is unconstitutional, they argue, because courts no longer allow 'stereotyped and/or antiquated assumptions about homosexuality and gender rôles.' To such reasoning. L'Osservatore Romano replied: 'Attempts to give to marriage new contents and aspects are simple moral aberrations which cannot be approved either by human conscience or, especially, by the Christian conscience.' Neither can they be endorsed as a matter of jurisprudence or social politics. And simply at a practical level, a woman is a better wife than a man.

A bizarre case recently surfaced in a tiny West Java village when the local undertaker revealed that a respected farmer who had died leaving a wife and two children had really been a 'she.' Under police questioning, the wife finally avowed that she had found out three nights after the wedding that her alleged husband really was a woman. To hide her shame, she continued the relationship and her 'husband' allowed her to have two children by another man.

In 1982, a New York state appellate court upheld the right of a 32-year-old Manhattan man to adopt his 43-year-old homosexual lover with whom he had been living for the last three years. New York does not recognise homosexual 'marriages' but it does permit adults to adopt one another which is often done to facilitate an inheritance. In this case, the purpose was to keep an apartment whose lease covered only one of the men and members of his immediate family. The judge declared that the New York incest statute did not apply.

Homosexual parents of both sexes have been awarded child custody rights and have been found 'fit' as adoptive parents. In April 1983, San Francisco Mayor Dianne Feinstein overwhelmingly defeated an attempt to force her from office because she sponsored a bill to ban hand-guns and vetoed a law related to 'live-in' lovers. The law would have given homosexuals and other unmarried couples in the city the right to collect health insurance given to the husbands and wives of city employees.

Homosexuality and US Immigration Law

On account of the classification of homosexuality as a disease, the American immigration regulations barred the entry of homosexuals, but the present wording of the statute prevents an automatic exclusion of homosexuals. A British journalist who came to San Francisco in 1980 for the annual Gay Freedom parade was refused permission to enter the United States when he stated that he was a homosexual. But a US district court ruled that Congress expressly required public health service medical certificates verifying that self-declared homosexuals were afflicted with 'a psychopathic personality, sexual deviation, or mental defect' before barring their entry to the United States. The 9th Circuit Court of Appeals upheld the decision. Before 1979, the Immigration and Naturalisation Service (INS) was permitted to exclude certain classes of aliens, including homosexuals, from entering the United States. The guidelines stipulated that homosexuality had to be verified by a public health service doctor. But in 1979, the Surgeon General discontinued health service inspections of suspected homosexuals claiming that homosexuality was no longer considered a mental disorder and determination of homosexuality was not a medical procedure. The INS maintained that it was in their agents' discretion to permit or deny entry to homosexual aliens, based on the aliens' voluntary statements (agents were not allowed to ask aliens their sexual preferences). The court's decision established that the INS cannot exclude homosexual aliens without medical certification of psychopathic personality, sexual deviation or mental defect.

But in May 1984, the US Supreme Court rejected without comment an appeal by a homosexual man against the refusal of a federal court in Texas to grant him citizenship, thereby upholding the law under which homosexuals are classified as psychopathic personalities and their applications for citizenship are atuomatically turned down.

Homosexuality in Anti-discrimination Laws

The prohibition of discrimination because of homosexuality has created difficult problems. The say-so of the government cannot decide the moral qualification of homosexuality and the government has no right to order individuals or private organisations to disregard moral considerations. It is indeed a strange contradiction that the military can maintain its ban on homosexuality while private organisations are forbidden to take homosexuality into account.

A typical incident was the attempt of two groups of homosexual students to force Georgetown University (an institution run by the Jesuits) to grant them 'university recognition.' The groups relied on the Human Rights Act of the District of Columbia which forbids discrimination. The act bans discrimination 'including but not limited to discrimination by reason of race, colour, religion, national origin, sex, age, marital status, personal appearance, sexual orientation, family responsibilities, matriculation, political affiliation, physical handicap, source of income and place of residence or business.' Georgetown's administration refused 'university recognition' because it could be construed as an endorsement of the groups' assertion that homosexuality is an equally moral alternative to heterosexuality which is contrary to Catholic teaching. The groups' lawyer argued that the university was a corporation, just a business like any other, which could not decline to abide by the human rights act because of its religious affiliation. The suit was an attempt to use government power to compel a private academic institution to subscribe to the doctrine that homosexuality is a matter of moral indifference. The university won in the first instance but on appeal, the Supreme Court of the District of Columbia held that religious convictions could not be used to thwart civil rights legislation, overturned the verdict of the lower court and ordered the university to recognise the homosexual groups.

On 1 April 1985, the US Supreme Court upheld the ruling of a Texas court that Texas A&M University had violated gay students' rights to free speech and association by refusing to fund and provide meeting facilities to a homosexual student group. The university had based its refusal on university regulations and state law declaring homosexual conduct illegal. The court decided that gay groups have a right to equal access to forums at state universities.

A similar clash occurred in New York where, by order of Mayor Edward Koch, all city contractors were required to sign a pledge that they would observe the city's ban on discrimination against homosexuals. The Salvation Army refused to sign the pledge. 'We do not discriminate against hiring homosexuals but we just cannot sign the pledge as a matter of our national policy,' the Salvation Army's chief of New York operations declared. The city threatened to withdraw $5 million worth of contracts it had with the Salvation Army to run day-care and old-people centres. The Catholic Archdiocese of New York chose to forego the city subsidies rather than to observe the city's ban. In June 1985, the state Supreme Court ruled that the mayor had overstepped his authority and that his order was invalid.

A California Court of Appeals overturned a state Superior Court decision recognising the right of the Boy Scout movement to enforce its by-laws excluding girls and homosexuals. The Appeals Court held that expelling a member because he was a homosexual was arbitrary and violated the common-law right of fair procedure.

The ruling raises the question how far public authority can force individuals and private organisations to refrain from discrimination. While equality is a basic postulate for the operations of the government and its organs, there is no similar obligation for private individuals and the non-discrimination requirement can be an undue limitation of individual freedom. The decision of the Superior Court that the Boy Scouts did not have to open membership to everybody was correct and the Court of Appeals was wrong in requiring some kind of 'fair procedure' different from the observance of the rules of the organisation.

Homosexuals and AIDS

Homosexuality received unwanted publicity from its connection with AIDS. The deadly disease first appeared in the homosexual communities of New York, San Francisco and Los Angeles around 1978 and, by 1983, it had spread to 35 states and 33 foreign countries, including France, West Germany and Denmark. By the beginning of 1984 the disease was claiming an increasing number of victims in Central and West Africa, notably among people from Zaire, Chad, Uganda, Burundi and Rwanda. Some of the cases treated in Belgium dated back to 1979. As of January 1987, the worldwide number of AIDS victims was put at 38,401. The disease has also spread to the clergy. No specific numbers are known but priests, brothers and ministers have been reported suffering from AIDS and some have died.

An important factor in the spread of AIDS and other diseases is the frequent change of partners among homosexuals. Diseases caused by fungi, viruses and bacteria are prevalent. Of sexually-transmitted diseases, gonorrhea, urethritis, venereal growths, syphilis, hepatitis and herpes simplex are frequent. Male homosexuals are particularly prone to intestinal disorders because they combine oral and anal sex. Amebiasis (dysentery caused by the protozoan Entamoeba histolytica), giardiasis (intestinal disorder caused by the protozoan parasite Giardia lamblia), shigellosis (bacillary dysentery) and enteritis are among these diseases.

Acting on a proposal of Mayor Dianne Feinstein, the San Francisco municipal council closed 14 bath-houses and sex clubs catering to homosexuals. The decision was reached despite considerable objection after investigators found that these facilities encouraged indiscriminate sexual contacts which helped spread AIDS.

After winning a third term, New York Mayor Edward Koch vowed to shut down homosexual bars and bath-houses that allow open oral and anal sex under new state regulations instituted by Governor Mario Cuomo forbidding 'unsafe sex.'

In August 1985, the Los Angeles City Council unanimously approved a bill providing penalties of up to six months imprisonment for discrimination against AIDS victims. The penalties apply to employers who dismiss, refuse to employ or segregate people with AIDS, landlords who refuse to rent a home to someone with AIDS or try to evict an AIDS patient, or medical personnel refusing health, dental or convalescent care to anyone with AIDS or thought to have the disease. The head of the city's Communicable Disease Control Unit, Dr Shirley Fannin, assured councillors that the disease could not be transmitted by casual contact among the city's 3 million inhabitants. This position has been somewhat weakened by the reports of infections through normal household contacts in Zaire.

The Office of Legal Counsel in the US Justice Department ruled that civil rights laws do not provide absolute protection to AIDS victims. If a person is dismissed from a job or excluded from a federal programme merely because he suffers from AIDS, his dismissal would be illegal if he is otherwise qualified for the position. If, however, the person is dismissed because of the employer's concern that he would spread the disease, the dismissal would be legal unless the fear of spreading it is solely a pretext for discrimination.

A decision of the US Supreme Court in March 1987 cast doubt on the legality of the position of the Justice Department. The case did not involve AIDS but tuberculosis, and the court ruled that the 1973 Rehabilitation Act against handicap discrimination can protect those with contagious diseases. The court, in a footnote, declined to decide whether carriers of the AIDS virus who do not actually have the disease might also be considered handicapped. But the court's broad language suggests that people who are suffering from AIDS will be able to use the handicap law as a protection against job discrimination.

The homosexual partner of actor Rock Hudson, who died of AIDS, sued Hudson's estate for $10 million. Hudson learned that he had AIDS in June 1984 but continued to have sex with the plaintiff for the following eight or nine months while denying that he had AIDS. There can be no doubt about the moral obligation to inform a sex partner of a communicable disease but the legal duty is uncertain. There are laws that cover liability for knowingly spreading communicable diseases and in a suit against a man who allegedly knew that he had herpes but did not tell his wife, a New York appellate court ruled that partners had a legal duty to inform each other about their venereal diseases. At present, Hudson's lover does not have the disease and blood tests were negative so that the claim would be for mental suffering. Whether juries would be sympathetic to homosexual victims seems rather doubtful.

7

Prostitution

TODAY'S SEX BUSINESS comprises two principal activities: prostitution and pornography. Naturally, there are connections, particularly because both may be controlled by the same criminal gangs. However, the personal, social, legal and moral problems involved are very different.

What is Prostitution?

Broadly speaking, prostitution can be defined as the exchange of sexual intercourse for money or any other material consideration. Prostitution is a mere business transaction and supposes the relatively indiscriminate availability of sexual gratification to individuals other than spouses or friends. Ordinarily, sexual gratification solely from visual or auditory stimuli is not considered as prostitution. Prostitution does not demand emotional involvement, imposes no liability and requires no effort on the part of the customer, usually the man, to please his partner. On the other hand, prostitution invests sexuality with the aura of vice and creates the atmosphere of something immoral, suspect and dangerous which acts as an aphrodisiac for certain people so that a man who is impotent in true love functions sexually with unloved women.

Freud pointed out the dissociation of 'love' from 'lust' and explained that many men were unable to achieve orgasm with a woman they respect. They need the illusion of some kind of lewdness to get sufficiently excited. A similar dichotomy exists between the woman with whom a man wants to generate offspring, the mother of his children, and the woman or women with whom he wants to satisfy his sexual lust.

Prostitution answers to the demand for sex on the part of individuals who do not wish an affectionate attachment, who experience a temporary difficulty in forming a sexual relationship or who want sexual techniques their wives or customary sex partners refuse (for example, mouth-genital contact). Prostitution may exploit the economic situation of women and supposes the double standard of morality for men and women. It is also intimately connected with drinking, entertainment and dancing. Military installations have usually resulted in a considerable demand for prostitutes despite restrictive legislation.

SEL-M

Brothels

In their present form, brothels are supervised by an older female. One or more males also live on the premises to deal with unruly or homosexual clients. Some brothels cater to particular socio-economic or ethnic groups. Brothels may be restricted to certain districts and a given area may be almost wholly given over to prostitution. A 'house girl' is a prostitute belonging to a particular brothel. Since clients prefer novelty, prostitutes not infrequently move from one brothel to another. The brothel owner takes a percentage of the prostitutes' earnings which may range from 20 per cent to nearly all.

A call-girl has her own residence (sometimes shared with another prostitute for security and companionship) but has connections with an agent or office and may be associated with some kind of organisation. Recently, West German police arrested a couple who were running a call-girl ring behind the front of an escort agency employing 400 women with branches in every major German city and in New York, Switzerland, Austria, Italy, Greece, France, Belgium, the Netherlands and Britain. In return for a percentage of her earnings, a call-girl is notified where to meet each client (hotel room, home). Ordinarily, she is discouraged from developing contacts of her own. Independent prostitutes only pay hotel employees, taxi drivers, bartenders or procurers.

Establishments other than brothels which actually serve for prostitution are numerous. Bars may have adjacent rooms, massage parlours, Turkish baths, escort services or modelling agencies may be fronts for prostitution. Some establishments or girls within an establishment may specialise in certain sexual techniques such as sadomasochism. Sometimes, the girls do not provide coitus but masturbate the client. Bars may not go beyond obscene conversation and some degree of petting. Live sex shows may invite customers to participate but clients of peep shows content themselves with enjoying the exhibition of sexual activities which may range from actual or feigned coitus to poses of a nude woman. As Guy Talese remarks, men are endlessly fascinated with the naked female form.

Socialist authors maintain that prostitution is a piece of the merchandise fetishism of capitalistic society in which women are treated as merchandise. Women who accept this status of slaves should make it a weapon against the oppression by men but it seems very doubtful that a private revolt could change the unjust conditions.

How Did Prostitution Arise?

How did prostitution arise? There is no satisfactory answer to that question and it will probably be impossible to give just one answer. Prostitution seems unnecessary in sexually-permissive societies but sexual permissiveness is a very loose concept. Adolescents may enjoy great sexual freedom as, for example, Malinowski reported for the Trobriand islanders, but that does not exclude firm sex relations in adult life. Sacred or religious prostitution is evidenced in antiquity for many countries in the Near and Middle East, including Egypt, Canaan, Phoenicia, Babylonia, Assyria, Lydia and Persia, and was also practised in India, Numidia and West Africa. Temple prostitution was in vogue in Judah under King Manasseh (692-638 BC).

Under Oriental influence, sacred prostitution found entry into Greece where the best-known example was the temple of Aphrodite in Corinth in which the *hierodules* (temple slaves) served as prostitutes. Sacred prostitution took various forms. It has been explained as a rite by which women offered their virginity to a particular god. In the so-called Myletta rite in ancient Babylonia, every female was required to sit in the temple of the goddess Ishtar and accept coitus from the first male who threw a silver coin in her lap. Prostitution as a continuous obligation of a particular class of priestesses was customary in the Middle East.

Public Prostitution in Greece

Public prostitution began in Greece in the seventh century BC and in an arrangement ascribed to Solon, the prostitutes had to live in a fixed quarter. They were lightly dressed or naked from the waist upward. Private prostitutes were marked by their dress with a distinctive flower design and the light colour of their hair. A special class were the *heterae* (female companions), professional independent courtesans distinguished by physical beauty and intellectual culture. Generally, they were foreigners, slaves or free women who sometimes lived fashionably in a respected position. They were protected and taxed by the state and enjoyed greater freedom than the ordinary married woman bound to seclusion. Their homes were frequented by married men and they were often hired for symposia or family sacrifices. The *heterae* of Corinth and Athens were particularly noted for their beauty and culture. Phryne ('Toad,' nick-name of the Athenian courtesan Muesarete, fourth century BC) was the model for Appelles' picture of Aphrodite Anadyomene (Rising from the Sea) and probably also for the statue of Aphrodite her lover Praxiteles carved for the Cnidians. A marble statue of her created by Praxiteles stood in the temple of Eros at Thespia and a gilted bronze statue by the same sculptor at Delphi.

The attempts to make prostitutes identifiable by requiring them to dress in a particular way and/or to live in a restricted area were also made in Rome and later in medieval Europe. Similar measures were taken in China and Japan. Even if no legal restrictions are imposed, prostitution is often tolerated only in certain districts of a city and effectively barred from other neighbourhoods.

Rome

Ancient Rome licensed and taxed prostitution, which was already run as a business, with the help of slaves. Besides slaves, foreign women and freed women were engaged in prostitution; a free Roman woman had to notify the *aedile*. Under Tiberius, the calling became so popular that the senate prohibited women whose grandfather, father or husband belonged to the equestrian class from becoming prostitutes. In the times of the emperors, Rome is said to have had 45 *lupanaria* (brothels) and Pompeii had at least seven. The cubicles were dark and closed by curtains above which the name of the prostitute was posted. The prostitutes were naked or wore only light dresses.

Medieval Europe

From the sixth to the ninth century, the large vassals of the Frankish kings had their private brothels called *genecium* (gynaeceum — a dwelling used by women). All female serfs were liable to be abused by their lords, the king and his court. Sometimes, the maids, often with illegitimate children, deserted the manors and joined the 'vagabonding' whores of the Middle Ages. The *lex Ripuariorum,* compiled in the seventh century, tried to force prostitutes into the brothels of the cities, and the *lex Romana Visigothorum* (published in 506) contained an attempt at regulating prostitution.

In medieval Europe, prostitution was generally not prohibited from the eleventh to the fifteenth century. Princes, cities and church dignitaries owned brothels which were usually connected with bath-houses. Social and economic conditions were quite different for the vagabonding prostitutes and the inmates of public houses. The former were without protection and in double jeopardy because of their lack of legal status as well as the fact that they were dubbed street-walkers; the latter gradually succeeded in improving their position and by the end of the fifteenth century had been able to form their own guilds in most cities which incorporated them into medieval society. They were often required to wear a distinctive garb, for example, a special hat, a yellow cloak or a veil with green stripes.

Each brothel had its regulations, usually fixed by the owner, setting forth the rights and duties of the brothel-keeper (often a woman) and the prostitutes. The brothel-keeper usually was a manager hired by the owner who paid a weekly or monthly rent. He was often supervised by a man or woman selected from ordinary citizens. The rules laid down by Henry II of England prescribed that the brothel-keeper had to give any prostitute the right to leave who wanted to move to another whore-house or to give up her sinful life. He was not allowed to solicit customers, admit nuns or married women or hire sick women. Many regulations prohibited the admittance of local women as prostitutes. The ordinance of the city of Ulm decreed that all income was to be deposited in a box under the triple supervision of a whore elected as treasurer by the inmates, the brothel-keeper and another prostitute. The box was opened each week and its contents divided according to a ratio fixed by the city. A certain sum to which the prostitutes and the brothel-keeper contributed was always kept for emergencies, such as sickness.

There were also brothels not owned by cities but managed by keepers who were outside the medieval social system and therefore without legal status and protection. The inmates of these brothels, the 'free daughters,' were likewise without legal position. Emperor Rudolph of Hapsburg gave them a minimum of legal protection by a decree issued in 1278 and at times, prostitutes paid a special tax to the emperor for his protection.

Women made homeless by the demise of the Frankish *latifundia,* women made widows by the interminable wars or driven into poverty by the devastation of rural households furnished the largest contingent of the inmates of the urban whore-houses. But there always were numerous vagabonding harlots who plied their trade on the roads. They often were the daughters of families in 'infamous' trades (executioners, grave-diggers, skinners, musicians) who could not find husbands, the widows or daughters of fallen soldiers, escaped serfs or pilgrims in need of money. All through the Middle Ages, the vagabonding whores moved from fair to fair and converged on diets or councils. The diet at Frankfurt in 1394 attracted more than 800 prostitutes, and over 1,500 gathered for the council of Constance in 1415. During fairs, prostitutes enjoyed the 'freedom of the fair,' that is to say, they were free to ply their trade. Vagabonding prostitutes as a mass phenomenon continued until the beginning of the eighteenth century.

A particular class of prostitutes were the women in the trains of the medieval armies. About 5,000 prostitutes are said to have accompanied the first crusade. They combined the supply of all kinds of merchandise with personal services such as cooking, washing, cleaning and the care of the sick and usually were also available for sexual intercourse. A special officer, often of the rank of a captain, supervised these women and his functions were assigned to the provost marshal in the Thirty Years' War.

Privileges of Prostitutes

Prostitutes enjoyed a number of privileges. In many cities they were entitled to be present at all marriages and receptions. In return for the hospitality, they had to offer bouquets of flowers to the hosts. Until 1524, they had the right to dance naked, but adorned with flowers, with the journeymen of Vienna's guilds at the solstice festival for which they received three pounds of Viennese coins. In Würzburg, the mayor and his council dined at the brothel on the feast of St John. In Zurzach, the governor of Baden danced twice a year, at the fair of Zurzach, with the most beautiful of the prostitutes — the *regina bordelli* (queen of the brothel). When Emperor Sigismund came to Ulm in 1435, the city put the brothel at his disposal and arranged an illumination of the brothel for the emperor's reception. When a prince entered a city, the prostitutes had the right to receive him naked at the city gate. Such receptions are recorded for Emperor Sigismund in 1435, for Emperor Albrecht II in 1438, for King Ladislas Postumus in 1452 and for Charles the Bold of Burgundy in 1468. Naked *filles de joie* welcomed Louis XI when he entered Paris, and the naked inmates of the harbour brothels saluted Emperor Charles V when he came to Antwerp in 1520.

The syphilis epidemic of 1494 led to the closure of most brothels. London's last twelve bordellos were shut down by Henry VIII because of syphilis. Since the prostitutes were thought responsible for the spread of the epidemic, tolerance of prostitutes changed into persecution and the criminalisation of prostitution resulted in the association of prostitutes with criminals. Luther exhorted the authorities to follow the example of the kings of Israel and abolish all whore-houses. It was unworthy of Christians, he wrote, to keep public places of sin.

Renaissance

The Renaissance brought an enormous display of sexuality and in the Italian cities, courtesans not unlike the Greek *heterae* were available to the individual *cortegiano* (courtier) as well as for parties and festivities. At a banquet in honour of Pope Alexander VI, 50 renowned courtesans entertained the party with dances, first in exquisite costumes, then in the nude, and prizes were given to those of the guests who showed most manly prowess with the damsels. Some time during the Council of Trent, 300 'respectable whores' (*honestae meretrices quas cortigianas vocant*) were in town.

In the seventeenth century, the division of prostitution between the prostitution of the poor and that of the rich became dominant and led to the separation of the street-walkers from the courtesans, mistresses and the *demi-monde* of the salons. Out of the luxury brothels of the eighteenth century developed the 'specialised' houses of the nineteenth and early twentieth centuries.

A tax on prostitution was introduced in Athens by Solon and imposed by Caligula in Rome. It was abolished by Emperor Anastasios in 501 AD. In the Middle Ages, taxes were levied on brothels as well as on individual prostitutes. Pope Sixtus IV collected a tax of 20,000 ducates from a single brothel he had built. In Naples, the government leased the tax on prostitution to a renter who paid a lump sum to the city and, as part of the contract, had to protect the rights of the prostitutes against the city and individual citizens.

The relation between prostitution and economic distress seems to be a worldwide phenomenon and obtained in antiquity as well as in modern times. Poverty is worse than prostitution, and social, moral, religious and legal restrictions have never and nowhere eradicated the sex trade. Private prostitution has competed with public or licensed prostitution wherever regulative restrictions were enforced and where poverty became a strong motive for disregarding social or moral taboos.

Abolition Movement

The economic misery and the social upheavals accompanying the Industrial Revolution led to an enormous increase in prostitution. In the nineteenth century, and particularly in Victorian England, not only the contrast between rich and poor was extreme, but the efforts to abolish prostitution coincided with a flourishing white-slave trade. The abolition of prostitution was part of the social movement aimed at removing the legal disabilities from women (Married Women's Property Act), admission of women to higher education and improvement of their social position (abolition of the Contagious Diseases Acts of 1864-9 which made women in garrison towns subject to compulsory examination for venereal disease). A leading feminist of the period, Josephine Elizabeth Butler, wife of the canon of Winchester, was largely instrumental in the abolition of public prostitution in England in 1886. A year earlier, in 1885, a correspondent of the French newspaper *Figaro* counted 500 prostitutes between the ages of 12 and 15 on the 300 metre-long stretch of road from Picadilly Circus to Waterloo Place. A thriving trade in children and virgins extended beyond Europe. There were brothels that used girls only once. For defloration, a man could get a girl who sacrificed her innocence voluntarily, a girl who had to be raped, a girl who was bound up to facilitate the rape, a girl who was crying or a girl who had been anaesthetised. If the customer so desired, he could be present when a doctor examined the girl for the intactness of the hymen. After defloration, the girls were released but they usually had nowhere to go but into prostitution.

Present Conditions

Following England, the movement to abolish prostitution was successful in Holland, Norway and Denmark. The suppression of prostitution has been the aim of international efforts and the League of Nations as well as the United Nations worked towards this goal. The UN Universal Declaration of Human Rights and the Convention for the Suppression of Traffic in Persons and of the Exploitation of the Prostitution of Others proclaim this policy. A report drafted under the auspices of the UN Economic and Social Council called for international cooperation in identifying world prostitution networks. It listed traffic of North-African women to Europe, South Americans from Argentina to Melbourne, Hawaiian and Californian women to Japan and Thai women to Switzerland as forms of procurement masquerading as marriage markets. It also attacked the so-called sex tours in which the services of a prostitute are included in the price of the plane ticket. In most cases, the report said, prostitution involves a procurer in one guise or another.

In the United States, the federal Mann Act (White Slave Traffic Act, 1910) prohibited the transport of a woman across state lines ('interstate traffic') for immoral purposes, and the anti-racketeering legislation passed in 1961 reinforced this prohibition. Brothels are illegal in most states. In Nevada, however, brothels were made legal in two counties as recently as 1972. They must be located 5 km out of town and marked by a sign saying 'Guest Ranch — Men Only.' The largest whore-house in Nevada, the Mustang Ranch, which has 109 rooms, a swimming pool and a tennis court on a 15-acre site, was recently put up for sale. The owners put on a price tag of $25 million and the girls who work there evidently thought that the place was worth it: they split their fees (a minimum of $60 an hour) with management.

There are laws against procuring, soliciting and living on the earnings of a prostitute, but the vice trade flourishes. Estimates put the number of women in the United States who have been used in prostitution at 400,000 or 500,000. The average age of working prostitutes is twenty-two, the average age at which women start working as prostitutes is seventeen; 63 per cent of the prostitutes had run away from home, 80 per cent had been victims of sexual abuse, 80 per cent have pimps and 83 per cent have no savings or other financial resources.

New York police estimates that a call-girl ring organised by the 'Mayflower Madam' (Sidney Biddle Barrows) may have grossed over $1 million a year. Her three escort services were advertised in the *Yellow Pages* and accepted payment by credit card. Police seized the names of 3,000 clients when they raided the office. In an agreement reached in court, the prosecutor's office dropped felony charges and allowed Mrs Barrows to plead guilty to a misdemeanour charge of promoting prostitution. She was fined $5,000 but could keep $150,000 in profits from the escort services.

Police in San Jose, California, broke up a prostitution ring that kept computerised dossiers on 12,000 businessmen from around the world who visited northern California. The ring which coordinated five escort services employed 117 prostitutes who carried credit card imprinters to allow customers to charge the $160 an hour 'escort service.' The operation took in more than $25 million in eight years of operation.

Organised crime groups with ties to the Far East have been expanding their operations in the United States, importing thousands of women from South Korea and Taiwan and shuttling them through a network of American brothels. Authorities have been investigating the possible involvement of American servicemen abroad who may have received up to $10,000 for sham marriages that enabled Asian women to enter the United States. These women then agreed to 'indentured servitude' as prostitutes for as long as six months. Other visas allegedly were obtained by bribing a US consular official in Taiwan. The Asia-linked syndicates operated not only in major cities such as Los Angeles, San Francisco, New York, New Jersey and Denver, but also ran five 'health spas' in Farmington Hills, a Detroit suburb.

The New York vice squad arrested the pastor of 'The Church of Sharing' who ran a brothel under the guise of a religious club. The church had never held a religious service but, under the slogan 'sharing and loving,' solicited 'parishioners' to join its 'religion-in-action' club known as the 'Midnight Interlude.' A New York psychiatrist operated a brothel under the guise of a sex clinic and had the medical insurance companies of his customers pay for the 'sex therapy' sessions. In a similar ploy, West German tourists who had patronised brothels in Thailand, Sri Lanka, the Philippines and some African and Middle East countries submitted claims for repayment of 'hospital bills.' The insurance companies got wise to the fraud and in some cases, the money was recovered.

American prostitutes organised 'prostitutes' rights' groups and wanted to persuade delegates to the 1984 Democratic National Convention in San Francisco that prostitution is a human-rights and labour issue and that their right to work should be protected by law. Prostitution is legal in Peru and the warehouse-like brothels in Lima are said to employ about 50,000 prostitutes. According to the International Abolitionist Federation, millions of women and children are kidnapped, cheated and sold into prostitution and slavery, shipped to remote corners of the globe by flesh traders who beat them, rape them and give them no opportunity to return home.

Prostitution is widespread in Asia. Bangkok, the Mecca of sex fanatics, is populated by 60,000 prostitutes and shelters 350 go-go bars, 130 massage parlours and 100 dance halls in addition to pleasure hotels, transvestite night clubs and live sex shows. Escort services for visiting foreigners are advertised daily in the Thai English-language press: 'Pleasant, charming, young, lovely, well-trained, cheerful and efficient lady escorts' cost $80 a night. Many of these escorts are students and bar hostesses. The availability of bargain-priced sex attracts about 60 per cent of the two million tourists coming to Bangkok. Outside Bangkok, 450,000 prostitutes are kept in brothels, bars and tea-houses. The International Commission of Jurists estimated Thailand's total prostitution population in 1982 at 700,000 and said that the situation raised serious human-rights problems. Poverty was considered the main cause. Girls as young as 12 are sold into slavery for $90 per body. The going price for deflowering a 12-year-old virgin was $100. If the girls escape, they are caught by the police and brought back.

Thailand introduced the registration of prostitutes in 1906 but no new brothels were licensed after 1948 and no new prostitutes registered after 1956. Prostitution was outlawed in 1960. Women arrested for soliciting face a 300 baht ($13.50) fine, but for every 1,000 women taken into custody, only one or two procurers are arrested. The most popular women can earn as much as 30,000 baht ($1,350) a month; average earnings are 7,000 baht ($315) in Bangkok and 1,000 baht ($45) in the countryside.

About 5,000 Thai girls are said to have been lured by white-slave traders to Hong Kong and about as many to Macao. They were offered high salaries in the 'service industry' but ended up by being forced into prostitution. Officials in Hong Kong and Macao acknowledged that Thai prostitutes operated in their areas but thought the numbers overstated. Hong Kong police believe that most of the women are recruited in Bangkok by syndicates which arrange for work permits with their Hong Kong connections. 'They know full well what they are going to do before they arrive in Hong Kong,' a police officer was quoted as saying. According to a newspaper story, officers of the Hong Kong vice squad sent to raid a brothel succumbed to the charms of the girls and took off their clothes.

In the People's Republic of China, prostitution which the Communist Party claimed to have stamped out, has become widespread, particularly in southern coastal areas. Western journalists have reported cases of prostitution since 1979 but recently Chinese officials, too, have voiced concern over the reemergence of professional prostitution. Prices are low by western standards, ranging from 1 to 8 yuan (35 cents to $2.75). The younger the prostitute, the higher the price, and ever younger women are induced to take up the trade. In Guangdon province, regulations published in 1981 impose fines from $35 to $1,000 on people who keep the company of prostitutes while the women are subject to detention and made to sign a pledge to repent.

The Japanese have been branded with reproach for their sex tours to Bangkok and Manila but Australians, West Germans, Arabs and other nationals also visit these cities. Usually, the Japanese do not parade their conquests through Manila streets as some westerners do who provide the visual evidence of the rape of the Philippines to the average Filipino and the other tourists. Philippine authorities are particularly worried about foreign tourists luring children into prostitution, including paederasty and the performance of sexual acts for pornographic films. Recently, an American petty officer was found guilty on 13 counts of carnal abuse of children by a Navy court-martial in the Philippines. Most of the girls with whom he had had intercourse were between the ages of 12 and 14. One was a girl of nine who had already been deflowered by another sailor. Many of the girls in the neighbourhood of the Subic

US Navy base are suffering from venereal disease. An estimated 16,000 bar girls registered at the social hygiene clinic of Olongapo City are tested weekly for venereal infections and other diseases.

An estimate of the Ministry of Labour of the Philippines put the number of prostitutes catering to the tourist demand at 150,000. Children aged from as young as 7 to 16 are bought by recruiters scouring the provinces who offer parents 200-400 pesos ($11-12). They promise factory jobs but actually channel the children into prostitution with many of the older girls being sold to Japanese *yakuza* (gangsters).

In the Philippines, Indonesia, Burma and Sri Lanka, prostitution is mainly an urban phenomenon but in India, about two-thirds of the prostitutes are from rural areas. Prostitution is still associated with girls dedicated to temples and in some communities, certain girls are consecrated as prostitutes. Prostitution is illegal in India, and all forms of religious prostitution are forbidden by law. In northern India, many dancing girls still become prostitutes while due to the general lawlessness in the state of Tamil Nadu, nearly 25,000 women have been abducted and forced into prostitution in the six years to 1983. In markets for women, a girl as young as 12 can be bought for as little as 2,000 rupees ($155). Indian health officials stated that most of the 2,000 prostitutes in New Delhi came from Nepal. Brothel owners and customers were said to ward off disturbing police raids by bribes.

In 1981, a member of the Congress (I) Party denounced the exploitation through marriage of young Indian Muslim girls by Arab visitors. Bombay, Bangalore and Hyderabad are the favourite places for marriages between old though rich Arabs, mostly from the Gulf states, and Indian girls, often as young as 14. The Arab bridegroom is charged 2,000 to 3,000 rupees ($155-232) for the wedding performed by a local *kazi* (the Arabic *quadi,* or judge in Muslim communities). The girls are taken to various Arab countries, divorced and sold after a few days of pleasure. Some of the girls never reach the Middle East; they are ditched in Bombay where they are sold to Arabs in five-star hotels for a few nights. Others are made to work as maids.

In the first six months of 1982, about 400 such marriages were performed in Hyderabad. The Indian government instructed the Hyderabad police to crack down on marriage brokers. A prospective bridegroom now must deposit $3,000 in the name of the girl in a local bank before he can marry her. But if the parents are willing to sell their daughter, the police can do little about it. A Saudi national was prosecuted for marrying five under-age girls within a period of five weeks in 1980. In a pre-dawn sweep, police in Islamabad arrested nearly 100 women for prostitution. The women who worked under the cover of dancing girls — itself a crime — were to be tried in Islamic courts and faced flogging in addition to lengthy jail terms.

In Iran, a special court and an 'anti-sin squad' have been created to combat prostitution, drinking and sexual perversion. As mentioned above, under the *Sharia* (Islamic law), adulterers are stoned to death, unmarried fornicators are lashed in public, as are imbibers of alcohol. Homosexuals and sodomisers are dropped to death from the highest spot in town. Although the Iranian authorities enforce the Koranic law, it is not clear to what extent the Islamic penalties are applied. The government claimed that thousands of prostitutes had been rounded up, reeducated and given factory jobs.

In Indonesia, polygamy is a contributing factor to prostitution. Men are permitted four wives, and if they want to marry a new woman, they divorce one or more wives without concern for what happens to them later. Many of the wives thus divorced turn to prostitution. Prostitution was abolished in mainland China after 1949. In Malaysia, Hong Kong and Singapore, measures to prevent prostitution are enforced by the police and the immigration authorities.

Anti-Vice Legislation

In Britain, much of the anti-vice legislation was directed against brothel keepers, procurers and pimps. Following the recommendations of the *Wolfenden Report,* the Street Offences Act of 1959 for the first time prohibited all street solicitation and loitering by prostitutes. Prostitution itself is not an offence, and if the prostitute lives by herself, her room is not a brothel (defined as premises used by at least two women for purposes of prostitution). There has been much criticism of the present legal situation. 'It is absurd to send prostitutes to prison for an offence which has no victim. This reflects a deep-seated double standard.' And prison often hastens the return to the street of prostitutes to pay bills that accumulated while they were in jail. There is no law against 'curb crawling' by male motorists seeking women in the street.

The community council of Southampton, England, found itself completely helpless against the sex industry and wondered whether the situation would not be less chaotic if brothels were licensed or permitted. This view has often been voiced in countries in which brothels are illegal but the experience in countries with licensed prostition shows that the legalisation of brothels does not do away with street-walkers. In West Germany, the number of prostitutes has been estimated at 60,000 because 'amateur' prostitutes such as housewives, working women and students compete with the women in the so-called Eros houses.

West Germany allows prostitution, brothels and sex shops, but prostitution is punishable if pursued in the vicinity of a school or other places destined to be frequented by persons under 18 years of age or in a house in which persons under 18 live in a way constituting a moral danger to such persons (Penal Code Art. 184b). Prostitutes are also punished if they habitually offend against a prohibition to engage in prostitution at certain places either always or at certain times (Art. 184a). In Munich, a city ordinance banned prostitutes from almost 80 per cent of the city whereupon a group of prostitutes appealed to the Bavarian constitutional court complaining that their constitutional freedom of action had been violated. The president of the court declined to act saying that it would be incompatible with the dignity of the court to decide where brothels could be built. A police expert claimed that of the 400 to 500 prostitutes in Munich, only about 180 worked in brothels.

France ended state registration of prostitutes, closed the *maisons de tolérance* and outlawed solicitation in 1946 but in the same year, a card-index system for all prostitutes was introduced and registration for the purpose of hygiene (contact tracing and treatment of venereal disease) enforced. In 1948, prostitutes were made subject to examination even before their occupation was proved which practically meant a return to state registration. Because little was done to rehabilitate the inmates of the brothels, conditions became worse than before because the prostitutes moved to the streets where they were arrested for soliciting. The battle of wits between the prostitutes and the police has touched off many zany episodes. It was proposed that brothels should be allowed at least in the neighbourhood of army barracks. The French Foreign Legion has its own bordellos at all its camps. The facility is run in military fashion. The women arrive each day at 5 pm and leave at 9 pm. They get the basic pay of a private plus monthly commissions based on the *jetons,* the counters bought at the door with the price determined by rank.

As in other countries, 'amateur' prostitution increased also in France. Recently, the police discovered a child prostitution ring run by the children themselves and comprising children between the ages of 8 to 13.

In a letter to Yvette Roudy, then minister for women's rights, Paris call-girls demanded an end to police harassment by clearly defining their status. They complained that judicial vagueness concerning their activities encouraged abuse of police powers and led to street prostitution. The French penal code provides that anybody who encourages or protects prostitution is guilty of procurement. Prostitution itself is treated with ill-defined tolerance. The call-girls may pursue respectable day-time careers as models, secretaries or university students or be the wives of notaries or academics and they claim that their nocturnal profession is one of choice. 'Our activities are very discreet and we disturb nobody,' one of the signatories of the appeal said. 'We pay taxes and we bring a lot of foreign currency into France through our international clientèle. And yet we are prosecuted. Why can't the authorities leave us in peace?'

Prostitution has been legal in Holland since the early 1970s and a law passed by the Dutch Parliament in April 1987 abrogated a 1911 ban on pimping and legalised brothels. Local authorities are allowed to fix their own rules on the locations where brothels can be established and on standards of safety and hygiene. The law ended what was termed a tolerance policy which permitted prostitution in established red-light districts but otherwise enforced a ban on brothels. Amsterdam has 200 sex clubs and 6,000 prostitutes. But the voluntarily-registered prostitutes are augmented by a legion of illegal street-walkers who often ply drugs to support their own habits or those of their husbands, boyfriends or procurers.

In Sweden, prostitution is no crime but the country's highest fiscal court ruled that the commercial offering of sexual services is professional enterprise and, like any other enterprise, liable to taxation.

Israeli newspapers follow a very liberal policy in accepting advertisements for their lonely-heart columns. They print ads for party-swappers, sadomasochists, homosexuals and prostitutes. Some newspapers have two columns, one for *shidduchim* (matches), the other for *hekeruyot* (acquaintances). In Austria, however, newspapers stopped accepting 'contacts' ads which gave phone numbers, addresses and prices (usually 300 schillings — $17) of prostitutes.

Switzerland banned brothels in 1942 when the penal code was revised but there have been proposals for their reintroduction. The proponents think that such a step would help to contain sexual disease, homosexuality and criminal violence.

Prostitution itself is not prohibited in Switzerland and recently, the country's highest federal court overturned the decision of a cantonal court and ruled that a prostitute unable to work after a traffic accident was entitled to compensation. The world's oldest profession might be immoral but was not illegal, the court reasoned.

The government of the Australian state of Victoria introduced legislation to allow prostitution in massage parlours that meet zoning requirements (at least 40 metres away from schools, Scout or Girl Guide centres or other places where youth under 18 regularly gather).

Under the pretext of combating prostitution, Zimbabwe police, aided by soldiers and members of Prime Minister Mugabe's African National Union Party Youth Brigade, in October and November 1983, arrested hundreds of women, including married and single women, foreign teachers and school-girls. Police raided night clubs, movie theatres, hotels, supermarkets and homes and picked up women indiscriminately in the streets. While real prostitutes had been tipped off in advance, irate husbands had to produce marriage certificates to get their wives released from police custody.

Launching a crackdown on prostitution, Gabon President Omar Bongo ordered police to round up prostitutes and turn them over to the troops. 'When they have had five or six soldiers on top of them, these women will understand that you mustn't street-walk in Gabon,' he was quoted as telling gendarmerie officers. The president was reported to have said that all prostitutes were foreigners and to have asked certain ambassadors to stop their compatriots from soliciting in Gabon.

Prostitution in Old China

Among the accounts on prostitution in old China, 'The Record of the Gay Quarters' contains sketches of prostitutes and their patrons with a selection of their poems. The location is Ch'ang-an, China's capital from 192 BC to 904 AD, near the modern Sian in Shensi province. Nara and Kyoto were modelled after Ch'ang-an which, however, was much larger, measuring over six miles from east to west and five miles from north to south. The author, Sun Ch'i, who lived near the end of the T'ang dynasty, relates the life story of a courtesan with whom he fell in love but whom he refused to marry. She was of humble origin but eager to learn and had been taken to the capital ostensibly as an opportunity for improving herself. She was left at a house of prostitution where she was trained and made into a courtesan after her virginity had been sold to a government official. Other women, from good families, entered the profession because their parents were deceived by spurious betrothal arrangements. The girls underwent rigorous training in the feminine arts and had to gain skill in dancing, composing poetry, playing musical instruments and conducting drinking parties, but good looks, wit in conversation and agreeable manners were valuable assets. The women who lived in the same house were considered to be family members and the 'daughters' adopted the surname of the 'foster mother,' an older prostitute who had become manager. But they were also given special personal names after they joined the profession suggestive of their calling (the special names used by modern Chinese prostitutes were called 'flower names'). In one of Ch'ang-an's thriving gay quarters, courtesans were allowed to attend religious lectures three times monthly at a Buddhist temple, after paying the foster mother a fixed sum for the privilege. Men often made arrangements with their favourites to meet them at the temple during these lecture periods.

Prominent courtesans were free to choose their friends and lovers. It was customary to purchase a courtesan's time for strolling about with her in the public parks along the Hwang Ho (Yellow River). Outstanding courtesans were selected as stewardesses for banquets. Entertaining at drinking parties seems to have been an at least equally important part of the courtesan's work as providing sexual enjoyment. A woman who could engage in this profession when she was over 30 years old was considered fortunate.

No moral stigma was attached to frequenting the gay quarters and the social position of courtesans, although low, was higher than that of modern prostitutes. Many gained fame because of their literary accomplishments and sometimes courtesans became the wives or concubines of their lovers.

T'ang literature also includes many references to the gay quarters of Yangshow, a flourishing trade centre in T'ang China, where the houses of prostitution were on a grand scale.

Prostitution in Old Japan

In Japan, the Heian noblemen shared the addiction to the pleasures of drink, love, poetry and music, but no accounts on organised gay quarters are extant. Temple prostitution *(miko)* existed in ancient times and public prostitution developed in the Kamakura era (1192-1333 AD). Toyotomi Hideyoshi (1536-1598) tried to suppress private prostitution and in 1598, licensed quarters called *yûkaku* opened in Kyoto's Yanagimachi. In order to limit prostitution to a confined area under strict supervision, the Edo authorities established a *yûkaku* district in Fukiyamachi where the first (Moto-) Yoshiwara was installed in 1618. The establishment was later transferred to Senzoku near Asakusa where the new (Shin-) Yoshiwara was completed in 1657. It remained the centre of public prostitution until 1957.

By 1679, there were over one hundred *yûri* (licensed quarters) throughout the country. The most famous were Shimabara in Kyoto, Yoshiwara in Edo and Shinmachi in Osaka. The gay quarters constituted a world of their own. Yoshiwara consisted of about 150 houses with some 3,000 courtesans, and a large population of attendants, dancing girls, musicians, panders, jesters and tradesmen also lived in these compounds. The organisation was generally modelled on Shimabara where prostitutes were divided into two classes, *age-jorô* and *mise-jorô*. The *age-jorô* were professional entertainers who lived in the house of their employer and were summoned to nearby houses of assignation *(ageya)* to entertain their customers. The second class of prostitutes, the *mise-jorô*, plied their trade in the houses *(mise,* literally, shop) where they lived or were called to outside tea-houses *(chaya)*.

In both classes of courtesans, a strictly defined structure developed. In most *yûri,* the *age-jorô* were divided into three grades, with the rank depending on looks, cultural achievements, seniority in the district and the ability to please customers. The top grade was *tayû* (later called *oiran);* they were to be found only in the five leading *yûri,* Shimabara (Kyoto), Shinmachi (Osaka), Yoshiwara (Edo), Maruyama (Nagasaki) and Kanayama (Sado Island). Apprentice girls were always in attendance on the higher ranking courtesans; they were the forerunners of today's *maiko* (young dancing girls in Kyoto) who remain virgins until some rich customer pays for the privilege of deflowering them. Once a year, the *tayû* paraded through the streets in a gorgeous procession. The high-ranking courtesans were in a position to turn down unwelcome customers; sometimes, a single customer would rent their services for an entire year.

Costs varied from town to town but were uniform for the same class in the district. Sometimes, services were divided between a day period and a night period. The fees for the courtesans were quite substantial, between 30 and 74 momme of silver (1 momme = 3.7565 g; at present silver prices, this would be equivalent to ¥7,650 to ¥18,870); in addition, fees had to be paid for the attendants. According to Ihara Saisaku, the expense of a first visit to a Kyoto *tayû* would come to 551 momme, and he warns that the pleasures of the gay quarters can prove ruinous.

Just as today, prostitution flourished in many forms and guises. Besides the registered prostitutes, there were several kinds of street-walkers and the attendants (*yuma*) at public bath-houses and hot springs often engaged in prostitution. It was one of the services available at the *chaya* which catered to the needs of the travellers at the stations of the *go-kaidô* (five great roads).

When a woman died in the Yoshiwara establishment, her parents were generally notified, but when the parents were unknown or lived far away, the woman was usually buried in the cemetery of the Buddhist temple Jokanji. Between 1664 and the early years of the Meiji era, about 20,000 prostitutes were buried there. Because the burials were conducted with little ceremony, the temple became known as *Nagekomi-dera* (dumping temple). Another burial ground of prostitutes was Dotetsu or Kôganzan Saihôji.

Male prostitution is recorded as early as the Heian period (794–858 AD) and professional catamites (*chigo*) lived in Buddhist monasteries. Centres of male prostitution existed in Kyoto, Osaka and Edo.

Meiji Era

Public prostitution was ostensibly abolished in 1872. According to some writers, the occasion was the reply of the captain of the Peruvian ship, *Maria Luz,* who was accused of illegal confinement by the Japanese authorities when he sought to recapture Chinese coolies who had escaped. The contracts made by the coolies, he said, were no different from those made by the courtesans in Yoshiwara. Whereupon the *yûkaku,* where prostitutes were kept, were suppressed. But in the following year, the authorities in Osaka issued business licenses for *kashi-yashiki,* and brothels reappeared everywhere under this new designation. In 1882, Gunma Prefecture abolished public prostitution (brothels) but placed private prostitution under the supervision of the morals police (*fûki keisatsu*) which practically created a system of public prostitution. The Licensed Prostitution Control Regulation of 1900 recognised public prostitution while prohibiting private prostitution. This regulation intended to stop the exploitation and mistreatment of prostitutes and prevent the spread of venereal disease.

A campaign by social reformers led by the Salvation Army called for 'self-emancipation.' A strike by prostitutes (*shinome no sutoraiku,* 'daybreak strike') and numerous desertions rocked the industry but the pre-war Supreme Court (*Taishin-in,* Court of Cassation) decided that

SEL-N

prostitutes have the freedom to leave but that they must first pay their debts which, of course, they were unable to do. It was only in 1955 that the (post-war) Supreme Court declared debts contracted prior to their release from bondage to be invalid.

During the war, the Japanese army set up brothels in the occupied territories. By the end of the war, about 80,000 women were employed in this system. Most of them were Koreans who had been conscripted for this purpose, but there were also indigenous women and, for officers only, Japanese prostitutes who were no longer usable in Japan. Under the Occupation, a memorandum of 1946 prohibited licensed prostitution and ordered the rescission of the Regulation of 1900 and related local ordinances. But even prior to the arrival of General MacArthur's troops, a special organisation had been created to supply 'comfort girls' *(ian-fu,* the same as the designation of the prostitutes who had accompanied the Japanese Imperial Army) to the Occupation forces. According to a report, the cabinet of Prince Higashikuni decided to build a 'human dam' in order to protect Japanese women against a sexual assault by the Allied forces coming to occupy Japan. Prince Konoe entrusted the superintendant general of the Metropolitan Police Department with organising what became in effect state-run bordellos for the Occupation forces. The Recreation and Amusement Association (ARAA) was established with a capital of ¥100 million (1945 yen). Initially, a pool of 5,000 women was considered necessary but the number of professionals was insufficient (at the end of the war, only 66 brothels with 356 inmates were left intact in Tokyo) and a system of public recruitment of non-professionals was adopted. The Home Ministry requested the prefectural governors to establish brothels for the exclusive use of the Occupation forces. The prostitutes lived in what were popularly called red-light districts. They had to serve a minimum of 12 'customers' a day but sometimes their workload came to 60. Private prostitution also continued openly until the Anti-prostitution Law of 1956.

The 'human dam' strategy seems to have been only partially effective. In the months from August to December 1945 alone, an estimated 150,000 women were sexually assaulted by Occupation personnel.

An Imperial ordinance promulgated in 1947 made pandering and procurement punishable but did not stop prostitution. The Child Welfare Law of 1947 provided stronger protection for minors and the Employment Security Law of the same year was meant to facilitate the search for jobs but had little immediate effect due to the disastrous economic conditions.

Prostitution Prevention Law

Largely as the result of the efforts of women members of the Diet and women's organisations, the Prostitution Prevention Law was enacted in

1956. The law prohibits public solicitation, procurement, the leasing of rooms for prostitution and enticement to prostitution. Prostitution is defined as 'sexual intercourse with undetermined partners against remuneration or the promise of remuneration' (Art. 2). To engage in prostitution and to become the partner of a prostitute are prohibited (Art. 3) but not punishable actions. To procure a mistress is not punishable unless the woman has sex indiscriminately against remuneration. Solicitation and procurement by advertising and similar means are also punishable. The major emphasis of the law is on punishing activities aiding prostitution, or preventing the exploitation of women and the operation of brothels.

Among the actions made specifically punishable are inducement to prostitution by pressure, abuse of family relations, threats or violence, receipt of all or part of the earnings from prostitution or arrangements to this effect by the procurer, advance payments or other financial advantages and contracts for the purpose of inducing a person to engage in prostitution, knowingly providing a place for prostitution or furnishing rooms for the purpose of prostitution as a business. The measures intended to prevent the establishment of brothels are set forth in Article 12 which prohibits the establishment of a business for the purpose of having people live in a place occupied, controlled or assigned by oneself and have those people practise prostitution. The courts have interpreted the word 'live' to mean to stay with the owner of the establishment so as to be available to customers. Prostitutes may have their own living quarters but if they report regularly to a certain place and there wait for customers they are considered to 'live' there for the purposes of this law ('commuting prostitutes'). But a place only furnished with a telephone does not fall under the prohibition of the law. Also punishable is to knowingly supply funds, land or buildings for operating a brothel. The provisions of the law are applicable to the officers and employees of a corporation and fines can be levied on the corporation as well as on the actual perpetrators of the criminal acts. Article 17 of the law allows women aged 20 years and older who have been sentenced to be committed for penal servitude or confinement for offences against Article 5 (solicitation) and other crimes and whose sentence has been suspended to a women's guidance home for a period of six months. Under the general rules of Japan's Code of Criminal Procedure, the public prosecutor can refrain from indicting prostitutes and instead place them under the care of 'protective offices' staffed by probation officers, police women, social workers, and so on.

Article 182 of the Japanese Criminal Code makes it a punishable crime to induce a woman who does not customarily commit obscene acts (who is not a prostitute) to have sexual intercourse for the purpose of gain.

The police handles the sex business in connection with the entertainment business mainly under the aspect of enforcing the Anti-

prostitution Law and the Law Regulating Businesses Affecting Public
Morals. In 1984, 10,000 cases of violation of the Anti-prostitution Law
were investigated and 3,270 people arrested. Violations included 643 cases
of solicitation (640 arrests), 5,428 cases of procurement (1,331 arrests),
577 cases of leasing rooms for prostitution (503 arrests), 135 cases of
running a prostitution business (327 arrests) and 3,417 other violations
(469 arrests). Violations of the law probed in 1985 numbered 11,647 cases
involving 3,167 people.

Patterns of Japan's Sex Business

The abolition of brothels and the prohibition of providing facilities for
prostitution has led to the proliferation of substitute establishments. The
regular hotels try to keep out prostitutes but the so-called 'love hotels'
(which rent rooms on an hourly basis) and motels are extensively used
for prostitution. In the absence of general regulations, local governments
have imposed restrictions on love hotels. In Osaka, where 345 love hotels
were operating at the beginning of 1984 (nationwide, there may be about
10,000 love hotels), construction of new love hotels is not allowed within
110 metres from schools and social welfare institutions. A similar
ordinance has been adopted in Nagoya.

In a survey (end of October 1984) covering all places connected in
some way with 'public morals,' the police listed 1,707 Turkish baths
with closed cubicles, 795 massage parlours, 839 dating clubs and lovers'
banks, 341 strip-tease theatres and nude photo studios and 327 peep
shows. Places providing food and drink falling under the provisions of
the Law Regulating Businesses Affecting Public Morals numbered 96,978
(3,082 cabarets, 917 night clubs, 36,421 bars, 42,974 eating places and
13,584 other establishments). Late-night eating and drinking places
included 31,934 bars not classified as businesses affecting public morals,
63,541 taverns, 151,080 snack bars, 2,787 pubs, 38,708 coffee shops and
tea parlours, 70,472 eating places and restaurants, 50,825 *sushi* and *soba*
shops and 8,786 other businesses. Amusement establishments coming
under the law numbered 46,017 (30,160 *mah-jongg* parlours, 13,399
pachinko parlours, 2,458 other businesses). Game centres not covered by
the law numbered 41,166. On suspicion of violating the Anti-prostitution
Law, police raided 105 Turkish baths (1,529 violations, 522 arrests), 292
massage parlours (1,497 violations, 807 arrests), 391 dating clubs and
lovers' banks (4,156 violations, 1,168 arrests). Police investigated 1,117
cases of public obscenity (1,241 arrests) and 1,961 cases of sales of obscene
objects (other than books, etc.) (1,673 arrests). On obscenity charges, 89
strip-tease theatres were raided (153 cases, 483 arrests) as were 79 nude
photo studios (318 cases, 402 arrests). In 934 cases of illegal gambling,
4,494 people were arrested and 7,326 gambling machines confiscated.

In 1984, police discovered 6,962 violations of laws and ordinances
by late-night eating and drinking places. They included 2,120 violations

of business hours, 1,486 cases of unlicensed entertainment, 1,415 cases of employment of minors, in 125 cases, businesses had failed to post prices, 125 sold alcohol to minors and lighting was insufficient in 100 establishments. There were 508 violations of the Labour Standards Law, 146 offences against the Anti-prostitution Law and 92 infractions of the Child Welfare Law. Despite these efforts, the police have not even come near to suppressing the sex business.

Dating Clubs and Lovers' Banks

The nearest to organised prostitution are dating clubs and lovers' banks. Establishments calling themselves *detô kissa* (dating coffee shops) or dating pubs charged each customer an admission fee of ¥2,000 to ¥5,000. This entitled him to as many cups of coffee or drinks as he could swallow in 20 minutes. In some places, the customer could choose one of the girls present, in others, the girls were assigned by the shop, but in all places, the girls could turn down the customer. If the girl agreed, the customer paid a go-between fee which varied from ¥3,000 to ¥10,000 and was billed as a charge for 'fruit.' The girl would accompany the customer to a nearby hotel where he could avail himself of her services for exactly two hours. He paid the girl between ¥18,000 and ¥20,000. In 1983, there were 696 dating coffee shops, dating clubs and lovers' banks.

A survey based on the police investigation of 676 women for alleged prostitution found that 42 per cent of the women were dispatched to their clients by dating clubs or lovers' banks, 19.5 per cent worked at Turkish baths, 14.8 per cent were street-walkers, 12 per cent worked at cabarets or night clubs and 11 per cent at massage parlours, 9 per cent were housewives, another 9 per cent held conventional jobs such as office work and 4 per cent were students. The average age of the women was 29; teenagers accounted for 14 per cent, 44 per cent were in their 20s, 20 per cent in their 30s, 12 per cent in their 40s and 5 per cent were over 50. Nearly half, 49 per cent of the women, said that they engaged in prostitution to earn a living, 14 per cent had to support a family, another 14 per cent wanted money to buy clothes, for travel or leisure, and 11 per cent needed money to repay debts. Women resorting to prostitution for their living were most numerous among those working at night clubs and among street-walkers while many of those working at Turkish baths wanted money for leisure.

Some dating clubs and lovers' banks use the membership principle. A 27-year-old woman organised a club called Roppongi Tribe (Roppongi is one of Tokyo's liveliest night districts) which brought together the seekers and providers of love for cash. The young men and women offering their services must be single, between the ages of 18 and 25, and contribute ¥30,000 to the club. They can then make their own deals with the club's members who are introduced to them. The members, people seeking sex partners, must be at least 35 years old, married, and pay an entrance fee of ¥200,000. Another lovers' bank had 90 female members for hire of whom 65 were Japanese and 25 foreigners. Of the foreigners, 80 per cent were Caucasians but some were Filipinas. Male members who paid an admission fee of ¥80,000 could choose among four girls, those who paid ¥150,000 were given an unlimited choice.

Osaka police broke up a dating club ring controlled by Masao Kikutani, leader of the Kikumasa-gumi, a gang affiliated with the Yamaguchi-gumi, Japan's largest criminal syndicate, and arrested Kikutani and six other gangsters on charges of violating the Anti-prostitution Law and the Child Welfare Law. Kikutani had opened nine dating clubs in various blocks of flats in June 1983, hired about 150 young women, some of them runaways, and had them engage in prostitution. Customers were charged ¥20,000 to ¥30,000 per session, and in over two years of operation, the gang had supposedly earned over ¥1 billion and made a net profit of ¥420 million. Kikutani's operation was said to have been the largest of about 350 dating clubs in Osaka.

The reputedly classiest outfit engaged in introducing well-heeled men to amenable young women, the 'Adam and Eve' lovers' bank, had 135 registered patrons and a roster of girls including 135 university undergraduates, 71 students in professional schools and 56 office workers. Among its members were 53 dietmen, 21 lawyers, 18 businessmen, 14 executives of major companies, 12 physicians, 6 performing artists, 5 members of the liberal professions and 3 professional athletes. Membership costs between ¥300,000 and ¥500,000, depending on the type of service requested. Some of the girls not only earn big money but graduate from prostitute to mistress. A university senior received ¥500,000 a month from her patron, a member of the Liberal-Democratic Party, in addition to dresses and other gifts. Another girl was given the same amount in cash in two monthly instalments. The money was in a brown envelope and she had to count each bill while her benefactor was watching. A 20-year-old co-ed lived in a one-room luxury apartment her lover, also a politician, who paid her ¥500,000 a month, had bought for her. As of October 1983, 106 lovers' banks were in operation, about 30 of them in Tokyo.

Police arrested a 25-year-old woman who had been the nominal operator of a lovers' bank and earned ¥250 million in two years of operation. The bank had 1,006 male members, many of them company directors and doctors, while the 1,402 female members included some high-school students and government employees. The membership fee was ¥200,000 for men and ¥50,000 for women. Indicted for violation of the Anti-prostitution Law, the woman and her associate claimed that they just introduced members to each other and had nothing to do with what the parties did thereafter. But the Tokyo District Court found the defendants guilty because they were aware that the members would have sexual intercourse after being introduced to each other and that the men would pay the women for their services.

There have been cases in which the membership lists of dating clubs and similar outfits have been stolen and used for attempts at blackmail.

Massage Parlours, Turkish Baths

The abuse of sex for promoting business has greatly increased the opportunities for prostitution which easily becomes a part-time job of hostesses in night clubs, bars, cabarets and other establishments. Turkish baths and massage parlours often provide 'special services' which may be masturbation or intercourse. The operators instruct the girls to dispose of birth control devices outside the establishment and not to involve the proprietor or proprietoress when questioned by police. The operators frequently rotate the girls to different branches. The Turkish bath owners have been trying to attract wealthier customers by making their establishments more luxurious. One result has been the creation of the so-called *mantoru*. The expression is a contraction of 'mansion,' the Japanese idiom for western-style apartments (flats), and 'turoko' (Turkish). It means a Turkish bath operating in an apartment building. Nationwide, 592 such establishments were in operation in 1983. One of the leading shops called 'Love House - American Lady,' featured a photo gallery of 60 girls, charged a membership fee of ¥10,000 and demanded ¥15,000 for what was described as 'play': a rubdown in the bathroom and subsequent mutual petting in the bedroom. For these services, the girl received ¥7,000. The customers, some 150 a day, choose to have amateurs as partners, not professionals. The Japanese police are worried about the influx of 'amateurs,' including bar hostesses, housewives and college and high-school students, into prostitution connected with Turkish baths, massage parlours, dating clubs and lovers' banks.

The association of Turkish bath operators decided to change the name of their establishments when a Turkish scholar, Nusert Sanjakli, complained that the name was damaging the reputation of his country. In 1985, the association announced that the establishments would be called 'soapland' (a name chosen from about 2,220 suggestions) and the attendants known as 'soap ladies.'

Recently, a massage parlour on wheels made its appearance in Tokyo. Depending on the preference of the customer, the vehicle called 'Pink Shuttle' can move through the streets or park in a quiet spot. The service starts with a manicure and ends with a massage by a minimally-clad girl. The basic charge is ¥7,000; the service costs ¥6,000 for 50 minutes and ¥8,000 for 70 minutes.

While, at least originally, mate-swapping was a private affair in the United States, it has become a label attached to some form of prostitution in Japan where men and women answering ads are brought together for 'mate-swapping parties' for which they pay (sometimes, only the men pay, sometimes, the women have to pay, too).

Strip-tease

Strip-tease and other sex shows can be prosecuted under Article 174 of the Criminal Code which prohibits 'public obscenity,' and the performer as well as the organiser or promoter is punishable. The definition of 'obscene act' used by the courts includes highly subjective elements: 'Actions stimulating and arousing or satisfying the sexual desires of the performer or others which offend against the normal sense of sexual shame of the ordinary man and are contrary to the right sense of sexual morality.' Acts falling under this prohibition are the exposure of the genitals and sexual intercourse. 'Public' means in front of a number of people, and the courts have interpreted this to include actions in closed rooms if an undetermined number of people have access, even if restricted to the members of an organisation.

Strip-tease shows may feature sexual acts in which the audience is invited to participate. The pressure to lure more customers to sex shows has led to crude representations of obscenity. Recently, the police arrested a dancer and the promoter of a burlesque show in which the dancer stripped on the stage and performed an act of bestiality with a stud horse aroused by two mares brought out on the stage.

Popular with less affluent customers were topless and bottomless coffee shops. Bottomless ('no panties') shops first appeared in Kyoto, expanded to Osaka and then became the rage in Tokyo where almost 200 bottomless coffee shops opened within six months. Typically, the waitresses would wear nothing but fishnet stockings and 'teeny weeny' bikinis. The excessive competition caused a crescendo in the debasement of the girls: customers could pat their breasts or their buttocks or paint on these parts. Sometimes, the panties of the waitresses were auctioned off. Legally, coffee shops operate under the Food Sanitation Law which requires a licence from the prefectural governor. The police wanted to put coffee shops under the Law Regulating Businesses Affecting Public Morals which would give police greater control because approval by the Public Safety Commission is necessary.

Waitresses are not allowed to entertain guests; entertainment is only permitted in establishments licensed under the Law Regulating Businesses Affecting Public Morals which covered seven categories: cabarets, night clubs, bars, tea-rooms, pachinko (slot machine) parlours, mah-jongg parlours and snack bars. As of October 1984, bars and cabarets numbered 97,072, snack bars 418,000 establishments.

A revision of the law prepared by the National Police Agency and passed by the Diet in August 1984 went into effect on 13 February 1985. The law brings sex businesses such as peep shows, massage parlours, love hotels and motels, rental rooms and adult shops under the purview of the law. All these businesses must apply to the Public Safety Commission for registration and police can take 'administrative measures' against these establishments. They are banned from hiring minors or having minors enter their premises. Such businesses are not allowed to operate in areas adjacent to schools, to put up obscene posters or other advertisements, or to force clients to enter their establishments. These restrictions also apply to movie theatres showing pornographic films and burlesque shows. Zoning regulations prepared by the prefectural governments are to circumscribe the areas in which these businesses can operate. In Tokyo, the existing establishments can continue in operation for the life-time of their present owners but new businesses will be restricted to the Yoshiwara area, the pre-war 'red-light' district. Except for love hotels and motels, all establishments must close by midnight. Establishments found to have allowed minors to enter will be ordered to suspend business for up to eight months.

A survey of the Metropolitan Police Department found that in the year from February 1985 to February 1986, the number of massage parlours in Tokyo decreased from 281 to 243, that of adult shops from 490 to 456, and that of rental rooms for couples from 757 to 737. A total of 109 sex-related establishments went out of business in the city since the new law went into effect. In the same period, 'administrative punishment' has been meted out to 159 establishments of which 145 were cabarets and bars. In 1985, the police arrested 6,575 people in connection with 5,465 cases of violation of this law.

The Association to Cope with Prostitution Problems in Japan, an umbrella organisation comprising 18 women groups and Christian bodies, had opposed the new law because it failed to abolish establishments such as massage parlours and seemed to give them official recognition. The Japan Federation of Bar Associations claimed that the new law gave the police 'unnecessarily expanded authority and power.' The revised law could revive the pre-war practice of having uniformed police posted in movie theatres and carry out midnight identity checks in hotels.

The National Police Agency reported that most prefectures have enacted ordinances imposing severer restrictions than the new law. In most prefectures, youths under 16 are not allowed to enter game centres after 6 pm. The zoning regulations banning sex businesses from the neighbourhood of schools, libraries and child welfare facilities have been extended to include hospitals by 44 prefectures, 25 prefectures have added museums and four prefectures sports facilities. The operation of massage parlours with private rooms has been prohibited by 19 prefectures and 22 have forbidden private massage rooms. Shiga Prefecture has banned strip-tease theatres and Kumamoto Prefecture has outlawed rental rooms.

Night Clubs

Night clubs range from seedy places where hostesses have to masturbate customers in tiny cubicles to genteel palaces where lecherous remarks to hostesses are not tolerated. Everywhere, hostesses are often propositioned but never forced into prostitution. Their main complaints are salaries — too low — and the money they have to spend on clothes, although many establishments provide clothing.

The bar and night-club clientèle consists largely of expense-account spenders, physicians, lawyers, patent attorneys, authors and artists, teachers of flower arrangement, shop owners and operators of small plants. Most hostesses loath the job but stay on for the money.

Hot-Spring Resorts

Reminiscent of the old-style prostitution are some of the places in hot-spring resorts where women acting as *geisha* actually are prostitutes. Hotels in resort towns customarily engage *geisha* for entertainment, and since there is a shortage of professional *geisha,* they recruit housewives to fill the vacancies. If the employment also involves prostitution, the fee paid by the customer is split 50:50 between the hotel and the amateur *geisha*.

Foreign Competition

In a hot-spring resort in Nagano Prefecture, the local *geisha* numbering 230 mounted a campaign to drive out the foreign 'entertainers' whose competition was threatening their livelihood. Taiwanese had first been employed as waitresses in 1979 but, reinforced by Filipinas and Thais, they began to function as 'hostesses' in inns and hotels in 1982. Because of their youth and gentle manners, the foreigners found growing favour with customers, and on weekdays, about 100, on Saturdays and Sundays, up to 300 operated in the town. A contributing factor in the popularity of the foreigners was the tendency of some *geisha* to show their disdain of the farmer-type clients. Sometimes, customers would ask management to get rid of the *geisha* even if that meant it would cost them money and replace them with South-East Asian entertainers. Some hotels offered all-inclusive rates for a one-night stay, two meals with *sake* and the constant company of a 'hostess.' Prices ranged from ¥50,000 to ¥70,000 of which ¥30,000 was billed as 'companion fee.' This amount was split between the inn, the woman and her 'agent.'

The *geisha*-house operators, incensed at the competition appealed to the police. A crackdown resulted in the deportation of 14 women; the rest moved to a neighbouring town where they remained on call but charged ¥5,000 for taxi fare and an additional ¥5,000 as a 'risk insurance' premium.

The influx of foreign women is a special feature of Japan's deprofessionalisation of the sex business. It started with foreign hostesses.

Thousands of American and European women work or worked in bars and night clubs in Tokyo's Ginza, Akasaka and Azabu districts and in other cities. Much of this work is illegal because these women usually enter on tourist visas and are not allowed to engage in paid work. But for a long time, the police hardly intervened. As an immigration official explained some years ago: 'Nobody suffers from hiring a foreign hostess. The bar prospers because of her presence. The woman has no financial worries during her stay in Japan as she is earning money. The clients are happy and have nothing to complain about. We hear little about these women.' This was the situation when these women made their own arrangements for after-duty services. But then, gangsters moved in and a regular slave trade developed. American women are recruited largely on the West Coast, in Los Angeles, San Francisco, San Diego, Las Vegas and Seattle. The girls are mostly sent to Tokyo, Osaka, Kyoto and Sasebo but also to places in the countryside like Chiba. The FBI undertook an investigation into an alleged ring that was suspected of having sent 12 Portland teenage girls to Japan to perform in live sex shows. California 'talent agents' find victims by placing ads in reputable trade papers for entertainers to work abroad. They recruit singers, musicians and dancers with minimal talent and great dreams, preferably blonde and tall with blue eyes, in their early twenties, dumb or naïve. Usually, employment in large hotels or night clubs is offered. Once in Japan, the girls are forced to dance in the nude, perform in live sex shows and engage in outright prostitution. If they refuse, they are beaten, their clothes are taken away and their money is stolen.

A promoter accused by an American entertainer of having tried to rape her, having failed to pay her and being associated with gangsters denied these charges and said the woman made these accusations because she knew that they would hurt his reputation. In his view, there were three motives for foreign entertainers to come to Japan: to make money, to seek an opportunity for success which eluded them at home, and to enjoy a trip abroad. While the first reason induces them to work hard, the second motive may cause trouble because they over-estimate their talents and become frustrated with the treatment they get.

The importation of women from the Philippines for 'work' in Japan is largely controlled by gangsters. The illegal employment agents have extended their activities and in addition to the female 'Japayuki,' men are brought into Japan for work on construction sites and other menial labour. The traffic also involves the smuggling of drugs and weapons. In the summer of 1986, Philippine immigration authorities deported some 38 members of Japanese crime syndicates who were involved in recruiting female entertainers for prostitution, gun running, illegal possession of drugs and other violations of the law.

There are about 500 promoters bringing foreign entertainers to Japan or promoting their domestic engagements; about 50 are members of the

Association of International Entertainment promoters. An English-language brochure distributed to entertainers brought to Japan by members of the association lists the telephone numbers of all immigration offices in Japan under the notice: 'Please contact the following offices if you are forced to engage in an activity other than that permitted under status of residence.'

Exploitation is crass. A Filipina who earned ¥900,000 a month was paid only ¥150,000 and Taiwanese women were made to serve as prostitutes and forced to take two customers every night. A Filipina engaged as a dancer by a Filipino in Manila had to perform in live sex shows and work as a prostitute. She told authorities that ten more Philippine girls between 18 and 20 were kept at a club in Chiba. In Tokyo alone, foreign women working illegally in cabarets, snack bars, strip-tease joints and similar places were estimated at 800, mostly from South-East Asia.

Some time ago, police broke up a prostitution ring which lured women from Chile to Japan. The ring attracted customers by placing ads in newspapers for a dating club and had the Chilean girls engage in prostitution at Tokyo hotels for ¥30,000 a session. The girls who were kept under the supervision of a Chilean woman were given only ¥1,000 a day for meals.

The basic principle of the Japanese immigration authorities in granting work visas is to let no alien fill a job that could be performed by a Japanese. There are three vague categories of work visas: technicians, skilled labourers and entertainers. The immigration regulations stipulate that an entertainer must be invited by a sponsor, that the entire schedule in Japan must be fixed (dates and locations), and that the entertainer must have a return ticket. The visa can be renewed at least once.

According to immigration statistics, about 27,000 performers were given visas for entering Japan in 1982, but bona fide artistes formed a small minority. The main operating bases of the so-called agencies recruiting women ostensibly for entertainment are Manila and Bangkok. In the same year, immigration officials detained 1,889 women working illegally in Japan. In 1985, 7,653 people were arrested for violations of the immigration laws. They included 6,592 who had overstayed their visas. Of the 5,411 who had accepted unauthorised employment, most worked in bars and other entertainment establishments ostensibly as dancers or hostesses. They included 3,927 Filipinas, 1,073 Thais and 427 Taiwanese. Most of the women are in their 20s or 30s; about half of them earn less than ¥300,000 a month and 10 per cent make less than ¥50,000.

Sometimes, groups of foreign women arriving with tourist visas are refused entry. Recently, the police arrested four Koreans and three Japanese for arranging faked marriages of Korean women to Japanese so that the women could extend their stay in Japan.

The growing involvement of gangsters in the white slave trade prompted the American authorities to investigate the activities of Japanese gangs in the United States and the Japanese immigration officials stepped up the deportation of women suspected of prostitution. Gangsters often instruct the women to state that they are only in transit and intend to proceed to some other destination.

Adolescent Prostitution

Some years ago, the revelation of the existence of prostitution rings organised by and consisting of high-school girls shocked the country. In some cases, an outsider, such as a service-station employee, started the operation, but in other cases, the girls acted on their own and introduced customers to one another. The desire to have spending money was the principal motive.

Motives for Prostitution

High-school girls and college students are also numerous among the girls working in topless and bottomless coffee shops. The mentality of the girls can be gathered from the answers of over 20 per cent of the high-school girls interviewed on work attitudes that they considered prostitution and jobs in Turkish baths or bottomless coffee shops as acceptable forms of part-time work. They did not understand why it should be bad. 'There is nothing wrong in using one's own body for earning money. It is my own body, so it should be of no concern to the police or the government. As long as I am young, it's not a bad business to work as a prostitute.' A co-ed who worked part-time in the sex business commented: 'I don't think it's particularly shameful. It's something everybody is doing, and I'm doing it as a job. If it's bad to accept money, a housewife is worse. She takes the husband's entire salary and moreover puts on airs.'

This attitude may confirm the assertion of psychologists that no woman becomes a whore without inner readiness but it hardly suggests that disappointment, the impulse of revenge or the lack of I-you relations in childhood constitute the presupposition of such behaviour.

In the last analysis, however, women turn to prostitution for only one reason — money. They certainly do not enjoy their work. There is nothing exciting or glamorous about it, and many prostitutes are physically brutalised by their customers as well as their pimps. Even for an expensive call-girl, it is the most dangerous and demeaning way any woman can earn a living.

In the mid-1970s, most of the women who engaged in prostitution wanted to make money for a definite purpose. Some planned to open a snack bar or a boutique, others dreamed of touring foreign countries and there were women who took care of their lovers. All thought of earning as much money as quickly as possible and took as many customers as possible. But a few years ago, the attitude of many girls changed. They wanted to move out of the tiny rented rooms in dingy neighbourhoods and take up residence in a nice apartment in a 'mansion.' They could make a comfortable living by having one or two customers a day or working two or three hours in a Turkish bath. But there were always women who just wanted to have spending money.

The view that prostitution is a legitimate profession seems widely held by those who engage in it. Chinese prostitutes in Malaysia expressed the conviction that the selling of sex was not an immoral act. The same as in Japan, prostitution was institutionalised in old China. A daughter selling herself into prostitution in order to help her family was praised for her filial piety, and patronising prostitutes was not socially reprehensible.

Police regard discotheques and game centres as hotbeds of juvenile crime and as places where connections for prostitution are made. In Tokyo, 403 discotheques were registered as cabarets or night clubs but nearly 600 others were not so registered.

Small notes glued to the walls of public telephone booths give the telephone numbers or even the addresses of girls willing to sell their services and often fliers with this kind of information are put through private letter boxes. So many handbills of massage parlours and money-lenders are pasted in phone booths in neighbourhoods such as Shinjuku, Shibuya or Ikebukuro that the booths are dark inside. But in some places, local gangsters control the phone booths in their area and remove all notices for which they are not paid.

Male Prostitution

Male prostitution is a very different business from female whoredom. While homosexual prostitution is common, male prostitutes catering to heterosexuals are rare. Even in the old times, very few male brothels existed. The 'call-boy' system is hardly used. Most male prostitutes are of the independent type. There are no pimps and no large organisations. The male prostitute clings to the self-protecting image of himself as a 'real' and heterosexual man who engages in homosexual relations only for money. Actually, the hustler has a substantial homosexual component; otherwise, he could not achieve erection and orgasm. Male prostitution is the reverse of female prostitution: the female prostitute feigns a passion she does not feel, the male prostitute conceals a passion he does feel.

Different from male prostitution are the 'host clubs' catering to females. In these establishments which are the reverse of the clubs in which hostesses massage the male egos, good-looking young men bestow their attentions on women tired of doing exactly the same thing to male patrons. The host clubs get 50 per cent of their clientèle from among bar hostesses and 40 per cent from Turkish bath masseuses; only 10 per cent are non-professionals. The top earner in the New Ai host club in Shinjuku's Kabuki-cho earned ¥4 million a month and his monthly expenses of ¥800,000 were covered entirely by tips. Most hosts make between ¥200,000 and ¥500,000 a month. They work from 1 pm to 5.30 am. Women please men by following their lead while men must take the lead if they want to satisfy women. A professional host turns down all invitations from the opposite sex that might result in emotional entanglements: 'Once you go to bed with a customer, you begin losing others.'

A different kind of host club was broken up by the police when they arrested the operators of a night club catering exclusively to women for violating the Anti-prostitution Law and the Child Welfare Law. The club recruited teenage boys as club hosts through newspaper ads and charged them ¥15,000 for being listed as club hosts. The women paid ¥10,000 an hour for the companionship of the host at a place designated by the customer.

Entry into Prostitution

Entry into prostitution may be coercive if women are forced into it through the white-slave trade or involuntary if girls are sold by their family or seduced daughters cast out by their parents, but in advanced countries, entry is largely voluntary although often prompted by poverty or economic difficulties. Nowadays, prostitution can be a full-time occupation or a part-time job.

A German survey on the social background of prostitutes found that 82 per cent came from broken families and 42 per cent had been in reformatories. The parents of over half belonged to the middle class, mainly skilled workmen and artisans; daughters of government officials, company employees and professional soldiers accounted for 20 per cent, those of farmers and shop-owners for 10 per cent and 6 per cent were children of unskilled workers. Sometimes, an older girl becomes the mentor of a new entrant. The motivation is almost always financial, also if entry is not related to a financial emergency. Money possesses an emotional character for prostitutes and becomes the substitute for sympathy, affection and tenderness.

Entry into prostitution means absorption by a sub-culture, adoption of a new set of values and relations, and a new pattern of behaviour. The majority of prostitutes assume a professional attitude which stresses the compartmentalisation of business and private life. A client should be sufficiently pleased to induce him to come back but experiencing sexual arousal or orgasm is unprofessional, fatiguing and inefficient. Some clients may be bothersome and others nice, but to allow affection to develop is foolish and emotional involvement can cause disappointment and hurt. In private life, a prostitute may have a lover, often the procurer or pimp, and she may even have a family. Australian prostitutes were said to be good mothers because they have more time to look after their children and have flexible 'working hours.' Pregnancy and venereal disease are some of the occupational hazards. The incidence of venereal disease is much higher for prostitutes than the average. Prostitutes ordinarily are not criminals. Only desperate or disreputable, low-class independent strumpets resort to stealing, robbery, fraud or blackmail, but the association with criminal gangs is often exploited by the police. Criminal organisations can provide better protection from law and social action than any individual or small group but the relationship is financially onerous and punishment is often meted out if the relationship is broken.

Exit from Prostitution

The exit from prostitution is not always voluntary. Prostitutes age more rapidly than other women; the physical burden, alcohol and irregular sleep and meals contribute to a fast decline which is accelerated by the loathing or even hatred of one's own life. Some prostitutes end in mental institutions and cases of kidney diseases are frequent. Their vanishing attractiveness forces prostitutes to cater to lower and lower classes of clients.

Some prostitutes try to make their exit by marriage. Particularly noteworthy is the tendency of prostitutes to marry ex-convicts. Four classes of women are said to marry former prisoners: prostitutes, women with an exaggerated mother instinct, hypersexual women and arrogant women eager to bring deviants back to the right path. Recidivism is about 10 per cent higher than average for ex-convicts who marry prostitutes. Some of the women try to save enough money to start some kind of business, a bar, boutique or some kind of eating place. Only few can keep up premium payments on life insurance.

How to Deal with Prostitution

What public authority should do about prostitution is an unsolved and probably unsolvable problem. Morally, prostitution is wrong, for the prostitute as well as her client, but 'what consenting adults do sexually in private should be of no concern to law,' and this would include prostitution. The Christian ideal of restricting sex life to marriage has never been realised, and a definition of public morality supposes a society with uniform moral standards which is certainly not the case in the West. Public morality, as noted above, is not a question of morality but of mores. The task of government is not to shape and define what society regards as decent or indecent but to shield the public against harm, injury or injustice that might arise from the disregard of decency. Applied to prostitution, this means that the government should protect individuals from being forced into prostitution, suppress the commercialisation of prostitution, above all its control by criminal gangs, prevent the exploitation of children, guard individuals from solicitation and contain the spread of VD. But the government has neither the duty nor the right to stop an individual who wants to engage in prostitution or to buy sex from doing so.

Japan's Anti-prostitution Law is an imitation of the West. In Japanese tradition, no social opprobrium was attached to frequenting gay quarters. Today's police control of public morals has nothing to do with public safety and is entirely ineffective in protecting children and adolescents against smut. Outside Japan, the failure of public authority to suppress vice sometimes induces individuals or groups to take 'positive' action. Recently, feminists in Oslo launched a campaign publishing the names of the clients of prostitutes on posters in underground stations.

Broadly speaking, there are two approaches if public authority decides to do something about prostitution, positive or negative action (the modern state rarely considers the option of doing nothing, because the bureaucracy is always attracted by the vanity of showing its power).

The negative approach means prohibition and the choice of the action to be made illegal should be (but not always is) determined by the possibility of enforcement. If prohibitions cannot be enforced, their effect is to drive violation underground which may make it easier for criminal organisations to obtain control and use it for coercion and extortion. The prevention and suppression of vice rackets constitutes a very important task in the field of public morality, but the suppression of organised crime does not require the prohibition of prostitution. On the contrary, prohibition creates conditions attracting criminal exploitation of sex. Even in advanced countries, the police are not always above venality.

A positive approach to prostitution means regulation by registration or licensing of individual prostitutes and/or houses of prostitution. It does not necessarily mean the promotion of prostitution or its organisation as a state enterprise. The protection of public health, particularly against VD, by regular inspection and the exclusion of criminal elements are usually given as reasons for a system of registration. There may be a certain possibility of attaining these goals if private prostitution can be prevented, but this is hardly the case. On the other hand, licensing of prostitutes and brothels creates the impression of public approval of the sex business. Legality, however, does not prejudice the question of morality, and in a pluralistic society, public authority cannot be blamed on moral grounds for allowing prostitution. As long as there is the view that prostitution involves a debasement of women and a defilement of the personal nature of sex but does not constitute part of the common value system of a community, a woman should be free to make money with her body if she so desires.

SEL-O

8

Pornography

FROM A LEGAL POINT OF VIEW pornography may be, at least in countries of a liberal persuasion, the most controversial of the sex businesses. Authors, artists and the producers of movies and video cassettes claim freedom of expression, the ordinary citizen resents being told by police or government officials what he can read or see, and it would be a threat to culture if Philistines were to control expression (according to Friedrich-Karl Kienitz, the Philistines were better than their reputation which has been hurt by their description in the Old Testament). Governments and the defenders of what they call public morality want to see the community protected against the purveyors of smut and stress above all the perils pornography creates for the young and adolescents. The problem today is not only that minors are introduced to sex by its warped representation but also that children are exploited for producing pornography. Of all pornography entering the United States from abroad, about half involves sex by children.

Definition

Such a statement naturally supposes that we know what pornography is, but this is exactly the problem. There is no definition of pornography that can claim universal validity. The word pornography is no help; it comes from two Greek words, *porne* meaning harlot, and *graphein* meaning to write, but its meaning is not restricted to the written word and extends to all forms of representation with the sole objective of displaying sex and its variations.

Pornography and obscenity are not the same. In the language of the courts, obscene means offensive to the common sense of decency and modesty of the community, suggesting or arousing sexual desires or lust and corrupting public morals. Pornography intends to produce sexual arousal. Whether the material is visual (a picture in a magazine or the description of sexual conduct) or auditory (a song or a voice on a telephone), it intends to cause or promote sexual excitement. Erotic art is addressed to creative imagination and distinguished from pornography by the interposition of thought between audience and object. Pornography appeals to sexual fantasy and aims directly at sexual gratification while erotic art is meant to evoke an imaginative identification with the sexual representation.

A definition of obscenity which was used also by American courts until its final rejection by Roth v. US (1957) was formulated in 1868 by Sir Alexander Cockburn in the case of Regina v. Hicklin. The test of obscenity, Chief Justice Cockburn said, was not the intention of the authors but whether the tendency of the matter charged as obscenity was to deprave and corrupt minds open to such immoral influences and into whose hands the publication might fall. The determination was based on the impact of certain parts of the writing on susceptible individuals. The test of morality was what a father could read aloud in his own home.

In Britain, the Williams Committee (Home Office Committee on Obscenity and Film Censorship, Bernard Williams, Chairman, 1978) defined pornography as a description or depiction of sex involving the dual characteristics of (1) sexual explicitness, and (2) intent to arouse sexually. Canada's Fraser Committee (Special Committee on Pornography and Prostitution, Paul Fraser QC, Chairman, 1985) decided that definition was simply futile. The uncertainty and subjectivity of the definition of pornography was admirably expressed in Justice Potter Steward's classical dictum in Jacobellis v. Ohio (1964). He wrote: 'I have reached the conclusion ... that under the First and Fourteenth Amendments criminal laws in this area are constitutionally limited to hard-core pornography. I shall not today attempt further to define the kinds of material I consider to be embraced within that shorthand description; and perhaps I would never succeed in intelligently doing so. But I know it when I see it, and the motion picture involved in this case is not that.' When the ship on which Justice Steward served as a Navy Lieutenant in World War II lay in port at Casablanca, he had seen much of the locally-produced pornography his men bought; so he called it his 'Casablanca Test.'

In the same case, then Chief Justice Earl Warren stated the rationale for prohibiting hard-core pornography declaring that there is a 'right of the nation and of the states to maintain a decent society.'

Today's preoccupation with sex is partly the result of the puritanical repression of sex in western society in the nineteenth century. The treatment of sexuality in legislation, administration and jurisprudence seems to have been based on the premise that sex should not appear in public. 'Public morality' was identified with the most narrowly interpreted norms of Christianity. The growing secularisation of society and its ideological and moral pluralism made the clash betwen old rules and new aspirations unavoidable.

Representation of Sex in the Past

It can certainly not be maintained that the explicit representation of sex is a modern development, and in antiquity, much of the display of sex was connected with religion. The Egyptian god Min, a god of fertility and harvest and the personification of the masculine principle, was represented with phallus erect and a flail in his raised right hand. Roman maidens offered their virginity to the gods by riding on the ithyphallic statue of Mutunus Tutunus and later the phallus marking the statues of Priapus was used in the same way for piercing the hymen before the bridal night. Much of Greek and Roman art was obscene, not only by nineteenth-century standards; many of the murals dug out in Pompeii depict sex scenes. The phallus has been a religious symbol in many cultures (Muslims and Buddhists have never practised phallus worship), and the term ithyphallic was specifically applied to the phallus carried in the ancient festivals of Bacchus. In the Middle Ages, some statues of saints invoked for help in sterility had prominent genitals, and women who wanted children squatted on the statue and let the phallus slide into their vagina. The most famous examples of sexually-explicit art are the reliefs adorning some Indian temples built from the tenth to the twelfth centuries, notably the Vishvanata temple at Khajuraho (central India). The linga as the symbol of Shiva and yoni as the symbol of Shaktri have been mentioned above. Thor Heyerdahl found more than 20 large limestone phalluses in the 4000-year-old ruins of a temple he discovered on one of the Maldive Islands. Phallic symbols abound in Japan, and the *shunga* (erotic pictures), often used for preparing brides for the wedding night, left nothing to the imagination.

The Renaissance brought an explosion of eroticism, not only in art and literature but even more in daily life. Moral norms almost ceased to be the canons by which to live and became only the rules by which to repent the excesses of sensual gratification. In England, censorship hunted irreligious or seditious publications, but a successful prosecution for the publication of indecent matter (*Venus in the Cloister* or *The Nun in Her Smock*) in 1727 made this a misdemeanour indictable under common law (Dominus Rex v. Curll).

In the eighteenth century, titillation largely replaced the robust affirmation of sensuous pleasure of the preceding era but it was left to the Victorian morality of the nineteenth century to make the repression of sex the signature of an entire civilisation. The Obscene Publications Act of 1857 was the first statutory prohibition of purely sexual material, but the act did not contain a definition of obscenity, and the century which opened with the Marquis de Sade and ended with Sigmund Freud was by no means devoid of sex. It brought the kind of pornography in which sex is commercially exploited 'with no redeeming feature.' The commercialisation of the display of sex may be the main difference between art and pornography. Nineteenth-century artists continued to indulge in the representation of the sensuously exciting together with the sensually repulsive, and a curious phenomenon was the predilection of painters for lesbian scenes which lasted into the twentieth century.

Also, still with us, are the attitudes and prejudices created by the nineteenth-century system of censorship which did not abolish pornography but blocked serious and truthful discussion of sexual problems. Alfred C. Kinsey's reports *Sexual Behaviour of the Human Male,* 1948; *Sexual Behaviour of the Human Female,* 1953, stirred a wave of moral indignation, and the American customs stopped a large collection of material on European pornography Kinsey had gathered with great difficulty.

Obscenity seems to have been part and parcel of human history. A linguist, Reinhold Aman, who studied expressions of vulgarity in 200 languages going back 5000 years found that obscenities have been used in all these languages to express every kind of emotion: anger or contempt, surprise or amusement, sorrow or joy. His conclusion: 'All people are rotten.'

Obscene Literature

There has always been obscene literature because there has always been obscene thought. Sexuality, just as aggressiveness, cannot be expunged from society. Smut has nothing to do with literature or culture but in modern society, the fight against smut must be carried out within the confines of the law and with the means sanctioned by law. Opponents of state intervention claim that action against obscene literature today can become action against all literature tomorrow. Freedom, it is said, is indivisible; if freedom is limited, it is no longer freedom. This, of course, depends on the definition of freedom and its distinction from licence and licentiousness. Freedom presupposes tolerance, and tolerance, again, is not divisible. But tolerance does not exclude opposition, and opposition implies the possibility of suppression. Recently, the mayor of Minneapolis vetoed a city ordinance which would have allowed women to sue for damages on the grounds that pornography degrading women violated their civil rights. The ordinance would have permitted law suits against the sellers and producers of material presenting women as dehumanised sex objects who enjoy pain or humiliation. The law, the mayor said, would have infringed on the right of free speech and made it impossible for legitimate bookshops, cinemas and museums to operate.

In itself, nakedness is not shameful. The human body is not obscene. Copulation, mankind's most ancient and most natural ritual, is not obscene. Obscenity depends on the manner of representation, and it is impossible to establish norms for something that challenges the boundaries of imagination. But there are too many cases where the absolute worthlessness of filth is beyond doubt. Art cannot negate the protection of youth, and this protection necessarily involves the curtailment of what might be claimed as freedom. On the other hand, if people want to get sexual arousal by reading dirty books, looking at lewd pictures or seeing blue movies, it is only a question of their own conscience and nobody should have the right to stop them. If men use pin-up girls or centrefold pictures to find sexual satisfaction, it is nobody else's business.

Effects of Pornography

The effect of pornography on the libido are ambiguous. The rôle of pornography in masturbation and rape has often been mentioned but an Arizona State University psychologist, Douglas T. Kenrick, said that sex magazines may have the effect of turning men away from their partners. Men exposed to the pictures of strikingly-attractive women in magazines such as *Playboy* and *Penthouse* may develop unrealistic expectations and experience less sexual arousal from their mates. But two women psychologists, Claire Coles and Johanna Shamp, reported that women who read sexy novels make love 74 per cent more often than those who do not read romance stories; they have sex an average of 3.04 times a week compared with 1.75 times by non-readers. The researchers also found that housewives who read erotic novels had more sexual fantasies and were more satisfied with sex than non-readers. But the sample on which these findings were based was small (interviews with 48 housewives and working women) and as one of the psychologists remarked, it was not clear whether their reading made women more interested in sex or whether women with strong sexual desires were more likely to read and be stimulated by erotic works.

Deleterious Developments

Testimony before the Senate Permanent Sub-committee on Investigation in November 1984 disclosed that almost all child pornography was imported into the United States. Most of it came from Denmark, Sweden and the Netherlands and included everything from graphic photos of infants to packaged child-sex vacation tours. Child-sex package tours to Sri Lanka, Thailand and the Philippines were offered in 1982 in the Netherlands, West Germany, Japan and the United States. Describing how explicit and perverted the material was, a special customs agent, holding up a magazine, said: 'The youngest child, if I can estimate the age, is about 18 months. A full-grown man is attempting to penetrate the 18-month-old girl.'

There has been relatively little discussion of erotic music. Love songs and marriage songs have been called obscene not because of their melodies but because of their lyrics. The music, therefore, may become erotic by association. But the message conveyed by more than a third of rock videos is sexual violence. The state attorney brought charges of 'public scandal' against Spain's state-controlled television for broadcasting a pop song advocating prostitution. The song, 'I like being a hooker,' was performed by the four-member female band Las Vulpes on a Saturday afternoon programme viewed by adolescents and children.

In an agreement reached in November 1985 between the Parents Music Resource Centre and the Recording Industry Association of America, the recording industry undertook to label albums containing explicit sex, violence, drug or alcohol abuse and glorification of the occult with the words 'explicit lyrics' or 'parental advisory' or else to print the actual lyrics on the album jackets.

The sphere of pornography has been extended by 'Dial-A-Porn' services. By dialing a number with a certain prefix, taped erotic messages in which a female voice describes a variety of sex acts can be heard or a partner for obscene conversation can be contacted.

Pornographic TV shows or radio plays constitute an extension of visual or auditory pornography on a commercial basis, but the diffusion of citizens band radio has created a private field of 'air pollution.' Male operators boast of their female conquests and many couples discuss the intimate details of their sex lives on the airwaves.

In the United States and Europe, the 'video nasties' have emerged as a major problem but in Japan, pornographic magazines, particularly pornographic 'comics,' constitute the crassest form of pornography freely accessible to young readers. Magazines for teenage girls are full of articles on foreplay, sex positions, masturbation, abortion and similar topics, and these magazines are passed around among fifth- or sixth-graders of elementary schools. Some of these magazines have been described as 'too provocative even for adults.'

Regulation in Japan

Japan's Liberal-Democratic Party has drafted a bill which would regulate the sale of publications and other materials 'impeding the healthy growth of youth.' Sex magazines would be kept out of the reach of young people by banning the sale of publications 'harmful to youth' to customers under 18. Publications featuring pornography, descriptions and pictures encouraging cruelty and violence or inducing other crimes would come under this ban which would extend to books, magazines, pictures, movies, films and recorded tapes. The bill eschews the most crucial problem by providing that the criteria for deciding what is immoral will be determined by government ordinance. Bookstores will be required to keep 'harmful' publications separate from 'ordinary' books inaccessible to minors. Sales of pornographic magazines by vending machines on streets will also be prohibited.

Actually, all prefectures with the exception of Nagano have ordinances regulating the sale of obscene literature, but these regulations have been ineffective. Osaka Prefecture plans to revise its 1957 Youth

Protection Ordinance. The new ordinance will require 'voluntary' restraints by bookstores, sellers of toys and cars, owners of restaurants, show places and game parlours not to harm 'the sound growth of youth.' By asking for 'voluntary' restraints, the ordinance tries to avoid infringing on the freedom of speech and expression but there are also compulsory provisions. Automatic vending machines cannot be installed within a 100-metre radius from schools and the prefectural government must be informed where such machines are located. The governor can order the removal of any pornographic posters, photos, magazines or toys from the view of passers-by. The ordinance also prohibits indecent sexual acts or other obscene conduct with youth aged 17 or less. (Here again, the crucial question of who is going to fix the standards for deciding what pornography is remains unanswered.)

Movies are subject to self-administered censorship by a film industry review board which enforces a code of ethics forbidding the presentation of 'promiscuous sex relations and abnormal sexual activities.' The Motion Picture Ethics Regulations provide that the representation of things which established custom generally requires to be covered, or vulgar representations likely to cause the viewers' disgust should be avoided. Restraint is to be used in showing nakedness, dressing and undressing, nude dancing, mixed bathing, sex organs and excretion. The board advises caution in handling 'bedroom scenes and outrageous activities' so as not to incite indecent passions of the audience. The passions of the audience, of course, are not their real reason for counselling caution but the censorship of the police and its ludicrous standards.

Video cassettes have created an enormous problem for the protection of children not only against explicit sex but also against the glorification of violence. Even if such cassettes are not sold to minors commercially, the video cassettes available through the enormous black market network may be seen by children at home.

Photo meetings at which young women, often professional models but also non-professionals, pose in the nude are very popular. Such meetings are arranged by photo clubs or camera shops. Recently, the former chief of the Kôfu Police Station published a volume of nude pictures largely taken on such occasions.

Women's Attitude to Pornography

Many women consider pictures of nude women as an insult and a sexist abuse. In order to show that pornography degrades women, the Feminist Film Studio of Canada's National Film Board produced a movie entitled 'Not a Love Story.' The film includes interviews with women in peep shows and strip joints, a couple that performs sexual intercourse eight times a day in a Times Square theatre, prostitutes, dancers, publishers and theatre owners. Its scenes include nude dancing and naked women bound and strung up on meat-hooks. The overall effect of the movie is strongly anti-pornographic; it shows that pornography is simply not erotic.

As with prostitution — women's attitude differs with regard to pornography. Some women contend that the female body is nothing to be ashamed of and that posing in the nude is just as honourable a way of making a living as serving tea in an office or washing dishes. The dissociation of *sexus* from *eros* constitutes the basic problem of the degradation of sex. Pornography implies the divorce of sex from the totality of man, the loss of its status as an inviolable attribute of the personal dignity of man. Sex has become the vehicle of profiteering. Sex is used for marketing, not only to draw attention but to associate the coveting of the sexual appetite to the greed for material possessions. The fusion of sex with violence and cruelty serves to satisfy at the same time prurience and sensationalism.

The diffusion of video cassettes has brought a significant change in the attitude of women to pornography and in its production. Because men, instead of going to movie theatres, took porn videotapes home, wives and girlfriends began to join them in looking at the sex tapes. The male customers, therefore, had to choose products which accommodated female repugnance against cruel sex, bondage and other sado-masochistic mayhem. Just as women want copious foreplay, they like a romantic story line and a gradual build-up to the sex scenes. Women feel safe when looking at pornography in the comfort of the home. As a porno producer put it: 'The VCR put porno where it belongs: in people's bedrooms.' Out of this shift have come not only couples films but also porn in the feminist style in which female sensuality and sexuality inspire the erotic episodes.

How to Curb Pornography?

On the other hand, the movements to ban pornography are not without problems. Protests such as demonstrations, marches, boycotts, picketing or distribution of leaflets are not always free from excesses and may hurt legitimate business. Movements such as the 'Moral Majority,' 'Morality in Media,' 'Citizens for Decency Through Law,' or 'Clean Up America' sometimes take stands that other people find arbitrary. They try to remove objectionable books from public and school libraries, to ban explicit teenage sex education and rock music. In Illinois, legislation was proposed to make librarians liable to criminal prosecution if they allowed minors access to harmful materials. Pages have been cut out from biology textbooks because they are 'too explicit.' The question always recurs: what is 'too explicit' and who is to decide on what is obscene? It is difficult to find suitable books for sex and drug education because someone will somewhere object to something. Books used for sex education in school may be read by six- or seven-year-olds, and sex-education films usually meet with protest at least on the part of some parents.

The approach of making effective protection of adolescents against pornography the standard of general sex control is basically wrong. While it may be legitimate to prevent the access of adolescents to what is called obscene and to protect them from being drawn into sex prematurely and in a way harmful to their growth, this should not be accomplished by prohibiting everything that might be called obscene. The protection of minors is not the only and not even the most important consideration in dealing with sex. Problems of sex are not only the province of doctors, psychologists, psychiatrists, clergymen, law-makers, police, prosecutors and judges, but also of writers and poets, painters, sculptors, dancers and other artists. Max Lerner wrote of Henry Miller: 'He was a writer who dealt with sexuality and the erotic as a crucial part of life,' and it would be absurd to reduce the relevance of this crucial part of life to an article of the criminal code and to have everybody deal with sex according to the canons of 'public morality' formulated by the police. But freedom from police control presupposes the moral maturity of the adult and his/her adherence to norms respecting human dignity. It also requires a public conscious of the cultural environment and the importance of the wholesomeness of all manifestations of human creativity.

The basic objection against the regulation of pornography other than the access of minors to smut is that some people decide what other people may or may not read or see. A policeman or a customs inspector looks at a 'dirty' picture and determines that it should be withheld from the 'public.' Judges view an 'obscene' film and decree that it should be banned. These people are not different from other people and if they see pictures or read books or view films, why shouldn't other people do so? The state has no business to interfere with the sex life of the individual unless it constitutes a violation of criminal law. Nobody has ever demonstrated the relevancy of banning pornography to the public order and the common welfare (if the question of the protection of minors is excluded). As a moral question, pornography is of no concern to public authority; unless there exists a special relationship, no adult will try to regulate the morality of somebody else. As a question of public morality, the dictum of Seneca applies: 'What the law does not prohibit, modesty does.' Decency is a matter of self-discipline, and self-censorship is the only practical way to keep pornography out of the home.

Representation of Violence

The question is entirely different for violence and cruelty. Violence, including sexual violence, is usually inflicted on somebody else and therefore essentially a social problem which directly involves peace and security in the community. Violence in entertainment portrays the most vicious and savage acts and even common forms of human behaviour and the encouragement of aggressiveness by the violence and cruelty shown on television and in motion pictures and resounding in the lyrics of rock music is not and cannot be counterbalanced by a condemnation of the misuse of force.

The International Coalition Against Violence in Entertainment (ICAVE) charges that American TV has been an important factor in the increase of violence in the United States. ICAVE recently released a 22-year study intended to establish a cause-and-effect relationship between TV violence in the 1960s and criminal convictions in the 1970s and 1980s. Compared with a generation ago, there were 3 times more murders per capita, 5 times more rapes and 6 times more assaults. TV and cinema violence, ICAVE says, is the cause of at least 25 to 50 per cent of violence worldwide.

It is misleading to link pornography to violence without qualification. Despite the proliferation of pornographic films and the flood of some of the grossest sex in comics, Japan's rates of sex crime compare favourably with most western countries. The reading of the comics with the most explicit portrayal of sex may provide an outlet for sexual fantasies.

Legal Measures

In New Delhi, women marchers protested against the increasing number of soft-porn films depicting women as 'sex-hungry seductresses' and 'objects to be consumed, abused, debased, raped and destroyed.' The Indian Cinematograph Act of 1918 was originally meant to check subversion against the British Raj. It was amended along the lines of the American Hays Code in 1952, refocusing vigilance from political subversion to sex. While Indian films could show murder, torture, rape, sadism and other forms of degeneracy and brutality, on-screen kissing remained prohibited until a few years ago. The result was that the hero couldn't embrace, kiss or make love in a normal fashion and while physical intimacy was banned, sadism and violence were made the common form of communication between the sexes.

Iran boycotted the Los Angeles Olympic Games which were not broadcast on television but the pictures in foreign magazines sold in Iran meant a lot of extra work for Islamic censors. The thighs and bottoms of women athletes were covered by a few rough brushes with a black pen because the exposure of female flesh or the body's curves is considered un-Islamic. Pictures of bikini-clad women also fall foul of the censorship standards.

In the Gulf states, a video cassette recorder boom started in the mid-1970s and ten years later, the region was said to have the world's highest per capita number of sets. Pornographic and horror films are banned in the Gulf but despite strict vetting of all incoming tape material, pornography is finding its way into the homes and officials fear that it will encourage anti-Islamic behaviour among young people. Bahrain, regarded as a relatively free society, closed three of the island's 107 shops renting video films in October 1984. Saudi Arabia has banned the showing of films in hotel rooms and a magazine, *Video 14,* dealing with the latest Arab and western releases, was forced to stop publication in November 1984 after only a few issues because of objections to photographs of women and film stars.

A censorship law prohibiting everything from hard-core pornography to stories that disparage Mexicans or use poor Spanish grammar went into effect in Mexico in November 1982. The law, which extends also to video cassettes, prescribes that sex magazines must be sealed in plastic and bear labels identifying them as 'material only for adults.' Nudes may not appear on the front or back covers of books, magazines or newspapers, and photos showing pubic hair are prohibited. Also outlawed are adventures in which the protagonists elude the law, flout established institutions and achieve success in business. A five-man censorship commission can confiscate any material it judges an affront to proper customs or morals or that encourages vice.

In West Germany, the Penal Code contains detailed provisions making pornography inaccessible to minors (Art. 184, Par. 1), and these prohibitions also apply to broadcasting (Par. 2). The propagation and exhibition of pornography showing violence, the sexual abuse of children or bestiality are generally prohibited (Par. 3). The government intended to revise the law for the protection of youth in public so as to guard minors not only against movies but also against video cassettes and games offering pornography, featuring horror or glorifying war or violence. The amendment would also prohibit the sale of wine and beer in vending machines accessible to minors.

Publications describing in a cruel and inhuman way violence against human beings and thereby glorify or extenuate violence or incite to racial hatred are prohibited by Art. 131 of the Penal Code.

West Germany's film industry has a code of voluntary self-regulation which links the release of movies to certain age limits (6, 12, 16 and 18 years). Video cassettes are screened by the Federal Review Office.

In a so-called 'Green Paper,' the European Community has examined the legal measures taken for the protection of youth in the different countries of the EC. New regulations have been adopted in some countries against the 'nasties,' pornographic video cassettes. Denmark and Luxembourg have almost no legal restrictions for protecting minors. Italy adopted restrictions on the admission of minors to movies in 1962, with different limits for children under 14 and under 18. In Holland, regulations differentiate between children below 12 and below 18 years of age. Britain passed legislation regulating the media for the protection of minors in 1981 and France has been imposing legal restraints on radio and television programmes since 1982.

In view of the difference in tradition and the variety of moral convictions and religious beliefs, a uniform European law for the protection of minors seems very unlikely.

In Sweden, a public decency law was scrapped in the 1960s and pornography is protected under the press law and the freedom of expression guaranteed in the constitution. Hard-core pornography has broken all bounds of decency and scenes of violence and brutality against women have become commonplace in magazines and video tapes. In an interview in January 1986, Swedish Minister of Justice, Sten Wickbom, complained that some manifestations of pornography clearly transgressed the limits of what could be reasonably tolerated by society.

The rating system established in 1968 by the Motion Picture Association of America distinguishes five categories. Motion pictures rated 'G' are considered suitable for the general public and admission is open to people of all ages. Some of the language in such movies may go beyond polite conversation but violence is minimal and there are no nudity or sex scenes. Films rated 'PG' (parental guidance suggested) are deemed suitable for all ages but parents are warned that some material may not be suitable for children. There may be some profanity and more than minimal violence and, although brief, nudity may be present. Sex scenes are not explicit. A 'PG 13' rating indicates that parental caution is necessary, particularly with regard to children under the age of 13. Some material, such as one of the harsher sexually-derived words, may be inappropriate for young children. An 'R' rating (restricted) is given to motion pictures which may contain obscene language, violence, nudity, sexuality or drug use but do not show explicit sexual activity. Minors under the age of 17 are admitted only if accompanied by a parent or guardian. A film portraying explicit sex, brutal or sexually-related language or excessive and sadistic violence is rated 'X' and no one under the age of 17 may be admitted. A film which is not submitted for a rating by the MPAA cannot, without authorisation, use any rating except 'X.'

Britain's National Housewives' Association advocated a campaign to withhold part of the £51 annual TV licence fee in protest against the amount of sex in American soap operas such as 'Dallas' and 'Dynasty.'

American politicians and pressure groups are calling for curbs on cable television sex shows. In the movie theatres, anyone under the age of 17 is banned from X-rated films which show sexual intercourse. Cable, however, does not use the public air waves and therefore is not subject to the federal regulations applying to broadcasting and the standards of obscenity, indecency and profanity in television and cinema. Some cable stations provide a second box with a key which enables parents to block their children's access to offensive material and thus places censorship in the hands of the consumer. In New York, legislation requiring all cable networks to offer their customers a cable lock and key took effect on 1 January 1984. A few states have drawn up legislation to control sexually-explicit material shown on cable networks. But in Utah and Miami, such laws have been held unconstitutional by federal judges and appeals are pending.

Decisions of the US Supreme Court

The conflict between 'traditional' (that is, nineteenth-century) attitudes towards sex and the twentieth-century assertion of sexual freedom can be traced in the decisions of the US Supreme Court. The first anti-obscenity statutes were passed in Massachusetts in the seventeenth century. Obscenity, however, was not defined in sexual terms but rather as the religious crime of blasphemy. Laws used terms such as 'lewd,' 'obscene' or 'lascivious' indiscriminately and defined these terms as offensive to the common sense of decency and modesty of the community, or as tending to suggest or arouse sexual desires or thoughts 'in the minds of those who may be depraved or corrupted thereby' (typical of the 'holier-than-thou' attitude of this legislation) or offensive to modesty, decency or chastity.

The first erotic book banned in the United States was an illustrated edition of an English novel by John Cleland called *Memoirs of a Woman of Pleasure* — the book has often been referred to as *Fanny Hill* — which was prosecuted in Massachusetts in 1821 (and was the subject of a decision of the US Supreme Court in 1966).

Due to the federal structure of the United States, the federal government had no original jurisdiction over pornography until the Child Pornography Act of 1984. The obscenity cases reaching the Supreme Court were first those arising under the so-called Comstock Act, a law passed by Congress in 1873 which broadened the 1865 Mail Act and banned from the mails 'every obscene, lewd, lascivious or filthy book, pamphlet, picture, paper, letter, writing, print or other publication of an indecent character.' The law presaged the muddle of the following generations since, despite the accumulation of damnatory adjectives, it failed to give a definition of pornography.

The other route by which obscenity cases come before the Supreme Court is through appeals involving the First Amendment. This amendment restrains Congress from making any law 'abridging the freedom of speech or of the press,' and since the Fourteenth Amendment provides that 'No state shall make any law which shall abridge the privileges or immunities of citizens of the United States,' state legislation against pornography raises the question of infringing on the freedom of speech or of the press.

According to Justice William J. Brennan, who wrote the majority opinion in the case of Roth v. US (1957), obscenity, like libel, is not protected by the First Amendment. Obscenity, he maintained, is a category of expression that is not speech and can properly be banned. Justice Brennan developed a definition of obscenity by which he intended to protect serious literary works which had been impounded by the police and condemned by judges as pornography. In addition to D. H. Lawrence's controversial novel *Lady Chatterley's Lover*, works such as *Ulysses* by James Joyce, *Sanctuary* by William Faulkner, *God's Little Acre* by Erskine Caldwell and *Tropic of Cancer* by Henry Miller have run foul of obscenity laws which was one of the reasons why Justices Black and Douglas maintained that printed material, as distinguished from pictures and films, should not be prohibited. 'The test that suppresses a cheap tract today can suppress a literary gem tomorrow,' Justice Douglas asserted.

Black and Douglas were First Amendment absolutists. In their views, courts and legislatures were barred from abridging any form of expression, including sexually-explicit material. 'If the First Amendment guarantee of freedom of speech and press is to mean anything in this field, it must allow protests even against the moral code that the standard of the day sets for the community.' Black and Douglas thought that it was impossible to define obscenity so that all laws banning it were necessarily vague and unconstitutional. No obscenity law had ever been clear enough to enable a person beforehand to know whether he was acting illegally. 'Whatever obscenity is,' Justice Douglas wrote, 'it is immeasurable as a crime and delineable only as a sin. As a sin, it is present only in the minds of some and not in the minds of others, and it is entirely too subjective for legal sanction.'

The definition of obscenity developed by Justice Brennan in *Memoirs of a Woman of Pleasure* v. Massachusetts (1966) required the prosecution to prove that the material was 'utterly without redeeming social value' in order to be considered obscene.

The United Nation's Convention for the Control of the Distribution and Sale of Obscene Literature gives no definition of obscenity because no agreement could be reached on a universally valid definition.

In a 1934 decision holding James Joyce's *Ulysses* obscene, a New York superior court modified the definition of obscenity incorporated in the English case of Regina v. Hicklin (1868) which declared an entire literary work obscene if any part of it was obscene and inappropriate for youthful readers. Such a standard reduced the works accessible to adults to the level of minors and was the ideal instrument for achieving the purpose for which obscenity laws have generally been used, to suppress unpopular ideas. The court held that the criterion for obscenity was not the content of isolated obscene passages but 'whether a publication taken as a whole has a libidinous effect.' At one time, the Supreme Court was almost unanimous in holding that printed material without illustrations could never be obscene (Kois v. Wisconsin, 1971), but this position failed to become explicitly accepted. With regard to pictorial material, the court, in 1957, overturned a ruling by Postmaster General Summerfield which had banned the nudist magazine *Sunshine and Health* from the postal service. In the opinion of the court, pubic hair and genitals were representative of an 'idea' essential to the nudist movement and therefore unassailable under the law.

Obscenity Test

In the case of Roth v. US (1957), the majority opinion stated that the test for obscenity was whether to the average person, applying contemporary community standards, the dominant theme of the material taken as a whole appealed to the prurient interest. Obscenity which was beyond the protection of the First Amendment meant only material which was 'utterly without redeeming social importance.' It was on the basis of the Roth decision that a federal judge, in 1959, rescinded the ban on *Lady Chatterley's Lover*. Lawrence had written this book as a 'phallic novel' in which he explored the 'mystery of masculinity,' and he regarded it as an affirmation of physical love against puritanical suppression. In line with the Roth decision, the Supreme Court, in 1964, ruled that a French film *The Game of Love*, was not hard-core pornography and could not be banned (Jacobellis v. Ohio), and in a 1966 opinion, (*Memoirs of a Woman of Pleasure* v. Massachusetts), Justice Brennan explained that a book or film or magazine could be classified as legally obscene only if it was simultaneously guilty of each of three offences: it had to appeal to the average person's prurient interest, it had to be 'patently offensive' to the average adult, and it had to be 'utterly without redeeming social value.' Prosecutors, therefore, had to prove that there was nothing of social significance in a work which prompted pornographers to include medical reports or quotations from Shakespeare to provide the redeeming social feature.

A major shift in the Supreme Court's treatment of pornography came with the 1967 ruling in the case of Redrup v. New York. Robert Redrup, a Times Square newsstand vendor, had sold two paperbacks entitled *Lust Pool* and *Shame Agent* to a plain-clothes policeman. He had just been filling in for an acquaintance who had taken the day off due to illness. Redrup was charged with violation of Section 1141 of the Penal Code of the State of New York which forbids the sale of any 'obscene, lewd and indecent book.'

In its decision, the court gave up its effort to define obscenity and declared, in its most liberal ruling ever, that any material held not obscene by a majority of the justices regardless of their personal definitions of obscenity was protected by the First Amendment. The Redrup ruling and subsequent reversals of numerous obscenity convictions on the basis of Redrup created a backlash and Congress adopted legislation that established the President's Commission on Obscenity and Pornography. The task of the Commission was to examine 'the effects of obscenity and pornography on the public, particularly minors, and its relationship to crime and other anti-social behaviour.'

President's Commission on Obscenity and Pornography

The report of the Commission published in 1970 disappointed the sponsors of the legislation that had created it. The Commission expressed its belief that there was no warrant for continued interference by the government with the full freedom of adults because extensive empirical investigation, both by the Commission and others, provided no evidence that exposure to or use of explicit sexual materials played a significant rôle in the causation of social or individual harms such as crime, delinquency, sexual or non-sexual deviancy or severe emotional disturbances.

The report denied the relationship of pornography with sex crimes, disclaimed that the pornography business was dominated by the mafia, and advocated that the US government, which annually invested millions of dollars in taxpayers' money to harass and prosecute pornographers with questionable results, should abolish all laws that sought to deprive adults of the right to sell and read any and all so-called obscene material.

A minority of the Commission published a violent dissent (Hill–Link Minority Report) and President Nixon totally rejected the recommendations of the Commission. An upshot of the Commission's work was an unauthorised edition of its report adorned with 546 illustrations of every imaginable type of sexual activity. William Hamling, the publisher of the spoof, was convicted by a California court of sending obscene material — a brochure advertising the illustrated Presidential Report — through the mail. His conviction was upheld by the Court of Appeals and finally, in 1974, by the Supreme Court.

In its report, the Commission stated that obscene films and erotic pictures highly aroused men as well as women, and that often women who thought they were not aroused actually were. The arousal, the report commented, might lead to increased sexual activity but did not change a person's basic behaviour and sex patterns. The Commission contended that there were no recorded instances of sexual aggression, homosexuality, lesbianism or sexual abuse of children attributable to reading or viewing erotic stimuli.

Meese Commission

In May 1985, US Attorney-General Edwin Meese III announced the creation of an 11-member commission for investigating pornography and drawing up recommendations for the control of production and distribution of sexually-explicit material. Meese declared that pornography had changed radically since the presidential commission proposed repealing most laws against pornography 15 years ago, that more and more emphasis was placed on extreme violence and that cable TV and video recorders had made pornography available at home at the mere touch of a button or at the dialing of a telephone.

In hearings held in Washington, Chicago, Houston, Los Angeles, Miami and New York, the Commission inquired particularly into child pornography and the links of pornography with organised crime. In their testimony, a former actor and two former actresses described adult film-making in the flourishing X-rated movie industry as a brutal business involving the use of drugs and threats to force women into performing dangerous and painful sex acts. Because the pay is good — cash per sex act —, there is no dearth of performers but many lives are destroyed with actors and actresses ending up hooked on drugs or alcohol.

Los Angeles was said to have become the pornography capital of the world, with its porno industry generating more than $550 million annually. The members of the Commission were shocked by the perversity of the sado-masochistic material and the extent of the commercial production of child pornography. Among the materials the Commission was shown were slides of a man being castrated, writhing women trussed in iron and chains and smeared with faeces and people having sex with animals.

In February 1986, the Commission mailed a letter to 23 retailers saying that it had received testimony that the addressee was involved in the sale or distribution of pornography and invited the company to respond to the allegations prior to drafting the final report section on identified distributors. Failure to answer the charges would be accepted as an indication of no objection. What the letter did not say was that the list of distributors had been supplied by the Rev. Donald Wildmon of Tupelo, Missouri, a Methodist minister and founder of the National Federation for Decency.

As a result of this letter, some stores such as 7-Eleven stopped selling *Playboy* and *Penthouse*. *Playboy,* together with the Magazine Publishers Association and other groups, sued the Commission, demanding retraction of the letter and a statement explaining its intentions. *Playboy's* lawyer charged that the Commission's letter was intended to intimidate the magazine because it couldn't do so using the law. No jury has ever found *Playboy* to be legally obscene under the guidelines laid down by the Supreme Court.

Thrifty Drug which operates 582 discount and drug stores in California and eight other western states ceased to carry *Playboy, Penthouse* and *Playgirl* magazines. Other chains, such as People's Drug, Dart Drug and Rite-Aid also discontinued the sale of 'adult' magazines.

Report of the Attorney-General's Commission on Pornography

The 2-volume, 1960-page Report of the Attorney-General's Commission on Pornography was published on 3 July 1986. It divided pornography into five categories: child pornography, sexually-violent material, sexually-degrading material, non-violent and non-degrading material, and 'mere' nudity. The material labelled non-violent but degrading fosters a lax and tolerant attitude towards rape although it does not necessarily arouse violence. The Commission found no evidence that erotica which it described as neither violent nor degrading promoted violence but still thought that they were not in every instance harmless.

The Commission viewed the problem of child pornography as the most serious development since 1970 (when the President's Commission on Obscenity and Pornography compiled its report). Its findings concerning the relation between pornography and violence contrast sharply with those of the President's Commission. Pornography, the Commission thinks, has become more violent and explicit and it asserts that there is a causal link between violent pornography and aggressive behaviour towards women. Moreover, sexually-violent pornography leads to a greater acceptance of the 'rape myth' in its wider sense — that women enjoy being coerced into sexual activity and enjoy being physically hurt in connection with sex. But two members of the Commission, Judith Becker, director of the Sexual Behaviour Clinic at the New York State Psychiatric Institute, and Ellen Levine, editor of Women's Day, objected to the attempt to link pornography and violence and in an 18-page rebuttal asserted that there is no proof of a causal link. Their opinion is shared by many researchers who hold that the purpose of pornography is to produce sexual arousal or excitement, not to produce violence. Below, are some of the Commission's findings.

Harm Caused by Pornography

The report devotes much space to demonstrate the harm caused by pornography. In addition to discussing the impact of the various categories of pornographic material, it details the rôle of pornography in child abuse, rape, forced sexual performance, battery, torture, murder, imprisonment, sexually-transmitted diseases, masochistic self-harm, prostitution, suicidal tendencies, fear, anxiety, feelings of shame and guilt, degradation, abuse of alcohol and drugs. Among the social harms, the report lists loss of job or promotion, sexual harassment, financial losses, defamation and loss of status in the community, promotion of racial hatred, loss of trust within the family and harassment in the work place. In a summary of its findings, the Commission states that all kinds of harm are found in sexually-violent materials and in materials depicting sexual activity without violence but with degradation, submission, domination or humiliation. All commissioners agreed that some materials in the category of sexual activity without violence, degradation, submission, domination or humiliation may be harmful and some commissioners agreed that not all materials in this category are not harmful. But this classification constitutes a very small segment of the total pornographic materials. All commissioners agreed that some materials in the category of nudity without force, coercion, sexual activity or degradation may be harmful, and some commissioners agreed that not all materials in this classification are not harmful.

Child Pornography

Following an investigation into the traffic in child pornography, Congress approved the Protection of Children from Sexual Exploitation Act of 1977. The act prohibited the production of any sexually-explicit material using a child under the age of 16, if such material was destined for, or had already travelled in, interstate commerce. 'Sexually explicit' was defined as any conduct involving sexual intercourse of any variety, bestiality, masturbation, sado-masochistic abuse, or lewd exhibition of the genitals or the pubic area. The prohibition was directed against the transportation, shipping, mailing or receipt of child pornography in inter-state commerce for the purpose of sale or distribution for sale. The penalties for violation of the provisions of the act were made applicable to parents or other custodians who knowingly permitted a child to participate in the production of obscene material. The enforcement of the 1977 act was seriously impaired by its 'for sale' requirement and its limitation to 'obscene' child pornography.

In 1982, the US Supreme Court, in New York v. Ferber, upheld the constitutionality of a New York law prohibiting the distribution of materials depicting children 'in actual or simulated sexual intercourse, deviate sexual intercourse, sexual bestiality, masturbation, sado-masochistic abuse, or lewd exhibition of the genitals.' Child pornography can be banned even if it is not legally obscene. The decision meant approval of laws in 20 states which prohibit material showing children in explicit sexual conduct. The social evil of child pornography is so great, the court said, that states can prohibit its distribution regardless of whether it is obscene under the standards of the court. Child pornography is rampant in the United States; one ring supplied films and magazines to over 30,000 subscribers.

Because the 1977 act proved to be of limited practical value, Congress approved a revision of the act in 1984. The Child Protection Act of 1984 removed the requirement that inter-state trafficking, receipt or mailing of child pornography be for the purpose of 'sale' to be criminal and eliminated the 'obscenity' restriction of the 1977 act. The age limit of protection was raised to the age of 18. The definition of 'sexually explicit' was slightly modified. Written materials were excluded from the application of the law and only 'visual depictions' of real children were made punishable.

Nearly all states have now prohibited production of child pornography and many have prohibited distribution. Most states make parental consent or accession to the use of children in sexually-explicit materials illegal and many ban financing, developing, duplicating or promotion of child pornography. But the first appellate district in Ohio found the state law prohibiting possession of child pornography unconstitutional (Ohio v. Meadows, 1985). The state could not punish the mere private possession of magazines depicting minors engaged in sexual activity, the court held. New York v. Ferber was different because it dealt with distribution and not mere possession of child pornography.

The report discusses the difficulties involved in the prosecution of child abuse and endorses two suggestions for mitigating the impact of the trial on child witnesses. States should establish procedures for the closed-circuit televising or videotaping of victims' testimony under circumstances which ensure procedural fairness while minimising the trauma to the child-abuse victim. In questioning a child witness, prosecutors should be allowed to use language appropriate to the age of the child and the child should be permitted to answer in terms with which they feel comfortable. Children should also be allowed to use anatomically-correct dolls, if necessary, to demonstrate the manner in which they were posed or molested.

Performers

The report notes that so far too little attention has been given to the performers in hard-core pornography and that the difference between the photographic image of actual sexual conduct by real persons and a written description or drawing of such conduct has been overlooked. The interpretation of the constitutional limitations on pornography has been based solely on the effects of sexually-explicit material on viewers and the public. It was only in New York v. Ferber that the court extended its analysis to the 'private interests' of the performers — in this case children. Filming explicit sexual activity of children not only harmed them because of the sexual abuse involved but also because the material produced constitutes a permanent record of the child's participation and the harm to the child is aggravated by its circulation. Furthermore, the continued existence of a market for such material makes it more likely that children will be abused in the future.

Performers for pornographic films are recruited through modelling agencies or advertisements. Young men and women answering advertisements seeking 'models' only later discover that nudity or sexual intercourse is involved in the work. Others enter from nude dancing or prostitution. Model agents receive a flat daily fee for each model provided and furnish producers with books containing pictures of available models. But it also happens that women are physically coerced to participate in the production of hard-core pornography, and others have been forced to engage in sexual activities during performances to which they had not agreed beforehand. Some pornography is produced by pimps through the rape of prostitutes; the rapes are photographed and the photographs used to secure the continued submission of the prostitutes. But they are also sold to and published in pornographic magazines without their knowledge and consent. Coercion is also used to get models to perform sex acts they do not want to perform. But force does not seem to be a normal part of 'mainstream' pornography production and largely incidental to bondage, sado-masochism and home-made non-commercial pornography.

Women who enter pornography voluntarily are well paid. Female performers earn $350 to $500 per day of performance, males $250 to $450. Performers may also be paid on the basis of the number and type of sex acts in which they engage — for example, $250 per sex act. Well-known 'stars' may earn from $1,000 to $2,500 per day of performance. Payment is in cash, and fringe benefits such as medical insurance are unknown. Models sign a standard release form giving the film producer or photographer complete ownership of and unlimited rights to the material produced. They have no guarantee of future employment.

The single most common feature of models is their youth. Female models appearing in 'mainstream' commercial pornography are rarely over 30 years old or even in their late twenties and many begin performing in their teens, while male models apparently can enter and remain in the industry for somewhat longer.

Workdays are 12 to 14 hours long, with videos requiring three and X-rated movies seven days to shoot. A performer is expected to engage in at least two sex scenes a day. In the production of 'mainstream' pornography, females are required to perform homosexual as well as heterosexual acts but women do not engage in sex in male homosexual pornography.

The work exposes performers to numerous health risks. The promiscuity inherent in the work — any one model may have 20 to 30 different sex partners every month — involves the danger of contracting sexually-transmitted diseases, and performers are not permitted to use condoms or other 'safe' techniques. Only established 'stars' can be choosy about their partners.

Drugs constitute another threat to the health of performers in pornography. Although the drug problem is not limited to particular classes, certain groups are more liable to drug abuse than others and the physical and psychic pressure of their work and their situation induces performers in the sex industry to turn to drugs.

Pornographic modelling affects the personal life of the performers also in their social relations. Romances or family ties are often strained and even destroyed. Many female models live with highly-abusive husbands or boyfriends who treat them like prostitutes. Models may suffer rape or demands to submit to agents or producers and may drift into becoming call girls.

From a legal point of view, all performances which include actual sexual intercourse constitute a form of prostitution. Where persons are paid to have sex, it is irrelevant that the act is for display to others. Under the International Convention for the Suppression of the Traffic in Persons and of the Exploitation of the Prostitution of Others (1949), the 'employers' who make models engage in sexual intercourse should be made liable to prosecution. The Convention provides that the state should punish any person who procures, entices or leads away, for the purpose of prostitution, another person, even with the consent of that person, or who exploits the prostitution of another person, even with the consent of that person.

Dial-A-Porn

Dial-A-Porn available in the United States can describe two types of obscene statements made over the telephone. In the first case, the caller dials a number and talks to an individual who tries to conform to the caller's preferences for sexual conversation which may last up to 45 minutes. The caller pays a per minute rate and is billed on his credit card. In the second type of transaction, a call is placed to a number with the '976' prefix. These numbers are part of the Mass Announcement Network Service (MANS) and provide the caller with a pre-recorded, sexually-explicit message. The caller is charged on his monthly telephone bill. The provider of the message receives a payment from the telephone company revenues which is calculated according to the local tariff, the telephone company retains the remainder.

The Dial-A-Porn recordings include graphic descriptions, complete with sound effects, of homosexual and lesbian acts, sodomy, rape, incest, excretion, bestiality, sado-masochism and other sexual acts involving adults and children. Dial-A-Porn numbers are advertised in pornographic magazines, newsstand racks, in local general purpose stores or on public notice boards. They can easily be discovered and used by minors without the knowledge of their parents.

In an amendment to the Communications Act of 1934, Congress prohibited the use of the telephone to make obscene or indecent communications for commercial purposes to anyone under the age of 18 except in accordance with regulations issued by the Federal

Communications Commission. The FCC's regulations, announced in 1984, allowed sexually-explicit recordings if the message was made available only between the hours 9.00 pm to 8.00 am eastern standard time or, in the case of 'live' messages, if the caller made prepayment by credit card.

The regulations were challenged by Carlin Communications, Inc., a New York firm, and on review the US Court of Appeals for the Second District found them invalid. The government had a compelling interest in protecting minors from salacious material, the court acknowledged, but the FCC regulations were not best suited to meet these objectives which could be achieved by less restrictive alternatives.

In October 1985, the FCC published new regulations under which Dial-A-Porn services had to require either an authorised access or identification code or obtain pre-payment by credit card before transmission of a sexually-explicit message.

Carlin Communications again went to court and in April 1986, the Court of Appeals granted their petition and set aside the regulations as applied to Carlin. The court relied on statements from New York Telephone that access or identification codes were not technologically feasible in the New York telephone network and that the FCC's conclusion that the access code requirement was the least restrictive means to regulate dial-a-porn was not supported by the record. The ruling leaves the possibility open that access codes may be permissible outside New York. The court suggested that the installation of blocking devices on the customer's terminal equipment could be used to block access to one or more pre-selected phone numbers but blocking may not be available to all telephone customers and few parents would know which numbers to block. Minors would still be able to make calls from telephones not equipped with blocking devices.

Cable Television

A new problem has arisen with the advent of cables and satellite television services. Major services offer adult programmes including soft-core movies, night club acts and concerts, but local access channels show lesbianism, homosexuality, sadism and masochism, and commercials where viewers can see naked men and women for hire. As mentioned above, the federal government maintains that cable can be regulated only by the states. US District Judge Bruce Jenkins who overruled the Utah law banning films on cable which included nudity stated: 'There is no law that says you have to watch. There is no law that says you have to subscribe to a cable television service.' The basic problem is whether the government can censure materials only seen in the privacy of the home.

The Cable Communications Policy Act of 1984 provides penalties for transmitting over any cable system any matter which is obscene or otherwise unprotected by the Constitution of the United States. But the Federal Communications Commission maintains that cable services can be controlled adequately within the home to assure that minors do not have access. Because the individual need not watch undesirable programmes, the government has no compelling interest in further intrusion.

The cable television industry recommends the use of 'lock-boxes' as a means of parental control over programmes viewed by children. But in a suit involving the FCC's authority to regulate broadcast contents, the Supreme Court decided that the availability of lock-boxes does not prevent the FCC from regulating obscenity on radio and broadcast television (FCC v. Pacific Foundation, 1978).

To cope with the increase in pornography attributable to the spread of cable television (which has made it a $6 billion a year industry), conservative religious and political leaders urged President Reagan through the group 'Morality in Media' to appoint an anti-pornography coordinator for better law enforcement by the FBI, the Justice Department, the Postal Service and the Customs Service.

If the experience of the cable TV industry is a guide, there exists a wide gap between what the courts consider community standards of objectionable obscenity and what the 'public' wants to see. Most complaints, the industry says, demand hotter, more passionate action.

In a 1986 referendum, voters in Maine rejected a proposal to make producing, selling, possessing or promoting obscene material a state crime punishable by up to five years in jail. The courts would have to decide what was obscene. The vote was 68 per cent against and 32 per cent for the proposal.

The report makes 92 specific recommendations, and although it rejects censorship and efforts to expand the legal definition of pornography, it calls for the enactment of federal laws to make it easier to seize the assets of pornographers and laws to be used against producers who pay performers in pornographic films. Definitions of obscenity should be revised, punishment made more severe and measures taken to combat the rôle of organised crime in pornography. The Federal Communications Commission should restrict pornographic cable television shows and 'Dial-A-Porn' telephone services. In order to suppress the 'kiddie-porn' industry, the Commission proposed to make the knowing possession of child pornography a felony. It also called for citizen action against stores that sell obscene materials.

The report contains a 246-page section providing excerpts from the bawdy dialogue in pornographic films and graphic descriptions of pictures in pornographic magazines. It gives lists of 2,325 separate magazine titles, 725 book titles and 2,370 films found in 16 'adults only' stores surveyed in six cities (Washington DC, Baltimore, Miami, Philadelphia, New York and Boston).

The report has found a mixed reception. It is symptomatic of the moral militancy in many American communities and the crusade to reaffirm family values. Under President Reagan, government officials from federal to local levels have shown willingness to help enforce traditional values. Civil libertarians were apprehensive of an invasion of moral vigilantism which would erode the constitutional right of free speech and infringe on privacy. The report raised old questions: has the state power to enforce the morality of its citizens? To what extent can the government regulate private conduct? Should the state actively promote the values cherished by the community? How should these values be defined?

Recent US Supreme Court Decisions

The Supreme Court's liberal interpretation of obscenity found its last expression in the case of Stanley v. Georgia (1969) which held that obscenity was largely a question of personal privacy. In Justice Thurgold Marshall's opinion: 'If the First Amendment means anything, it means that the state has no business telling a man, sitting alone in his own house, what books he may read or what films he must watch.' The court held that the mere possession of obscene matter cannot constitutionally be made a crime. The court rejected the contention of the state of Georgia that to eliminate the traffic in pornography, it is necessary to ban the mere private possession by an individual. But before the court could develop the privacy doctrine to its logical conclusion, the change in the composition of the court by President Nixon's appointment of Warren E. Burger as Chief Justice (1969) and three associate justices in the following two years reversed the liberal trend in obscenity cases. In later decisions, the court rejected the argument that Stanley created a right to import or receive obscene material for private use and in 1985, the US Court of Appeals for the Eleventh District upheld the conviction of a defendant who had received child pornography from Europe through the post.

Miller v. California

The first important decision in which the Nixon court could assert its interpretation of pornography was Miller v. California (1973). Chief Justice Burger relieved the prosecution of the burden to show that material was 'utterly without redeeming social value' and made it incumbent on the defence to prove that a work possessed 'serious literary, artistic, political, or scientific value.' The case involved a pornographic brochure which had been posted to an unsuspecting restaurant manager and his mother and the definition of obscenity was the crucial issue in the case. Material could be found obscene where the sexual acts were 'actual or simulated' as long as the act itself was 'patently offensive.' Obscenity was present when all of the following three conditions were met: (1) That the average person, applying contemporary community standards, would find that the work, taken as a whole, appealed to the prurient interest in sex. (2) That the work depicted or described, in a patently offensive way, sexual conduct specifically defined by the applicable law. (3) That the work, taken as a whole, lacked serious literary, artistic, political, or scientific value. Chief Justice Burger summed up the gist of the Miller decision when he wrote: 'This much has been categorically settled by the Court, that obscene material is unprotected by the First Amendment.'

The decision replaced the 'national standard' in the interpretation of obscenity laws by 'community standards.' The lower courts should be allowed to be more flexible in defining what was obscene. In a society priding itself in supporting pluralism and diversity, the decision maintained, there was no sound reason for the law to say that, what was found tolerable in the portrayal of sexual activities in Los Angeles or Las Vegas, must be accepted in Maine or Vermont. Such reasoning may be appropriate for local regulations on nude bathing but can only create confusion for publications or films distributed nationwide.

The decision made every state and every local community the arbiter of acceptability and all sex-related literary, artistic and entertainment production had to be reduced to the lowest common denominator of tolerance to escape local censorship. Chief Justice Burger, repudiating the findings of the Presidential Commission, wrote: 'Although there is no conclusive proof of a connection between anti-social behaviour and obscene material, a legislature could quite reasonably determine that such a connection does or might exist.' Which means that the prejudices of a bunch of politicians can determine the standards of freedom of sexual expression.

In a later decision (Smith v. US, 1977), the Court ruled that the question whether a work lacked serious literary, artistic, political, or scientific value was never to be determined by local standards; the frame of reference must always be national.

In Paris Adult Theatre I v. Slaton, the defence claimed that no one under 21 years of age was admitted and that showing films to consenting adults was protected under the right to privacy. Chief Justice Burger, writing for the majority, stated: 'We categorically disapprove the theory, apparently adopted by the trial judge, that obscene, pornographic films acquire constitutional immunity from state legislation simply because they are exhibited for consenting adults only. This holding was properly rejected by the Georgia supreme court.'

Later decisions of the US Supreme Court have made no contribution to the twin problem of how pornography should be defined and why the publication of pornography should be banned. In 1981, the court refused to review the obscenity conviction of the producers and distributors of the film *Deep Throat*. The film portrays the sometimes humorous, sometimes sad and frequently explicit efforts of a young lady to achieve sexual satisfaction. *Deep Throat* was produced by the Peraino brothers of the Colombo crime family for $25,000 and is reliably estimated to have grossed $50 million as of 1982. Joseph, Anthony and Louis Peraino all became millionaires and used the proceeds from the film to build a vast financial empire in the 1970s.

In March 1987, the Supreme Court, by a 7-2 vote, affirmed the ruling of a federal judge upheld by a federal appeals court that declared unconstitutional a 1983 Utah law prohibiting cable television programmes that contained indecent material but were not legally obscene. The lower court had found the Utah statute vague and too broad and also held that regulation had been preempted by federal law.

Zoning Codes

In addition to federal and state law, establishments of the sex industry and the distribution and sale of pornography are also being regulated by zoning codes and local nuisance, anti-display and civil rights ordinances.

In June 1981, the Supreme Court ruled that individual states may ban topless dancing in bars and other places where liquor is served. Although the court had decided in some cases that nude dancing may be protected by the First Amendment, it upheld a New York law forbidding liquor-licence holders from staging nude dancing. The states, the court reasoned, have complete authority to regulate when and how liquor is sold. On the other hand, the court, in Schad v. Mount Ephraim, quashed an attempt to use the zoning power to keep nude dancing and other forms of sexually-explicit entertainment out of the cities. In 1976, the court had upheld a Detroit zoning ordinance that banned adult bookstores and movie theatres from clustering together in downtown areas or near residential neighbourhoods (Young v. American Mini Theatres). But the 1981 decision explained that the Detroit zoning ordinance had the effect of 'merely dispersing, but not excluding' adult theatres. The location can be restricted so that cities and towns can keep all forms of commercial entertainment out of purely residential areas but they cannot, as Mount Ephraim, N.J., had done, banish all live entertainment within their borders. The court recognised that nude dancing was part of the freedom of speech protected by the First Amendment.

In 1986, the court reaffirmed that a city can use its zoning regulations to restrict adult entertainment, movie theatres showing X-rated films and adult bookstores to a less developed section of the city in order to protect the 'quality of life.'

Newport, Kentucky, across the Ohio River from Cincinnati and known as 'sin city,' passed an ordinance requiring that night-club dancers wear at least panties or G-strings.

Nuisance Laws

Some states have enacted so-called 'public nuisance laws' which give local communities the power to close down theatres showing or stores selling sexually-explicit materials. While nuisance abatement suits have been successfully brought to stop the exhibition or dissemination of specific books, magazines or movies, the Supreme Court rejected the application of nuisance statutes to prevent the future exhibition of unnamed films in an 'adults only' pornographic theatre (Vance v. Universal Amusement Co., 1980). In November 1981, the Supreme Court struck down a portion of a Washington law which allowed temporary closure before any court findings of obscenity. Nuisance actions have also been brought based upon lewd activity, assignation or prostitution occurring on the premises where obscene material is sold or exhibited.

Anti-Display Statutes

Statutes and ordinances have been enacted to restrict the public display of sexually- explicit materials in order to protect minors. The US Court of Appeals for the Tenth Circuit upheld a Wichita, Kansas, ordinance which restricted the display of material 'harmful to minors' and required that in places accessible to minors such material be kept behind devices known as 'blinder racks' so that the lower two-thirds of the material is not exposed to view (M.S. News Co. v. Casado, 1983). A Minneapolis, Minnesota, ordinance provided that any material whose cover, covers, or packaging, standing alone, was harmful to minors had to be blacked from view by an opaque cover. The booksellers contended that the requirement of a sealed wrapper was unduly restrictive because it abridged an adult's right to peruse the materials which were harmful to minors but not to adults. The court, however, decided that any inconvenience suffered by adult patrons was not sufficient to render the restrictions unconstitutional (Upper Midwest Booksellers v. City of Minneapolis, 1985).

Civil Rights Actions

Pornography as a civil-rights violation constituted the gist of an ordinance enacted by the city of Indianapolis, Indiana, in 1984 to prevent and prohibit all discriminatory practices of sexual subordination or inequality through pornography. The ordinance defined pornography as 'the graphic sexually-explicit subordination of women, whether in pictures or in words.' Discriminatory practices for which the ordinance created a civil remedy included trafficking in pornography or coercing a person into a pornographic performance.

The constitutionality of the ordinance was challenged in court and in American Booksellers Association v. Hudnut (1984), the District Court found that the ordinance regulated speech that was protected under the First Amendment. Otherwise free speech could be regulated to protect women from the humiliation and degradation in pornography if required by compelling reasons. The court came to the conclusion that women were capable of protecting themselves from being harmed by pornography. The US Court of Appeals for the Seventh District upheld the decision of the District Court (1985). When the city of Minneapolis appealed to the Supreme Court, the court summarily affirmed the judgement of the Court of Appeals (1986). As mentioned above, a civil rights ordinance adopted by the city council of Minneapolis was vetoed by the mayor.

Nude Pictures

Personal nudity has been involved in two problems, first, the right of preventing one's nude picture from being published and, second, the right to have one's nude picture published. Typical of the first situation was the suit brought by film star Brooke Shields and her mother to prevent commercial use of nude photos taken when Miss Shields was ten years old. They lost the suit and New York State Supreme Court Justice, Edward Greenfield, chided Mrs Shields for having pushed her daughter's career too hard. She was maternally protective but exploitative at the same time, the judge said.

In Faloona v. *Hustler* magazine (1985), the Fifth Circuit Court ruled that children whose nude pictures, including one showing the plaintiff child holding her vagina open facing the camera, appeared in adult magazines, had no right to revoke the mother's consent to publication.

A cartoon and depiction of a famous boxer in the nude was held actionable because of its effects on the boxer (Ali v. *Playgirl,* Inc., 1978). The Court of Appeals for the Fifth Circuit upheld a judgement against *Chic* magazine for publishing a nude picture of a woman whose consent had been obtained by fraud (Braun v. Flynt, 1984). The same court sustained a judgement against *Hustler* magazine for the reckless publication of a nude photo which had been stolen from the subject's home (Wood v. *Hustler* Magazine, Inc., 1984).

The opposite problem has come up when public officials have posed for publications featuring nude pictures. A New York female police officer was suspended and formally charged with misconduct when her nude picture appeared in a girlie magazine. She contended that the picture had been taken before she joined the force. A 25-year-old Springfield, Ohio, police officer was suspended indefinitely for having posed nude for *Playboy* magazine. The divorced mother of a 7-year-old boy maintained that she had done nothing wrong. In the Philippines, Filipina movie actress Tatchie Agbayani was sued for obscenity and 'bringing shame' to Philippine women when her nude picture appeared in the German edition of *Playboy*. Another Filipina actress was prosecuted for having her nude photo published in a local magazine.

Regulation of Pornography in Other Countries

In Britain, the 1981 Indecent Displays (Control) Act applies literally to what is 'exposed' in displays and on magazine covers. The law is designed to remove salacious film advertising and outrageous magazine covers but does not touch on what is shown inside the cinemas or printed in magazines. This is still subject to the confused legislation on what is legally obscene. The UK theatre censorship was abolished in 1968 but the director of the National Theatre was prosecuted for gross indecency when, in the play of Howard Brenton entitled *The Romans in Britain,* three armed Roman soldiers confront three naked druids of whom one is raped. The British Board of Film Censors vets films for exhibition in public places but has no power to control the material traded on video cassette recordings. Gross offence against decency in this form may be subject to the Obscene Publications Act of 1959.

In an attempt to clean up the capital, the General Purpose Committee of London's Westminster Council voted to close 42 of the 62 sex shops in the Soho red-light district.

In accordance with the prohibition of censorship in the Fundamental Law of the Federal Republic of Germany, the legal restraints on pornography were abolished although restrictions can be imposed for the protection of minors. Some years ago, ten prominent women filed suit against the German magazine *Stern* because they found the magazine's pictures of women on its cover 'demeaning and insulting.' They demanded that the magazine stop representing women as mere sex objects and giving male readers the impression that 'men could arbitrarily dispose of women and dominate over them.' They felt injured 'in their honour and personality' and contended that the magazine's pictures reduced women to 'sexual usabililty' and suggested 'female subordination and male domination.' The court turned down the complaint because it had no foundation in existing legislation. Although the suitable representation of women in public and in the media was a worthy cause, it was beyond the competence of the court.

Political Implications of Anti-Pornography

The ban on pornography is frequently linked to political censorship. Under the 1974 Publications Act, South Africa maintains a three-tier censorship system which controls not only pornography but anything incompatible with 'apartheid.' At the local level, three-member censorship committees whose members are not identified review all films planned for distribution and books, posters and records which draw complaints. The higher levels comprise the Administrative Directorate of Publications and the Publications Appeals Board. A work may be banned if any part is ruled obscene or harmful to public morals, blasphemous, a cause of ridicule or contempt to any social group, harmful to race relations or prejudicial to the safety of the state or peace and good order. The ban can extend not only to the distribution but also to the possession of the material. Every week, the Directorate issues a list of newly banned items. Over 13,000 books, films, records, posters and other items have been banned. (The former 'Index of Forbidden Books' of the Catholic Church contained about 5,000 titles). In recent years, the sexual standards were somewhat liberalised. Bare black breasts were considered acceptable and naked white breasts were sometimes passed. By now, film censorship has become more tolerant of sex and swearing; full frontal nudity and four-letter words are no longer taboo. But the political repression remains unchanged and affects black writers as well as rebel Afrikaners who challenge white supremacy.

In Brazil, media censorship banned women in bikinis, people in panties or underpants, advertising underwear and programmes with shocking scenes such as people in bed together, adultery and free love as well as violence. In view of Rio de Janeiro's bacchanalian carnival, some of the restraints seem rather ludicrous.

Greece's socialist government which came to power in 1981 abolished censorship of films and songs. A committee at the Undersecretariat of Press and Information which screened all films and checked the lyrics of songs before public circulation went out of existence. All films can be freely shown for adults but for viewing by minors under 18 years of age, films must be submitted to a special committee which can grant a general public certificate. Public prosecutors, however, can still take legal action against cinema owners if a film offends against public morals.

The Egyptian Ministry of the Interior confiscated 3,000 copies of an unexpurgated edition of *Thousand and One Nights* and charged a publisher and three booksellers with violating the pornography law by printing, importing and distributing the book. A Cairo judge agreed with the government, ruled that parts of the classic violated morals, fined the defendants and ordered the destruction of the confiscated books and the printing plates. After pondering the issue for over a year, the court of second instance decided that at least the expurgated edition which is on sale in bookstores and probably in the hands of students is not pornographic.

The People's Republic of China imposed a nationwide ban on importing, copying, selling or playing reactionary or pornographic tapes and videotapes. Theatres, schools, enterprises and other establishments are not allowed to show videotapes from Hong Kong, Macao, Taiwan and other countries. Every individual must register videotape recorders and videotapes and the authorities determine which tapes may be kept.

The Manila International Film Festival of 1983, sponsored by the then Philippine's First Lady, Mrs Imelda Marcos, caused a sharp protest by Jaime Cardinal Sin, archbishop of Manila. The strict official censorship system was set aside for the event and the cinemas went on a binge in showing hard-core pornography including films previously banned, such as 'Virgin People,' a film in which a seventeen-year-old Filipina actress, Pepsi Paloma, appears nude in torrid love scenes. Some producers restored sex scenes cut by the censors and a producer was reported to have shot some extra scenes to take advantage of the censorship holiday. Ordinarily, the Philippines censors, like their Japanese counterparts, cut out everything in which pubic hair is visible.

When Cardinal Sin criticised the suspension of censorship, Mrs Marcos replied in a news conference: 'Pornography is not in the vision, but in the minds and hearts of the people.' She remarked that she was sorry that this cheap pornography had affected some fragile senses and expressed the opinion that youths who had been inculcated with proper values would not be destroyed by one or two bold movies.

In his rebuttal, Cardinal Sin went beyond the issue of pornography and attacked the Marcos régime for arrogance and oppression. 'There is a climate of fear pervading our country,' the Cardinal said, so that 'the people now prefer to think no evil, see no evil and hear no evil.' Referring to a new decree strengthening the powers of government censors, he charged that 'to suit its own ends, the government will not hesitate to use power in a capricious and arrogant manner, to treat the people like idiots and expects to get away with it.' — 'If pornography is wrong, then the suspension of the law was an unjustifiable abuse of authority. If pornography is not wrong, then the new presidential decree is an unwarranted limitation of the people's freedom. Either way, there is a dismaying demonstration of the arrogance of power.'

The people? At least the male part of Manila's population jammed the over 100 cinemas, queuing for hours and then sharing seats or squatting in the aisles to enjoy the brief respite from public control of morality.

Japan's Legal Provisions

In Japan, the Criminal Code contains two articles related to 'public morality' and pornography. Article 174 concerns 'public obscenity' and says: 'A person committing an act of public obscenity will be punished with penal servitude of less than six months or a fine of less than 500 yen (the fines are adjusted by a multiplier) or alternatively with confinement or a police fine.' Article 175 prohibits the distribution of 'obscene literature' and stipulates: 'Persons distributing, selling or publicly exhibiting obscene books, pictures or other things will be punished with penal servitude of less than two years or a fine of less than 5,000 yen or alternatively with a police fine. The same applies to a person possessing them for the purpose of sale.' The law does not give a definition of 'public obscenity' or obscene books or pictures. ' Pictures' also includes photos and films, and 'other things' is understood to refer to sculptures, records, tapes, and so on.

A provision in the 'Minor Offences Law' subjects to detention or a police fine 'a person indecently exposing buttocks, thighs or another part of the body at a place open to public view and in a manner liable to cause aggravation to the public' (Art. 1, No. 20). This law also prohibits voyeurism by decreeing the same punishment for 'a person who without justifiable reason secretly peeps into a person's dwelling, bath, dressing-room, toilet or other place where people usually are without clothes' (Art. 1, No. 23). While the courts have often tried to define the meaning of obscene publications, they have had less occasion to elucidate the meaning of indecent exposure.

What censorship laws generally overlook is that the production of obscene materials may involve much more serious problems than their distribution and sale. This is particularly true for child pornography but applies also to the production of blue films and tapes which may involve sexual exploitation by gangsters or other criminals.

Japanese Court Decisions: Lady Chatterley's Lover

A landmark in Japan's obscenity jurisprudence was the *Lady Chatterley's Lover* case in which the translator and the publisher of the Japanese translation were indicted for violating Article 175 of the Criminal Code. The Tokyo District Court, in a decision handed down in 1952, held that ordinarily, distributing a literary work having artistic value is not punishable under Article 175 but that various parts of the book (the prosecution had listed 12 sexual scenes as pornographic) were very close to what was clearly obscene writing. The book stimulated the sexual desire of the reader and destroyed or weakened the control of reason over sexual impulse. The publisher who had promoted the sale of the book with sensational advertising was fined but the translator was judged not guilty because the court found that he expected the book to be bought by persons who would read it as literature. Thus, the court concluded, he did not participate in the criminal act of the publisher.

The decision was appealed by both the prosecution and the publisher. The Tokyo High Court sustained the conviction of the publisher and reversed the acquittal of the translator who, the court held, was to be considered a co-principal because he translated the work at the request of the publisher and the manuscript was printed without alterations.

Furthermore, the court said, the lower court was mistaken in assuming that the book became an obscene publication by virtue of the methods of sale and advertising; the translation in itself was an offence against Article 175 of the Criminal Code.

In 1957, the Supreme Court declared that it had often emphasised the limitation of such rights as the freedom of speech by the public welfare and asserted that 'there can be no doubt that the protection of the sexual order and the maintenance of a minimum degree of sexual morality constitute the contents of public welfare.' The standard which the court used in determining the obscenity of *Lady Chatterley's Lover* was 'to wantonly arouse and stimulate sexual desire, to impair the normal sense of sexual shame of the ordinary man, and to offend the right sentiments of sexual morality.'

What the court actually meant by 'obscene' was the description of sexual intercourse, fore- and afterplay, kisses, embraces, changes in the sex organs, the thoughts, desires, feelings and utterances of the partners related to sexual activity and reflections couched in realistic terms.

With regard to the obscenity charge, the court recognised some artistic quality in the sexual passages pointed out by the prosecution which distinguished the book from Japanese pornography (*shunga*) but even so the court found them bold, detailed and realistic: 'They contravene the principle of privacy in sexual conduct and offend the feeling of shame to such an extent that one would hesitate to read them aloud not only in the family circle but also at a public meeting.' Artistry and obscenity, the court held, belong to separate and different spheres and are not incompatible. A certain level of artistry does not necessarily absolve a work from obscenity.

The conviction of the translator was a flagrant misconstruction of the wording of Article 175. It is completely arbitrary to consider the translator as a co-principal with regard to the 'distribution, sale or exhibition' of a book unless he is a partner in the publishing firm. The law does not forbid the writing, printing and publication of obscene literature and the cooperation of a translator does certainly not extend to distribution and sale.

What Has Obscene Literature to do with Public Welfare?

A question that must be raised in connection with the standard applied by the court is 'what has it to do with public welfare or the public order?' A person who does not want to be sexually aroused or who feels ashamed by sex is not obliged to read obscene books or see blue films. The court proclaimed that the law and the courts were called upon to fulfil a 'clinical' rôle in stemming moral depravation. In the Middle Ages, when church and state were two powers regulating the same community, morality was a public concern, and in Calvin's Geneva or the Puritan communities

of New England, public authority policed the morals of the citizens.
But, as one of the judges in the case of *Lady Chatterley's Lover* pointed
out, to enforce morality by law and punishment is 'judicial heresy.'

Moreover, the standard relied on by the court is entirely subjective.
How can a court determine what the 'normal sense of sexual shame of
the ordinary man' is? Or, another expression used by the court, what
the commonly accepted idea of society (*shakai tsûnen*) is? The courts do
not undertake public opinion polls and if they did, the results would be
completely irrelevant. The thinking of the 'ordinary man' or 'society' do
not represent an objective standard, and it is impossible to say to what
extent the ideas of the 'ordinary man' are influenced by prejudice,
ignorance or superstition. Man's moral convictions are a question of his
conscience, and he may form his conscience on the basis of the moral
value system of his religion or church, or of philosophy, the teaching of
his guru or the drivel of a demagogue. For the pluralistic, 'neutral' state,
a religious value system has no binding force. In a country in which the
majority of the citizens belong to the same religion or in Europe where
the Christian tradition has shaped the social value system, a certain
uniformity of views remains but this has no legal significance. For a
correct solution of this problem, it is important to understand that man
belongs to society not as male or female but as a human being, and that
his sexuality is of no concern to the public order. (That only men fight
as soldiers is a social custom which has never been a universal norm.)
Man's sexual sphere is essentially man's personal sphere, and his sex life
belongs to his private life. There is no principle which says that man
cannot conduct his private affairs in public but this still leaves unanswered
the question whether and when sexual acts and sexual performances
offend against the public order.

Religion's presumption that it had the right to regulate what people
do with their bodies in bed and that it could pass judgement on the
manner and purpose of sex has been widely repudiated. Whether a book
stimulates the sexual desires of readers or weakens the control of reason
over sexual impulses should be of no concern to the police or the judiciary.
As mentioned above, the protection of minors is a different problem
which should be solved in such a way that neither the police nor the
courts can tell adults what they can or cannot read or see. That is none
of their business. On the basis of the principles of a free and pluralistic
society, police and courts should protect the freedom of every adult to
read and see what he wants.

There is no question that sex offences (as defined in the Criminal
Code) are incompatible with the public order. It is also true that public
authority has the right and the duty to protect minors against undesirable
and premature exposure to sex (what this means and how it should be
done is a difficult problem). But that all public manifestations of sex
should be banned is an untenable position in any society. In the United

States, the basic contest has been whether public display of sex is obscene and therefore not protected by the First Amendment (on account of the interpretation that obscenity is not covered by the First Amendment). In Japan, the court battles always involved the question 'what is obscene?' because the courts have generally upheld the constitutionality of the prohibition of the sale of obscene literature.

'The Underlay of the Sliding Door of the Four-and-a-Half-Mat Room'

One of the cases in which the definition of obscenity was the major point of contention involved the ban of a story reputedly written by a well-known author of the Meiji era, Kafu Nagai, entitled 'The Underlay of the Sliding Door of the Four-and-a-Half-Mat Room' (the room is in a *geisha* house). The story had been reprinted in a magazine, and the editor of the magazine together with the president of the publishing company were prosecuted for violation of Article 175 of the Criminal Code. The case went all the way up to the Supreme Court and the defendants were found guilty in all three instances. The Tokyo District Court had based its ruling on the definition of obscenity in two prior obscenity cases, *Lady Chatterley's Lover* and *Glory of Vice* (a translation of a work of the Marquis de Sade). The Tokyo High Court, in 1979, upheld the district's court decision, rejecting the defendants' arguments that the definition of obscenity was vague and obscure and that Article 175 of the Criminal Code was unconstitutional. The court ruled that the story portrayed sexual intercourse in a lewd and realistic manner and that, even if its amusing style was taken into account, the work as a whole appealed to the prurient interest. Also, 'according to today's commonly accepted ideas of society,' the court declared, the work was obscene. The standard for this evaluation, the court said, was 'a lewd and realistic description of the genitals or the sex act' and that the description was given in such a way 'as to appeal to emotional sensations or the senses.' A book is obscene in the meaning of Article 175 of the Criminal Code if, seen in its entirety, it stimulates the lasciviousness of the reader and moreover is, on the basis of the social ideas of the time, disgusting, seriously stimulating sexual desire and injuring the sexual shame of the ordinary person. As a safeguard, the decision added that medical books did not fall under the definition of obscenity and that humorous or sensual novels although they might be written in a way appealing to the senses were exempt if their descriptions of sex organs and sex acts were not too lascivious. Hinting at the modification of the Hicklin rule by the *Ulysses* decision in the United States, the court said that it was not proper to lift special passages out of the entire work and evaluate obscenity out of context. Some immoral or uneducational passages would not make the entire work obscene. The court brushed aside the allegation of unconstitutionality without giving a convincing reason for the constitutionality of the censorship contained in the provisions of Article 175.

The decision of the Supreme Court delivered on 28 November 1980, kept closely to the definition of obscenity given in the 1957 *Lady Chatterley's Lover* case. As points to be considered in evaluating a work, the court listed 'the extent and manner of lewd and detailed description related to sex in the work in question, their ratio to the entire work, and the connection between the thoughts expressed in the work and the sex descriptions, the degree to which the sexual stimulation is moderated by the structure and unfolding of the work as well as its artistic value and ideology. From this point of view, it must be decided whether seen as a whole, the work appeals to the prurient interest of the reader or not. 'Basically, however, the court reaffirmed the three criteria distilled from the *Lady Chatterley's Lover* decision: 1. Whether the work overwhelmingly stimulates and excites sexual desire. 2. Whether it injures the normal sense of sexual shame. 3. Whether it offends against the right sentiments of sexual morality. The court found that the story gave a lewd, detailed and realistic description of scenes of sexual intercourse in an exciting style, and that these descriptions constituted, quantitatively and qualitatively, the bulk of the story, and that the structure and unfolding of the work and its literary and ideological value consisted mainly in appealing to the prurient interest of the reader. A comprehensive evaluation of these points showed that the prohibition of the sale of obscene books provided for in Article 175 of the Criminal Code applied to the story.

On the same day, the Supreme Court turned down the appeals in two other obscenity cases. The first involved the owner and manager of a bookstore who had displayed copies of the magazine which contained the story 'The Underlay of the Sliding Door of the Four-and-a-Half Mat Room.' The accused had been found guilty of keeping obscene material for sale in the first and second instances and the Supreme Court rejected their appeal. In their defence, the accused had maintained that they had not read the magazine which contained the allegedly obscene story. To which the Tokyo High Court replied that they must have heard that the police had confiscated the issue of the magazine as obscene and that the story was generally regarded as pornography. In the opinion of the court, therefore, the action of an administrative agency (the police) creates the presumption of illegality. To the objection of the defence that this amounted to self-censorship, the court remarked that bookstore owners generally remove from their shelves works against which the police had taken action: 'it is popular wisdom not to approach dangerous things.' Such an attitude may be common sense in a totalitarian state; that the Japanese judiciary considers this as normal shows how deep-rooted the authoritarian ideology is in Japan and how superficial the much-vaunted

) post-war conversion to democracy has remained.

A third decision rendered on that day turned down an appeal from the ruling of the Osaka High Court that had overturned the verdict of 'not guilty' of the Osaka District Court. The lower courts with their generally younger judges are sometimes more liberal than the judges on the higher courts who do not want to jeopardise their promotion. The suit involved a novel entitled 'Love Juice for Two' written by folk singers and published in a folk magazine. The district court had reasoned that 'in a consideration of the commonly-accepted ideas of society, the readership must be taken into account' and that in view of the sexual environment of the young readers, the novel was not obscene. But the Osaka High Court did not want to have any truck with this relaxation and found that the novel contained lewd sexual descriptions exceeding the limits of the permissible on the basis of the socially-acceptable ideas.

The 'Four-and-a-Half-Mat Room' trial had an amusing sequence. Because the decision did not include the sequestration of the magazine seized by the police as evidence, 641 copies had to be returned to the publisher. But the police were unable to give back all copies. Some had been burned, some had been damaged by water, and others had just disappeared. Which might show that law-enforcement officers are not beyond the appeal of pornography.

'L'Empire des Sens': Why is Pornography Bad?

A new height of judicial partiality was reached when the Supreme Court rejected the protest of a film producer and a publisher against the confiscation of a book that had been cleared of the charge of obscenity by the Tokyo District Court. The book contained the synopsis of the plot and 28 still photos of a film edited in France in order to evade prosecution in Japan. The film, entitled *L'empire des sens,* gained wide acclaim when it was shown at the Cannes Film Festival of 1976 and was awarded the British Film Institute's grand prize. It was banned in several European countries and shown in Japan only in mutilated form with thirty of its 108 minutes cut. The film's scenario was based on an incident that had actually happened in 1936 in which a woman killed her lover and cut off his genitals (hence the Japanese title *Ai no Corrida,* Bullfight of Love). The police had seized the book and charged Nagisa Oshima, the producer of the film, and the president of the publishing company with the distribution of obscene material. Eight pages of photos, the police charged, depicted lovemaking 'too nakedly.' (The number of pages with offensive photos was later increased to twelve). Oshima charged that the book had been made a scapegoat for the film and was an act of revenge of the prosecutors because they had been unable to stop the showing of the film.

The Tokyo District Court failed to answer Oshima's challenge 'why is pornography bad?' but considered two questions with regard to the three criteria of the *Lady Chatterley's Lover* decision: 1. Is the lewd and realistic description of sex organs and sex acts done in a provocative way which excessively arouses and stimulates sexual desire? 2. Is it lewd to such an extent that it injures the sexual shame of the ordinary man because, as a whole, it appeals to the prurient interest?

The court recognised that the notion of obscenity was undergoing changes because commonly-accepted ideas of society differ depending on time and place and that also in the same society, such changes may occur. Applying these general considerations to the notion of obscenity in Japan, the court said: 'In Japan, too, the extent of sexual display has bcome bolder, sexual displays formerly considered taboo are shown openly and the extent has grown. The consciousness of the ordinary man has gradually become accustomed to such sexual displays, and it cannot be denied that a change is taking place in which also manifestations that are explicit and bold compared with former times are affirmed and accepted.'

The changes which led the court to find the defendants not guilty apparently did not impress the police. When the publisher on the strength of the verdict of the district court brought out a new edition of the book, the police swooped down and confiscated it. Angrily, the producer and publisher appealed to the Supreme Court but the court upheld the high-handedness of the police: 'Since the decision of the first instance is not final, it is not legally binding on the prosecuting authorities' — which is a good indication of what the rule of law means in Japan. Oshima retorted: 'The Japanese constitution forbids censorship but does not forbid pornography. The concept of obscenity only exists in the minds of prosecutors and judges. I have always said that Japanese customs, (that is, the censorship of books entering the country) and censorship are nonsense and stupid. The Japanese people agree with me, yet our protests are useless.'

The prosecution appealed the verdict of the district court but the Tokyo High Court, in June 1982, upheld the lower court's ruling that the book was not obscene by today's standards.

Another pornography case in which the Supreme Court maintained the old obscenity standards against their relaxation by a lower court involved videotapes produced by the film-maker Nikkatsu for motels and the so-called love hotels. The Tokyo District Court had decided that compared with adult movies and porno magazines in general circulation, the videotapes could not be considered obscene. But the Tokyo High Court overruled the district court: 'The standard for holding something obscene is not the average of the consciousness or feeling of the ordinary citizen but a normative standard.' The Supreme Court, in turning down the appeal of Nikkatsu, stated that there was no rational reason for changing the obscenity definition established in the *Lady Chatterley's Lover* decision and that on the basis of that definition, the tapes were obscene.

The trouble is that the definition of the *Lady Chatterley's Lover* case did not establish rational and objective criteria of pornography but were a jumble of abstractions which could be used whenever the courts wanted to find something obscene. The definition is not based on the text or contents of a book but on the impression it is supposed to make on the reader which is purely a matter of judicial speculation. What the sense of sexual shame of the ordinary man or his sense of sexual morality means is a semantic enigma. The 'commonly accepted ideas of society' or the 'right sentiments of sexual morality of the ordinary man' are entirely without normative value. They would at most be data of social psychology but constitute no standard and are worthless for defining legal rules.

The courts not only failed to find a rational answer to the question 'What is obscenity?' they never came to grips with Nagisa Oshima's challenge 'Why is pornography bad?' and the basic problem why the common welfare requires the prohibition of pornography. Morally speaking, impurity or unchastity is the violation of an objective norm (such as, 'Thou shalt not commit adultery') in 'thought, word or deed.' This is a question of the individual's conscience and of no concern to society. But obscenity prohibited by the Criminal Code is necessarily related to society — otherwise, there is no reason why it should be in the Criminal Code. Why, then, should the state intervene because a man (or a woman) is sexually aroused by reading a book or experiences an orgasm by seeing a movie? This is completely irrelevant to the common good (the protection of minors is a different problem).

Prohibition of Pornography: Accommodation to the West

Nagisa Oshima maintains that the portrayal of feminine eroticism and sexual pleasure is a Japanese tradition that has been lost with the modernisation of Japan. His assertion is supported by Ronald V. Bell who pointed out that Japan's police, prosecutors and judges are not defending Japan's traditional moral values but the standards of prudery accepted by the Meiji oligarchy in order to avoid being looked upon as barbarians by westerners. Japan's autochthonous sex culture has been suppressed by an élite applying borrowed standards of civilisation to cultivate their ambition for progress. The Meiji oligarchs copied French or German codes in order to attain international respectability and gain recognition as a modern nation. In essence, however, Japan remained a feudal and patriarchal society, and since the Confucian tradition provided no separation between the public order and individual morality, the government dictated the moral standards of society. The pre-war ideology exalting allegiance to the Emperor as the foundation of all duties only increased the confusion between law and morality. Even today,

Japanese courts tend to base their decisions on the inner moral culpability of the accused rather than on the legal construction of his actions.

The Japanese never understood the sense of the Christian restrictions on sex but imported the ban on pornography with the other sexual prohibitions taken over from western legal systems. Because these regulations were invented by societies that had lost their natural nonchalance in matters of sex, public nudity was classified as obscene. Among the rules of thumb used to make the legal proscriptions workable for ordinary law enforcement officials is the ludicrous rule that a picture is obscene if it shows pubic hair. The obsession with pubic hair is typical of the puerile and imbecile attitude of Japan's censorship. The cartoons in pulp magazines, particularly in the 'adult comics,' are full of violence, sadism and virulent hatred of women and are more degrading of women than frontal nude photos and even beaver shots, but such magazines are sold without interference.

In the first case involving pictures, the Supreme Court, on 8 March 1983, rejected three appeals from defendants who had been found guilty of selling obscene books. These so-called 'vinyl books' contained pictures of nude or scantily-clad women and sex scenes. Because the police confiscates publications in which pubic hair or sex organs are visible, these parts had been blotted out with black ink.

Nevertheless, the court found that, although the books could not be classified as hard-core pornography, the blocked-out areas were small and insufficient, and the obscenity remained clear, crass and explicit. There was little redeeming artistic or ideological value and the pictures appealed to lascivious curiosity.

In a concurring opinion, one of the judges wrote that a distinction should be made between hard-core and quasi hard-core pornography. The prohibition of hard-core pornography involved no constitutional problem but quasi hard-core pornography could not be uniformly made subject to criminal law. Works could have a scientific or artistic value or involve political messages. Their prohibition would constitute undue interference with the freedom of expression. Furthermore, the 'social common sense' which the court uses as premise for its definition of obscenity is changing. The court maintains a rigid idea of 'social common sense' which upholds the 'non-publicity of sex' in order to prevent the moral decay of society. But this attitude is inappropriate because the actual conditions of society are changing. 'If the collections of photos involved in this case are seen in the light of the actual conditions of Japan's present society, it is not impossible to arrive at the conclusion that they do no longer fall under obscene pictures.' Like all bureaucrats and most other people, judges are loath to admit that they have been wrong.

In the discussion of pornography, much emphasis is placed on its deleterious effects on children and adolscents and their premature exposure to sex. Actually, children react to nakedness and the display of sex in an uncomplicated matter-of-fact way. An Indian mother of a boy and a girl whose husband was posted to Tokyo was appalled by the display of nudity on posters and in magazines and the flood of sex on television. She tried to shield her children from the exposure to nudity but after some time she gave up. The children no longer showed any curiosity and were unperturbed by the pictures.

In its first decision on child pornography, the Supreme Court, in December 1984, held that the mere representation of the genitals of children could be obscene so that the display and sale of such material was punishable under Article 175 of the Criminal Code. Part of the publications had been imported from abroad and obviously not considered obscene by the customs authorities but later found obscene by the police. In some photos, the offending parts had been blackened out but the lower court held that the ink could easily be removed and that the representation remained obscene. The Supreme Court upheld the conviction without discussing these points.

Censorship of Imported Books and Pictures

The vetting and confiscation of material imported from abroad is a particular form of Japanese censorship. Article 21, Paragraph 1, No. 3 of the Customs Tariff Law gives the chief customs inspector the right to prohibit the importation of 'books, pictures, carvings and other articles impairing the public order and good morals.' Japan's constitution forbids censorship (Art. 21, Par. 2) but does not say what censorship is which in turn has led to a number of cases contesting the constitutionality of the provisions of the Customs Tariff Law and a number of decisions making a mockery of common sense and jurisprudence.

Generally speaking, censorship means the previous examination of publications for the purpose of suppressing what is deemed objectionable on military, political, moral or other grounds, but there is no reason to suggest that the constitutional prohibition of censorship does not extend to subsequent censorship. The prohibition of importing publications certainly interferes with the freedom of information and the remedy provided by the Customs Tariff Law, the filing of a complaint with the administrative agency which decreed the prohibition (Art. 4) is in its very nature ineffective. No official will admit that he has been wrong and still less that he has been stupid.

The constitutionality of the prohibition of importing publications deemed harmful to public morals by the customs inspectors has been contested in the courts but the results have only shown the absolute incomprehension of the higher courts of the questions of individual rights and their blind support of the government bureaucracy. In a suit which started in 1969, a book importer sought the nullification of the notification of the chief inspector of the Yokohama Customs House rejecting the import application of 392 volumes of a book entitled 'Sun-Warmed Nudes' showing pictures of nude women on the basis of Art. 21, Par 1, No. 3 of the Customs Tariff Law. In a first round, the Yokohama District Court turned down the complaint of the importer on the ground that the determination whether a book could be imported or not did not constitute censorship. The Tokyo High Court, in an amazing display of legal quibbling, found that the determination of the chief customs inspector whether a book could be imported or not was not an administrative determination and therefore not subject to an administrative suit. Even the Supreme Court found it impossible to sustain their *tour de force* of judicial illogic, declared, in December 1979, that the determination of the chief customs inspector was an administrative determination and therefore a measure against which a suit could be brought. The court quashed the decision of the Tokyo High Court and remanded the case.

The Tokyo High Court's decision, announced on 24 December 1981 can only be called a brazen disregard of the letter and the spirit of the constitution. 'The constitution,' the court said, 'does not absolutely prohibit all systems formally appearing as censorship. The customs inspection is an indispensable system for protecting the morality of our country and the soundness of society and is not censorship prohibited by the constitution.'

A similar suit brought by a Sapporo office worker had a similar result. The man had ordered pornographic films and publications from Sweden and other countries but the material was confiscated at the Sapporo Central Post Office. When his complaint was rejected by the chief inspector of the Hakodate Customs House, he filed suit with the Sapporo District Court. The court decided that the customs inspection was censorship prohibited by the constitution but ruled that the addressee was not entitled to the possession of the materials as long as they were in the possession of the Post Office. The decision maintained that censorship was constitutional under extraordinary circumstances when there was a clear and imminent danger to the public welfare or a clear threat to the minimum requirements of the sexual order but that such an exceptional situation did not exist in the present case.

On appeal, the Sapporo High Court, in July 1982, overturned the decision of the district court and ruled that in terms of 'formal logic,' the inspection of the customs authorities might constitute censorship but that not all forms of censorship were banned by the constitution and some forms of censorship were necessary and unavoidable in order to protect public morals. The addressee, Naokatsu Matsue, died before the Supreme Court ruled on the case.

When is Censorship not Censorship?

In its decision on two cases on 12 December 1984, the Supreme Court affirmed the constitutionality of the customs censorship. In addition to the Sapporo case, the court decided the Yokohama case which had been before it in December 1979 when the court reversed a ruling of the Tokyo High Court that the Yokohama importer had no legal grounds to sue the customs authorities.

In order to arrive at its decision that censorship by the customs officials is not censorship, the Supreme Court adopted a restrictive definition of censorship ('an act of an administrative authority having as its object the expression of an ideological content aiming at the prohibition of all or part'). The court did not give the slightest reason why the constitutional prohibition of censorship should be restricted to preceding censorship and to the expression of an ideological content. Since foreign publications are barred from entering Japan, the ban on obscene literature may appear as previous censorship infringing on the right to know, but because these publications previously appear abroad, the ban does not mean all-out previous prohibition of publication and the customs censorship does not constitute an antecedent restraint.

The court reaffirmed its position that the prohibition of obscene literature does not clash with the constitutional guarantee of the freedom of expression because this guarantee is not absolute and the freedom of expression can be curtailed in order to protect the common welfare which also justifies the curb on the influx of obscenity from abroad. The restriction of imports of obscene materials by the customs proceedings does not conflict with the constitutional provisions.

The Customs Tariff Law dates from 1910 when autocratic government could blithely trample on individual rights and the censorship provisions were used mainly to confiscate communist and other politically undesirable literature. The court took great pains to explain that the expression 'books, pictures, carvings and other articles impairing the public order and good morals' could reasonably be limited to mean obscene books and pictures which would bring it into accord with the prohibitions in Article 175 of the Criminal Code and meet the objection that the prohibition was vague.

Needless to say, the standard of jurisprudence exemplified by these decisions is abysmally low. The courts fail completely to protect the people against arbitrary actions of the government and wanton legislation. No attempt is made to justify the assertion that the constitution does not say what its words say. Japan's pre-war experience was reason enough to prohibit censorship pure and simple, with no ifs and buts. That an individual's possession of pornographic film or the sale of 392 volumes with pictures of nude women should endanger the public order is so absurd a proposition that it can only be uttered by people completely devoid of common sense.

An American who moved to Japan sent a box with his belongings by sea mail from San Francisco to Fukuoka. One of the items in the box was *The Joy of Sex*, a sex manual. He received a letter from the Moji Postal Matters Office informing him that they could not allow the book to enter Japan. He was told that he had three choices: (1) To give permission to the customs authorities to abandon the book, whereupon he could receive the remaining contents of the box. (2) Not to give up the book. In that case, the box with all its contents would be sent back to San Francisco. (3) To file a complaint.

The book contained no pictures although there were sketches of various ways to make love. But even if it were pornographic, why does a book owned by an individual and not for sale 'disturb the public order or corrupt public morals?'

The Japanese customs authorities' imbecile censorship of imported materials drew an official protest from the French government when a local publishing company was forced to sanitise four photos by a renowned French photographer. The French note signed by External Trade Minister Michel Jobert said Japan's administrative attitude was astonishing and beyond understanding. In its reply, the Japanese Ministry of Finance stated that it handled the photographs in a fashion fitting local sexual manners and culture. The 'Japan' the ministry had in mind has obviously not the slightest similarity with today's Japan.

Shuichi Tsuchikawa, a collector of *ukiyoe*, produced a documentary film entitled *Shungakô* (Thoughts on Erotic Pictures) based on his own collection and those of his friends in the United States. The film deals with prints of Utamaro Kitagawa and Kunisada Utagawa, two famous artists of the Edo period. The Tokyo Custom House banned the import of the film because it was obscene and Tsuchikawa applied to the Tokyo District Court to have the ban rescinded. The court, however, rejected his claim that the prints were art and should not be classified as obscene. Presiding Judge Kazutoshi Yamamoto ruled that *shunga* aimed at appealing to sensual tastes and that the original character of the prints has not changed. 'Although the plantiff's sincere efforts to make an artistic documentary film has somewhat helped to reduce the degree of obscenity, the pictures nonetheless are not acceptable according to prevailing social norms,' the judge said.

Police Censorship

Typical of the overbearing attitude of Japanese officials and their interference with the freedom of expression were some happenings in 1969. The Tokyo High Court found Tetsuji Takechi, the director of the film *Black Snow*, personally not guilty of obscenity but declared the film obscene (the legal foundation for such a verdict seems rather dubious).

Shortly after this decision, Masao Araki, chairman of the National Public Safety Commission, warned the Japan Film Producers Federation, the National Federation of Entertainment Environmental Sanitation Associations and the Motion Picture Ethics Commission, that in case of suspicion of obscenity, he would have not only director and producer, but also the members of the Motion Picture Ethics Commission and the theatre owners prosecuted.

In the same year, the Metropolitan Police Department directly informed Toei Motion Picture Co., that a film distributed by the company was obscene and had six scenes cut from the film, a clear case of police censorship.

The zeal with which the police try to suppress obscene publications would be worthy of a better cause. To judge from the efforts of the authorities, the 'vinyl books' must have been the incarnation of all evil. The trade coined the name vinyl book for magazines with salacious pictures and titillating titles wrapped in plastic covers to prevent browsers from taking a free peek at their contents. According to the police, vinyl books were on sale in 3,080 shops at the end of December 1984. About 1,000 shops have gone out of business or stopped the sale of such books in the last three years. On the suspicion of selling obscene literature, 576 stores were raided in 1984, and in connection with 715 cases of law violations, 792 people were arrested and 516,142 volumes confiscated.

Video tapes depicting sex came into circulation in the latter part of 1982. In 1984, video tapes considered obscene by the police were sold in 2,371 stores. Police searched 397 of these stores, detected 879 cases of law violations, arrested 692 people and confiscated 68,538 tapes.

Under prefectural ordinances for the protection of minors under the age of 18, 25,799 books and magazines and 10,285 films or plays were designated as harmful and their sale to minors or the admission of minors prohibited.

The police may have good reasons for its campaign against pornography but sometimes the rule of law suffers in the process. A Tokyo model who had been placed second in the 1980 Miss Nude World Contest in Canada and who posed for pornographic magazines featuring nude women was arrested on a charge of using stimulants and sentenced to a suspended three-year prison term. When she continued to work as a nude model, the police arrested her again on the ground that she had cooperated in the publication of obscene magazines. Since there is no law against posing for nude pictures, the arrest was patently frivolous and illegal; obviously, the police intended to frighten the girl out of the business.

One of the curious by-products of the suppression of pornography is the development of the art of 'sterilising' objectionable pictures and films, a process in which young people, including girls, spend long hours sanitising material from which they are to be protected. In one of the

American convictions under the Comstock Act, a publisher, Lew Rosen, was held guilty because the magazine he had sent through the mail featured pictures of attractive women partially covered with lamp black that could easily be removed by the subscriber at home. In 1980, a Tokyo dealer in porno magazines was found guilty of selling and possessing for sale obscene literature because the censor marks covering the genitals of under-age nude foreign boys and girls could easily be removed with paint thinner. And 'photographs where the sexual organs are prominent are clear examples of an infringement of concepts of sexual morality.'

What makes the campaign of Japanese officialdom against pornography a dubious undertaking is not only the absence of any objective standard of obscenity but also the completely arbitrary way in which the authorities sometimes enforce what they consider the law while generally they let things go because the law is impossible to enforce. Hard-core pornography is largely an underground operation and its products are of such a low standard that nobody would buy them if they were not prohibited. Blown-up photos of the union of male and female genitals, actual or faked intercourse, the pictures of poor girls who take off their clothes and get photographed in the nude to make a living document the vulgarity of a society which can hardly be corrupted by more of the same obscenity. The level of so-called 'adult entertainment' is so deplorable because producers are faced with a double handicap. First, they think that they must compete with hard-core pornography while, secondly, they must stick to a format that will pass censorship. Video cassettes to be sold through legitimate channels such as camera shops, audio equipment stores, electric appliance stores, supermarkets and department stores must be approved by the Video Ethics Association whose censors are said to be stricter than those of the Motion Picture Ethics Commission. Because people cannot buy what they want to see or read, they can be made to buy things they would rather not see or read. What people want is eroticism, the beauty of sex and the romanticism of sexual love but all they get is smut.

9

Rape

Indecent Assault

AS COMMONLY UNDERSTOOD, rape is the act of forcing a woman by actual violence or the threat of violence to have sexual intercourse. In a wider sense, any act of sexual intercourse forced upon a person is called rape. The technical term 'statutory rape' means sexual intercourse with a girl under the age of consent. Articles 176-189 of Japan's Criminal Code are related to sexual behaviour towards other people. Indecent assault on males or females 13 years of age or older is punishable if it involves violence or threat; if the victim is under 13 years of age, it is punishable in all cases (Art. 176). The law does not give a definition of 'indecent assault' which creates the same difficulties in interpretation as those mentioned above in the discussion of obscene literature. In American terminology, the expression 'indecent liberties' is often used which means actions that the 'common sense of society' regards as indecent and improper but does not necessarily involve an attempt at sexual intercourse or relate to the private parts.

An American court convicted a man who had grabbed a sales clerk in a department store by the arm and waist, pulled her close and kissed her on the cheek of simple assault and sentenced him to a $110 fine and four hours of community work. Japanese courts have interpreted indecent assault to include touching genitals or breasts (also above the clothes), forcing a kiss on a woman or making her take off her clothes.

Unfortunately, the law has little effect on the behaviour of Japanese males. The *chikan* is a very common phenomenon. On crowded trains, men press against women, unashamedly rub their groins against the woman's body, touch her genital region or her breasts. Western women have been particularly bitter in their complaints of being subjected to all sorts of indecencies in public places; they have been pinched, grabbed, accosted and a woman reported that a man exposed himself in front of her and ejaculated on her. Western women who have learned from their mothers 'never let a strange man touch you' protect themselves from gropers, if necessary by biting, kicking, scratching or screaming. Japanese women generally prefer to ignore a *chikan* rather than draw attention to themselves. They do not move, offer no resistance, and never appeal for help. Bystanders pretend not to see and sometimes seem to disapprove if a woman resists. The best way to protect oneself against a *chikan* on a crowded train, a foreign woman found out, was to step as hard as possible on the aggressor's foot, which was most effective with high-heeled shoes.

Article 177 of the Japanese Criminal Code prescribes the punishment for rape and statutory rape. Guilty of the crime of rape is a person, who, by violence or threat, has sexual intercourse with a female 13 years of age or older; statutory rape (the Japanese code does not use this term) means sexual intercourse with a female under the age of 13.

Definition of Rape

Rape includes two elements, the use of violence or threats and intercourse. Violence or threats are meant to overcome the resistance of the victim. In the case of indecent assault, the violence is usually identical with the assault and no violence different from the assault is involved. If the victim ceases to resist (for example, if she takes off her clothes herself and submits to intercourse), the act remains rape if the woman ceases to resist under the influence or as the result of the preceding violence or threats; otherwise, it is attempted rape.

The Federal Supreme Court of West Germany declared in a rape case decision that to lock a woman up in a room or constrain her freedom of movement in similar ways does not amount to violence. Such an interpretation may be theoretically correct as a judicial abstraction but conflicts with the realities of life.

Rape is usually associated with physical violence but there are forms of coercion that force women to become partners in sex (for which they remain morally responsible: 'coactus — or, in this case, coacta — tamen voluit'). In their book *The Lecherous Professor,* Linda Weiner and Billie Wright Dziech have collected interviews with students, faculty, alumni and administrators detailing the harassment female students are subjected to, the threats of lower grades, the promises of higher ones and other hazards co-eds encounter. The study asserts that 20 to 30 per cent of female students can expect to be sexually harassed during their college years. In a Harvard University study, 49 per cent of non-tenured faculty women and 41 per cent of women graduate students said they experienced sexual harassment. Unwelcome advances were received by 34 per cent of the undergraduate women.

The element of intercourse is present if the attacker inserts his penis into the vagina of the victim, irrespective of ejaculation. In Japan, rape and indecent assault are only prosecuted upon a complaint of the victim, but these crimes are prosecuted *ex-officio* if two or more persons joined in the attack. The rationale of these provisions is that in the latter case, publicity is hardly avoidable while in the former case, the victim might prefer to keep the affair from becoming public. Basically, this approach is wrong because it facilitates the continuation of criminal activities and may make it more difficult for the victim to overcome the psychological trauma.

Indecent assault against a person who has lost consciousness or is unable to resist or has been made unconscious or unable to resist is punishable as quasi-indecent assault and the same applies to the rape of a woman in the same condition (Art. 178). This crime, too, is usually only prosecuted if a complaint is made. Under this article, the courts have punished the rape of feeble-minded, of sleeping women (such as a woman who thought an intruder to be her husband and offered no resistance), and of physicians making patients believe that their actions were part of the treatment.

A soft-spoken 50-year-old man claiming to possess occult healing powers persuaded over 50 women to be treated by him and used the occasion to violate them. The police twice tried to have him convicted on the strength of Art. 178 of the Criminal Code but each time he was acquitted. The court found that the defendant had not used threats, force, drugs, or any other forcible means but that the women had yielded to his persuasion. There is no provision in the Criminal Code making sex obtained by fraud punishable (fraud is only a crime if a monetary value is involved, Art. 246).

In England, a psychiatrist was struck from the medical register after two women patients had told how he used hypnosis, love fantasies and drugs to seduce them in his consulting room.

Rape Between Spouses

Rape between spouses is a very difficult problem. Coercion to extramarital intercourse is a constituent element of the definition of rape in the German Penal Code but a survey of the Allensbach Institute for Opinion Research reported that 2.5 million West German wives are raped by their husbands each year and all women who fled from their husbands and found refuge in a women's home at Heidelberg had been raped by their spouses. Women organisations, therefore, want to have sexual intercourse forced on a spouse made punishable but there is strong opposition to such a measure. Wives would gain a weapon to secure unfair advantages in divorce procedures and the danger of false accusations could not be excluded.

In the United States, 25 states and the District of Columbia have made marital rape punishable, but prosecutions are relatively seldom because it is difficult to prove a case if the couple is not separated.

A 20-year-old wife made legal history in Japan when she succeeded in prodding a reluctant law enforcement apparatus to indict her husband for assault and battery as well as rape. According to press reports, the wife fled to the home of her parents in September 1984 in order to escape from the constant mistreatment by her 24-year-old husband. But the following day, the husband, accompanied by a friend, came to the place and dragged his wife into a car. On the way to the home of the husband's parents where they had been living, the car stopped in a wooded area. The husband first beat and kicked his wife and then raped her, and while her husband pinned her down, his friend likewise raped her. A month later, the wife appealed to the police for protection, started an action for divorce and also filed a formal complaint with the police about the rape. Because gang rape must be prosecuted irrespective of a complaint (Criminal Code Art. 180, Par. 2), the prosecutors were forced to act and in February 1985, the husband and his friend were arrested and indicted.

In December 1986, the Tottori District Court sentenced the former husband (the couple got divorced in April 1985) of the raped woman to 2 years and 10 months in prison, and his accomplice to a two-year prison term. The prosecution admitted that there was no precedent in Japan for convicting a husband of raping his wife and that there was considerable legal opinion denying that a husband would be criminally liable for forcing his wife to submit to intercourse against her will but that the double rape by the husband and his friend constituted a different situation. Another factor was that the marriage had already broken down when the rape took place.

Penal servitude for life can be imposed if indecent assault or rape results in death or injuries (Art. 181). The supposition is that the attacker had no intention of killing his victim; if he intended to kill, he is guilty of two crimes, rape (or indecent assault) and murder. Injuries are often the result of intercourse (particularly in the case of minors), and infection with a venereal disease is also regarded as an injury. The injuries need not necessarily be inflicted by the attacker; for example, the victim may attempt to escape by leaping out of a second-floor window. In the case of suicide of a rape victim, it may be difficult to establish the causal connection, especially if the suicide occurs only after a considerable period of time. If sadistic attacks are clearly linked to sexual assault, they can be punished under this article, but proof of this connection is often difficult. Cases such as cutting women on crowded trains with a razor, spilling ink, paint or acid on a woman's clothes and throwing acid in a woman's face can be prosecuted as infliction of bodily harm (Art. 204) or destruction of property (Art. 261).

A report submitted by the Criminal Law Revision Committee to the British Parliament recommended to extend the crime of rape to cover husbands and wives living apart, extend the penalty for attempted rape from seven years to life, allow incest between brother and sister aged 21, and lower the minimum age of consenting homosexuals from 21 to 18. The minimum penalty for indecent assault on a woman should be raised from two to ten years, as it is already for assault on a male. A maximum of five years applies if the assaulted female is under 13. The members of the committee voted 9 to 8 to maintain the current law on forcible sexual intercourse in the case of a married couple living together which is treated as assault, not rape. Women, the committee held, have the right to decline intercourse on the risk of divorce. The Women Against Rape Organisation protested against the exclusion of forcible intercourse in the home from the classification as rape.

A Swedish commission preparing a new sexual offences code had called for a separate category of sexual compulsion depending on the behaviour of the woman prior to the crime. The proposal met with furious opposition which prompted the government to scrap the proposal. A new commission with a female majority expanded the concept of rape to include acts similar to intercourse, homosexual rape and rape of a man by a woman.

Under reform legislation proposed by New Zealand's Labour government in August 1984, the term 'rape' was replaced by 'sexual violation' defined as forced sexual intercourse, forced oral sex, forced anal sex and violation by means of an object. The spouse immunity clause which usually protects a husband from being charged with raping his wife has been eliminated and sex by coercion made a criminal offence.

In 1983, the Bangladesh military government passed a new law under which any person found guilty of kidnapping or abducting a woman of any age for the purpose of prostitution, intercourse, rape or similar immoral activities will receive a maximum penalty of life imprisonment at hard labour. Cruelty to women, by husband or lover, attempted murder or coercion to get dowry from a wife or her parents is punishable by a maximum sentence of death.

The American Psychiatric Association dropped a proposal to classify rapist behaviour as a mental illness (calling it 'paraphilic coercive disorder') in its Diagnostic and Statistical Manual when feminists and victims' rights groups protested against this obfuscation. At the same time, the Association decided to place two other contested additions to the list of mental illnesses, masochistic behaviour (referred to as 'self-defeating personality disorder') and pre-menstrual distress (labelled 'pre-menstrual dysphoric disorder') in an appendix rather than in the text of a revised edition. The proposal is a typical example of the tendency to metamorphose exceptions into the norm.

Deviational rape is a form of sadism in which the man is aroused by the struggle and agony of the woman and his perception of hurting her gives him satisfaction. Psychologists attribute these aberrations to fantasies of revenge or a feeling that women are inferior and not worthy of decent treatment. Such attitudes may derive from childhood experiences in which the boy was humiliated by women or subjected to punishment which he considered unjust. Psychoanalysis explains deviational rape as an attempt to force a rejecting mother into sexual relations. There have been cases in which masochists suddenly turned into sadists and killed their attackers.

Rape of Men

Traditionally, rape has been limited to assaults by men on women, but two researchers, Dr William H. Masters of the Masters and Johnson Institute, and Dr Philip M. Sarrel, associate professor at Yale University School of Medicine, reported eleven cases of sexual assault on men by women. Masters and Sarrel distinguished four categories of assault: one or more women using the threat of physical violence or death to force men to sexual acts; seduction of a boy by a female baby-sitter, housekeeper or tutor; incest; aggressive sexual approach to an adult male by a domineering woman who intimidates or terrifies her victim.

Masters termed a 'sexual myth' the belief that it would be almost impossible for a man to achieve or maintain sexual arousal if he were assaulted by a woman. The raped males reacted emotionally and physically to their experiences in the same way as female victims. They developed immediate impotence and lost self-esteem and confidence, rejected intimacy and were extremely loath to admit the experience. They recovered after treatment.

In June 1984, Utah police arrested Miss Joyce McKinney, a former British beauty queen who, in 1977, had followed a Mormon missionary, then 21, from Utah to England, kidnapped him with the help of a male accomplice, chained him to a 'wedding bed' and forced him to have sex with her. She had come to Salt Lake City allegedly to find an ending for a book she was writing on the 1977 incident but was harassing the man, now a Western Airlines employee, married and father of three children.

Incidence of Rape

Rape is one of the most frequently occurring sex crimes and everywhere, the number of rapes reported in police statistics is far from that of actual rapes. The London Rape Crisis Centre estimates that only one out of every four rape victims goes to the police and the producer of a Canadian film on rape surmised that there were about 20 cases of rape behind each reported case in North America. The US crime statistics for 1981 listed 81,500 rapes. A government report released in 1985 put the number of rapes and attempted rapes in the ten years up to 1982 at over 1.5 million but added that about half of US rape victims never report the crime because they distrust the legal system or fear reprisals. In 1985, reported cases of rape numbered 138,000, 2.38 per cent of all violent crimes.

The incidence of rape in the United States rose from 20.5 cases per 100,000 population in 1971 to a high of 36.4 cases in 1980 (1981: 35.6 cases), and the share of rape in the total of violent crimes went up from 5.2 per cent in 1971 to 6.2 per cent in 1981. Naturally, these figures do not take into account the numerous cases of rape that remain unreported. According to the US Department of Justice, the incidence of rape (including unreported cases) in 1982 was 140 per 100,000 females age 12 and over. On the same basis, the victimisation rate was 250 for age 12 to 15, 390 for age 16 to 19, 250 for age 20 to 24, and 230 for age 25 to 34. Of all rapes, 29.0 per cent occurred in the victim's own home, and 38.1 per cent in streets, parks, parking lots and other public places. The assailant was a stranger in 63.9 per cent of the cases, somebody known to the victim in 36.1 per cent. Unmarried, divorced or separated women are the most frequent victims of rape. The greatest number of rapists were between 25 and 44 years of age. Nearly one-fifth of rapes were committed by two or more attackers.

A special form of rape, the so-called date rapes, has become a major problem. A date between a soft-spoken woman raised to be polite and an aggressive male not inclined to take a no at face value may end in sex being forced on the woman. A survey of two campuses found that 20 per cent of the women had been forced into sex during their college years or before and most of these cases were date rapes. Many of the victims did not report these incidents to the police and many avoided using the term rape in describing their experience. Date rapes sometimes occur after the victim has taken drugs or over-indulged in alcohol which may make their recollection hazy and clouds the issue of consent when a case comes to trial. The defence will assert that the woman gave her consent but doesn't remember.

Estimates put the yearly total of rapes in the United States at a quarter of a million of which only a fifth was reported and only one in sixty resulted in a court conviction. Rapists served less than one-third of the average sentence of nine to ten years in prison. Many rape victims thought the short time served was not worth the anguish the judicial process evoked. Changes in the law have altered the situation. In Michigan, where the reform has been most sweeping, the number of convictions rose from 10 per cent to 19 per cent of the rape arrests. Courts now impose 30- or 50-year sentences, and some judges make the terms consecutive rather than concurrent.

In West Germany, rapes reported to the police number 7,000 a year which means that on average 20 women are raped each day. But the actual number of rapes may be three to ten times higher. In some jurisdictions, about half of the rape cases are discontinued for lack of evidence.

A survey of the Urban Institute found that about one in ten American women has been raped and that an additional 10 to 20 per cent have experienced rape attempts. Over half of the rapes took place indoors, no weapon was involved in 70 per cent of all cases and there was no injury besides the rape itself in the same percentage of cases.

Researchers claim that most rapes are not committed in a sudden impulse of sexual passion but are premeditated. They also maintain that the chief motive of rape is not the satisfaction of sexual lust but the assertion of power. Rape is a crime of violence even more than a sex crime. The attractiveness or clothing of the victim is of little importance; most rapists cannot remember what their victims looked like. Nevertheless, women's way of dressing may be a factor. In Japan, half of the cases of indecent assault and rape committed in elevators occur in the three months of May, June and July.

Gang Rapes

Gang rapes constitute a special form of sexual violence. In the New Bedford, Massachusetts, bar-room rape case, a 22-year-old mother of two was subjected to successive rapes and sexual abuse on a pool table for two hours. Four of the rapists were still lingering at the bar when the police arrived; they were later convicted of aggravated rape. Two men who had urged them on were also arrested but were found not guilty. The most depressing fact was that none of the bystanders intervened to end the terror. Two of the defendants testified that the woman had willingly participated in sex, and the community of Portuguese immigrants sided with the defendants. Audience passivity when witnessing a rape is sometimes referred to as the Kitty Genovese syndrome, after a historic New York case. Gang rapes have become a problem on the campuses of American Universities, particularly in connection with fraternities and the members of athletics teams. Alcohol abuse is frequently involved in these cases.

Rape in Japan

In Japan, there have been several waves of sharp increases in rapes committed by adolescents. In the years after the war, rapes jumped to three times the pre-war level and 54 per cent of the rapists were juveniles. In 1968, of 10,930 persons arrested for rape, 4,437 were minors; by 1971, the number had decreased to 2,465 out of 6,575. The number of cases declined through the seventies but was somewhat higher in 1981 than in 1980. In 1981, the total number of rapes amounted to 2,735; of the 1,007 juveniles arrested for rape, the highest percentages were registered for the groups from 16 to 18 years (16 years: 22.9 per cent of the cases, 17 years: 22.1 per cent, 18 years: 22.0 per cent). Of 85 cases of indecent assault, rape or robbery committed in elevators in the first eleven months of 1982, seven were committed by minors. Rapes numbered 1,615 in the eleven months from January to November 1986.

Compared with other large cities, Tokyo has few rape cases. Of a total of 256,055 crimes reported to the police in Tokyo in 1982, 388 were rapes which corresponded to a ratio of 4 rapes per 100,000 population. Police solved 85.6 per cent of the reported rape cases. In 1981, the ratio of rapes was almost as low in London (5 per 100,000 of population) but considerably higher in West Berlin (25) and very high in American cities

(Los Angeles 88, New York 55, Chicago 42).

Recidivism, Rape Patterns

There seems to be a tendency towards repetition in rape. Dr Bernice Sandler, director for the Project Status and Education of Women at the Association of American Colleges, expressed the view that the number of sexual harassment cases has increased because more incidents are reported. 'This isn't a widespread practice by a lot of men,' she said. 'It is a man harassing a large number of women.' Some of the court cases confirm this opinion. A church-going Christian who gave Bible classes at an old people's centre was sentenced to 142 years in prison for rape attacks on 11 women ranging in age from 24 to 71. An Australian doctor was charged with having drugged seven female patients and then sexually assaulted them. An Ohio internist was sentenced to 151 to 665 years in prison for raping and terrorising 30 women. An innocent look-alike served five years for two of those rapes. An American psychologist found that 6 to 8 per cent of US psychiatrists and psychologists have sexual relations with their female patients although the practice is unethical and illegal. Of the patients involved, 50 per cent developed strong fear or distrust of men or therapists, 11 per cent had to be hospitalised and 1 per cent committed suicide.

Rape is part of the violence of war and one of the atrocities committed above all by conquering armies since ancient times. An official of the UN High Commission for Refugees stated in December 1983 that since 1980, pirates had raped almost 2,300 women on the South China Sea, another 600 women had been abducted and 1,400 people of both sexes had been killed.

Ugandan government troops were said to have abducted schoolgirls and married women, raping them and forcing them to become their 'wives.' Husbands trying to resist abduction of their wives were shot. Soldiers who had too many women auctioned them off for $10 or $15. Officials of the International Red Cross aided by some army officers rescued ten schoolgirls, all younger than 15, and five women who had been held for weeks and raped by soldiers in the Ngogolo barracks north of Kampala.

The story of a woman member of a Japanese activist group illustrates the experiences of many young women whose engagement in ideological causes brough personal grief. She charged that women were used as sexual playthings by male comrades; they were raped and 'treated like insects.' The assaults took place in the group's office in an apartment building with other apartments all around. Group loyalty prevented them from resisting. 'If we had screamed, we would have been evicted.' Each woman was raped by four or five men at a time, and more than 30 women met this fate.

In an entirely different but also typical set-up, a 14-year-old Indian girl who was sent to work for a family in Malaysia was raped by the head of the household. The girl said nothing because she thought that it was 'part of her job.' It was only when she became pregnant that her parents learned of what had happened.

A West German industrialist was sentenced to 10 years in prison and his wife to a six-year prison term for having imprisoned and tortured a 17-year-old girl. As soon as the girl arrived at the house where she was to take care of the children, she was forced to strip and was then handcuffed and chained to the wall of a windowless basement cell. For the next 15 months, she was subjected to rape, torture and forms of sexual abuse so brutal that the police could not believe her tale when she managed to escape.

The lower house of the Indian Parliament passed a new law in December 1983 prescribing a minimum of seven to ten years' imprisonment for rape and directing that the accused must prove that sexual intercourse followed the victim's consent. The courts have to presume absence of consent when the victim states so in her evidence. The maximum punishment for rape continues to be life imprisonment. The law was prompted by anti-police protests after a case in which policemen shot dead a woman's husband and then paraded her naked through the streets of a town in Uttar Pradesh before raping her.

Some years ago, the women of an Indian village were raped by the police. The occasion was the complaint of a widow living in the village of Narainpur in the state of Uttar Pradesh whose two small children had been run over by the bus of a rich entrepreneur. Since the village supported the claim of the widow, a police force of 24 men raided the village, looted and set fire to the houses, and raped the women from grandmothers to little girls. The authorities first ignored the incident which only came to national attention when Prime Minister Indira Gandhi personally distributed money to the victims and had herself photographed with a weeping grandmother.

In another case, a 15-year-old girl called as a witness to a police station near Nagpur was raped by two policemen on duty in the toilet. The Bombay High Court imposed a 5-year jail term but the verdict was overturned by the Supreme Court on grounds of insufficient evidence. Since the girl's body showed no marks of mistreatment, the court ruled, the girl must have submitted voluntarily.

New Delhi women are annoyed by what is called 'Eve-teasing,' meaning pinching, striking or otherwise harassing women, which is particularly common on crowded buses. A 1978 ordinance required bus drivers to take women complaining of Eve-teasing — and everyone else on the bus — straight to a local police station and turn the culprit over, but neither this nor other measures stopped the molestation and a new bill provided for seven to 15 days in jail.

President Mohammad Zia ul-Haq amended the penal code and

authorised courts to sentence to death or life imprisonment anyone found guilty of using criminal force against a woman, including stripping her naked or exposing her to public view.

Allegations of rape of minors by the police have also been made in the Philippines.

Parents usually tell their children not to talk to strangers, to stay away from unusual places, and to avoid physical violence, but according to police, sexual crimes against children are committed by someone the child knows. Only one out of five children is misused by an unknown. Crimes are most likely to occur in familiar settings such as schoolyards or playgrounds. Children are particularly open to confidence tricks, threats and bribery.

In the rape cases reported to West German police, one-third of the victims knew the attacker. Only 6.2 per cent of the victims in the rape cases handled by German courts had never met the attacker before while in almost 70 per cent of the cases, the victim knew the aggressor.

Investigation of Rape

Many women do not report rapes because they are afraid of the ordeal of police interrogation and the court proceedings. A German woman reporting a rape to the police was told: 'You must have enjoyed it. You are not married, so once in a while you need something like this.' Another woman said: 'Never again. The questions the public prosecutor and the judge asked were simply lascivious. It seemed they greatly enjoyed having an occasion to probe into sex.' And the conclusion of another woman: 'They (the police) think you are neurotic. They believe the criminal more than the victim.'

A report on London's Metropolitan Police Force (Scotland Yard) by independent investigators accused detectives of getting drunk on duty, making sexist jokes about women constables and acting indifferently towards rape victims. Other shortcomings were racial prejudice, accepting bribes, faking overtime and bullying suspects.

When London police opened a hot-line to Scotland Yard to track down two rapists working together they received 140 calls. The two men wearing track suits staked out car parks or alley-ways, dragged their victims to secluded spots where the women were often raped at knife-point by both attackers. Many women had failed to report the assaults because the rapists took their addresses from their handbags and threatened them with reprisals if they reported the crime.

Faked Rapes

The confession of a young woman whose faked rape story had sent a young man to jail showed that police caution in handling rape cases is not unfounded. Cathleen Crowell Webb, now married and the mother of two children, had sexual intercourse with a boyfriend when she was 16 and feared that she had become pregnant and would be thrown out of the home where she was living. She made up the rape story and picked a young man, Gary Dotson, out of the photographs the police showed her. The young man was sentenced to up to 50 years in prison and had spent six years behind bars when the woman could no longer live with her qualms of conscience and confessed that the alleged rape had been a fabrication. Despite the recantation of her testimony by the accuser, the judge who had presided over the original trial refused to overturn the conviction and the Illinois governor rejected pleas for executive clemency. After a number of hearings, the governor commuted Dotson's sentence into the six years of prison he had already served but Dotson was denied a retrial.

The psychic traumas of rape victims are serious and deep-seated. Many women shy away from men and frequently frigidity results. It is impossible to forget, and the thought 'all men are pigs' is behind the attitude towards men.

Trivialisation

The psychic damage to rape victims contrasts sharply with the tendency to trivialise rape, to treat it as a joke or to react with doubts or disbelief to complaints. Balzac remarked: 'It is impossible to thread a needle if the needle does not keep still.' An Arabian story makes the same point; a sword cannot be sheathed if the scabbard is wagged. Such comparisons are wrong but they reveal the thinking behind the assumption that a woman cannot be raped as long as she resists. In his review of the book, *Endless Rapture: Rape, Romance and the Female Imagination* by Helen Hazel, former White House speechwriter Aram Bakshian Jr. termed rape 'a cherished fantasy of many women.' The expression angered women and in an interview, Mr Bakshian explained that he had been misunderstood. 'The rape being discussed was rape as a theme of female fiction,' he said.

The cavalier attitude of many men to rape transpired in an episode involving a Japanese politician. Shumon Miura, a member of the Liberal-Democratic Party, a former essayist and subsequently chief of the Cultural Affairs Agency, wrote in the December 1984 issue of a sports magazine: 'When asked why I jog, I say "It would be a shame for a gentleman to rape women but it is a shame if a man does not have the physical strength to rape a woman."' In the May 1985 issue of a women's magazine, he commented: 'I wish rapists would attack those promiscuous women. For these women, it would be nothing more than tumbling into a puddle.' And he was quoted as boasting, 'I think I have enough physical strength to rape a woman.'

When taken to task in a meeting of the Education Committee of the

House of Councillors, Miura tried to brush off the matter by asserting that he was just joking. But when some committee members insisted on an apology, he bowed to the committee and said, 'I should not make any practical jokes.'

The sexist remarks and particularly the lack of repentance and the failure to realise the grossness and immorality of his statements apparent in his apology would be political suicide abroad but hardly ruffled Japan's political establishment which, under the influence of the so-called 'money politics,' has degenerated into a legally sanctioned replica of the country's equivalent of the mafia, the *yakuza*.

'You are to blame because you are a woman,' seems to be the preposterous reasoning behind the tendency to blame the victims of sexual assaults for the crime. In a recent incident, which happened at about 11 pm in mid-winter, a drunk, later identified as a 47-year-old high-school teacher, accosted a 39-year-old dancer who was waiting for a train at a railway station in a town near Tokyo. She tried to evade him but he followed her yelling, 'You idiot!' When he persisted in his attempt to embrace her, the woman put her luggage on a bench and gave him a shove. He staggered and fell off the platform onto the tracks. Some of the 100 or so bystanders who had ignored the woman's cries for help tried to pull the man up but he was caught by an oncoming train and killed. The police arrested the woman for manslaughter. The fact that she had put her luggage on the bench, they said, was proof that her action exceeded the limits of legitimate self-defence. It showed, the prosecution claimed when the woman was indicted, that the man had ceased to molest her and that there was no immediate threat.

What to Do When Attacked

What women should do when attacked has been the subject of a sharp debate. Should a woman fight or play for time? The basic advice of the film *How to Say No to a Rapist and Survive* (Frederic Storaska) is: play for time, use your wits, and go along with the rapist until you have a chance to react safely. But many women oppose this strategy and counsel: scream, run or struggle immediately! A rapist will flee 50 per cent of the time if the woman resists quickly. Women who are passive, or who cry, try to talk their way out of being raped, play on the attacker's sympathy or make themselves look less appealing are more likely to be raped. Resistance or immediate flight notably increases a victim's chance of escape but it also increases the odds on sustaining heavy injuries. Another objection of feminists is: We are concerned about the self-image of a woman who responds with feigned affection to a rapist but is still unsuccessful in avoiding rape. Then, what about her guilt, her anger, her feeling of being used? Moreover, non-resistance will weigh heavily against a woman if the case comes to trial. In German jurisprudence, the view prevails that resistance of the victim is a comstituent element of rape.

Many women have stated that they felt unable to do anything — as if they were paralysed. The overwhelming consciousness of fear blocked out any other thought. One woman compared herself to a rabbit remaining motionless in the middle of the road hypnotised by the lights of an oncoming car.

According to a German study on sex crimes, resistance was successful in only 7 per cent of 93 cases whereas 80 per cent suffered more or less severe injuries and in 4 cases, the victims were killed. If the women did not resist, about half of the assaulted women were otherwise not hurt but 23 per cent sustained serious injuries.

A New York Girl Guide group has been organising courses in self-protection., The courses are given for two age groups, from 8 to 11 and from 12 to 17 years. The girls learn that they have a right to say no to an adult request, to refuse to answer questions on the telephone, to lie to protect themselves and to run away, scream, bite, kick and hit at strangers who might approach them on the street. Among the rules of conduct for avoiding trouble are: don't talk about the money you are carrying and keep your bus passes and valuables in your pockets rather than in your school bag. Don't hesitate to hand over your possessions if someone threatens you; personal property is not worth risking your life. Don't travel home by the same route every day (a recommendation somewhat hard to follow) and try to travel with friends whenever possible. Check to see if you are being followed by looking at the reflections in shop windows or by crossing the street. Get to know where the fire and police stations are in your neighbourhood and the hours of the local shops because shops are good places to run to when you need help.

The girls are also shown how to use things they might be carrying like umbrellas or key rings for defending themselves but the police think that threatening situations vary so much that it is difficult to draw up a general rule whether to use a weapon or not. For self-defence, whistles, spray cans or gas pistols have been used, but defence may invite greater violence and unsuccessful defence involves the danger of a direct attack on the life of the victim.

The difficulties encountered by rape victims have prompted the establishment of private organisations providing assistance. In the United States, the Rape Crisis Centres offer help; in West Germany, the *Notrufe für vergewaltigte Frauen* talk with victims, accompany them to the police or to a doctor, prepare them for the trial and care for the psycho-social stabilisation of the victims.

A researcher at Carnegie Mellon University reported that victims of crimes such as rape or burglary are subject to delayed mental ailments similar to those experienced by Vietnam war veterans. The symptoms of the 'post-traumatic stress syndrome' are anger, rage, wanting to be alone, loneliness, despair, nightmares, insomnia, inability to eat, paranoia or flashbacks. Occasionally, the result can be alcoholism or violence, including suicide. The victims may suffer a 'second wound' if they are improperly treated by police, social workers, psychiatrists or psychologists.

Investigation, prosecution and punishment of rape have been the object of severe criticism. Police interrogation and court procedures can be cruel experiences, and punishment inflicted on the criminals was often light. Rape victims who went to the police said they felt that they were on trial: their sexual past and practices were considered an open book by judges and lawyers.

Rape Shield Laws

Since the late 1970s, however, more than 40 states have passed rape shield laws. The new laws protect the victims testifying in court from having their sexual histories raised in court, thus preventing defence attorneys from making the victim's sex life and her consent the subject of the trial. Rape has been redefined to apply to both sexes and made independent of the difference of sex, that is, homosexual rape is covered by the law. The requirement that the victim prove that she had resisted to the utmost of her ability has been dropped and corroborating evidence is no longer needed. Nevertheless, testimony by a third party may make a critical difference in the actual trial. In the New Bedford gang rape case, a bystander's testimony was decisive for the conviction of the assailants. An attack in which some object is used instead of a penis is punishable as sexual assault and so is an attack which stops short of penetration.

As a result of a change in Illinois law, making consent to rape an 'affirmative defence,' the defendant has to prove that the victim agreed to sexual intercourse. This forces him to take the stand and makes him subject to cross-examination and questioning on his criminal record.

Handling of Rape Cases by Police and Courts

In Japan, the police seem more interested in prying into the private life of the victim than in identifying the attacker, particularly if the victim is a foreign woman. They offer little sympathy and less protection and usually no female police officers are available for investigation.

A British television documentary two weeks after the notorious rape trial at Ipswich (discussed below) showed policemen interrogating a woman who said she had been raped. How often did she usually have sex? Was she menstruating regularly? Had she ever been a prostitute? Three police officers surrounded the grey-haired woman and subjected her to an inquisitorial examination far beyond the facts of the case. Said one of the policemen: 'I'll agree that you've had sex this afternoon. But I think you've been a willing party to it.' After some more badgering, the woman refrained from filing a complaint. While it is understandable that the police do not want to investigate unfounded accusations, it is not the job of the police to probe into the sex life of the victims.

For defence lawyers, the credibility of any witness in rape cases is fair game. Defendants often claim that their victims enticed them into the crime. The strategy works; judges sometimes impose light penalties on a rapist if they feel that the victim's behaviour was imprudent, such as accepting a lift in a car from a stranger.

Police, prosecutors, judges, parole officers and the medical staff of institutions are blamed for being too soft on sex offenders, particularly on those with a record of repeated sex crimes. Treatment with drugs, castration or the extirpation of the supposed sex centres in the brain give no guarantee against recidivism and exaggerated concern for the human rights of convicted criminals exposes innocent people to the risk of becoming victims of maybe uncontrollable impulses.

Greek feminists, fed up with the ineffectiveness of the legal process, organised vigilante groups and attacked rapists released by the police. They charged that often nothing was done when women reported rapes to the police and that penalties for rape were grossly inadequate. Until recently, Greek law treated rape as an offence against public decency rather than as a crime against an individual and law enforcement, the feminists complained, reflected the attitudes of a male-oriented society.

Since the Hinckley trial, the plea of not guilty by reason of insanity has come in for sharp (and well-deserved) attacks. The threat to innocent victims if killers are left free was illustrated when a former policeman, found not guilty by reason of insanity after psychiatric tests in the killing of his first wife in 1975, killed his second wife in 1983.

Just as in the cases of child abuse, the present court procedures are unsuited for handling rape cases. Judges, prosecutors and attorneys seem to welcome the opportunity to wallow in verbal salacity — probably to demonstrate that they are sexually mature. Defence lawyers try to show that the woman provoked or instigated the rape or was a willing partner so that often the victim and not the rapist seems to be on trial. The impudent ribaldry of some West German defence lawyers was so atrocious that the proposal was made to stop the direct questioning of the victim by the defence and arrange for the lawyers to address her through the judge which was assumed to protect the woman from the most sordid obscenities. Judges sacrifice the protection of the human rights of the victim to a chimeric notion of a fair trial.

The shortcomings of the handling of rape cases have been highlighted by some recent trials. In the squalid east-end of Glasgow, three teenagers raped a young mother whom they subsequently slashed with a razor — the cuts required 168 stitches. The police charged the attackers, one of whom had confessed, with rape and attempted murder and gathered more than 40 witnesses to testify. But the crown office, competent in

Scotland for prosecuting serious charges, decided against bringing the case to court. The Scottish solicitor-general later said that the case was dropped because a psychiatrist had advised that a court appearance would have a traumatic effect on the woman — she might commit suicide. (The psychiatrist denied having made such a statement.) The prosecution also said that the woman had been unwilling to take the witness stand — a claim that the woman denied. The woman's lawyer instituted a private prosecution (the last successful action of this kind in Scotland had been in 1909). One of the teenagers was jailed for 12 years; the others were given suspended sentences on lesser convictions. The solicitor-general for Scotland resigned (January 1982) after being rebuked by Prime Minister Margaret Thatcher and jeered in the House of Commons over the handling of the case.

At Ipswich, crown court judge Bertrand Richards levied only a fine (£2,000) on a man who had pleaded guilty to rape. Usually, rape carries a jail sentence but because the victim, a 17-year-old girl, was hitch-hiking alone after midnight, the judge found that she was guilty of 'contributory negligence' — in plain language, 'she asked for it.'

The judge's injudicious observation provoked a wave of protests from all quarters. Prime Minister Thatcher commented: 'It is absolutely vital that women should have confidence in the ability of the law to protect them against this violent, detestable and odious crime, and to see that persons are found guilty should they commit it.'

Mr Jack Ashley, Labour MP for Stoke-on-Trent, the constituency in which the girl lived, asked Lord Hailsham, the Lord Chancellor, to intervene. Lord Hailsham's reply: 'Contributory negligence does not, of course, constitute any defence of rape, nor in my view, in the absence of actual sexual provocation, should imprudence on the part of the victim operate as a factor of mitigation in reduction of sentence.'

The chief justice recommended that convicted rapists be jailed in almost every case. The precariousness of the women's situation has been pointed out by Lord Wheatley, lord justice clerk, the top criminal judge in Scotland, in rejecting appeals from two rapists. He stated: 'There seems to be a feeling at the present time among the male community that any female, young or old, is fair game for their sexual activities, whether the unfortunate woman is a willing participant or not.'

Imprudence of Victims

Imprudence on the part of the victim was the main factor in the gang rape of a Finnish dental student on Hawaii in 1979. The girl had been waiting for a bus in Nanakuli Beach Park when she was accosted by some boys and voluntarily accompanied them to their surfside tent and smoked marijuana with them. Later, more than a dozen local punks, in age from 12 to 17, raped her repeatedly all night long.

SEL-S

The five youngest attackers were judged guilty by the Hawaii family court and dispatched to a juvenile prison. The case against four teenagers who had signed confessions at a local police station came to trial in 1981. After deliberating for only five hours, the jury found all four not guilty. The judge, accepting the verdict, complimented the jurors: 'They were very conscientious. They followed the law.'

The defence lawyers had thought the case so hopeless that they had tried but failed to plea-bargain with the prosecutor. The court threw out the confessions because they had been signed without the presence of the defendants' lawyers. The case hinged on the single issue central to nearly every rape prosecution: the victim's degree of resistance.

The verdict was an affront to common sense. No woman asks for a night of torture. The eruption of local outrage against the verdict induced Governor Ariyoshi to propose a revision of the law and adopt the rule of many mainland states that rape victims have to prove only that force was used or threatened and not that they tried to fight off the attacker.

California's Proposition 8

The softness in legal thinking has obscured the principle that the aim of the prosecution in rape cases (the same as in murder) should be punishment and retribution rather than rehabilitation. Judicial leniency or rather irresponsibility was the main factor which led to the approval of Proposition 8 by California voters in September 1982. The sponsors of Proposition 8 which contained a revision of the state's criminal procedures packaged as a 'Victim's Bill of Rights' charged that the government was not protecting the people and was turning vicious criminals loose every day. The revision greatly limited the right to bail and made public safety the first consideration in granting bail. Under the old California law, a judge setting bail could only consider the likelihood that the defendant would show up for trial.

The immediate occasion for formulating Proposition 8 was the murder of a rape victim by her attacker, Harvey Lee Heishman III, who had spent six years in jail for three rapes, raped an Oakland woman, Nancy Lugassy, in 1979. As he left, Heishman warned the woman not to go to the police. She did, and he was arrested. After he posted a $1,500 bond, Heishman tracked down Lugassy and killed her.

In January 1982, the US Supreme Court rejected the death penalty for sex crimes against children when it refused to reconsider reinstatement of a Florida law that allowed capital punishment for people over 18 who were convicted of rape or other sex crimes against children under the age of 12. The law had been struck down by the Florida Supreme Court which was of the opinion that the death penalty for rape involved punishment disproportionate to the kind of harm done. That may be true as an abstract proposition but, at least in the case of recidivists, a short prison term constitutes neither commensurate punishment nor adequate protection of society.

Judicial Idiocy

In another case of idiotic judicial thinking, the Nebraska Supreme Court vacated the death sentence of a convicted murderer and ordered the lower court to resentence him, that is, to spare his life. The man had seen the picture of an attractive woman in a newspaper with a story announcing her coming marriage. He did not know the woman but tracked her down, stalked her and when he knew that she was alone in her home, he got into her house and overpowered her. She pleaded for her life but he stuffed pieces of clothing down her throat, wrapped a nylon stocking around her neck and choked her until she was unconscious. After sexually abusing her, he found that she had a faint pulse. He dragged her into the bathroom and drowned her. He was later arrested and sentenced to death but Nebraska state law says that capital punishment can only be inflicted if the murder is especially heinous, atrocious and cruel or shows exceptional depravity by ordinary standards of morality and intelligence. The state Supreme Court, in a 4 to 3 decision, decided that this murder was not of the nature described in the state law. No wonder people think that the courts are soft on criminals.

In Beijing, a man was executed who had evaded capture for 11 years and raped or molested 85 women and girls. In Shanghai, four men were sentenced to death after having been convicted of rape. One of them had raped four girls aged between 7 and 10. Other rapists received life sentences. But in Japan, a man who had strangled a 17-year-old girl when he attempted to rape her on her way back from school got away with an 18-year jail term (which he had appealed up to the Supreme Court).

California is one of eleven American states that punish only males in statutory rape cases (unlawful sexual intercourse with a minor). A teenage boy forced a 16-year-old girl to make love to him on a park bench. The girl told her story to the police and the boy was charged with statutory rape. The defence challenged the prosecution on the ground that in punishing only males in statutory rape cases, California law violated the equal protection clause of the constitution. Three state courts rejected the plea, and the US Supreme Court, in 5 to 4 decision, upheld the state courts. The majority reasoned that singling out males for punishment made sense because women suffer disproportionately deep consequences from sexual activity. A criminal sanction imposed on males thus serves to roughly equalise the deterrents on the sexes.

Another indication that the male establishment is not sufficiently aware of the atrociousness of rape was the proposal of the UK Criminal Injuries Compensation Board (a panel of 50 legal experts including 29 judges) in March 1982 to give rape victims about £2,250 in compensation for their suffering. A spokeswoman for the Women's Aid Organisation branded the proposed sum as 'a meager amount that adds insult to an injury which has immeasurable consequences.' In comparison with the financial awards for other injuries, this could only encourage men to continue viewing rape as an 'insignificant and minor crime.'

Since the guidelines would give a man 'facially scarred' in a criminal attack £4,000 and a woman £6,500, a spokeswoman for a rape counselling centre commented: 'This award (for rape) is pathetically low. In practical terms, the psychological damage to a woman is certainly equal to the damage and pain caused by a bad facial scar.' There can be no doubt that rape may have lasting physical and psychological effects.

How a cohesive society reacts to an outrage against its women can be seen from the story of the revenge the sons of Jacob took on the Hevites for the rape of their sister Dina by Sichem (Gen 34). Feuds lasting for generations originated from the violation of a woman. They had nothing to do with the esteem of virginity in the Christian sense but were a manifestation of the primordial urge of the group to protect its women.

Psychiatry and Rape

Programmes of sex therapy for compulsory sex offenders such as rapists and child molestors intend to increase normal sexual response and eliminate deviant behaviour. In Oregon State, where sex offenders account for 17 per cent of all prisoners, the treatment determines the offender's deviant arousal pattern by recording his response to slides and narrative tapes of sexual situations, measured by an instrument called penileplethysmagraph (which records the swelling of the penis). Once the pattern has been determined, the same slides are shown and the tapes played while the inmate is subjected to a putrid odour through a tube placed in the nose. The machine then records whether the reaction to the smell diminishes sexual response. Through the aversion treatment, the 60 to 100 per cent arousal in response to deviant fantasies was reduced to 20 per cent. But most of the theories on which the treatment is based are complete poppycock without any relation to reality. The release of compulsive sex offenders into freedom for their compulsive urges and irresistible temptations has sometimes been outright irresponsible and often stupid.

In a trial of a 29-year-old man who pleaded guilty to two rape-related charges, psychiatrists testified that the defendant had received too much sexual stimulation as a child because his mother, a topless dancer, used to walk around the house scantily clad. He was sentenced to 10 years' probation and a $10,000 fine after indicating his willingness to undergo injections of Depo Provera, a treatment dubbed by the media 'chemical castration' because the drug reduces the sex drive. The heir to a chemical company who had raped his step-daughter from the time she was seven until she ran away from home when she was 14 pleaded no contest. In addition to five years probation (the first in the county jail), the judge who rejected surgical castration because it would be 'cruel and unusual punishment' ordered the use of Depo Provera.

George F. Will opposes castration as punishment for rape. 'Therapy can not substitute for punishment,' he says, 'unless all crime is considered a manifestation of sickness.' While Will is right in rejecting drugs and psychotherapy as a replacement of retribution, castration, if imposed by law and not by judicial improvisation, can be an appropriate additional punishment for rape. The rapist's violation of the victim's personality is more cruel than the violation of the rapist's personality by making him sexually less dangerous to society.

West German authorities confiscated a video game awarding points for 'successful rape.' In the first part of the game, made in Japan and imported to Europe by an Italian firm, four female figures are pursued by a naked man who is steered by the player. A policeman with a dog patrols the scene. If the man traps one of the women without being intercepted, the game moves to its second phase, a close-up of forced sexual intercourse. A second player then competes for points by trying to assault any of the women before they can reach a police station.

10

Venereal Disease

Social Dangers of VD

VENEREAL DISEASE (VD) is a comprehensive appellation of diseases characteristically transmitted by sexual intercourse. There are a number of diseases of the reproductive system of both men and women not related to sexual activity, some of which are due to infections (for example, puerperal infection, tuberculosis, balanitis, posthistis, elephantiasis, prostatitis) but these diseases involve no social problems. VD has engaged much public attention on account of the social questions it raises. Although the major venereal diseases such as syphilis, gonorrhea and herpes are highly contagious, it is practically impossible to enforce a quarantine of sufferers as would be the case for typhus, plague or diphtheria. A reporting system obliging physicians to notify health authorities of VD cases may ensure that an individual continues treatment but does not prevent the spread of the disease. Moreover, different from syphilis and gonorrhea which are curable, no cure is known for herpes and AIDS (acquired immune deficiency syndrome) so that every new case adds to the pool of sufferers and potential transmitters.

Venereal disease is not only a threat to sex life but may endanger the life of the victim and of children of infected mothers. To the individual, VD is not just a minor irritant. If syphilis remains untreated, its tertiary stage is incapacitating or fatal in about half the patients showing tertiary symptoms. Permanent disability from arthritis may be the result of untreated gonorrhea. As mentioned above, herpes simplex is incurable at least at present, because it is caused by a virus and not by a bacillus so that antibiotica do not work. In addition to the recurrence of the attacks of irritations, sores and blisters, herpes simplex is lethal in up to 60 per cent of infected newborn infants, and of the surviving babies, 50 per cent carry the risk of blindness or brain damage. Infected mothers may transmit congenital syphilis to their children, and the gonococcus may cause eye infections in newborn infants.

Spread of VD

Venereal disease is spreading all over the world. It is difficult to assess the actual extent of VD. Reporting requirements are not uniform and even in developed countries, statistics do not cover all forms of VD. In Japan, for example, the Venereal Disease Prevention Law requires reporting for syphilis, gonorrhea, soft chancre and lymphogranuloma inguinale. In 1984, the number of reported cases of venereal diseases exceeded 15,000, the highest number since 1969 when it amounted to 17,600. The 1984 figure included 13,500 cases of gonorrhea, 1,640 cases of syphilis, 106 cases of soft chancre and 9 cases of lymphogranuloma inguinale. But there was a considerable increase also in other venereal diseases, such as herpes and chlamydia. In Osaka Prefecture alone, the total number of cases of venereal diseases was over 24,000. One reason for the increase in VD is that the use of contraceptives by women has superseded the use of condoms by men. Thanks to better treatment, these diseases have become less fatal. Deaths from syphilis declined from 660 in 1970 to 104 in 1983. Male VD patients who visited the 102 hospitals (out of 230 hospitals with urology and dermatology departments) responding to a 1983 survey numbered 15,667, 31 per cent over the preceding year, female VD patients 5,920, up 37 per cent. The largest group of patients suffered from nonspecific urethritis (36 per cent), followed by gonorrhea (28 per cent), candidiasis (10 per cent) and syphilis (6 per cent). Gonorrhea, primary syphilis and herpes were most common among male VD patients, trichomoniasis and candidiasis among women. About 70 per cent of the male patients had been infected through contacts with women working in massage parlours while half of the women contracted VD from their husbands.

The Institute of Public Health conducted a survey on eleven sexually-transmitted diseases treated in the six-month period up to the end of February 1985 at 26 medical facilities in 12 prefectures, including Tokyo and Osaka. Of the 5,096 male patients, 71.1 per cent had been infected at massage parlours or other sex-related establishments, 11.7 per cent had contracted the disease from girlfriends, 4.9 per cent on overseas trips and 4.6 per cent each from their wives or other females. Of the 1,383 female patients, most of whom were bar hostesses, 59,5 per cent had been infected by male customers, 20.3 per cent by their husbands and 1.6 per cent by other men.

In the United States, chlamydia and herpes are not reportable diseases. Estimates put the number of new chlamydia trachomatis cases at about 4.5 million a year. Treatment (with tetracycline or erythromycin) must be continued for about two weeks in order to be effective. Estimates of new cases of genital herpes range from 200,000 to 500,000 a year, with several million (between 5 million and 20 million) recurrent cases. A significant portion of the 200,000 cases of hepatitis B were sexually transmitted. New cases of gonorrhea came to 1 million in 1984 and another 1 million may have gone unreported. New cases of syphilis amounted to 90,000, and those of AIDS to 4,500. A spreading disease is venereal warts, with an incidence of about 1 million cases in 1984. The warts, caused by the papilloma virus, are transmitted through the secretions exchanged during intercourse. They are linked with malignancies affecting the cervix, vagina, vulva, penis and anus. The warts can be transmitted to a baby during delivery and lodge in the larynx, trachea and lungs.

In Britain, new cases of VD numbered about 500,000 in 1981. Thailand has one of the world's highest rates of venereal disease. Estimates put the number of people suffering from syphilis, gonorrhea and other sexually-transmitted diseases at 3 million, out of a population of 50 million. This figure has been disputed by Mr Suwan Wongsarojana, permanent secretary of Thailand's Ministry of Public Health, who stated that the incidence of syphilis and gonorrhea was reduced from 0.5 per cent of the population to 0.05 per cent in the last decade and that the incidence of venereal disease among prostitutes who make weekly visits to public VD clinics is less than 20 per cent.

Almost everywhere, venereal disease is infecting lower age groups, particularly youth between the ages of 15 and 25. In Japan, gonorrhea is the dominant venereal disease among students. It has spread from senior to junior high-school students. Transmitters are not limited to the student population; students have been infected by sexual intercourse with bartenders or salesmen of teaching materials as well as the customers of student prostitutes. The increase has been faster in rural areas than in the large cities.

Medical experts in the United States think that the fear of herpes and AIDS has slowed down the sex revolution. Unmarried people, in particular, have changed their behaviour and avoid the casual choice of sex partners for fear of contracting herpes or AIDS.

The infection scare has drastically altered life in gay neighbourhoods in the United States. Store clerks wore plastic masks, one store owner had plastic gloves for all homosexual customers to put on before they touched any merchandise. Still another had a special register for 'Gays Only.' AIDS victims found that their social life was in ruins; their friends shunned them and treated them like pariahs.

Factors favouring the spread of VD include the migration of manpower, tourism, urbanisation and particularly the greater sexual freedom. In western countries, the rise in gonorrhea reaches a peak in late summer and early autumn (August, September) while new cases decline in winter and early spring. The increase in venereal disease slows down in times of economic recession when people have less money for sexual promiscuity.

Generally speaking, diagnosis of VD is reliable and treatment effective but the emergence of drug-resistant strains of gonorrhea and syphilis caused apprehension. For syphilis, the evidence is still inconclusive, but penicillin-resistant strains of gonorrhea were discovered in London and in the United States in 1976 and also appeared in the Philippines where US personnel contracted gonorrhea which could not be cured by penicillin and the back-up drug spectinomycin. This form of gonorrhea, known as penicillinase-producing Neisseria gonorrhea (PPNG), grows an enzyme that destroys penicillin. Out of the 1 million reported cases of gonorrhea in the United States each year, about 5 per cent are PPNG, but the percentage is said to be much higher in the Philippines and in Thailand.

An experimental drug, norfloxacin, was tested on US navy men in the Philippines and proved very effective against drug-resistant strains of gonorrhea.

Origin of VD

The origin of venereal disease is obscure. The possibility of infections by bacilli and viruses constitutes one form of the susceptibility of the human organism to disease, and just as other organs are liable to infection, so are the sexual organs. Contagious diseases are generally transmitted by contact with an infected person or object so that, medically speaking, the spread of venereal disease by sexual intercourse is nothing special. That venereal diseases are set apart as a special class is due to social rather than medical considerations, for venereal disease is frequently propagated by extra-marital sex.

One theory holds that syphilis was formerly unknown in Europe and that it was introduced from Haiti by the sailors who accompanied Christopher Columbus on his first voyage to the New World. Some skeletons of pre-Columbian Indians are said to show vestiges of the disease. Although there are indications that syphilis existed in Greece and Rome, the disease was extinct in Europe when it erupted in Barcelona in 1494 and rapidly spread through Spain, Portugal, France, Germany, Switzerland and Italy. According to a different opinion, many cases thought to be leprosy in earlier centuries were actually syphilis. The first epidemic of syphilis occurred in 1495 in the French army besieging Naples (whence the French called syphilis the '*mal Napolitain*' whereas others referred to it as the '*mal français*'). In the first quarter of the sixteenth century, millions are said to have died of syphilis.

Because it is spread by social contact, venereal disease is often referred to as social disease. Actually, venereal disease is a social problem in more than one sense. In the United States alone, the treatment of venereal diseases costs at least $2 billion a year.

Moral and Legal Problems in VD

The spread of VD is aided by ignorance, carelessness and irresponsibility. As a matter of fact, most men used to be infected by promiscuous pre-marital intercourse while most women caught such diseases post-maritally from their husbands. But this pattern is a thing of the past. The social, psychological and economic factors that promoted sexual freedom also encouraged sexual promiscuity and helped to spread VD. While people were eager to pick up new sexual techniques, the inadequate health and sex education failed to sufficiently stress sexual hygiene. Shame often makes people suffering from VD reluctant to seek medical help. Relatively few avail themselves of the counselling services provided by telephone advisory centres although the advice is confidential and no caller is asked his or her name.

Venereal disease involves sometimes difficult moral and legal problems. It seems evident that somebody who suffers from VD has the moral duty to inform his or her partner before having sex relations or when contemplating marriage. While the moral obligation may be clear, the legal duties are murky. In the United States, most states have laws requiring blood tests for syphilis before marriage as well as blood tests of pregnant women to protect their babies from congenital syphilis which can be prevented while the child is still in the womb. In December 1982, the wife of a Kansas City bank president filed a $6 million ($1 million in actual and $5 million in punitive damages) lawsuit in the federal court charging that her husband had caused her permanent and progressive injury by failing to warn her that he had herpes. Similar suits were brought by an Oakland woman against her estranged husband and by a retired Iowa school teacher against her divorced husband. It is understandable that a wife seeks damages from a husband who contracted herpes from an extra-marital affair but it is hard to see the rationality of a suit brought by a woman against a man with whom she had a casual encounter. It is strange that people who reject established social norms should invoke the law to get damages for something they claim is outside the law. If sex is a private matter and none of the law's business, it seems absurd to establish legal rules on the right to information of the infected and balance this right against the right to privacy of the infector in a casual sexual relationship freely sought by the parties.

It may be argued that somebody who has relations with a prostitute should be aware of the possibility or even probability of VD (an application of the old principle 'caveat emptor' — let the buyer beware?).

Genital herpes can be lethal to a baby who contracts it at birth. The virus can strike the child's central nervous system or damage internal organs. One out of every three newborn babies with herpes will die, 27 per cent will survive but suffer severe retardation, and 6 per cent will be mildly retarded. Because of the risks involved, doctors perform Caesarian operations on 54 per cent of all pregnant women with herpes, although the disease may not be active at the time of delivery. Most newborn babies with herpes are born to women who are unaware that they have the disease.

If husband or wife contracts a venereal disease, he or she has the imperative duty of informing the other party, and the same obligation seems incumbent on people living together without formal marriage. A doctor should remind his patient of this duty and should take it upon himself to advise the partner of his patient whenever he is not sure that his patient has disclosed his condition. The protection of an innocent person who has the right to know from possible harm takes precedence over the duty of professional secrecy. A doctor also has to comply with the legal provisions on reporting communicable diseases. There can be no doubt that the public interest in preventing the spread of contagious disease outweighs the right to privacy or the protection of the reputation of the patient.

The South Korean government drew up a bill which made regular tests for venereal disease a condition of employment for civil servants and the employees of hotels and restaurants. The measure aimed at eradicating sexually-transmitted diseases before the influx of foreign visitors for the 1986 Asian Games and the Olympic Games in 1988.

Frightened by the spread of VD, the San Bernardino city council passed a law obliging prostitutes and their customers to undergo a venereal disease test and providing a six-month jail term in case of refusal. The law has been attacked as an attempt to pry into people's sexual activities but has been defended as a necessary step for protecting the community against VD which has reached epidemic proportions.

Some progress has been made in recent years in the treatment of the two venereal diseases which are still incurable, herpes and AIDS. The drug acyclovir which had been most effective as an ointment in the treatment of first outbreaks of genital herpes was also approved by the US Food and Drug Administration for use in oral form. Israeli researchers have developed a gel laced with the antiviral agent idoxurin which proved more effective than other preparations in the treatment of cold sores of mouth and nose. British scientists at the University of Birmingham developed a vaccine which prevents the recurrence of the herpes sores and in this sense provides a cure. A drug called intervir-A makes the eruptions disappear quickly when applied to herpes sores and lengthens the time between recurrent outbreaks.

In animal tests, a drug called methoxymethyldeoxyuridine (abbreviated MMUDR) seems to lessen the severity of venereal herpes attacks and to halt the growth of the herpes virus but it will take time before it can be used on humans.

Data on AIDS

The World Health Organisation (WHO) announced on 13 February 1987, that a total of 40,536 cases of AIDS had been reported in 91 countries. With 29,575 victims, the United States accounted for three-quarters of the cases. The incidence was much lower in other countries. Of the 4,542 cases reported for Europe, France had the most with 1,253, followed by West Germany (875) and Britain (638). Brazil reported 1,012 cases,

Canada 809 and Tanzania 699. At about the same time, a spokesman for the Foreign Ministry of the Soviet Union told a news conference that 20 cases of AIDS had been diagnosed in the USSR, all of them among foreigners. Of the 20 victims, 19 were male homosexuals and one was a female drug abuser. Research on AIDS was carried out by a group of institutes of the USSR Ministry of Health and the Academy of Medical Science. But Dr Giorgy Khlyabirh, deputy minister of health, told the *Literaturnaya Gazeta* that there were 13 confirmed cases of AIDS in the Soviet Union and another 15 suspected of the disease had been isolated. Of the confirmed cases, 12 were foreigners and the other a Soviet woman. In Hungary, 107 people had been identified as carriers of the AIDS virus and one death from the disease had been reported.

Researchers estimated that 1 million to 1.5 million Americans had been infected with the virus of whom most appear healthy and have no symptoms. Overall, over 70 per cent of the victims were homosexual men, 13 per cent intravenous drug users, about 3 per cent Haitians and less than 1 per cent haemophiliacs. Over 60 per cent of the patients were from two states, New York and California. In New York City, where the largest number of AIDS patients live, 28 per cent of the recently diagnosed cases were heterosexuals and intravenous drug users.

In Japan, 36 cases of AIDS had been reported as of 19 March 1987 and 24 of the victims had died. Of the total number of victims, 22 were haemophiliacs and 11 male homosexuals. A woman suffering from AIDS, a Filipina prostitute, was deported in November 1986. The victims included three women, two Japanese and a Swiss. Carriers of the AIDS virus were estimated at some 11,000.

A grim picture emerged from the proceedings of the second annual AIDS congress held in Paris in June 1986 and attended by over 2,500 doctors and scientists. AIDS cases have been reported in 92 countries and while the number of officially-counted cases was about 30,000 (two-thirds of them in the United States), the World Health Organisation estimated that 100,000 was a more realistic figure and that worldwide, 5 million or 10 million people may harbour the AIDS virus. The disease is most widely spread in Africa, where according to an estimate of the World Health Organisation 50,000 people have died of AIDS. Private scientists, however, put the death toll at several hundred thousand and estimate the number of virus carriers at 5 million. Men and women suffer from AIDS in almost equal numbers and the disease seems to spread by heterosexual contact.

In mid-January 1987, 18 African countries reporting to WHO had a total of 2,324 AIDS cases. Uganda had the highest number with 766 cases, Uganda had 462 and Zambia and Congo 250 each. The figures for other countries were Central African Republic 202, Ivory Coast 118, Kenya 109, Ghana 73, Zimbabwe 57, South Africa 41, Malawi 13, Lesotho and Mozambique one each. But 12 African countries, including Zaire, failed to report to the WHO.

In blood tests on 304,000 US Army volunteers, 1.56 per 1,000 men and 0.62 per 1,000 women showed signs of infection. This means a male-to-female ratio of 2.5-1 which contrasts sharply with the 13-1 ratio for previously reported cases in the United States.

Speakers at the conference acknowledged that neither a vaccine nor a cure was in sight and nobody could offer an explanation why the disease was so rampant in Africa.

AIDS was first reported in Britain in 1983 and at the latest count (February 1987), 686 people had contracted the disease of whom 355 had died. The number of people having the AIDS virus was estimated at 40,000 but other estimates ranged from 50,000 to 300,000.

On the basis of earlier data, over half of 731 women diagnosed as suffering from AIDS were intravenous drug users and 95 had had sexual contact with men in the high-risk groups but 177 of the women got the disease from sources that could not be identified or were not in the established risk categories.

Analysis of AIDS

The disease results from the breakdown of the body's natural defences against infections so that usually harmless germs become killers. The collapse of the immune system is attributed to a disturbance in the production of lymphocytes. Their production is regulated by so-called T cells on which depends the formation of B cells which make antibodies. There are two kinds of T cells, helper T cells (also called T-4 cells) and suppressor T cells. If there are too many suppressor T cells and not enough helper T cells, the production of B cells becomes insufficient.

The AIDS virus which causes the disorder not only attacks the helper T cells and phagocytes but also uses them for producing new viruses. The virus consists of a small number of genes (DNA - deoxyribonucleic acid, or RNA - ribonucleic acid) encased in a protective coat of protein. The virus is a retrovirus which means that it uses RNA to pass genetic information to DNA as opposed to the usual information flow from DNA to RNA. After the virus penetrates a cell, the protein coat is removed and the activated genes make the cell produce new viruses. The AIDS virus reproduces and mutates at a much faster rate than most other viruses and frequently changes the structure of its surface antigens, either gradually or suddenly, and disappears after its work of destruction.

Because the body's immune system can no longer prevent the invasion of alien protein, germs, bacteria, viruses, protozoa, fungi and parasites can spread in the body. Although AIDS is thought to primarily knock out the B and T cells, it apparently also affects the antigen-presenting cells, at least in the skin.

The discovery of the virus and the development of a blood test for detecting AIDS infection have become the subject of a bitter feud between French and American scientists. The French team under Dr Luc Montagnier of the Pasteur Institute claims to have been the first to identify the virus which was called lymphadenopathy-associated virus (LAV). A team at the National Cancer Institute under Dr Robert Gallo isolated a somewhat different strain of the virus which was called human T-cell lymphotropic virus, type 3 (HTLV-3). The US Patent and Trademark Office acknowledged that the Pasteur Institute had filed a patent application seven months earlier than the National Institutes of Health. The decision on the rival claims involved millions of dollars in patent royalties on the blood test and possibly a Nobel Prize.

However, the lawsuit filed by scientists at the Pasteur Institute was promptly settled by an agreement between the US Department of Health and Human Services and the Pasteur Institute; the news was announced by President Reagan during a visit to Washington by French Prime Minister Jacques Chirac at the end of March 1987. Under the agreement, the two medical groups will share the patent on an AIDS test developed by US scientists. Each party will contribute 80 per cent of the royalties received to establish and support an international AIDS research foundation. The foundation will sponsor AIDS-related research and donate 25 per cent of the funds it received to education and research of AIDS problems in less-developed countries.

In order to clear up the confusion in the designation of the virus, a third party proposed the appellation human immuno-deficiency virus (HIV) but Dr Gallo refused to endorce the change.

Scientists at Harvard Medical School found that the AIDS virus reproduction starts in the RNA part of the cell invaded by the virus rather than in the DNA part. DNA generates RNA molocules which in turn generate the protein that determines the nature of the cell.

A new strain of the AIDS virus was isolated by the team at the Pasteur Institute under Professor Luc Montagnier and called LAV-2. Initially, the new virus was found in only two cases out of 2,000 patients tested (both patients were from Guinea-Bissau) and seemed close to a simian retrovirus isolated in 1985. According to Dr Françoise Barre-Sinoussi, LAV-2 is not encased in the same kind of protein as LAV-1 (HTLV-3) and a new blood-screening test must be developed because the human body forms different kinds of antibodies against LAV-2.

Dr Gallo reported that he found about 100 different forms of the AIDS virus and that up to 20 per cent of the genetic material in the virus can vary from person to person. Despite the differences, all samples isolated had enough common features to make them the same virus. But it will be difficult although not impossible to develop a universal vaccine.

The disease has attacked mainly five groups of people: homosexual men (in 1983, about 72 per cent of the victims in the United States, 87 per cent of those in Europe), drug addicts of both sexes who took their drugs intraveneously through needles, sufferers from haemophilia, other people who had blood transfusions and Haitian immigrants. In Africa, where 40 per cent of the victims were women, no significant correlation between AIDS and homosexuality was found. None of the African patients admitted to homosexual contacts or drug abuse and the disease seems to be transmitted by heterosexual contacts.

In about 40 per cent of the cases, AIDS leads to a deadly form of Kaposi's sarcoma, and homosexuals are also subject to a particularly virulent form of pneumonia (pneumocystis carinii pneumonia) caused by a parasite. Both these diseases were previously endemic in equatorial Africa. AIDS victims are also exposed to a form of herpes that attacks the central nervous system and a mycrobacterial infection that usually causes TB in chickens and pigs. Some AIDS victims show an increased vulnerability to other types of cancer, four times the normal incidence of lymphoma and a higher incidence of Hodgkin's disease and melanoma. A condition that often precedes AIDS is the lymphadenopathy syndrome (swollen lymph glands, fever, night sweat, loss of appetite). Patients infected with the AIDS virus but not (yet) exhibiting the severe symptoms of full developed AIDS are classified as suffering from ARC (AIDS-related complex).

The AIDS virus has been linked to a variety of fatal diseases spreading in many parts of Africa. Cases of an unusual fungal meningitis have increased more than seven times since 1977, and while formerly half of the victims of cryptococcal meningitis survived, the death rate is now 100 per cent. A new kind of Karposi's sarcoma progresses very quickly and is accompanied by mental dullness in some patients and by other infections in two-thirds of the patients. Antibodies to the AIDS virus were found in the blood of 5 per cent of Kenyans tested, 7 to 12 per cent of Zaireans and up to 18 and 20 per cent of Rwandans and Ugandans. Children died of measles and diarrhœal illnesses — diseases that would be easily treatable in the absence of AIDS.

AIDS may have been responsible for a conspicuous rise in tuberculosis during the past five years.

A British blood specialist, Dr Peter Jones, attributed the outbreak of the AIDS epidemic to blood supplies from Africa. The main source of African supplies was Zaire's capital of Kinshasa, situated in an area in which Karposi's sarcoma and other AIDS-related diseases are endemic.

A Sydney newspaper reported in 1985 that four Australian women had been infected with the AIDS virus through artificial insemination in 1982 with semen from the same donor. One of the women showed symptoms of the second stage of the disease (lymphadenopathy syndrome) while the other three had AIDS antibodies but no symptoms.

Unexplained remains the question of whether every infection leads to the specific AIDS symptoms within three or five years with death following in 85 per cent of all cases or whether the AIDS virus can retreat into some hiding-place where it stays up to 15 years and suddenly becomes active. A possible sanctuary is the brain because the AIDS virus is capable of penetrating a membrane called the blood-brain barrier (which prevents most drugs in the blood from reaching the brain). If it becomes active, it paralyses the nerves and finally destroys the brain, causing Alzheimer's disease and senile dementia.

Dr Richard Price of the Memorial Sloan-Kettering Cancer Institute reported that, in addition to wreaking havoc on the human immune system, AIDS can cause severe neurological problems. Many victims develop a form of dementia, not unlike Alzheimer's disease, that affects speech, movement and memory. In some patients, the dementia becomes a dominant aspect of the illness.

Tests

The development of a blood test for HTLV-3 has been hailed as a scientific milestone, but screening also creates great uneasiness, particularly among homosexuals. If someone is identified as having the AIDS virus in his or her blood, it still remains uncertain whether the individual will come down with AIDS him- or herself or whether he or she will transmit the virus and cause AIDS in someone else. The results of screening could be used by health authorities, insurers and employers to discriminate against people who may develop the disease even if they are healthy now and may never become ill.

A new test devised by Dr Jack Love detects the actual AIDS virus in patients. It uses a nucleic acid or DNA probe to show the presence of the virus in white blood cells. Earlier tests were only able to discover the antibodies which develop when the body tries to fend off the invading virus. The antibodies can show up any time from two weeks to several months after the patient has been exposed to AIDS. Some people who have the virus never develop antibodies.

New diagnostic agents which can be mass-produced detect the presence of AIDS antibodies in 45 minutes with almost 100 per cent accuracy.

A report in the Journal of the American Medical Association related that AIDS patients had abnormally high levels of a protein found in the blood and on the surface of most cells in the body. The protein, beta 2 microglobulin (B2M), is part of the immune system and this abnormality can be detected by a simple test two years before the symptoms of AIDS appear. But the test is not specific for AIDS because the level of the protein can be raised by other diseases as well.

Dr Jean-Claude Chermann tested mosquitoes, cockroaches, ticks, tsetse flies and other insects from Zaire and the Central African Republic. Virtually all of some 50 insects from Zaire were carrying the AIDS virus while only mosquitoes and ticks from the Central African Republic showed traces of the virus.

Although pathologists maintain that AIDS is only transmitted by the sperm, saliva, tears or blood of AIDS sufferers, an American study carried out in Zaire (where the disease is believed to have originated) suggested that infection by the deadly virus can occur through normal household contacts. The reseachers found that 17 per cent of the 204 people who shared homes with AIDS victims had antibodies to the virus in their bloodstream compared with 4 per cent of those who lived elsewhere. In the United States, AIDS has occasionally passed from infected mothers (intravenous abusers of drugs) to unborn or newborn children.

A study by the American Red Cross found that 0.17 per cent of over a million blood samples tested had antibodies to the HTLV-3 virus. This means that one in every 500 blood donors had been exposed to the virus. Extrapolated to the general population, the results would indicate that roughly 350,000 Americans might be potential AIDS victims although a person may be the carrier of the virus without contracting the disease. The estimates may be too low because only donated blood was sampled and blood banks discourage donation by high-risk groups (homosexuals, intravenous drug abusers) and the supplies did not include blood from New York and San Francisco, the two cities with the highest concentration of AIDS sufferers.

Treatment of AIDS

What the doctors could treat in AIDS patients were not the immediate effects of the virus but the secondary symptoms which appeared as a result of the breakdown of the immune system. This further weakened the general capacity of the body to cope with the invasion of germs which would otherwise be relatively harmless.

An important development was the discovery that the drug azidothymidine (AZT) stopped the AIDS virus from reproducing and attacking blood cells. AZT was first synthesised in 1964 as a possible anti-cancer drug but proved ineffective. Scientists at Burroughs Wellcome Co. discovered that the drug interfered with viral reproduction in AIDS-infected human cells in test tubes. AZT does not provide a cure but inhibits the chemical process by which the AIDS virus spreads. The AIDS virus is a so-called retrovirus containing single-stranded RNA. Alone, RNA lacks the ability to take over the cell's genetic machinery and make it produce copies of the virus. But retroviruses carry an enzyme called reverse transcriptase which enables the viral RNA to convert to DNA which instructs the cell to produce more AIDS viruses. AZT halts the manufacture of DNA because a human enzyme converts it into a 'false sugar' (that is, similar but not identical to the sugar used by the AIDS virus' reverse transcriptase for building a DNA strand), thus disrupting the DNA synthesis.

After clinical tests showed that AZT greatly reduced the deaths of AIDS victims, the US Public Health Service announced in September 1986 that the drug would be made available for distribution to patients suffering from pneumocystis carinii pneumonia although some uncertainties remained such as AZT's toxic side effects and dosage levels. Because AZT is able to penetrate the blood-brain barrier, it might possibly make the AIDS virus hidden in the brain ineffective.

In March 1987, the US Food and Drug Administration approved AZT for prescription use in the United States. Although the drug, marketed under the trade name Retrovir, does not kill the virus and has serious side effects, it has improved the short-term survival of AIDS patients with recently-diagnosed pneumocystis carinii pneumonia and some patients with advanced ARC (AIDS-related complex). The annual cost of the treatment with AZT for a typical patient ranges between $7,000 and $10,000.

The clinical tests confronted the researchers with an ethical problem. Was it right to give patients in the control groups placebos and thus prevent them from receiving the benefits of the treatment? Most clinical tests involve a moral problem because there is no absolute certainty that there will be no unforeseen effects. In this case, the question was not purely academic because in the first phase of the tests, there had been 16 deaths among the 137 patients receiving the placebos and only one among the 145 patients taking AZT. Nevertheless, doctors insisted that the use of placebos was the only way to find out whether there was an effect attributable to the drug and not to chance. A different problem is how long the treatment which requires a dose every four hours can be continued without more serious side effects than headaches or a decrease in the number of hematocytes.

The National Cancer Institute has been testing a drug, dideoxycystidine (DDC) developed by the American subsidiary of F. Hoffman-La Roche which, in laboratory tests, halted the replication of the AIDS virus, thus allowing the body's immune system to begin rebuilding. In tests on animals, DDC was slightly more effective and less toxic than AZT. Clinical tests and approval by the FDA will be needed before the drug can be marketed.

An American company ICN Pharmaceuticals Inc., arranged clinical tests of the antiviral drug Ribavirin which proved effective in preventing the development of AIDS in patients who had been exposed to the AIDS virus and had experienced enlarged lymph nodes.

Professor Chermann used a drug called HPA-23 to stop the AIDS virus from replicating. The US Food and Drug Administration approved the drug for limited testing in five American research institutions after actor Rock Hudson had gone to Paris for treatment with the drug.

Tests showed that using condoms during intercourse can prevent infection by the AIDS virus which cannot penetrate the membrane of the condom. Boston doctors tested two substances, gamma interferon and interleuken, for strengthening the immune system. Those substances which are natural human proteins, dramatically restored the microbe-killing power of blood cells taken from victims of AIDS in test tube experiments.

The Maripola Foundation of California found that the spermicide nonoxynol-9, a common ingredient of contraceptive creams and gels, kills the sexually-transmitted HTLV-3 virus in about 30 seconds. If confirmed in clinical tests, this could limit the transmission of the virus but would not help AIDS victims.

A study conducted by Bionetic Research, Inc., of Rockville, Maryland, showed that a disinfectant called Sporacidin, widely used in hospitals and by dentists to clean medical instruments, kills the AIDS virus. The Centres for Disease Control confirmed that Sporacidin also kills the hepatitis 'B' virus and the genital herpes virus.

In a joint project, researchers from Fukushima Medical College and Yamaguchi University Medical School discovered that glycyrrhizin, used for treating hepatitis and allergies, is effective in containing the multiplication of the AIDS virus. The effectiveness of the chemical, a component of licorice, which stimulates the human immune system, has yet to be confirmed by clinical tests but in the test tube, glycyrrhizin proved effective in saving almost 100 per cent of the virus-infected cells.

Professor Natan Trainin, a biologist at the Weizman Institute of Science, developed a treatment with hormones from the thymus of calves (later, a synthetic hormone was substituted) which reinforced the natural immune system but did not attack the virus itself. The treatment stopped the most serious infections in a 12-year-old boy, a haemophiliac who had contracted AIDS from blood transfusions.

French doctors at the Laënec Hospital in Paris treated AIDS patients with cyclosporine, a drug used to prevent the rejection of transplanted organs. They found that cyclosporine paralysed cells infected with the AIDS virus which, they said, prevented the spread of the disease and allowed the body to build up its immune system. Medical circles criticised the treatment as unproven and the announcement of its effectiveness as premature.

Handling of AIDS

The question whether AIDS should be made a notifiable disease has divided the medical world as well as politicians and the general public into two opposing camps. One side demands protection against a killer disease threatening the entire population, the other opposed any measures which would create an official record of the private life of citizens. Many American states have made reporting mandatory but others (for example,

West Germany) have no regulations. Switzerland requires reporting without disclosing the name of the patient.

California's 'Agnos Law' which makes it unlawful in California for a physician to disclose a positive AIDS test result without the patient's written consent is unjust because it enables the virus carrier to conceal his condition from people who have a right to know (spouse or other sex partner). The association of AIDS with homosexuality has resulted in giving undue protection to the privacy of AIDS victims at the expense of the protection of the public against a communicable disease. Reporting should be required for suspected or confirmed carriers of the virus as well as for AIDS patients.

The German state of Bavaria has prepared legislation which will introduce compulsory AIDS tests for people regarded as most at risk from the disease. The tests will affect prostitutes, drug addicts, prisoners, non-European Community nationals who apply for a residence permit and anyone suspected of being infected. Compulsory tests may also be given to applicants for public sector employment. Police have been given power to round up people who refuse to undergo a voluntary examination. Under existing German federal law, people with AIDS who knowingly expose others to the disease could be forcibly hospitalised or isolated in state institutions. They are also prohibited from sexual intercourse.

Officials of the US Centres for Disease Control suggested that the government might consider recommending mandatory blood testing for exposure to the AIDS virus for pregnant women, couples applying for marriage licenses, people seeking treatment for other sexually-transmitted diseases and all patients admitted to hospitales. The negative reaction to this proposal was very strong. Politicians, moralists, lawyers and public-health experts branded the idea as morally and legally wrong, enormously expensive and undemocratic. But there seems to be widespread popular support for compulsory testing of certain groups, high-risk groups as well as people in certain occupations (food handlers, health-care workers, teachers) and people applying for marriage licenses.

Japan's Ministry of Health and Welfare prepared legislation to prevent the spread of AIDS. The draft went through various modifications because of the disagreement on the protection of privacy and punitive provisions. In its final form, the bill requires doctors to report both AIDS patients and carriers of the virus to the prefectural government, giving age, sex, and source of infection. The doctor must instruct the patient (and his parents) in ways of preventing the spread of the disease. If the doctor fears that the patient may disregard his instructions and transmit the virus to others, he must notify the prefectural government of name and address of the patient.

The bill requires people infected with the virus to follow the orders of the doctor and bans them from engaging in sexual activity and donating blood. Prefectural governors are authorised to take the necessary steps to curb the spread of the virus by recommending or ordering medical check-ups of people infected, or suspected of being infected. If necessary for preventing the spread of AIDS, foreigners, including refugees, can be barred from entering Japan.

Public officials and doctors who fail to keep the secrets of AIDS patients can be punished with a maximum prison term of one year or a maximum fine of ¥300,000. People who refuse to follow a governor's order to undergo a medical check-up or who give false answers when questioned by medical examiners can be fined a maximum of ¥100,000.

What to do with pregnant women suffering from AIDS or infected with the AIDS virus poses a difficult problem. In some cases, doctors have suggested abortion. There is a 30 to 60 per cent probability that the foetus will be infected. In the United States, an estimated 300 children have been infected with the AIDS virus by their mothers. The intricacy of the problem was illustrated by a woman in Kochi Prefecture, Japan, who tested positive for the virus before her marriage and was advised not to marry and not to have children. She married anyhow, became pregnant and refused to have the pregnancy terminated. Her child was born healthy and free from the virus.

There have been cases in which hospital personnel have refused to assist AIDS sufferers and the school attendance of children with AIDS became a problem when some American communities tried to prevent them from attending classes. In some cases the courts have intervened and ordered that the children be allowed to go to school. In the West German state of Baden-Württemberg, two children suffering from AIDS were barred from the classroom.

The risk of infection of health workers exposed to AIDS patients seems remote. So far, there have been ten confirmed cases, nine in the United States and another in Britain. In five of the American cases, health workers accidentally stuck themselves with needles contaminated with blood; other contacts with blood caused the infection in the remaining four cases.

The United States is testing the armed forces for the AIDS virus; the screening also covers men and women enrolled in the service academies, those in college military programmes and those enrolled in officer candidate schools. West Germany screens all new recruits.

Dealing with AIDS is a serious problem for US prisons where a study group found 765 cases of infection among the inmates in the beginning of 1986. The bulk of the cases were concentrated in just 4 per cent of the nation's prisons.

The use of a common chalice for holy communion became a subject of concern in the Anglican Church around Christmas 1985. Medical authorities had advised the churches that the risk of catching AIDS when sipping from the chalice was slight, but some precautions should be taken. The chalice should be wiped and rotated after each communicant, communicants could take only the communion wafer or could dip the wafer into the wine. The risk would be less if the wine was of normal alcohol content. (Some non-conformist churches use so-called 'non-alcoholic wine').

The standing liturgical commission of the US Episcopal Church recommended continued use of the common chalice in communion services despite widespread fears of possible transmission of AIDS. Some parishes have discontinued use of the common cup, in other churches, communicants dipped the communion wafer into the sacramental wine rather than drinking from the cup. 'The practice undermines a principal symbol of Christian and Anglican worship,' the commission said.